# The Problem of Bureaucratic Rationality

# The Problem of
# Bureaucratic Rationality

## TAX POLITICS IN JAPAN

*Junko Kato*

PRINCETON UNIVERSITY PRESS

PRINCETON, NEW JERSEY

Copyright © 1994 by Princeton University Press
Published by Princeton University Press, 41 William Street,
Princeton, New Jersey 08540
In the United Kingdom: Princeton University Press,
Chichester, West Sussex

*Library of Congress Cataloging-in-Publication Data*
Kato, Junko, 1961–
The problem of bureaucratic rationality: tax politics in Japan /
Junko Kato
p.   cm.
Includes bibliographical references and index.
ISBN 0-691-03451-6
1. Bureaucracy—Japan.   2. Civil service—Japan.
3. Taxation—Japan.   I. Title.
JQ1647.K37   1994
354.520072'4—dc20   94-15825

This book has been composed in Times Roman

Princeton University Press books are
printed on acid-free paper and meet the guidelines
for permanence and durability of the Committee
on Production Guidelines for Book Longevity
of the Council on Library Resources

Printed in the United States of America

1   2   3   4   5   6   7   8   9   10

# Contents

# Tables

# Acknowledgments

DURING the long process of completing this book, I incurred large debts of gratitude to many people. I am afraid that my acknowledgments here will be much shorter than they should be, and that I have no adequate way to repay my indebtedness to these people. I am especially grateful to Susan Rose-Ackerman and Mike M. Mochizuki who were supervisors of my dissertation on which this book is based. In a variety of ways, Rose-Ackerman helped me to make this a study of political economy, as well as of Japanese politics. I was also privileged to benefit from Mike Mochizuki's expertise in connecting a theoretical scheme with empirical findings. I owe much to both of my supervisors for encouraging me to take an interdisciplinary approach in my study. I am also indebted to many faculty members in the department of political science at Yale University. Among them, I would like to express special thanks to David Cameron, David Mayhew, and Bruce Russett. David Cameron and David Mayhew have continued to stimulate my interests in comparative politics; Bruce Russett provided me with the opportunity to teach in the department while I was completing this book.

Many people also supported my research in Japan. For their comments and advice I would like to express appreciation to Seizaburō Satō and Wataru Ōmori, who were my first teachers of Japanese politics at the University of Tokyo. During the summer of 1989, when I conducted the first research in Japan, John Creighton Campbell organized a research group on Japanese politics among the Ph.D. students in Tokyo, invited me to join this group, and encouraged me to pursue my project. Susan J. Pharr also gave me very useful advice when I was about to begin the dissertation research.

The field research in Japan was also generously assisted by tax specialists and journalists who were well informed about tax theory or tax practice and by bureaucrats who were deeply involved in the tax policy-making process. They spent many hours giving me valuable information on Japanese tax reform. The bureaucrats of the Ministry of Finance were frank and generous about answering my questions, although most of my interviews were conducted in the summer of 1989 when the fate of their proposed consumption tax was most at stake. I also thank Hiroshi Katō, a researcher in the financial section of the Diet library at the time of my research in

ACKNOWLEDGEMENTS

Japan, for his photographic memory that helped me gain access to enormous amounts of detailed information on tax policies and tax politics. The University of California Press and the Organization for Economic Cooperation and Development gave me permission to include parts of their publications in this book.

Many colleagues advised me on my research and provided valuable comments on earlier drafts of the manuscript. Among them, I am especially indebted to Stephen Anderson, Takeo Hoshi, Jun Iio, Debbie Milley, Frances Rosenbluth, Robert Uriu, and Kuniaki Tanabe. My sincerest appreciation should be reserved for T. J. Pempel and Mathew D. McCubbins, who reviewed my manuscript for publication. T. J. Pempel's comments helped me to structure and tighten my argument for the final draft. In preparing the manuscript for publication, Kay Mansfield not only helped me edit it but also gave me continuous encouragement as one of my best friends. I am also grateful to Malcolm DeBevoise of Princeton University Press, who saw the potential of my manuscript at the predissertation stage and steered the way for its publication. I wish also to thank Jennifer W. Mathews and Timothy Bartlett of Princeton University Press for their gracious assistance and Rita L. Bernhard for her excellent copyediting. Finally, I thank my family and my friends who supported this project. Especially, I would like to express my appreciation to my parents, Chieko and Kiyoshi Katō, and to my sister, Toshiko Imamura.

Tokyo, Japan
September 1993

# Note on Conventions

IN THIS BOOK all Japanese names appear in Western order to avoid confusing readers who are not familiar with name order in Japan—family name first. I use macrons to express long vowels in Japanese names and words. But some geographical names (i.e., Tokyo, Osaka, and Kyoto) and the names of certain Japanese authors who write in English (e.g., my own name, Kato, which is written Katō in romanization) are exceptions to this rule.

Amounts of money expressed in yen are translated into dollar amounts. As a conversion rate, I use the annual average of the exchange rate in the year when the money was spent as a budget, measured as a deficit, and so on. Each annual average of exchange rate is taken from an appropriate issue of *International Financial Statistics*, Organization for Economic Cooperation and Development, Paris.

# *Abbreviations*

| | |
|---|---|
| CGP | Clean Government Party |
| DSP | Democratic Socialist Party |
| EC | European Community |
| GTSRC | Government Tax System Research Council |
| HC | House of Councillors |
| HR | House of Representatives |
| JCP | Japan Communist Party |
| JSP | Japan Socialist Party |
| LDP | Liberal Democratic Party |
| LDP PARC | LDP Policy Affairs Research Council |
| LDP TSRC | LDP Tax System Research Council |
| MOF | Ministry of Finance |
| MHA | Ministry of Home Affairs |
| MITI | Ministry of International Trade and Industry |
| MPT | Ministry of Posts and Telecommunications |
| NLB | New Liberal Club |
| OECD | Organization for Economic Cooperation and Development |
| PARC | Policy Affairs Research Council |
| SDL | Social Democratic League |
| SPCAR | Second Provisional Council for Administrative Reform |
| TSRC | Tax System Research Council both of the government and the LDP |
| VAT | Value-Added Tax |

# The Problem of Bureaucratic Rationality

# Introduction

IN APRIL 1993 President Bill Clinton implied that to finance the proposed health care reform, he would reconsider the introduction of the value-added tax (VAT) which he had ruled out the previous February. Whether the Democratic administration will implement this broad-based consumption tax remains to be seen, but one can expect that the president should handle this tax issue cautiously. Though it is an attractive financial resource for many industrialized countries that suffer from a budget deficit, the VAT is a hot potato for politicians. The experience of governments in other countries demonstrates this. The Progressive Conservative government in Canada spent a lot of nerves and political resources in the late 1980s to introduce the Goods and Services Tax (GST) as its version of the VAT. In March 1993, just one month before the announcement above by President Clinton, an issue involving the VAT forced the Australian Liberal Party, under the leadership of John Hewson, to lose the opportunity to take office. While Dr. Hewson, an American-educated economist, proposed a 15 percent consumption tax in the campaign for national parliamentary elections, Prime Minister Keating of the Labor Party, who had enraged voters with his economic management, deflected public attention to the tax issue by overtly criticizing his opponent's tax proposal, and thus restored electoral support for himself.

No other country, however, has experienced such a major tax policy change and such intense political turmoil as Japan when the VAT was introduced in 1989. In 1987 Japan was the only country, except the United States, among twenty-four members of the Organization for Economic Cooperation and Development (OECD) that did not have taxes on consumption generally applied to commodities (a general consumption tax) (Table Intro.1):[1] Eighteen countries already had the most developed form of a multistage tax, i.e., the VAT, and even the United States had a single-stage general consumption tax, i.e., a retail sales tax at the state level (forty-five states ranging from 4.25 percent to 8.25 percent). As these data show, Japan had been a peculiar case in which the government did not seek revenues from a broad-based consumption tax during the postwar period. The recent introduction of the VAT meant a major shift in tax policies.

The government's proposals for the VAT in Japan also incurred significant political costs for policymakers. In 1979 the prime minister proposed

3

TABLE Intro.1
General Consumption Tax in OECD Countries[a]

| | System | Number of Rates[c] | Rates (Percent) | | | | Principal Exemptions and Preferential Rates[b] | |
| --- | --- | --- | --- | --- | --- | --- | --- | --- |
| | | | Basic | High | Low | Average[d] | Basic Foods | Medicine and Drugs |
| Australia | WST[e] | 3 | 20.0 | 30.0 | 10.0 | 17.2 | Yes | Yes |
| Austria | VAT[f] | 3 | 20.0 | 32.0 | 10.0 | 31.0 | 10.0 | 10.0 |
| Belgium | VAT | 6 | 19.0 | 33.0 | 1.0 | 19.8 | 6.0 | 6.0 19.0 |
| Canada[g] | MST[h] | 1 | 12.0 | — | — | 18.7 | Yes | Yes, 12.0 |
| Denmark | VAT | 1 | 22.0 | — | — | 42.4 | 22.0 | 22.0 |
| Finland[i] | VAT | 1 | 16.0 | — | — | 33.8 | Yes | Yes |
| France | VAT | 4 | 18.6 | 33.3 | 5.5 | 24.6 | 5.5 | 7.0 |
| Germany | VAT | 2 | 14.0 | — | 7.0 | 20.8 | 7.0 | |
| Greece | VAT | 3 | 18.0 | 36.0 | 9.0 | 28.1 | 7.0 | |
| Iceland | RST[j] | 1 | 25.0 | — | — | n.a. | Yes | 25.0 |
| Ireland | VAT | 3 | 25.0 | — | 0.0[k] | 36.1 | 0.0 | 0.0, 25.0 |
| Italy | VAT | 4 | 18.0 | 38.0 | 2.0 | 19.0 | 2.0 | 18.0 |
| Japan | — | — | — | — | — | 6.4 | Yes | Yes |
| Luxembourg | VAT | 3 | 10.0 | — | 2.0 | 21.3 | | |
| Netherlands | VAT | 2 | 20.0 | — | 6.0 | 21.4 | 6.0 | 6.0 |
| New Zealand | VAT | 1 | 10.0 | — | — | 16.0 | 10.0 | 10.0 |
| Norway | VAT | 1 | 20.0 | — | — | 53.2 | 20.0 | 10.0 |
| Portugal | VAT | 3 | 16.0 | 30.0 | 8.0 | 24.0 | Yes | 20.0 |

| | | | | | | | |
|---|---|---|---|---|---|---|---|
| Spain | VAT | 3 | 12.0 | 33.0 | 6.0 | 12.1 | 6.0 | 6.0 |
| Sweden | VAT | 2 | 23.5 | — | 12.9 | 31.6 | 23.5 | 23.5 |
| Switzerland[l] | RST | 1 | 6.2 | — | — | 6.1 | Yes | |
| Turkey | VAT | 4 | 12.0 | — | 0.0 | 6.9 | 0.0 | 5.0 |
| United Kingdom[m] | VAT | | 15.0 | — | 0.0 | 22.3 | 0.0 | Yes |
| United States | — | | — | — | — | 7.6 | Yes | Yes |

*Source: OECD Economic Studies*, no. 10 (Spring 1988): 212.

[a] In January 1987.

[b] "Yes" denotes exemptions; figures denote rates. Exemptions from services typically include rent, banking, and property transfers. Sometimes preferential rates also apply to electricity and gas, passenger transport, and insurance.

[c] Number of rate classes, including zero rate where applicable

[d] Implied average rate of consumption tax (both general and specific taxes) relative to private consumption (1984 data).

[e] WST = Wholesale sales tax.

[f] VAT = Value-added tax.

[g] In addition, all provinces except Alberta have a retail sales tax, at rates ranging from 4 percent to 12 percent.

[h] MST = Manufacturer sales tax.

[i] In Finland, VAT applies to selected goods, hotels, and restaurants only.

[j] RST = Retail sales tax.

[k] 0.0 means zero tax rate.

[l] In Switzerland, 80 percent of general consumption taxes is collected at the retail level at a rate of 6.2 percent. There is also a WST at a rate of 9.3 percent on some goods.

[m] In the United States, there is no general consumption tax at the federal level, although forty-five states have RST at rates ranging from 4.25 percent to 8.25 percent.

such an indirect tax, and the public fury over this proposal resulted in a poor showing of the incumbent Liberal Democratic Party (LDP) in the general election of the Lower House of the Diet. The withdrawal of the tax issue from the public agenda symbolized the beginning of the austerity campaign by the Japanese government in the early 1980s, which ended with another failed proposal of the VAT from 1986 to 1987. Moreover, the third proposal of the VAT and the subsequent introduction of the new tax brought a change in the hallmark of Japanese politics since 1955—the long-term predominance of the LDP. Public opposition, which was activated after the passage of the new tax, crippled the LDP's control over the Diet for the first time since 1955: the LDP could not maintain a majority after the election of the House of Councillors three months after the implementation of the VAT system.

From the late 1970s to the late 1980s, the Japanese Ministry of Finance (MOF) continued to be a major advocate of reforming the tax system through a major indirect tax on consumption. During this period, the leadership of the incumbent LDP began to incline toward the introduction of the VAT that the MOF proposed. The case of tax reform in Japan, therefore, provides an arena for the examination of bureaucratic influence on democratic policy-making.

About a century ago, when bureaucracies began to attract academic attention in social science, Max Weber argued that both technocratic bureaucrats and party politicians would shape the politics of the modern state (Weber 1958, 77–128). Bureaucratic capability to solve complicated modern policy problems contributed to their increasing influence. Weber attributed the strength of bureaucratic organizations not only to specialized expertise and reliance on instrumental rationality among their members, but also to hierarchy and division of labor in their structure (Weber 1978, 956–1003).

Since Weber, much scholarly effort has been invested in the study of bureaucracy, and the political importance of bureaucrats has become the conventional wisdom in comparative politics. At the same time, the increasing complexity of policy-making in the contemporary world encourages politicians to become more familiar with technical matters and requires bureaucrats to pay attention to the political feasibility of policy proposals (Aberbach et al. 1981). The converging roles of bureaucrats and politicians in contemporary politics motivate much scholarly work analyzing the power relationship between these two major groups of policymakers.

This book is a contribution to the literature on the relationship between bureaucrats and politicians in contemporary industrial democracies.[2] This study will explore the possibility of bureaucratic influence over policy-making. It aims to show that, utilizing their unique position as policy experts in the government, bureaucrats achieve an advantage through active involvement in politics—especially by exercising their influence on policy discourse and political agendas. This argument runs counter to the conventional wisdom that elitist and technocratic bureaucrats increase their influence as they become more autonomous and insulated from political pressure. At the same time, the study maintains that bureaucrats can have a significant impact on policy-making only if they focus on the minimum imperative of a policy change that is critical for their interests, and collectively act for its pursuance. The strength of bureaucrats lies in their capability to make an effective consensus on such imperatives inside their organization and coordinate their action to cope with political pressure. In a democratic political system, the bureaucrats do not have a free hand to impose their favorite policies on politicians and voters, and thus they need to compromise if their critical interests are not at stake. Another consequence of political involvement by bureaucrats is, therefore, a decline in the technical consistency and effectiveness of policies that occurs when bureaucrats succumb to intense political pressure.

The argument in this book about bureaucratic influence on political agendas can be summarized in several points. The first concerns the relationship between bureaucratic influence and competent policy expertise. The conventional explanation assumes an overwhelming advantage for bureaucrats as policy specialists. This monopolization of policy information and expertise enables them to manipulate the political process and to override the popular will by tricking party politicians who are supposed to represent it.[3]

Contrary to this expectation, this study argues that sharing policy information and knowledge with incumbent politicians is compatible with the promotion of bureaucratic influence in policy-making. In this context, I also reject the link between insulation from political pressure and bureaucratic influence in the conventional explanation.

The overemphasis on monopolization of expertise and autonomy observed in the argument for bureaucratic dominance derives from its presumption of the apolitical nature of bureaucratic decisions. According to one line of thought, a bureaucratic policy decision is rational and superior to others in the sense that it relies on technocratic considerations and thus is effective in attaining certain policy objectives. Another view regards the bureaucratic decision as a purely economic decision—maximization of a certain utility function.[4] Differing from either of these positions, this study argues that a bureaucratic policy decision is closely related to organizational interests in a certain political context, and is thus in no way based on any "objective" standard like "effectiveness" of policies or maximization of a simple utility function such as the one expressed by the size of the budget.

Third, the bureaucratic decision is not solely concerned with the interests of individual bureaucrats or the promotion of influence of the bureaucratic organization. Rather, bureaucrats propose policies that make the promotion of their organizational influence compatible with technocratic considerations.[5] Bureaucrats recognize that no economic theory or policy science can determine a unique solution to a real policy problem. At the same time, however, they present a policy proposal by utilizing those technocratic ideas that support it and undermine other technocratic points of views that present alternatives to their proposal. This study calls such bureaucratic behavior "political." More specifically, bureaucratic advantage lies in their *political* use of technocratic ideas instead of in their allegiance to a technocratic idea itself.

The fourth point of my argument relates to the ultimate reason for bureaucratic influence over the policy process. Bureaucratic manipulation of the policy agenda requires organizational behaviors directed toward a certain policy objective or outcome. This study argues that whether the political manipulation leads to a desired policy outcome hinges on the effective coordination of the behavior of members of the bureaucratic organization. More specifically, the analysis will show that the bureaucracy is capable of pursuing organizational interests if favorable conditions exist both inside and outside its organization; it aims to identify these specific conditions that facilitate bureaucratic influence.

Several assumptions about bureaucratic behavior in policy-making constitute the framework of my analysis. First, bureaucrats rationally pursue their organizational interests in policy-making. I mean by *rational* that the bureaucrats are fully conscious of the importance of their objectives and intend to achieve them. The concept of rationality here is not the same as that of economic rationality or substantive rationality, that is, utility maximization of individual rational actors. A concept called "bounded rationality" or "procedural rationality" (Simon 1976, 1987a, 1987b), which is distinct from pure economic rationality, will be used to examine the adaptive behaviors of bureaucrats in choosing goals and objectives, selecting means, and employing strategies.[6] Simon points out that the limited nature of human rationality, that is, irrational elements—for example, a shortage of information, misperception, or miscalculation—and emotional effects bound the area of rationality. The concept of "bounded rationality" or "procedural rationality" refers to this type of human rationality, which is, nonetheless, "intentionally rational."

The concept of bounded rationality defines human rationality in relation to the structure of the environment. Individual actors perceive the environment as a simplified model of a real situation and conform their behavior to this model so as to achieve objectives. Organizations, which "are the least 'natural,' most rationally contrived units of human association," provide individuals with the "structural environment" in which they reach a consensus on common objectives, and rationally choose and coordinate behavior in order to achieve these objectives. That is, "individual human beings are limited in knowledge, foresight, skill and time so that organizations are useful instruments for the achievement of human purpose" (Simon 1987a, 199). However, organizations in real situations do not necessarily promote rational behavior among their members; rather, they often produce disarray among members. This is because "organized groups of human beings are limited in ability to agree on goals, to communicate, and to cooperate that organizing becomes for them a 'problem'" (Simon 1987a, 199). In this way, the concept of bounded rationality closely relates individual rationality to the organizational environment and makes rationality assumptions compatible both at the individual and organizational levels.

Although using the same concept of bounded rationality, the focus of this study differs from Simon's concerning the mechanism of decision making inside the organization. Using this concept, the study will analyze both the limitations and possibility of individual rationality in the organizational context, as well as of the rationality of the organization as a whole. More specifically, I analyze how a political organization—in this case, a technocratic bureaucracy—strategically influences the policy-making process and pursues its objectives. Whereas Simon explores problems of organizational design in relation to the limited nature of rationality and psychology of the organized, this study analyzes the rationality of organizations in terms of the relationship with other organizations. The premise of this study is that organizations, if they are organized to promote members' pursuance of organizational goals, are likely, in the long run, to gain influence over other organizations or unorganized individuals. More specifically, this study first explores to what extent and in what way bureaucratic organizations can be organized to facilitate members' rational behavior, and then influence and cope with other political organizations, especially a political party. In this sense, my study aims ultimately to explore the political influence of rationality exercised at the organizational level by a technocratic bureaucracy.

Second, this study assumes that a bureaucratic organization, if it has a consensus about organizational interests among its members, tries to achieve them through policy-making. The power interests of a bureaucratic organization are closely connected with its decisions on policy. This is not because bureaucrats are power-seeking Machiavellians, but rather because their attempts to achieve policy objectives go hand-in-hand with their pursuance of organizational interests. The theory relies ultimately on the following assumption about the relationship between policy-making and technocratic expertise: an objective definition of "social welfare" or "public interest" is impossible in policy-making; thus any definition of social welfare or public interest in a particular policy problem is always accompanied by a political intention to support some proposal and oppose the other. Bureaucrats are often motivated by a sense of duty or mission to seek to realize what they regard as the social welfare or the public interest. Their interpretations are inevitably related to their discretionary power and are influenced by considerations of power. In this sense, the bureaucrats' professional consciousness as policy experts does not necessarily obstruct their pursuance of power through policy-making.

Third, the present study assumes that the goal of a bureaucratic organization is to increase, or at least maintain, its discretionary power, but that the power of the bureaucracy is not measured quantitatively, for example, by budget size. In my study, the bureaucratic goal that bureaucrats pursue is quite different from that used by the rational choice theorists who assume that the primary interest of bureaucrats is to maximize the size of their budgets (Niskanen 1971). My study considers discretionary power to be influenced significantly by factors such as administrative procedures, the institutional relationship between the executive branch and the legislature, the decision-making routine, and party politics.[7] I examine the complex relationship between the power of bureaucrats and budget size and pay attention to the effect of institutions on political behavior. Thus, in this study, the goal of bureaucratic organizations to maintain their discretionary power is specified by referring to institutional factors that are particular to the bureaucratic organization—the Ministry of Finance in Japan, which is the subject of the study.

Fourth, the apolitical appearance of technocratic ideas leaves plenty of room for the bureaucrats to influence political discourse in favor of their desired policy outcomes. As technocrats inside the government, an extensive use of policy information and technocratic ideas serves to make their desired policies more legitimate. Their easy access to policy information and policy expertise does not directly guarantee their advantage in relation to other policymakers, that is, party politicians. But the bureaucrats gain a strategic advantage by claiming the "technocratic neutrality" of their position and by keeping their distance from any special-interest representation.

While strategic advantage derives from their administrative positions as technocrats, the biggest constraint on the implementation of a policy for bureaucrats comes from the opposition of the electorate—both special-interest groups and the unorganized voting public that the party politicians represent. An additional assumption about bureaucratic behavior can be drawn from the existence of this constraint. If bureaucrats choose an objective that they cannot achieve immediately, they rationally employ a strategy designed to lead, over time, to policy outcomes not otherwise obtainable. The bureaucrats first attempt to obtain reliable political sponsors for their proposed policies among incumbent politicians, influential representatives of special interests, or both. Then, the incumbent politicians who have given critical support for a bureaucratic proposal inform bureaucrats of the intensity of public opposition or possible compromise measures to facilitate the acceptance of the policy proposal. This study does not presume that bureaucrats are superior to incumbent politicians in collecting information about social interests involving a certain policy issue. Rather, it assumes that to achieve policy objectives bureaucrats need the cooperation of incumbent politicians who articulate social interests and alleviate opposition to the policy.

Sixth, the focus on the rational behaviors of bureaucrats does not imply the irrationality of the incumbent party or coalition of parties[8] that support bureaucrats' efforts to implement an unpopular policy. This study assumes that the party politicians, especially incumbent politicians, also rationally pursue their own interests. It will explore, then, a condition in which bureaucrats have a good chance of obtaining political support from incumbent politicians for their proposed policy that may have an adverse influence on their party's popularity. Support is obtained not because of the irrationality or ignorance of politicians, but because of different interests among individual members inside the party organization. First, the party politicians elected with a popular mandate have different interests as far as they serve their own election districts' constituencies. Second, there are also differences between the backbenchers, who often have weak electoral bases, and the experienced and leading members, who secure organized support and are more interested in promoting their reputations in the poli-cymakers' circle. To obtain party approval for their proposal, the bureau-crats take advantage of these potential conflicts inside the party.

The effective pursuance of organizational interests by bureaucrats also hinges on the coordination of the members' interests. Based on the assump-tions described above, the present analysis aims to identify specific condi-tions that give an advantage to bureaucratic influence. This study does not conclude that bureaucrats generally have an advantage over the party.

Instead of relying on abstract terms, this study will present the argument by closely relating to it an empirical case. More specifically, this study employs a concrete strategy for political analysis: it uses an "ideal type"[9] of a certain phenomenon to increase the understanding of it. I use the recent Japanese tax reform case to illustrate the influence of technocratic bureau-crats over policy agendas. In other words, the study does not provide an explanation for Japanese policy-making in general; rather, it is an analy-sis of bureaucratic influence over policy agendas in a setting in which the stable bureaucratic organization faces an unchanging incumbent party throughout a process, such as the Japanese tax reform case.

The MOF had planned the introduction of the major indirect tax since the early 1970s, and has worked continuously for its implementation since the late 1970s. Why was this unpopular new tax of interest to the MOF? How were the bureaucrats in the MOF able to persuade incumbent politi-cians to support a policy that threatened the dominant party's popularity with the electorate? How did the new tax finally overcome the public oppo-sition that had recurred during the reform process and even after the intro-duction of the new tax? These questions should attract one's attention to the Japanese tax reform.

A reconstruction of the reform process here will show that the new tax was closely related to the organizational interests of the MOF, and that the political maneuvering of the MOF bureaucrats led to its passage. Proposals for reform failed twice (in 1979 and in 1987) before a tax on consumption was enacted. The introduction of an apparently unpopular new tax cannot be explained by unchanging factors, such as the partisanship of the party government, institutionalized procedures of policy-making, and so on, under which proposals for new taxes had failed twice before. Additional factors unrelated to the MOF's political maneuvering—i.e., business cy-cles, foreign economic pressures, timing of elections, political leaders' per-sonal commitments, and so on—might have occasionally intervened in this process. However, the MOF's commitment to the implementation of a major indirect tax is the only factor that consistently and continuously affected the reform process which led to the final introduction of the unpopular new tax. The MOF persuaded the incumbent LDP of the value of the new tax on consumption, enlisted the support of big business for it, coped with the opposition from special interest groups, and influenced the policy discourse so as to alleviate opposition from the unorganized public.

The recent tax reform is exceptional among Japanese policy decisions in providing an especially clear-cut example of bureaucratic influence, and thus is an ideal case with which to examine bureaucratic influence. First, in Japanese politics, bureaucratic influence is commonly observed by scholars, though disagreements remain as to the importance of its role in policy-making. The modernization of the Japanese state has helped make active bureaucratic involvement in policy-making an integral component of contemporary Japanese politics. Muramatsu and Krauss (1984) draw two important conclusions by comparing the Japanese bureaucracy to those in other industrialized countries (the United States, Britain, France, and West Germany).[10] In Japan, where bureaucracy played a major role in modernization and authoritarian rule, the convergence of the roles of politicians and bureaucrats comes from the increasing power of politicians during the democratization process. However, in the Anglo-American countries, bureaucracy is more important in policy-making because of the growing complexities of policy-making in modern states in the mid-twentieth century. In these countries, the bureaucratization of policy-making is a relatively new tendency. Consequently, in Japan, the competence of the bureaucracy in the policy-making process has a longer history and deeper roots than in the Anglo-American and some Western European countries that modernized earlier than Japan. This study intends to show that even in Japan, whose bureaucracy has been considered strong, bureaucratic influence depends on contingent factors and does not constitute an institutional necessity. This presentation serves as a strong counterexample to the explanations that attribute bureaucratic influence to the monopolization of policy expertise and autonomy from political pressure.[11]

Second, during the reform process, Japan had a predominant party system that had been in place since 1955 in which the policy-making process was institutionalized between the bureaucracy and the party in power to an extent greater than in other systems experiencing frequent alterations in party government.[12] Under the predominance of the Liberal Democratic Party, policy-making that preceded the legislative process consisted of the interaction of bureaucrats and the same incumbent party and excluded opposition parties. Continuous control of the government by the LDP, as well as relatively strong party discipline, made it possible for bureaucrats to count on the passage of bills approved by the LDP leadership. Bureaucrats concentrated their efforts on obtaining the LDP's approval for a proposed policy.

In such a system, bureaucratic attempts to influence policy-making significantly change policy outcomes. An unchanging incumbent party provides stable circumstances in which bureaucrats can pursue their desired policies. But at the same time, the party itself is a coherent and competitive political organization that is not easily tractable for bureaucrats.

The Japanese bureaucracy also has a stable membership. The high-level civil servants in the Japanese central ministries, whom this study labels "bureaucrats," are not politically appointed but are recruited by examinations. They have working-life-long tenures, and almost all of them remain with the same ministry or agency for their entire working lives. In this employment system, the bureaucratic organization develops its members' loyalty by socializing newly entering members and by guaranteeing for all of them certain job opportunities (promotion to management positions) and security (working-life-long tenures in the ministry or in a related public or private organization). An unchanging incumbent party and the stability of the bureaucratic organization make the observations of interaction between the two groups easier.

Third, the tax reform case provides a good example of bureaucratic influence when the bureaucratic organization pursues a policy goal through effective cooperation with political leaders. The introduction of the new tax was an important policy goal which the MOF consciously pursued. Establishing a broad-based consumption tax was closely related to the MOF's organizational interest of increasing, or at least maintaining, control over the budget. The entire ministry made a deep commitment to the new tax. During the ten years of the reform process in this study, the MOF consistently put the highest priority on the introduction of a broad-based consumption tax.[13] Moreover, the new tax was a major policy change that would influence not only special interest groups but also the unorganized public as consumers. Before the introduction of the new tax, Japan had had no major indirect tax broadly based on consumption.

Fifth, there is reason to believe that the bureaucratic proposal for the introduction of the new tax was never a reflection of the incumbent party's view nor of certain social groups'. When the Ministry of Finance first proposed the new tax in the late 1970s, opposition came from every segment of society—the governing party, opposition parties, special interest groups, the unorganized public, and even from the other ministries. The incumbent party politicians, with few exceptions, uncompromisingly opposed the first

14

proposal for the new tax in the late 1970s. The intensity of the opposition in the first place, as well as its importance as a policy change, meant that the bureaucrats had significant obstacles to overcome in the implementation of the new tax. The unpopularity of the new tax required influence over the policy agenda by bureaucrats who had initiated the proposal.

Sixth, tax policy-making in Japan in the 1980s demonstrates how bureaucrats can adapt to a new situation in which party politicians increase their policy expertise and are more likely to intervene in policy-making. The new taxes on consumption were proposed from the late 1970s to the late 1980s as incumbent politicians increased their tax policy expertise, and the tax council inside the LDP increased its influence over policy-making. The introduction of the new tax was a result of the bureaucrats' successful adjustment to a new situation in which incumbent politicians became interventionists. The MOF relied on the specialized knowledge of incumbent politicians when it persuaded them of the value of the consumption tax. Enlisting their support, which might not have been obtained without their special understanding of tax policies, was critical for making the consumption tax a formal party decision. Because many party leaders who were familiar with tax issues came to support the reform, backbenchers' approval of it was ensured through party discipline. It was not a coincidence that the unpopular new tax was introduced after many incumbent politicians increased their policy expertise.

Chapter 1 introduces the framework of an explanation for the strategic pursuance of policy objectives by bureaucratic organizations. More specifically, it will explain how bureaucrats make the social welfare considerations of a policy compatible with their organizational interests, and how they decide to pursue a certain policy objective. Discussion of competing explanations of bureaucratic behaviors and different concepts of rationality will precede the introduction of this framework. Chapter 2 applies the theoretical scheme introduced in chapter 1 to the Japanese tax reform case; it relates the framework to the Japanese reform case and introduces the next four empirical chapters.

In chapters 3 through 6, I introduce the Japanese tax reform case as an empirical example of bureaucratic influence over policy-making. The major inquiries in my case study are (1) how, in the mid-1980s and again in the late 1980s, the Ministry of Finance could put on the political agenda an unpopular new tax that every segment of society had opposed in the late 1970s; and (2) why the incumbent Liberal Democratic Party accepted a policy which it had every right to expect would place its political fate at stake?[14]

Chapter 3 deals with the case of the first failed attempt to introduce the VAT in 1979, when the government demonstrated the necessity of tax increases to overcome a budget deficit and proposed the new tax. This presentation will demonstrate that all the social interests and party politicians (except the prime minister at that time) strongly opposed the new tax. The straightforward tax proposal drove the bureaucrats into a tight corner where they were forced to shelve any tax reform proposal for the time being.

Chapter 4 investigates the implementation of an austerity policy from 1981 to the mid-1980s. This austerity campaign, the Administrative Reform, was formally initiated by a blue-ribbon advisory council under Prime Minister Suzuki and was fueled by public criticism of the fiscal authority. But the Ministry of Finance effectively coped with this major policy agenda and steered the way to the next proposal of the new tax on consumption through implementation of specific fiscal and tax policies.

Chapter 5 presents the case of the second failed proposal for a revenue-neutral reform in 1987. At the time, the government combined the introduction of the new sales tax with an income tax reduction. The tax proposal failed again because of a failure to fine-tune the reform proposal inside the administration, especially to solve a subtle disagreement between the MOF and the prime minister at the time. In the electoral campaign, Prime Minister Nakasone promised not to introduce the new tax. Subsequently, the tax reform lost political legitimacy when it was believed that the prime minister broke his promise on the tax proposal.

Chapter 6 deals with the process that led to the ultimate introduction of the consumption tax in 1989 when the MOF, with the incumbent party's cooperation, shaped the new agenda for the tax reform. The study demonstrates how the government obtained the public's reluctant consent for the new tax by emphasizing that the tax reform would rectify tax inequity and secure financial sources for social security. Their claims were not, however, fully justified. The argument will show that this inherent weakness in the government's position generated active opposition to a new system of the consumption tax after it became effective in April 1989.

Chapter 7 summarizes the theoretical implications of the Japanese case for the study of bureaucratic behavior.

# Bureaucratic Rationality and Strategic Behavior: The Framework

AMONG political scientists there exists a widespread recognition that bureaucracy competes with the representative political body in influencing policy-making. Bureaucrats have an edge in an industrialized society where the formulation of policies requires specialized knowledge and training (Page 1985; Aberbach et al. 1981; Suleiman 1974). This view attributes the rising influence of bureaucrats to the increasing complexities of policy problems in contemporary democracies. That is, "bureaucrats, monopolizing as they do much of the available information about the shortcomings of existing policies, as well as much of the technical expertise necessary to design practical alternatives, have gained a predominant influence over the evolution of the agenda for decision" (Putnam 1973, 257).

At the same time, in the discipline there has persisted a view of the bureaucracy as a constituent of the "rational" state which has a strong arm to intervene in socioeconomic activities and regulate markets. Recently, economists have come to study the behavior of policymakers with increasing interest in the role of governments in economic management and have presented another version of the "bureaucrats-as-rational-actors" perspective. Social choice theorists have applied economic theory to the analysis of political phenomena and studied bureaucratic behavior based on the assumption of economic rationality.

In this chapter, first I will argue that bureaucratic influence over policy agendas is misunderstood because of incomplete specification of the rational behavior of bureaucrats in the organization. I will review these competing views in order to contrast them with my own approach. I assume that bureaucrats are rational actors, but the concept of rationality in my analysis is different both from "rationality" in the state-centered analysis and from economic "rationality." I will base my analysis on the concept of "bounded rationality" and show that bureaucratic influence depends ultimately on a sequence of behaviors that constitutes a process, instead of routine procedures and an institutionalized decision-making pattern that is embedded in a particular political system.

17

A CRITIQUE OF EXISTING THEORIES OF BUREAUCRACY

*Sociological and Political Analyses of Bureaucracy*

In political science and sociology, the institutional analysis of bureaucracy dates back to Weber's pioneering work (Weber 1978). Weber regards the bureaucracy as an important force in the modernization process. This historical perspective leads him to highlight two different aspects of a bureaucracy as a social institution. First, a bureaucracy is a more effective organization than those that preceded it because its rule depends on legal authority. Second, bureaucracy is a political organization in which technical knowledge and expertise in policy-making challenge the contemporary representative institutions of elected politicians.[1] Weber's analysis has a broad perspective that includes various historical and social factors, and his prediction of an increasingly powerful bureaucracy is prescient. However, he falls short of completing the explanation of bureaucratic behavior in policy-making. Assuming two conflicting aims for bureaucrats—promotion of their personal interests and concern for the welfare of the governed (utility consideration) (226)—Weber formulates the concept of instrumental rationality[2] to explain the organizational principle by which bureaucrats effectively exercise legal authority. But the analysis of bureaucratic behavior by instrumental rationality does not explain how bureaucrats increase their influence over policy-making nor what kind of interests, if any, they pursue in policy-making.

Some political scientists have begun to consider bureaucrats as a group of individual policymakers in a dynamic political context, but an emphasis on institutional analysis is persistent in the tradition of sociological and political analyses of bureaucracy. The questions posed by a seminal work by Aberbach et al. (1981) show this tendency very well.

> [W]e want to ask not about bureaucratic and political institutions, but about bureaucrats and politicians as policymakers. How are they different? Indeed, *are* they different? Do they come from different backgrounds? Have they different priorities? Do they consider different criteria when making decisions? Do they regard public affairs and the process of policy-making differently? Have they different world views? What do these differences, if any, imply for their relationships and for their performance as policymakers? What difference would it make if all important government decisions were made by civil servants instead of by party politicians, or vice versa? (3)

Assuming the Weberian proposition that the bureaucracy would become a competitive and even threatening partner with the representative body, political scientists study the individual characteristics of each group of actors. These include social background, ideology, education, as well as their priorities, goals, and objectives in policy-making. In order to learn how bureaucrats behave in general, scholars scrutinize the differences and similarities between bureaucrats and politicians, and examine what kind of relationship they have.

This kind of analysis of the bureaucracy is useful for understanding what social groups or classes provide two different groups of political elites, and how conflicting interests and values in a society are represented in policy-making by a recruitment process of the political elites. However, the focus on these differences between two groups of policymakers diverts the scholarly attention from what still distinguishes the two different groups of political actors. Thus, many sociological analyses conclude that bureaucrats and politicians have converging roles and often collusive interests. This conclusion identifies the general trend of a changing relationship between them as politicians have gained more policy expertise and bureaucrats have become more active participants in politics. But, at the same time, it says little about differences in organizations to which they belong—bureaucratic agencies and political parties.

### Bureaucracy as a Constituent of a Rational State

One of the most influential views in political science regards the bureaucracy as a constituent of a state whose actions are autonomous from social interests, and thus effective and rational for the purpose of their control. The recent attention to political institutions has revitalized scholarly interest in the state (March and Olsen 1984, 1989; Evans, Rueschemeyer, and Skocpol 1985). Though admitting the possible irrationality of such actions, this view often regards state actions as attempts to reinforce the public authority or interests of state officials, and thus considers them purposeful and consistent. Skocpol (1985) hypothesizes that "one (hidden or overt) feature of all autonomous state actions will be reinforcement of the prerogatives of collectivities of state officials," and that autonomous state activity "can never really be 'disinterested'" (15).

The rationality of state actions is of special interest to those who analyze the state's role in economic development. To consider the state's role in the economy, they distinguish between two economic systems: one based on the self-interested behaviors of individuals and the other on some substantive guidance and centralized authority. One example is found in Weber (1978, 109). He distinguishes the *market economy*, which "results from actions oriented to advantages in exchange on the basis of self-interests and where co-operation takes place only through the exchange process," and the *plan economy*, in which "economic action is oriented systematically to an established substantive order, whether agreed or imposed, which is valid within an organization."

Students of the industrial policies of contemporary democracies consider the state capable of providing such an order.[3] Some of them also assume that the state could have more influence over the economy than the mere provision or maintenance of order. This argument, which links active state intervention in the economy to the effective allocation of resources between industrial sectors, often uses Japan as an example. The typical argument is found in Johnson (1982). He makes a conceptual distinction between a regulatory or market-rational state and a developmental or plan-rational state. The regulatory state, a good example of which is the United States, is interested in regulatory functions, that is, maintaining competition and consumer protection to supplement price systems. The developmental state, represented by Japan, sets substantial goals for economic development, that is, it determines which industries ought to grow more and which are no longer important, and then actively pursues these goals. Another example of the argument is found in a comparative study by Zysman (1983) of financial markets of five industrialized democracies. Zysman regards Japan, as well as France, as prime examples of state-led growth systems in which government bureaucracy influenced industrial adjustment to a changing economic situation through financial markets. In these systems, he argues, the bureaucrats apply administrative rules and manipulate credit tax and trade policies on a case-by-case basis, facilitate efficient resource allocation, and promote the growth of more promising industrial sectors.

The literature cited above successfully investigates resources and opportunities that the bureaucracy, a constituent of the active state, has to influence industries and shows its interaction with the private sector. Though admitting the possible mistakes, misperceptions, and irrationality of bureaucrats, the literature maintains that bureaucratic actions are effective enough to contribute to industrial developments. But the goals of industrial adjustment and effective resource allocation are not as obvious in real situations as argued in the literature. According to the argument, bureaucrats pursue particularistic policies, that is, those that support specific industrial sectors or even particular firms for development. Not all the necessary information for implementing such particularistic policies can be obtained in a real situation. At the time of policy-making, even the available information is located in the private sector, not in the public sector. With this significant disadvantage, how can individual bureaucrats anticipate promising industrial sectors in future international markets and reach a consensus on effective policies to stimulate industrial growth?

The literature cited here, as well as works with similar arguments, often emphasizes intensive communication between private and public sectors through which bureaucrats obtain information on markets from industries and businesses. There are two plausible reasons why the bureaucrats can obtain information. First, they have special measures to force businesses and industries to collect as much information as possible, to provide it to the bureaucrats, and to ensure no noncompliance or tricks. Second, on the contrary, voluntary cooperation with the bureaucrats is beneficial to business and industry. The argument that supports the rational policy-making of bureaucrats seems to employ both reasons, but falls short of presenting them convincingly. It explains neither the measures by which the bureaucrats detect noncompliance and false or incomplete revelation of information by industries, nor a specific reason why cooperation with the bureaucrats is more beneficial for industries.

The literature emphasizes two observations: the resources and opportunities available to bureaucrats to influence markets, and the relatively effective resource allocation across industries of the country in question. It draws the conclusion that active state intervention is rational in the sense that it helps industries adjust to changing conditions of international competition. This conclusion is plausible if both strong arms of state bureaucracy and relatively good economic performance are observed in the same countries. However, there are more places for investigation—for example, why individual bureaucrats come up with effective industrial policies and why such policies often reach a consensus among members of the bureaucratic organization.

The literature that regards the state as a rational actor shares an interest with this study in the goal-oriented behavior of the bureaucratic organization. But, as described above, its focus diverges from the question of why bureaucrats are as rational as it contends. More precisely, the literature presumes the rationality of the bureaucratic organization without paying enough attention to the rationality question at the individual level, and to the coordination problem between the individual and organizational levels. The next section will review the economic literature that is built on the analysis of the self-interested behaviors of individual bureaucrats.

*Application of Economic Approaches to Studies of Bureaucracy*

BUREAUCRATS AS RATIONAL ACTORS

*Development of a Maximizing Bureau Model.*   The study of bureaucracy by economists began in the half-a-century-old subdiscipline of public or social choice theory. Public choice theory has extended the application of economic theory to subjects that had been of interest to political science, for example, the state, government, voters, politicians, and bureaucracy. Alternatively, public choice theory is interested in the impact of political institutions or political actors on the economy.[4]

Orthodox economics has continued to assume that the role of policymakers can be reduced to helping economic systems work well. This idealistic premise allows economists to avoid seriously considering the motivations of the policymakers themselves. Keynes, who first advocated active government intervention in the economy, presumes that a small and enlightened group of wise people make policy decisions.[5] Buchanan and Wagner (1977) argue that this premise is not different from the notion presented by Wicksell in 1896 that "their [economists'] role was one of proffering advice to a benevolent despot" (Wicksell 1958).

Instead of the aforementioned assumption in economics, public choice theory contends that policymakers are neither benevolent nor wise despots but egoistic and rational actors. Public choice theorists clearly distinguish between politicians and bureaucrats as groups of elites who can impose decisions *externally* on society, and the governed who are reactive participants. They analyze policymakers as well as the governed using the same basic decision-making model (Buchanan 1972a, 11–14).

Using this position, two founding fathers of public choice theory, Downs and Tullock, try to generalize the decision-making behavior of bureaucrats. Downs constructs a model in which five different types of bureaucrats pursue particular subsets of goals (Downs 1957).[6] At the same time, he analyzes bureaucratic organizations in a social context (for example, in terms of the recruitment of bureaucrats, the impact of bureaucratic organization on behavior, and so on), assuming that every bureaucratic organization's social function strongly influences its internal structure and behavior. Differing from Downs, Tullock argues that the most obvious characteristic of bureaucratic behavior is a desire for career advancement in the organization (Tullock 1965). In his explanation, bureaucrats pursue this goal rationally, that is, so as to maximize their utility, as is assumed in orthodox economics. But he also pays attention to the hierarchical relationship in the bureaucratic organization and defines "politics" as "social situations in which the dominant or primary relations are those between superior and subordinates" (Tullock 1965, 11). Consequently, both emphasize the importance of the organizational and social aspects of bureaucracies in order to explain a central concern of the theory of the state: bureaucratic decisions on the provision of public goods and budget.

The application of economic theory to bureaucratic study is, however, not limited to these two pioneering works. For example, Mueller (1989, 251 n. 3) says that "these earlier works do not attempt to develop a theory or model of bureaucracy from a public choice perspective. Instead, they use the economics methodology to examine various facets of bureaucratic organizations." Especially after Niskanen (1971), public choice theorists typically regarded the earlier works as incomplete models from the social choice perspective. Niskanen (1971) points out that Downs and Tullock stop "short of developing the consequences of maximizing behavior on the budget and output performance of bureaus" (8). He argues that a complete theory of governmental decision making should incorporate bureaucratic preferences, as well as the preferences of the governed. Consideration of these preferences in an account of public administration is, according to him, *not* compatible with the organic concept of the state, which regards the state as a product of certain historical or social situations.

Therefore, Niskanen, differing from the two pioneers, is exclusively concerned with the preferences of bureaucrats and of the governed in explaining the annual budget game. He assumes that monopolization of information concerning the cost of government services enables bureaucrats to pursue budget maximization rather than the maximization of the sponsor's (parliament's or constituency's) welfare.[7] He presumes the dominance of a monopoly bureau in a budget decision (supply side decision) and the secondary or even impotent role of the preferences of the governed (demand side). As a result, he makes the utility maximization of the bureaucrats closely associated with the budget (output) decision.[8]

While Niskanen explains the recurrent pattern of annual budget decisions and shows the short-term effect of the budget maximizing bureau, Brennan and Buchanan (1980) extend the monopoly bureau model to explain the nature of the state. In the same way as Niskanen's, their model defines the government as a revenue-maximizing Leviathan, and it rules out explicit consideration of electoral constraints, such as franchise, voting rules, legislative power, and so on. Differing from Niskanen, who presumes a bureaucratic dominance over popular representation, however, they explain the ineffectiveness of political constraints by the rational ignorance of voters and the vulnerability of voting equilibria under majority rule (Brennan and Buchanan 1980, 17–23). They present a theory of the state, then, in which the monopolistic bureau has central importance and taxpayers are primarily subjects of the governmental power to tax. From this position, they draw a normative conclusion that effective long-term constraints on government efforts to maximize revenue will not arise from popular representation under a contemporary democratic system, but require a constitutional limit on the power to tax.

The theories discussed above attribute expanding government output—which is presumed to be a result of divergence from an ideal level—to the monopolistic influence of bureaucrats on policy-making. Another important assumption is that the rational behavior of legislators and the electorate only weakly constrains the budget or revenue maximization of bureaucrats. Aranson and Ordeshook summarize this idea nicely:

> The monopoly bureau construct, in sum, takes some electorally-mandated level of public goods production or regulation as given and implicitly as desirable. Then it shows how, through various artifices such as the fiscal illusion, agenda control, or the substitution of different, and sometimes perverse, objective functions, bureaucrats expand jurisdictions and output beyond electorally mandated levels. The monopoly bureau literature may now be joined with the proposition that bureaus and agencies are engaged in producing private goods at collective cost. In this case, the beneficiaries are either the bureaucrats, who are the regulators themselves, or "high-demanders" of agency services, or both. (Aranson and Ordeshook 1981, 88)

The economists who study bureaucrats make two presuppositions in order to simplify our understanding of their decisions about government output. First, they presume that the budget or revenue maximization are the primary bureaucratic interests that influence budget decisions. Because of this assumption, economic studies ignore other plausible objectives of bureaucrats, especially the welfare considerations of their political masters—the politicians and the electorate—or what the bureaucrats define as social welfare. Second, they assume that both the maximization behavior of bureaucrats and the electoral pressure on politicians in a democratic society result in the expansion of government services and outputs.[9] Here, the concept of bureaucratic maximization of government output is theoretically consistent with the vote maximization of politicians by Downs (1957)—that is, "parties formulate policies in order to win elections, rather than win elections in order to formulate policies" (28). Thus, these theorists could argue that the strong pressure on expanding government service from the democratic process is highly compatible with the policy dynamics inside a bureaucracy. The first presupposition reduces bureaucratic behavior to that of a rational economic actor, ignoring other plausible objectives that may be of more interest to the bureaucracy. The second presupposition allows economists to slight the potential conflict between two groups of policymakers. Bureaucrats try to maximize revenue or budget and neglect increasing (per-unit) costs for the public service, while politicians try to provide their constituencies with as much benefit as possible from the given size of the revenue or budget. This construct means that politicians have neither incentives nor opportunities to control bureaucrats, and thus it denies a strategic relationship between bureaucrats and politicians. These two presuppositions provide the foundation of the monopoly bureau model.

Assumptions of bureaucratic dominance derived from a monopolistic position and the absence of political control over the bureaucracy are not as obvious as the maximization bureau construct presumes. In Niskanen's model, a suboptimal level of production of public service by bureaucratic maximization is attributed ultimately to the simple fact that each bureau monopolizes a supply of designated public service. The monopolistic position here means also the full-agenda control power of bureaus to make take-it-or-leave-it budget proposals and the lopsided information that only bureaus know about their own cost schedules and their sponsor's true demands. Based on this assumption, Niskanen does not need to consider seriously how bureaucrats manipulate policy agendas, but the assumption is too strong to be held in a real situation.

Using as a case the school budgets in local governments in the United States, Romer and Rosenthal (1978) show that the agenda-setting power of a bureau to make take-it-or-leave-it proposals does not necessarily guarantee strong control over voter decisions, as presumed by Niskanen, because "the level of supply that voters approve depends on the status quo position" (Romer and Rosenthal 1978, 29). Niskanen asserts that the legislature or the electorate as a funder "is assumed not to increase its potential power as a single buyer of the service, for either lack of incentive or opportunity" (Niskanen 1971, 45).[10] In contrast, Miller and Moe (1983), and Bendor, Taylor, and Van Gaalen (1985) show that a small modification of the monopoly bureau model, for example, a bureau's presentation of a unit price of supply output (a marginal cost schedule of public service) to a funder, will allow more representation of the funder's preferences in the resulting budget.

BUREAUCRATS AS AGENTS OF POLITICAL MASTERS

Going far beyond small modifications of the model of bureaucratic dominance, other public choice scholars view governmental decisions as subject to political control. While theories by Niskanen and by Brennan and

Buchanan view the state above its citizens and hold that decisions about public service are dominated by the preferences of individuals inside the government, the opposite view regards the state as the carrier of the public will. The latter view, which focuses on the linkage between public preference and policy decisions, is central to some normative and positive public choice literature (Arrow 1963; Downs 1957; Buchanan and Tullock 1962).[11] Although much of this work is institutionally impoverished, some scholars in this tradition have studied the bureaucratic relationship between the legislature and the electorate.

In American politics, scholars have recently begun to apply an economic approach to the positive analysis of policy making. Learning from pioneering studies about the relationship between the U.S. Congress and bureaucrats (Fiorina 1977; Mayhew 1974), scholars have tried to develop a bargaining model between Congress and bureaucrats (including executives). They have tried also to incorporate the strategic relationship between the electorate and Congress to it (Calvert, Moran, and Weingast 1987; Calvert, McCubbins, and Weingast 1989; Eavey and Miller 1984; Fiorina 1982; McCubbins 1985; McCubbins and Schwartz 1984; Miller 1977; Weingast 1984).

This approach, the so-called rational choice approach, shares the same premise as economists' works on regulation, for example (Becker 1983; Peltzman 1976; Stigler 1971). This premise is the linkage between social interests and policy decisions, which is regarded as a voting equilibrium (Shepsle 1979, 1986; Shepsle and Weingast 1981).

The election incentive of lawmakers, especially of congressmen at the federal level, is a critical assumption for studies using a rational choice analysis of the executive-legislative relationship, as well as of the internal dynamics of Congress. Desire for reelection motivates congressmen to represent their constituencies' interests. To serve well, congressmen need to check policy decisions made by the executive and administrative branches.[12] In this sense, rational choice scholars significantly modify the second assumption of the monopoly bureau model—the ineffectiveness of the political control of politicians over bureaucrats.

The principal-agent theory, one of the newly developed theories of the firm in economics,[13] is applied to analyze the Congress-bureaucracy relationship (a congressman is a principal and a bureaucrat is an agent), as well as the Congress-electorate relationship (this time, a congressman is an agent of her or his constituency). The principal-agent theory focuses on problems of control that arise from asymmetries of information between a principal and an agent and the imperfect observability of an agent's behavior by a principal.[14] Congress is the pivotal point of two different principal-agent relationships, and thus the voting equilibrium in decision-making procedures in Congress is of special interest to this approach.

Despite the common premise discussed above, however, the rational choice approach in American politics is significantly different from the economic literature in its treatment of the political process. Early economic literature on regulation regards policymakers as neutral intermediaries of social interests, that is, "politicians and bureaucrats are assumed to carry out the political allocations resulting from the competition among pressure groups" (Becker 1983, 396), on the one hand. On the other, the rational choice literature studies the relationship between the self-interested behavior of policymakers and political institutions. This approach *does not presume* that policymakers carry out social interests; rather, it *attributes* the linkage between social interests and policy outcomes to behaviors of individual policymakers under the influence of political institutions. This is the reason why the approach is often called the positive theory of institutions (PTI) (Moe 1990, 127).

To ensure the successful influence of social interests over policy decisions, the delegation relationship needs to favor the interests of principals in two different principal-agent relationships, that is, the one between the electorate and Congress and the other between Congress and the bureaucracy. To prevent Congress from making decisions against its interests, first the voters[15] change their electoral and financial support based on congressmen's contributions to their benefits.[16] Representation of their own constituency's interests is the one prominent goal for congressmen.[17]

The principal-agent approach in the legislative-bureaucratic relationship may be more controversial than its application to the relationship between the electorate and the Congress. That approach disputes the observation that bureaucrats autonomously make many policy decisions, and argues that their authority is a result of delegation rather than abdication by elected lawmakers. This delegation is observed through examination of a layer of principal-agent relationship embedded in institutionalized patterns of administrative and legislative procedures. The logic of congressional delegation is strong enough to force scholarship to reconsider the possibility of the persistent influence of social interests. But the approach does not necessarily comprehend all the possible cases and processes.

The first reservation about the conclusion drawn from this approach is its neglect of the role of political parties. The rational choice approach must pay greater attention to party influences over individual politicians' voting decisions, especially to the coordination of conflicting interests of party

27

members; their differing interests are ultimately attributed to different constituencies' preferences across election districts. Departing from the early neglect of the importance of parties,[18] the recent work using the principal-agent approach argues that the parties in the U.S. Congress (especially in the House) play very positive roles. Kiewiet and McCubbins (1991) show that the congressional parties serve to solve collective action problems and avoid voting cycles through coordination of their members' interests, and thus help the effective control by congressmen over bureaucrats in decisions on budget appropriations. Cox and McCubbins (1993) regard majority parties in the House as legislative cartels that aim at controlling the agendas in favor of interests of majority party members. Their findings are convincing enough to reject the so-called abdication hypothesis, and to refute the presumption of weakness of the U.S. political parties.

These findings, however, should not be overextended to a full rejection of potential conflicts between party-level decisions and individual members' interests if considering that the congressional parties do not have strict enough discipline to ensure party votes. For example, in Congress, party voting, in which a majority of one party votes against a majority of another, is not prevalent. Rohde (1991, 14–15) examined the ratio of party votes in terms of the proportion to total voting results in the House annually from 1955 to 1988, and reported that even the highest ratio was 64 percent (in 1987). If there is leeway for party members to vote independently of the majority decision or the leadership decision of the party, the members' compliance or agreement with the party decision may be interpreted as a voluntary one which serves to solve collective action problems. Strong enough discipline to require members to vote with the party on almost all bills, however, completely changes this complementary relationship between party influence and pursuance of individual interests. In many industrialized democracies with parliamentary systems, where the party discipline is strong and the party vote is a common practice, there remains a persistent possibility that party influence results in the repression of subordinate members' interests. Such systems certainly need a much more sophisticated mechanism of interest coordination to ensure a reflection of social interests in final policy decisions; even using such a mechanism, they produce more frequent examples of repression rather than coordination of line members' interests than the system with weak party discipline. Although the influence of constituencies' interests on policy decisions through the party organization is an important factor in congressional control over the bureaucracy, the possible distortion of social interest representation by rigid party discipline may allow some place for bureaucratic influence over political decisions.

Second, the rational choice theorists have identified the resources and institutionalized patterns of decision making by congressmen as the means to control bureaucratic activities. These means contribute to increasing compliance behaviors of bureaucrats but *do not guarantee* them. Thus some scholars argue that bureaucrats still may be able to take advantage of their expertise. Responding to this criticism, a recent study of the rational choice approach does not directly relate legislative control to a specific decision-making structure. Instead, it admits that bureaucrats have significant advantages because of their expertise, and tries to identify additional conditions that help the legislators to obtain useful and truthful information (Lupia and McCubbins, forthcoming).

These recent developments in the principal-agent approach complement the present study. My aim is to find conditions that facilitate bureaucratic influence over the above institutionalized patterns of policy-making and monopolization of expertise. If the "structure" of policy-making embedded in political institutions does not guarantee legislative control over bureaucratic (noncompliance) behaviors, we need to pay attention to bureaucratic incentives and behaviors that the previous rational choice approach does not directly investigate.

In this sense, this study examines the opposite side of the analysis from the existing rational choice perspectives: bureaucratic organization. Despite their quite different assumptions about bureaucratic behaviors, both the maximization bureau model and the principal-agent approach do not directly analyze bureaucratic organization. The maximization bureau model assumes that the self-interests of bureaucrats are simply associated with budget size that is quantitatively measured. Thus it avoids the problems inherent in organizations, that is, how to reach a consensus of organizational goals, make members aware of them, and coordinate members' behavior to pursue them. The maximization bureau model presumes no conflicts between the self-interests of individuals and organizational interests. Without some coordination mechanism or punishment-and-reward system, however, members may try to reap personal benefits rather than expand budget size itself.[19] Conversely, in the principal-agent approach, the assumption of weak incentives of individual members leads to little interest in bureaucratic organization. The approach neglects the possibility that the bureaucratic organization may be capable of the effective pursuance of organizational goals by the coordination of individual members' behaviors, if appropriate mechanisms of rewards and punishments are available.[20]

The above discussion shows that if we seriously consider the influence on individual decision making by organizations, that is, parties, bureaucratic ministries, and agencies, we need an alternative to the economic approaches developed thus far. In the next section, I introduce the concept of bounded rationality in the structured environment provided. I show that this concept can be used to analyze the rational behavior of individual members in the organizational context, especially career civil servants in bureaucratic organizations.

## RATIONALITY IN BUREAUCRATIC BEHAVIOR: SUBSTANTIVE AND PROCEDURAL RATIONALITY

The most critical difference in this study from the economic approaches thus far lies in the conceptualization of rationality. The following section compares and contrasts two different concepts: substantive or maximizing rationality in economics and procedural or bounded rationality. The discussion will show that the concept of bounded rationality is a more useful way to analyze the relationship between the rational behavior of individuals and organizations.

Generally, "*rationality* denotes a style of behavior (A) that is appropriate to the achievement of given goals, (B) within the limits imposed by given conditions and constraints" (Simon 1964, 573). The crucial difference between the concepts of rationality in economics and in the other social sciences lies in how they define goal-oriented behavior under given constraints. Simon summarizes: "In economics, rationality is viewed in terms of the choices it produces; in the other social sciences, it is viewed in terms of processes it employs" (Simon 1987b, 26). The goal sought by economic actors is utility maximization. They make choices to pursue this goal. Utility maximization in economics is *substantive rationality* in the sense that the economic actor is assumed to pursue and achieve objectives by choosing the best means from alternatives given by environmental conditions. The rival concept to this is *procedural* or *bounded rationality*, which tries to explain the process of choosing objectives, selecting means, and employing strategies to achieve objectives.[21]

Economic theory narrowly defines the concept of "rationality," that is, "consistent maximization of a well-defined function, such as a utility or profit function"[22] (Becker 1962, 1). In this formulation, some behavior is chosen from alternates and serves as a means to lead to each of specified outcomes with certainty or with probabilities (if an expected utility function is applied). If applied to bureaucratic behaviors, the model presumes that bureaucrats pursue the goal or a hierarchy of the goals defined by their utility function and use means that are most appropriate to achieve them.[23] The implicit assumption here is that the bureaucrats anticipate the consequences of their chosen behaviors or political outcomes resulting from employing alternative means, especially how other political actors will respond to their behaviors based on rational calculation. Other political actors, say party politicians, interest groups, the electorate, and so on, will behave as bureaucrats rationally expect. The critical point here is that this model presumes the existence of a "real situation" according to which rational behaviors are objectively defined.

The concept of "bounded rationality"[24] has a less strict and more realistic assumption than that of substantive rationality. This concept departs from an objective definition of rationality, as in the case of "substantive" rationality, and highlights the subjective nature of human self-interested behavior, that is, "behavior that is rational given the perceptual and evaluational premises of subjects" (Simon 1956b, 271). The analysis of bureaucratic behavior using this concept assumes that bureaucrats intend to be rational, and that they try to achieve their highest-priority goals by employing the most effective means within the confines of their present perceptions and evaluations. Here, the definition of rationality is inseparable from the premises of perception, selections, and evaluations that constitute the artificial environment for their decision making, and thus determine bureaucratic behavior. This study examines the decision making of the subjects of the study (primarily bureaucrats), and then defines rational behavior within these premises to study its impacts on policy-making.

The concept focuses on the subjectivity of goal-oriented behaviors. It distinguishes "between the rationality of perceptions themselves (i.e., whether the situation as perceived is the 'real' situation) and the rationality of choice, given the perceptions" (Simon 1956b, 271). This study does not present an objective definition of the real situation and then examine behavior in terms of the rationality that is defined within this "true" situation. Rather, it regards bureaucratic behavior as rational as far as bureaucrats conform their behavior to their perceived situations, and as far as they are conscious of their limited knowledge, and try to learn more. Therefore, bureaucrats, if they are rational, usually do not thoroughly specify policy objectives in the first place, nor do they canvass all the alternatives in order to choose the best means for achieving their goals.

31

If one accepts the limited nature of human rationality, the relationship between objectives and the means of achieving them in goal-oriented behaviors deserves further inquiry. For example, Simon defines this relationship as follows: "A means-end chain is a series of anticipations that connect a value with the situations realizing it, and these situations, in turn, with the behaviors that produce them. Any element in this chain may be either "means" or "end" depending on whether its connection with the value end of the chain, or its connection with the behavior end of the chain is in question" (Simon 1976, 74).

Defining the relationship between objectives and means is, however, more complicated in three aspects than was described above. First, the specification of objectives is far from perfect in actual human behavior, even though it is not completely irrational. The inability to collect all the necessary information and the lack of confidence in one's own preference and interest inevitably prevent people from specifying clear objectives in the first place (Simon 1976, 80–84). Rather, they realize their ultimate objectives only after they have learned more from their experience and interactions with the others.

Second, the relationship between the objectives and the means is reciprocal. One reason is that "the particular means used to attain this particular end" has "many consequences other than the specific end being sought, and these other unsought ends" have to "be given their proper weight in considering the desirability of the means" (Simon 1976, 65). The consequence of employing certain means is not neutral in the sense that its consequence cannot necessarily be reduced to achieving the given objective. Moreover, in some extreme situations, the means *could* even determine the objective; that is, because the available means are quite limited in the actual and specific situations that a person faces, the person may choose or specify the objectives for which the means are available.[25]

Third, because objectives cannot be completely specified at the beginning, and because objectives and means are reciprocal, "time" becomes important in explaining a series of actions in which rational thinking makes objectives and means correspond to each other. "Time" could influence procedurally rational behavior in two ways. Choosing some objective at a certain time is irrevocable in the sense that this decision shapes the situation the person faces and influences all the following decisions (Simon 1976, 67–68). All the above factors representing the complex relationship between objectives and means will be included in my model of bureaucratic and political interaction.

## Rational Behaviors of Bureaucrats: A Revised Image

Using the concept of procedural rationality, I analyze the objectives of bureaucrats and how they pursue those objectives in policy-making. I first define the bureaucratic objectives in policy-making as dependent on two important distinctions. One is the different levels at which bureaucrats determine their objectives, that is, the individual and organizational levels. The other concerns how the interests of their organization and social welfare influence bureaucratic objectives. The level at which the bureaucratic objective is defined and how objectives are related to bureaucratic decision making distinguish my theory from those of others.

### Assimilation of Individual Interests with Those of the Organization

The rational choice approach provides a simplified model that defines the bureaucratic objective exclusively at the individual level and in terms of self-interested behaviors. Some approaches in political science that are critical of the simple rationality assumption focus their analysis on the organizational process, presume that various actors seek different objectives in the bureaucratic organization, and are less interested in relating the objectives or intentions of policymakers to actual policy outcomes. A typical example is the "garbage-can" model, which denies any direct link between goals or objectives of policymakers and resulting policy decisions (Cohen, March, and Olsen 1972).

Differing from either of the above two positions, some studies explore the possibility that organizations promote rather than obstruct members' rationality. Emphasizing the limit of human rationality, Simon (1976) suggests that organizations could affect the limitations that bound the area of rationality of the person making decisions by presenting alternative ways of acting, reorienting values, and providing necessary information and knowledge (241–44). Stinchcombe (1990) relates organizational rationality to efficient processing of information rather than to maximization of a utility function narrowly conceived. He asserts that organizations or individuals in their organizational roles are likely to do better jobs than individuals outside the organizational contexts (347–51). Even in economics where the rationality is associated with individual behavior, that is, not behaviors in the organizational context, Williamson (1975, 1985) shows that economic organizations serve to economize trans-

33

action costs compared with market interactions by independent individual entrepreneurs.

These works raise the possibility that organizations provide a better environment for rational decision making for individuals. Common premises in these works are accepting the limited definition of the rationality, such as the one in the context of a "structured environment" (Simon 1956a) consisting of specific premises of decisions, choices, and evaluations, and attributing the roles of forming such environments to organizations; that is, "one function that organization performs is to place the organization members in a psychological environment that will adapt their decisions to the organization objectives, and will provide them with the information needed to make these decisions correctly" (Simon 1976, 79).

The psychological environment may be structured by individuals, but studying the function of organizations in providing such an environment is worth the political analysis. First, organizations are capable of placing ordinary people in a structured psychological environment. Without organizations, few people come up with views of surrounding conditions clear enough to integrate their decisions, direct their behaviors, and appraise outcomes according to the views. Second, if a majority of people's decisions and behaviors are organized in a certain direction, they are more likely to influence the behaviors of others. Organized behaviors are likely to have significant political impacts, and are thus worth investigating.

A major problem, however, is members' noncompliance with the organization's interests or goals. Members who have a limited capacity for perception and communication may not be able to conform their behavior to premises given by the organization. Conversely, the organization may not be able to provide clear premises to ensure the understanding of its members. Problematic also are measures by which members come to understand the organization's interests and how they pursue these interests.

This study presents a situation in which the organization, in fact, effectively facilitates members' compliance with organizational interests and promotes cooperation for their achievement. The bureaucrats are conscious of clear objectives; the entire organization cooperates to pursue them; and it knows how to coordinate members' behavior to pursue the objectives. Assuming the rational pursuance of policy objectives by bureaucrats enables the analysis to focus on the impact of technocratic knowledge on policy-making.

Bureaucratic objectives defined at the individual level consist of income, promotion, reputation, power, and job security, which derive from their occupations and become their own personal property in organizational activities. From this follow two questions: First, by what mechanism does the bureaucratic organization ensure members' compliance with organizational interests and coordinate their behaviors to promote it? Second, in what way does the bureaucratic organization make members conscious of organizational interests and inform them of objectives in specific cases of policy-making?

This study looks at a stable bureaucratic organization for which professional bureaucrats continue to work their entire working lives. It is most likely to reflect the ideal situation in which bureaucrats assimilate their personal interests into the organizational ones and coordinate their behaviors to achieve objectives on which they have reached a solid consensus. Long tenure is a prerequisite to make members' welfare dependent on the organization. In such an organization, assimilation of personal and organizational objectives is fortified by two different mechanisms.

First, the bureaucratic organization must devise a good incentive system to punish and reward members' contributions, so that effective pursuance of organizational objectives eventually furthers individual interests. The system also needs member accountability, that is, a clear basis for reward in the future. While promoting competition among members, nurturing their loyalty to the organization is achieved by guaranteeing job security (i.e., a certain level of promotions, management positions, and so on) to all members.

However, an incentive system cannot guarantee the effective pursuance of organizational interests. In real policy-making, agreeing on a policy and cooperating for its implementation are not easy tasks. In order to ensure easy consensus making and to coordinate members' behaviors, the organization shapes members' preferences toward a certain policy orientation (for example, a balanced budget, Keynesian fiscal orientation, and so on). The organization facilitates the formation of a specific preference by recruiting new members whose preferences are close to those desired and then further socializing them. Bureaucratic preferences are closely related to organizational interests: bureaucrats prefer policies that contribute to making the role of their organization important in policy-making and thus increasing its discretionary power. These preferences also influence their ideas on social welfare or public interest.

Pursuance of certain policy objectives often requires a sequence of coordinated behaviors that have long-term consequences, and during which members in charge will keep changing. The preference formation among the members enables the bureaucratic organization to continue the same commitment across different generations of members. By using "preferences as instruments of organizing" (Levitt and March 1990, 12) the organization makes each member similarly respond to contingencies in policy-making. This usage is a more efficient way to pursue organizational interests than relying only on the complicated hierarchy of a command-and-control system.

## Organizational Objectives: Social Welfare Consideration of Policies and Power Interests of Organizations

All existing studies, except those employing the strict rational choice assumption, demonstrate that bureaucratic organizations pursue multiple objectives. They most often isolate two objectives: increasing their (organizational) power and reflecting "social welfare" considerations in policy-making where social welfare is determined by the officials' technocratic ideas and specialized knowledge. Pursuance of power and the incorporation of technocratic ideas in policy-making are often regarded as conflicting objectives which the bureaucrats cannot easily make compatible. The assumption of the simultaneous pursuance of these objectives illustrates the complexity of the decision-making process inside the bureaucratic organization.

This study assumes that the bureaucratic organization tries to increase its discretionary power and, at the same time, to incorporate technocratic considerations into its policy-making activities. I argue that bureaucrats decide on a specific policy aim through a process that makes these objectives compatible. Technocratic consideration of policies does not give a fully convincing solution to policy problems; policy science or economic theory give valuable advice on policy problems, but they do not necessarily determine what is "the best solution" for a specific problem. This assumption coincides with the theoretical and empirical evidence of recent works; technocratic expertise cannot provide an "objective" policy solution that is free from politics (Fischer 1990; deHaven-Smith 1988). The public, as well as policy experts, disagree on interpretations of the "facts" or "problems" on which the analysis and evaluation of policies are based. In addition, policy analysis often leaves several alternatives that are equally justified from a technocratic point of view. In order to choose one alternative, therefore, the policymakers rely on another criterion, which this study assumes is the wish to enhance the power of their organization.

The lack of a unique scientific answer to policy problems also provides a different perspective from which to understand the role of policy expertise in policy-making. Some existing studies believe that the monopolization of policy expertise guarantees influence to policy specialists inside the government, typically bureaucrats. For example, Weber (1978) suggests that the power of the bureaucrat rests on two kinds of knowledge, "technical know-how . . . acquired through specialized training" and "official information which is only available through administrative channels and which provides him with the facts on which he can base his action" (1417–19). The rational choice theorists also regard policy expertise (by which they mean knowledge about others' preferences and status-quo conditions) as the ultimate factor that gives an advantage to bureaucracy and thus as a major concern for party politicians who desire effective control over bureaucratic activities. Incorporation of the concept of "uncertainty" does not change their conclusion. This is because "uncertainty creates the potential to exercise power; information provides the capacity to do so" (Mueller 1989, 248). In other words, the uncertainty of situations often makes information and expertise even more advantageous to bureaucrats.

Differing from these positions, this study argues that bureaucratic influence is derived from political usage rather than from the simple monopolization of policy information and expertise. Controlling information by the use of expertise is an important part of the exercise of bureaucratic influence here, but this argument differs from the view that bases bureaucratic advantage solely on the control of information. The bureaucrats develop information sources and combine policy data, which, if otherwise interpreted and formulated, might be used to support alternative policies. The bureaucrats control policy information and use technocratic ideas so as to highlight their favorable policy against other possible alternatives rather than to conceal "facts" or leave others ignorant or misinformed. To reject the possibility of an objective interpretation of policy problems, this study draws on the idea of bounded rationality, which denies the existence of an "objectively" defined "real" situation. According to this view, the bureaucrats have no need to have a strong hold on policy information because even complete policy information does not lead to an obvious policy choice.

## The Strategy

The previous section explained the interests of the bureaucratic organization and how they facilitate members' compliance and coordination to pursue them effectively. This section explains the strategies that bureaucratic organizations use to implement desired policies (which are consistent with their organizational interests) by influencing other political actors.

37

Unlike the strategies in one-shot games with perfect information, which can be defined at the beginning, the strategies introduced here are presumed to unfold over time and require a sequence of actions. In this study, bureaucratic influence over policy does not refer to their agenda-setting power to make take-it-or-leave-it proposals, as in some of the rational (or social) choice literature. There, agenda-setting power means that "no communication at all occurs between those who set agendas and those who vote on the proposals contained within them" (Altfeld and Miller 1984, 707), and thus is far from many real situations. Here, it is assumed that bureaucratic influence is exercised through interaction between party politicians and the electorate. Thus it can be revised and adjusted, depending on the bureaucrats' former experience and political socialization.

The first strategy involves the use of expertise to increase the possibility of a policy's implementation. Here, expertise means both (1) theoretical or abstract knowledge about the economic and social impacts of certain policies, and (2) practical knowledge about how policies are actually implemented. To provide expertise that is politically neutral, bureaucrats must present as many alternatives as possible. This is because a purely theoretical consideration of policies leaves several alternatives that are equally justified. There is no unique scientific answer to a specific policy problem. Alternatively, if bureaucrats want to present a favorable judgment for a certain policy, this is not a difficult task. Expertise can be used strategically to gain influence.

To lead to the implementation of a policy, the first step is to define the problem so that the proposed policy will be a good solution. Different interpretations of the same problem will support different solutions. Thus bureaucrats, who carefully interpret a situation and define a policy problem, are able to influence public opinion in favor of their proposed policy. For example, if there is a budget deficit, one can frame this problem as either excessive public expenditures, insufficient taxation to finance the necessary expenditures, or wasteful management inside the government. Different interpretations about the budget deficit are more likely to support different solutions: cuts in government programs, tax increases, or curtailments in administrative personnel and organizations, respectively. Moreover, some may think that the problem does not require solutions if government bonds finance the deficit without distorting resource allocation in the economy.

The next step is specifying a solution for the present problem among policy experts. The electorate often agrees that the policy problem, as it is presented, requires a solution, but may still disagree with the proposed solution. Consider a case of tax increase. Though public opinion may accept the necessity for tax increases, it rarely agrees on the kind of tax and on what social groups it will be levied. In such cases, bureaucrats highlight those aspects of the policy that are most favorable and increase the political legitimacy of the proposal. Using policy information, they can emphasize the expected merits of the policy while talking ambiguously about the points that are likely to cause opposition or controversy. Bureaucrats also gain relative support for a proposed policy by drawing public attention to the defects of other possible alternatives or by not giving serious consideration to them. They can appeal to the public directly through their proposals or indirectly through policy implementations. In this way, the bureaucrats change how the policy is proposed and politicized in order to increase the possibility of its public acceptance.

Whereas the first strategy aims to give reasons to support the proposed policy or to deprive its opposition of legitimate reasons, the second strategy is used to come to terms with opposition to the policy. It includes making compromises with special-interest groups and with politicians who represent the interests of the organized and unorganized electorate. There are two reasons for including political compromises in bureaucratic strategy here. First, in practical terms, bureaucrats are very likely to be exposed to political pressure when they propose policies, especially unpopular ones. Second, since bureaucrats are supposed to be controlled by popular representation in a democratic system, outright bureaucratic dominance over policy-making or an uncompromising attitude are likely to make their proposal appear undemocratic, and thus decrease the possibility of the public's acceptance of it.

Bureaucrats do not treat all the features of the policy as predetermined objectives to be achieved. In realistic and complex situations they lack information about other political actors. They are better off learning how politicians, interest groups, and the electorate respond to their proposals, while interacting with them. Unlike bureaucrats who specialize in policies and are concerned with their implementation, other political actors are less certain about how a specific policy influences their interests and how they should respond to it in the first place. As a policy becomes politicized, the electorate becomes more conscious of its interest and preference for it. Then, the party politicians respond to these expressed interests and policy demands. In a situation where all the features of a policy have been determined, bureaucrats cannot easily make political compromises with opposing groups that otherwise would be possible.[26] If they want to obtain the best result for their interests, these bureaucrats decide a clear priority order about the features of the policy and prepare for compromise, that is, they withdraw lower priority measures one-by-one, to cultivate opposition. They are flexible in compromising the unimportant features of the policy, while defending the attributes that are critical to their interests.

This strategy requires bureaucrats to distinguish between features of policies that are more important and those that are less important for their interests. At the same time, bureaucrats make policy proposals, especially at first, that leave room for compromises and the withdrawal or modification of measures with low priorities. To obtain others' approval or acceptance of their proposals and cultivate opposing groups, bureaucrats compromise in the unimportant features of policies, while defending those features with higher priorities. Bureaucrats must continuously adjust their proposals to ever changing political circumstances and to changes in opposing groups' and politicians' attitudes. This strategy of compromises, if successfully implemented, increases the possibility of implementing policies that preserve their crucial interests. The rationality assumption here means that the bureaucratic choice of primary policy objectives is most consistent with the organizational interests, that is, the achievement of the objectives that best serve to increase the discretionary power of the organization.

Therefore, bureaucrats may utilize compromises as instruments to achieve their high-priority objectives. At the same time, however, political compromises extended to the features of the policy that affect the critical interests of bureaucrats do result from concessions to political pressure beyond their control.

To distinguish between these two kinds of political compromise, this study presents three conditions necessary to conclude that bureaucrats actually influence policy-making and control policy outcomes. The first condition is that the policy change being proposed must have a significant political and policy impact. The bureaucratic proposal must bring a significant change to attract public attention to the policy. It also incurs political costs, that is, organized opposition, which is likely to be imposed on the party politicians who support it. Second, the policy outcome after the political compromises must be consistent with the critical interests of the bureaucratic organization that made the original proposal. The organization prefers this outcome to the status quo, that is, to no policy change. Third, opposing groups must have an alternative policy which they prefer to the one being proposed. Even groups that do not have such a clear alternative at least prefer the status quo to the policy outcome that would result from the bureaucratic proposal.

*Rationality of Party Politicians and Representation of the*
*Electorate's Interests*

To focus on the relationship between the bureaucratic organization and the party, this study assumes that the bureaucratic organization has interests independent of those in society. The bureaucratic organization does not intend to represent or protect any interest groups. To be consistent with this assumption, this study examines fiscal bureaucrats engaging in public financial management whose influence does not depend on their relationship with special interests.

In this section I present assumptions about incumbent party politicians and their representation of the electorate's interests. I maintain that those other political actors, especially party politicians, are as rational as bureaucrats in the sense that they try to implement policies in their interests and to avoid those that are unfavorable to them.

For purposes of comparison with bureaucrats in a stable bureaucratic organization, I consider politicians in a disciplined party with a majority power in the legislature for a long period. This setting means that both politicians and bureaucrats are situated in stable organizational contexts and that bureaucrats can formulate some expectations about the party's behavior. Bureaucrats constitute the primary policy staff for the incumbent party, and thus do not have a substantial competing body of experts inside the government. This situation is consistent with the observation of contemporary democracies except the United States in which the legislatures do not have independent policy staff strong enough to compete with bureaucrats. At the same time, the condition enables one to focus on the relationship between the bureaucratic organization and the political party inside the government. During this period, some incumbent politicians have gained specialized knowledge and policy expertise. This last assumption indicates some political constraint on bureaucratic behaviors: a long-term relationship with the same party imposes on bureaucrats a trade-off between increasing accountability of the party and more substantial political interventions in policy-making.

The party politicians are not simply intermediaries of social interests. I assume that they have two interrelated but still distinguishable interests: the representation of their constituencies' interests and increasing their influence among policymakers, including the party, the legislature, and the bureaucracy. As they increase their influence in this policy-making circle, reflecting the interests of their constituencies becomes generally easier. However, politicians' desire for constituency service does not necessarily go hand-in-hand with the pursuance of influence in policy-making circles. Clinging to representation of their constituencies' interests may be counter to their efforts to increase their influence. Their claim to serve the electorate's interests is often considered an inability to consider policies from a broader perspective, not only the one that is vaguely related to a majority of people's interest but also one that is allegedly concerned with the party's interests. Such a reputation is not good for party politicians wishing to establish careers as policy specialists in the long run.

In general, incumbent politicians with long tenures and stable electoral bases can afford to be concerned with increasing their influence in policy-making circles. They have obtained specialized knowledge and expertise primarily from exposure to and interaction with bureaucrats during long careers. Also, they want to distinguish themselves as policy specialists from backbenchers. They are inclined to accept a bureaucratic proposal if they consider it sensible in terms of their specialized knowledge and acquired expertise. Backbenchers with shorter tenures and weak electoral bases are more sensitive to the electorate's response to the policy. They are not easily persuaded by a bureaucratic proposal that their constituencies oppose. And, they may overturn the party decision if some leaders show understanding to them. However, they usually abide by the party decision because they are also concerned about their reputations inside the party. The only other option is to quit the party.

In this way, different members have different concerns about reelection and policy-making. Thus the disciplined party that maintains its coherence and acts as one body in policy-making may need to impose collective decisions on members by using strong discipline rather than by promoting voluntary compliance among them. This allows room for bureaucrats to obtain approval for an unpopular policy. To get the approval of the party with strong party discipline, bureaucrats concentrate their efforts on obtaining approval from party leaders who have secure electoral bases and are more concerned with policy-making than reelection. The incumbent party leaders obviously care about the reelection of a certain number of backbenchers to maintain majority power of the party in the legislature or to keep members under their personal influence inside the party. But since they lack firsthand information about line members' constituencies, their judgment about public opposition is less risk averse than the judgment of backbenchers themselves. Therefore, the study argues that the rational pursuance of the individual interests of politicians who share knowledge with bureaucrats may facilitate bureaucratic influence.[27] Neither monopolization of policy information by bureaucrats nor irrationality of politicians to misperceive their interests are prerequisites of bureaucratic influence.

Public opposition to a policy always constrains bureaucrats' behavior indirectly. The opposition from the electorate and special interests never directly influences the administrative careers of bureaucrats. The opposition concerns them if there is a possibility that the incumbent politicians will reject their proposed policy or block the policy from passing the legislature. Thus bureaucrats concentrate on obtaining approval from incumbent politicians. For this purpose, the bureaucrats try to obtain information from the politicians about opposition from or acceptance of interest groups, and especially the possibility of effective compromises with opposing groups. This dependence on the incumbent politicians to cope with special interests is another assumption of this study. This dependence may lead to the limitation of the bureaucratic strategy of cultivating public opposition. If the incumbent party fails to perceive the special interests and public opinion opposing a policy, the bureaucrats also underestimate opposition to it. Consequently, bureaucratic strategy falls short, and the policy may be stalled by unanticipated opposition.

The next chapter will show that the framework presented here can be applied to an empirical case—tax reform in Japan. This application will demonstrate that this theoretical framework explains the case without losing generality. At the same time, this application enables one to examine bureaucratic influence under the conditions of the Japanese tax reform case.

# Bureaucratic Rationality and Strategic Behavior: Japanese Tax Reform

WHAT ARE the conditions of bureaucratic organization and party politics that facilitate the strategic behavior of bureaucrats who are seeking policy objectives? Using the recent Japanese tax reform case, this chapter seeks to clarify the relationship between the power interests of the bureaucratic organization and its choice of policies, and illustrate how the organization seeks power interests through policy-making.

This chapter applies the theoretical framework presented in the preceding chapter to the analysis of the Japanese Ministry of Finance. It will show that the MOF wants a moderate amount of budget tightness in order to maintain control over public finance. It will also demonstrate that the ministry's power interest is closely related to its choice of the VAT as a tax reform alternative.

If the consensus and cooperation for a specific policy proposal is obtained inside the bureaucratic organization, the bureaucrats need to find political sponsors for their proposed policy. In the predominant party system of Japan, bureaucrats could count on the passage of their proposed policies in the Diet if the incumbent Liberal Democratic Party approved them. Thus bureaucrats first concentrated their efforts on persuading the leaders of the incumbent party that had relatively strong party discipline.

The final section discusses the relationship between bureaucrats and party politicians, as well as other political actors, opposition parties, and the electorate. The premise of this section is that these actors and organizations are not reactive subjects of the bureaucratic strategy to pursue policy objective, but are active in seeking their own interests. The success of bureaucratic strategy thus hinges on how the bureaucrats can exploit conflicting interests inside these competing groups and organizations. The section focuses especially on the relationship between the party and the bureaucrats after the party politicians with long tenures have gained specialized knowledge and policy expertise. I explore the possibility that the bureaucrats may persuade the politicians of the value of their proposals, paying attention to the differences among politicians of the same incumbent party, especially between experienced members and line members.

These factors, having to do with bureaucratic organization and party politics, are likely to facilitate bureaucratic influence, but they do not necessarily guarantee it. Bureaucratic influence is also affected by contingent factors. The discussion at the end of the chapter introduces the empirical analysis contained in chapters 3 to 6 to illustrate in what way and to what extent bureaucratic influence really worked in the Japanese tax reform case.

## STUDIES OF THE JAPANESE BUREAUCRACY

Before presenting the major argument, this first section reviews the existing literature on Japanese politics under the LDP's one-party predominance. This review will demonstrate that studies thus far have an interest distinct from the one proposed here, and fall short of analyzing the issue of central concern here—the influence of bureaucratic organizations in policy-making.

### Overview

Until the early 1970s, scholars commonly pointed out two characteristics of the Japanese policy-making process. First, the deliberation process in the Diet is not very substantial because the bureaucrats decide the rough line of policy before the government submits a bill to the Diet. Second, the politicians, especially those of the incumbent LDP since 1955, almost always legitimate these policies by majority support, and modify them only when it is expected that the proposed policies will disadvantage them in the elections. The incumbent politicians do not have clear ideas about policy-making in general, except when the policy in question is closely related to their constituency's interests. Based on this characterization, two different models can be distinguished. The first one relies on the elitist paradigm formulated by Mills (1959), and emphasizes the concentration of policy-making power within a small number of elites, including bureaucrats. This model assumes that the LDP politicians, bureaucrats, and big business compose a "triad" in which their conflicts and interests are coordinated through a decision on policy direction (Kaplan 1972; Yanaga 1968).

The idea of neocorporatism can be used also to reinterpret the triad model. In the theory of societal or liberal corporatism, which aims to explain the political systems of the advanced capitalist countries, especially in Western Europe, power is concentrated in a small group of representatives from major socioeconomic interests, labor and business, and governmental elites (Schmitter and Lehmbruch 1979; Berger 1981). According to Pempel and Tsunekawa, the corresponding group of represented interests in Japan includes big business and agricultural groups, but excludes labor (Pempel and Tsunekawa 1979). Their model, "corporatism without labor," presents the possibility of a form of elite coordination different from the corporatist systems observed in Western European countries.

Differing from the model of elite coordination, the second model is related to the statist idea, which emphasizes the state's autonomous role in politics (Nordlinger 1981; Skocpol 1979; Skowronek 1982; Stepan 1978). Since Tsuji's seminal work on Japanese public administration (1969), scholars have paid attention to the continuity of the political system before and after the war, and argued for the preservation of bureaucratic dominance in policy-making. The most notable example is the developmental state model presented by Johnson. He explains Japanese industrial policy from 1925 to 1975 by two characteristics of the bureaucracy—its strength in directing economic development and its autonomy in being insulated from even the most powerful interest groups (Johnson 1982, 44).

These two models both assume bureaucratic dominance, even though they also pay attention to their interaction with other political actors. More specifically, the former regards it as one of the equal partners in a triad, and the latter cites it as a dominant power in policy-making in postwar Japan. The maintenance of the LDP majority in the Diet from 1955 to the early 1970s was fully compatible with the bureaucracy's significant role in policy-making in these two views. The continuity of policies that pursued high economic growth was considered the consequence of the above relationship between bureaucrats and politicians, and, conversely, economic prosperity became an important reason for the stability of LDP rule. Consequently, these views in the early period do not pay much attention to the competitive relationship between bureaucrats and politicians. They maintain that consistent interests and the lack of sharp conflicts between them support a continuity of policies and stable party government.

Since the late 1970s, scholars have begun to modify and change their models of Japanese politics. The new perspective of bureaucrats as policymakers emerged in comparative literature on industrial democracies, and stimulated a new interest in the relationship between bureaucrats and politicians in Japan. In addition, the new dynamics of Japanese politics in the 1970s provided evidence that decreased the validity of the previous models.

First, there was a decline in popular support for the LDP, as indicated by opinion polls, a more reliable indicator of popular support than electoral voting. The opinion polls of party support held once a month since 1960 by Jiji Tsūshinsha provide the most reliable data and show a long-term trend of the party support.[1] The support rate for the LDP maintained a level of between 35 and 40 percent throughout the 1960s, but dropped to 24.7 percent in 1974. In tandem with the decline in the popular support rate, the LDP managed to maintain a majority of the Diet by making the successful independent conservative candidates enter the party after the elections (in the general elections in 1976 and 1979). Conversely, the opposition parties, especially the smaller Democratic Socialist Party, the Clean Government Party (Kōmeito), and the Japan Communist Party, increased their votes in the elections. The numbers of party-independent and floating votes that supported no party also increased. In the same opinion poll, throughout the 1960s, the rate of the independents in terms of party support increased from 7.4 to 17.8 percent; the rate increased further to 32.2 percent in the 1970s. Demographic change underlies the above electoral tendency.[2]

Second, the policy response of the parties further disadvantaged the LDP, which had already lost electoral support. The rapid socioeconomic changes that resulted from the high growth rate increased the necessity for implementing new policies. They included welfare policies that were aimed at redistributing the enlarging pie of economic prosperity, and environmental policies that were directed toward solving the problems of industrial pollution. While the LDP was slow in responding to these policy demands, emerging opposition parties—the middle-of-the-road Democratic Socialist Party and Clean Government Party, the conservative New Liberal Club, as well as the existing Socialist and Communist parties—advocated the radical expansion of welfare coverage for a higher quality of life at the expense of economic efficiency. These parties received more support from the increasing urban and industrial population. The control of local legislatures and governments by these parties led to the active implementation of the welfare program and environmental protection measures. The popularity of these policies facilitated the employment of similar policies by the LDP at the national level.

The political dynamics in the 1970s replaced the stability of LDP rule and the continuity of policies that had constituted the major pattern of Japanese politics until then. The LDP government began to expand welfare programs and implement environmental policies in the early 1970s, almost at the same time as the first oil crisis. Due to this policy change, the LDP could include the emerging social classes[3] in its new support group, while it tried to maintain its old support groups of agriculture and small and medium-sized businesses by nurturing their interests. Thus the LDP's flexible

47

response to new policy demands was one of the most important reasons for the restoration of its electoral support in the 1980s.[4] The continuing economic downturn in the capitalist world made people less demanding of policy changes than in the 1970s, and contributed to a conservative resurgence (Inoguchi 1990).

Scholars have studied the LDP's electoral response to changing policy demands of the electorate from two different viewpoints. First, by close analysis of the Diet process, they have found that deliberation in the Diet, even under the majority power of the LDP, has as substantial a meaning as in other parliamentary systems in Europe. Even though nearly all legislation submitted to the Diet is made by the government and most is passed, the bills are frequently modified as a result of compromise between the governing LDP and opposition parties (Mochizuki 1982). Some scholars observed that the pattern of compromise was more institutionalized in the 1970s, when opposition parties threatened the LDP majority, than before. During this period, the LDP rarely employed unusual parliamentary procedures, for example, the snap vote (*kyōkō saiketsu*)[5] by which the incumbent party forced a vote despite the disagreement of the opposition parties. The opposition parties ceased using *gyūho senjutsu* (literally, the "cow-walking tactic") in which an enormous amount of time in casting votes was taken up by walking slowly.[6] (Krauss 1984; Satō and Matsuzaki 1986, 121–30). Both measures were more frequently observed in the 1960s.

Second, many scholars argue that under its long predominance, the LDP has gradually accumulated knowledge and experience about policies which the bureaucrats have thus far monopolized. The LDP's rising policy-making power enables it to represent constituencies' interests more effectively, which is crucial for maintaining its power, on the one hand. On the other hand, some LDP Diet members have sometimes become autonomous and confident enough to pursue their own ideals or beliefs in policy-making, even at the expense of the opposition of the electorate and special interests. The bureaucrats still provide most of the policy information to the politicians and "write" most of the bills. But the bureaucrats now expect the LDP dietmen's opposition or criticism when they explain government legislation at the LDP Policy Affairs Research Council (PARC) before it is submitted to the Diet (Nihon Keizai Shimbunsha Henshūbu 1983). Scholars have different views on the present power balance between the incumbent politicians and the bureaucrats, but they agree that the LDP has an increased influence in policy-making in terms of its relationship with bureaucrats (Muramatsu 1981; Inoguchi and Iwai 1987; Satō and Matsuzaki 1986).

Pempel's (1982) analysis of policy-making by "creative conservatism" is useful to interpret these changes in comparison with the previous studies. In his analysis of policy-making in Japan, Pempel focuses on the interaction between the Japanese strong state (represented by the bureaucracy) and the conservative coalition in society that is assumed to support elitist and exclusionary politics in the previous views. Based on his rich case studies, including changes in policies and politics in the 1970s by the LDP government, however, he points to the LDP's creativity in policy-making and its flexibility in response to social demands. In this sense, his work bridges the perspectives in the early period and those after the 1970s.

Based on the new evidence, some scholars have modified the previous models. The increased focus on the relationship between the state and society in Japanese studies corresponds to the new interest in comparative politics—which means the shift from a focus on the state's role in the statist idea to the broader interest in the relationship between the state and society in "new institutionalism" (Evans et al. 1985; Gourevitch 1986; Hall 1986; Katzenstein 1985). For example, building on the developmental state model of Johnson (1982), Okimoto (1987, 1989) shapes a more complicated model of economic development. This model analyzes the bureaucracy in its relationship with the party and the private sector, and also pays attention to the independent influence of industrial organizations and party politics on policy formation. Samuels (1987), using the government-industry relationship in energy markets as a case, further extends the argument on subtle interactions between the public and private sectors. The question he asks on the Japanese state intervention in the economy is "not why the Japanese state is so pervasive in the economy but why the pervasive state is so congenial to private firms" (Samuels 1987, 260), and he interprets the public-private relationship as politics of "reciprocal consent." Friedman (1988) also employs a model of flexible production (Piore and Sabel 1984) whose perspective encompasses the state and society and provides a new explanation for the Japanese economic "miracle," that is, rapid economic growth.

Many variants of the pluralist model have marked a complete departure from the statist approach and constituted the dominant view of Japanese politics in the 1980s. The pluralist paradigm itself was one of the most influential in explaining the political system in Western democracies during the last decades (Dahl 1961, 1971, 1982). The focus on the party role in interest representation, however, distinguishes the pluralist idea in Japanese politics from that in American politics. The explanation of the LDP's ability to adapt to changing policy demands is the most important element

49

of the Japanese version of the pluralist idea. The examples are "bureaucracy-led mass-inclusionary pluralism" (Inoguchi 1983), "patterned pluralism" (Muramatsu and Krauss 1987), and "canalized pluralism" (Satō and Matsuzaki 1986). The literature relies on the observation of increased sensitivity to policy demands and more refined policy expertise by the LDP for the formation of the pluralist model.[7] That is, the LDP represents its constituency's interests by using the party organization. It forms compromises with the opposition's representatives, and proposes policies that the bureaucrats, insulated from the electorate, never do. Moreover, according to the new models, substantially increasing knowledge and experience make the LDP politicians more comparable with the bureaucrats as policy experts. These models show that two different elements constitute Japanese policy-making. One is the institutionalized relationship between the LDP and the bureaucrats that excludes the opposition parties and the electorate. The other is the concentration of communication channels for special-interest-group representation within the LDP. This enables the LDP to respond sensitively to various interests through party organization and support groups in order to incorporate them into the policy-making process.[8]

Since the mid-1980s, other scholars also began to argue for the more important role of the party in Japanese politics. While pluralists interpret the institutionalized patterns of policy-making (including party organization and the party-bureaucracy relationship) in terms of a central role of the incumbent party, these scholars seek evidence of the LDP's political influence in public policy-making, the dynamics of party systems, and the party's relationship with constituencies. For example, Calder (1988) broadly perceives the state as a political order under a conservative hegemony including the organization of social interests, and defines a crisis to this order as "a 'prospect of major loss or unwanted change that threatens the established order,' meaning operationally the continued political preeminence of the ruling party" (123). He explains major shifts in several public policy fields from 1949 to 1986 as compensation measures that emerged from the pluralistic rivalry of the elites by which the conservative party government (since 1955, the LDP government) curries the favor of underrepresented interests at the time of the political crisis. Campbell focuses on welfare programs whose postwar expansion have been considered to test the incumbent party's capacity to incorporate a wide range of interests. He then shows that policy sponsorship by party politicians is a crucial factor to explain policy-making (Campbell 1992).

An attempt has also been made to examine Japan's party dynamics in a comparative perspective. The first comprehensive study of the predominant party system in a comparative perspective (Pempel 1990) includes Japan as the most clear-cut case of party predominance and provides an understanding of an "uncommon democracy" under more than forty-five years of the LDP's rule. In comparison with similar cases of conservative hegemony in Western Europe, Mochizuki (forthcoming) also examines the postwar political history of Japan as a case of creation, development, and stabilization of one-party predominance. His perspective is more critical of the democratic nature of Japanese politics than other arguments that pay new attention to the LDP; he considers the LDP's capacity to represent social interests, especially labors', as limited.

To conclude the survey of competing explanations of Japanese politics under the LDP dominance, one needs to mention the most recent and radical perspective—the application of the rational choice approach to Japanese politics. The gist of the idea behind this approach, despite differences in emphasis and focus from one study to another, is that reelection incentives of politicians (backbenchers) of the LDP play a central role in the explanation of policy results and changes. Studies employing this approach (McCubbins and Noble, forthcoming a, forthcoming b; McCubbins and Rosenbluth, forthcoming; Ramseyer and Rosenbluth 1993) apply the same principal-agent perspective that is used to study American politics. Identifying a layer of principal-agent relationships in policy-making, the rational choice theorists in Japanese politics reinterpret the decision-making procedure as the result of delegation by the incumbent party to bureaucrats. They argue that the constituencies watch their representatives work for their interests. Backbenchers police the party leadership to assume that it reflects their constituencies' interests in party decisions, and the party leadership ensures bureaucratic compliance with the party decision. Attaching prominent importance to the individual rationality of reelection-seeking politicians makes this approach most challenging to the conventional view of a strong state and bureaucracy in Japan.

Though each has an original perspective, the recent studies similarly present the more competitive relationship between politicians and bureaucrats and emphasize the relative decline of bureaucratic power vis-à-vis politicians. I agree with them on this point, but I argue for the possibility of bureaucratic influence with more political attention to and intervention in policy-making. In the next section, I contrast my view of bureaucratic influence with the existing explanations by using the tax reform case.

51

## Existing Approaches and the Proposed Approach: A Comparison

The Japanese government's tax reform effort for the late 1970s to the late 1980s is certainly an important case to study because it not only introduced the major tax policy change that affected all the constituencies through the VAT but also brought about the LDP's first failure to retain a majority in one House of the Diet. The existing approaches, however, fall short of offering a convincing explanation of the entire process of the tax reform from the late 1970s to the 1980s. More specifically, they fail to explain why a broad-based consumption tax, which the formidable opposition had twice prevented from being implemented, was finally institutionalized in 1989.

Their failures to explain this major policy change can be attributed to misperceptions of the nature of bureaucratic influence and incomplete understanding of bureaucratically rational behavior. This study, instead, explains the consumption tax in 1989 as a result of the influence of technocratic bureaucrats. The nature of bureaucratic influence illustrated in the tax reform case clashes with existing views of Japanese politics, and is consistent with premises and implications in this study's approach.

### THE PLURALIST APPROACH

The pluralist approach explains the policy-making process by focusing on the new policy expertise and the resulting increased political intervention by the LDP politicians. From this perspective, the ten years of the tax reform process, involving three government proposals, may be interpreted as a process in which the MOF bureaucrats have apparently decreased their dominance over tax policy-making at the expense of the increased influence of the LDP. Two facts appear to support the pluralist explanation in the tax reform case. First, the LDP has become more active in its influence over tax policies, and thus is now capable of changing the technocratic and complicated measures that had been left to the bureaucrats. Second, the LDP politicians have actually influenced the substance of tax policies. When it was finally introduced, the consumption tax included many compromises in tax-filing measures, pushed by the LDP politicians to protect the interests of small and medium-sized self-employed businesses and distributors.

A crucial difference between the pluralist approach and the present study's approach is in how one observes the influence of technocratic bureaucrats. The pluralist explanation has developed from a criticism of the elitist approach or the statist view that had dominated Japanese political studies. Thus, relying on observations of more frequent modifications and changes of bureaucratic proposals by the LDP, it tends to draw the conclusion that the power of the incumbent party has increased at the expense of the bureaucracy in the government (*tōkō seitei*). This pluralist approach is interested in a shift from bureaucratic influence over other political actors (including the LDP) to an active role of the incumbent party in policy-making.

The approach proposed here focuses on the possibility of bureaucratic influence when the LDP gains policy expertise. More precisely, the study, assuming a certain degree of incumbent party influence over the tax reform, investigates to what extent and in what way bureaucratic influence will persist despite the political intervention. Observation of the political intervention—though it appeared frequently and intensively—is not enough to lead to the conclusion that the influence of politicians exceeds that of bureaucrats. To examine bureaucratic influence, one needs to know whether political intervention changes the features of a policy that are critical to bureaucratic interests. To answer this, my approach specifies which features of the proposed tax on consumption were most important for the bureaucrats and then answers whether they were preserved or modified by the politicians' influence. Later in this chapter I elaborate the MOF's most critical interests in the introduction of the new tax.

THE STATIST APPROACH

Another possible account of the tax reform is provided by the so-called statist approach, which emphasizes the bureaucracy's dominant influence over policy-making. Here, I have in mind the approach offered to study industrial policies (Johnson 1982; Zysman 1983; Okimoto 1989). This approach is the most fully developed and influential among political scientists for explaining the strong Japanese state. It explains Japanese economic development—a shift from one industrial sector to another, increasing international competitiveness of industries, development of highly technological sectors, and so on—by the industrial policies implemented by the Ministry of International Trade and Industry (MITI). Its emphasis on the technocratic superiority of the Japanese economic bureaucrats in making effective industrial policies may appear to some readers to parallel this study's interests in the technocratic bureaucrats of the MOF. However, this study is *not* the MOF version of the statist approach. Differing from an approach that emphasizes the strength of the Japanese state, this study does not associate bureaucratic influence with the political institutions peculiar to Japan. The Japanese political system has several conditions that serve to favor bureaucratic influence. But these conditions do not necessarily guarantee bureaucratic influence over policy-making. I clarify these conditions in the following sections, and then show that whether these conditions actually help bureaucrats exercise power over policy-making depends on contingent factors.

This study differs in an important way from the statist approach in terms of its understanding of technocracy and the extent of organizational analysis. In some statist approaches, the bureaucrats are excellent technocrats, not only because they successfully attain the goals that they pursue but also because their attained goals are considered "rational"—for example, efficient resource allocations across industries that ultimately lead to Japanese industrial development and international competitiveness. Reservations inherent in the approach—possibilities of mistakes and misjudgments—do not change the basic argument that the industrial policies made by bureaucrats are an important factor in explaining Japanese economic development.

In the statist approach, it is possible to postulate the bureaucratic goal that is not specifically defined as rational, and many statists simply assume that the state pursues the goal that represents the interests of its constituents, that is, government officials and bureaucrats. However, even in such a setting, the statist analysis says little about the bureaucratic organization, especially the question of why individual members in the organization cooperate to pursue that goal or why the organization can act in a unified way. This is because the approach is overtly concerned with the state's relationship with a society. The statist approach's presumption of the rationality of a bureaucratic goal is closely related to this relative indifference to the internal organization of bureaucracy. If the approach posits a goal that is obviously consistent with the interest of the entire nation, it need not explain why bureaucrats endorse that goal and how the goal emerges from a process inside the organization.

The framework being developed here differs from the statist approach in two ways. First, it assumes that bureaucrats try to achieve policy objectives that satisfy the technocratic consideration and at the same time increase the bureaucrats' organizational interests. Second, the present study investigates in what way the bureaucratic organization determines its goal and ensures the members' cooperation for its pursuance. I also argue that bureaucrats' technocratic expertise aids in political maneuverings to lead to desired policy outcomes. In other words, the bureaucrats' strength is not inherent in the institutional setting that allows them to control policy information, monopolize expertise, and insulate political pressure, but rather in their capability to maneuver the situation.

## THE SOCIAL COALITION ANALYSIS

Though the pluralist and statist approaches concern the relationship between the LDP politicians and bureaucrats, both of them are also interested in the party or bureaucratic coalition with social interests. For example, in Muramatsu and Krauss (1987) and Okimoto (1988) such a tendency is prominent. Another work, not classified as either statist or pluralist, is primarily concerned with changes and shifts in the social coalitions that it regards as determinants of a configuration of the parties and policy outcomes (Mochizuki, forthcoming).

The analysis of social coalitions is important in many cases of policy-making because any policy change in a democratic setting should accompany an approval, or at least an acceptance, of a significant size of the electorate. But this analysis is weak if it is ambiguous about the cause of the shift of the social coalition that supports a certain policy change, that is, whether it is the result of political maneuvering involving that policy or of some other social and economic change. In relation to the first point, it is important to examine what conditions ultimately make the social coalition shift to a certain policy change or to what extent this change is consistent with the interest of such a coalition both in prospect and retrospect. The analyses of the process and content of the tax reform in this study is especially concerned with these questions instead of simply pointing up the emergence of a new social coalition backing a policy change. This is discussed more thoroughly at the end of this chapter, using the empirical observation of changing attitudes and shifting coalitions of social interests in the Japanese tax reform case.

## THE RATIONAL CHOICE APPROACH

The rational choice approach and the approach presented here are similar in two ways. First, both aim to reject the idea of bureaucratic autonomy and insulation from politics. Second, both are interested in the rationality of policymakers. A close look at these similarities, however, permits one to distinguish between the two approaches.

First, this study denies the bureaucratic dominance in a rather different way from the rational choice approach. I reject the bureaucratic dominance view by showing that bureaucratic influence does not work in the way the view contends. More specifically, bureaucrats influence policy-making neither in insulation from political pressure nor under a convergence of interests with the politicians.

In the rational choice approach, bureaucratic dominance is replaced by

55

effective political control over bureaucracy as a fundamental determinant of policy-making. The approach gives central importance to politicians' reelection incentives that work as an effective control over pursuance of bureaucratic interests in policy-making. In other words, both the rational choice perspective and the bureaucratic dominance view agree that bureaucratic influence depends on institutionalized factors, a decision-making procedure, or a monopolized policy information and expertise that leaves politicians uninformed. The rational choice approach disagrees with the bureaucratic dominance view in terms of the consequences of interaction between the politicians and bureaucrats. To refute the possibility of bureaucratic dominance, the rational choice studies then show that decision-making procedures ensure bureaucratic compliance with party position.

This study agrees with the rational choice approach that bureaucratic dominance is *not* a stable component of the Japanese political system. Paying special attention to bureaucratic organization, however, this study explores the possibility of bureaucrats' rational pursuance of organizational interests in policy-making. I am especially interested in the conditions in which the bureaucratic ministry has been successful in coordinating members' behaviors to pursue a common interest. I will now introduce the Ministry of Finance in the Japanese tax reform as an example of an organization that rationally pursues its own objectives.

## ORGANIZATION AS AN ENVIRONMENT TO PROMOTE RATIONAL BEHAVIOR: THE MINISTRY OF FINANCE IN JAPAN

What organizational interests does the MOF seek through policy-making, and how do these interests influence its choice of policies? To answer these questions, first I will explain the internal structure of the bureaucratic organization, which facilitates the rational pursuance of objectives that its members have agreed on. Then I will show that the MOF, which is in charge of both budget expenditures and tax revenues, is interested in seeking a moderate budget tightness. The last part of this section will clarify how the MOF's interest in controlling the budget size is related to the attempt to reform the tax system through the introduction of the VAT.

### The Internal Structure of the Bureaucracy

Why do bureaucrats assimilate their personal interests into the interests of their organization? How do the interests of the organization benefit a wide spectrum of fiscal bureaucrats? Answers to these questions are obtained by investigating the internal structure of the bureaucratic organization.

In the case of the MOF in Japan, systems of recruitment, training, employment, and promotion increase the internal coherence of the organization and facilitate the members' personal commitments to it. Recruitment of bureaucrats by a competitive and objective examination, and extensive education and training of members in the early stages of their careers, contribute to making a highly selective, homogeneous, and competent group of policymakers. The so-called (working) lifetime employment system of the ministry makes the membership of the bureaucratic organization stable. The system of promotion is very competitive but is based on seniority, and guarantees certain job securities to all members; it nurtures the members' loyalty to the organization and increases their incentives to work for it. Their personal interests, that is, income, promotion, job security, and prestige, are deeply connected with the ministry. How much they contribute to the ministry greatly influences the achievement of their personal interests.

Each mechanism can be further specified. The recruitment and employment system of bureaucrats in Japan has two institutional characteristics: open entry by competitive examination and very little lateral mobility after entry. Most bureaucrats are recruited by examinations; the examination results determine most of their future careers—which level of job will be attained and to which agency or ministry one will belong.[9] Three different levels of examination at the time of recruitment distinguish so-called career officers (whose influence and role this study analyzes) from noncareer officers. The bureaucrats who aspire to top positions have to pass the highest level of examinations, and those who will occupy intermediate and lower positions are selected, respectively, by the intermediate and lower levels of examination. The assignment to specific organizations is based on the judgment and evaluation of the personnel authorities of each agency and ministry through examinations and interviews. This recruitment system is designed to be both competitive and open. However, it results in the selection of a quite homogeneous group. The MOF, which formerly recruited about twenty new career officers annually and now recruits about twenty-five, has an especially high level of homogeneity. A majority of career officers are graduates from one of three national universities (Tokyo, Hitotsubashi, and Kyoto).[10] Among its members, more than 50 percent are graduates of the faculty of law at the University of Tokyo and, if one includes graduates from different departments of the same university, this number amounts to more than 80 percent (Jin 1986, 90–91).[11] Because of the intense competition in the examinations, career officers already have a sense of responsibility and the self-confidence of selected elites on entering the administration. This tendency is especially strong in the MOF, which is considered to be one of the most competitive ministries to enter.[12]

When they enter the administration, bureaucrats (referred to as "career officers" hereafter in this study if there are no additional explanations) are further socialized as future top officials by job training. After assisting their seniors for two years, half of the new officials go to the United States or Europe in order to study language and economics at the graduate level. Those who stay in Japan use an entire year to study economics at the graduate level in a curriculum specially designed for them and taught by professors of the universities from which most of them graduated. The ministry provides an opportunity for graduate-level education to its members who embark on administrative careers immediately after graduation from college. The ministry does not expect that new members have had any specialized knowledge or training. Actually, it is almost impossible to find a recipient of a Ph.D., and is rare to find even one with a master's degree in economics or policy sciences among new members at the time of entry to the ministry.

What does the opportunity for post-entry education and training imply for the coherence of the bureaucratic organization? Why does the ministry not employ more qualified members or require candidates to finish certain training before joining? The first reason is that such post-entry investments in human capital will be rewarded. In the Japanese government, all the bureaucrats work for a single ministry or agency. The ministry provides intensive post-entry education and on-the-job training, assuming that almost all the bureaucrats will remain working for that ministry their entire working lives. The organizations exchange members for one or two years for further training or experience, but it is clear that the bureaucrats are always working for their own home ministry or agency.

Second, the ministry's special education and training systems are designed not only to help bureaucrats study academic disciplines to enable them to qualify as policy specialists, but also to nurture the same attitudes about policy-making. Obtaining an economic education while working in the administration does not make them strict interpreters of economic theory. The bureaucrats often emphasize the importance of common sense rather than theoretical consistency or elegance. They have a deep suspicion of neoclassical economic theory, which tends to regard the financial behavior of the government sector as a function of the market economy. They claim they nurture their own sense that guides their decisions through their experiences in public financial management and knowledge gained from their experience within the organization.[13] Based on the ministry's day-by-day experience, with its long history that dates back to the late nineteenth century, the bureaucrats think it important to put the public financial system under their control. Of course, the bureaucrats do not ignore specialized knowledge or understanding of technocratic aspects of economic policies. But they are not impartial interpreters of technocratic ideas; rather, they are entrepreneurs who use technocratic ideas to realize what they believe to be a good policy.

The career course of bureaucrats after socialization and training is based on seniority. After serving as a section chief (*kakarichō*), in the fifth or sixth year from the beginning of their careers (a majority of them are then twenty-seven or twenty-eight years old), they become chief of the tax office in a small city with the support of experienced and older noncareer officers.[14] After a seventh- or eighth-year-training period, they begin to serve as assistant directors (*kachō-hosa*) under directors (*kachō*). After this stage the career course that the most successful of them follow is almost determined, and they are further selected at several stages. For example, assignment to a position in the budget bureau and minister's secretariat are considered promising signs: the former is in charge of budget making and the latter is directly in charge of all personnel matters up to general directors. All the career officers usually get positions as directors, but a clear distinction is made between important positions and others. Usually, seven executive director positions (each of seven bureaus has one executive director position) and three executive directors in the minister's secretariat are considered important; among them some positions are more important than others (Jin 1986, 112). Those who are assigned to other positions are likely to leave the ministry positions subsequently and get management positions in local or related organizations. Only some of them remain as candidates for future general directors (*kyokuchō*). Usually, one person among those who entered the ministry in the same year will become a vice minister; upon this person's appointment to the highest position, all the remaining members who entered the ministry in that year will leave positions inside that ministry. In other words, an administrative vice minister is most senior, that is, the oldest member in the ministry (among career officers). In this sense, the seniority system is completed from the bottom to top among bureaucrats who are on the fastest career track.

The procedures for selection for promotion can be summarized as follows. First, the system is under the control of the ministry, and very few possibilities for outside intervention exist.[15] There are negligible possibilities for intervention into the personnel matters of the ministry by politicians. Only the minister and two (parliamentary) vice ministers are politically appointed and changed by the frequent reformulation of the LDP cabinet. Even though these three political executives are formally in charge of assignments of and promotions to all the positions, bureaucrats are usually able to work independently of their substantial supervision when deciding promotion or recruitment inside the ministry.[16] The ministry's control over members' promotions helps to foster members' reliance on the organization.

Second, the career system encourages competition for promotion among bureaucrats. The bureaucrats usually change their affiliation to a section, division, and bureau once every two years, and are required to learn policies quickly and to become generalists.[17] In the pluralistic competition between sections and bureaus at the same horizontal levels within the same ministry, the bureaucrats have plenty of opportunities to show their competence in pursuing the interests of their assigned parts. The members improve their own chances for promotion by protecting the interests of their section, division, bureau, and ministry. In this sense, the bureaucrats have clear criteria for measuring contributions that increase the possibility of their being promoted.

Third, even though the competition is so intense that only a few of them attain the highest positions, the system promises a certain degree of job security to all the members, and maintains their loyalty. In addition to a seniority system, all the career officers reach management positions. The ministry or the personal relationship developed through administrative careers guarantee jobs for retired bureaucrats in the private sector or in the half-private and half-public sectors. Because of this job security, bureaucrats maintain a solidarity as selected members of the same ministry in spite of high competition for promotion.[18] Members who entered the ministry in the same year, that is, those who are in the same "class," have a strong solidarity. They are generally proud of having a classmate who reaches a top position in their year, because it is considered proof that they are part of a pool of candidates of high quality. Having a "classmate" who has held a position of vice minister also gives a substantial advantage to the remaining members' jobs after retirement, and so on (Jin 1986, 119–20; Nihon Keizai Shimbunsha 1992, 171). In this way, the intense rivalries for promotion among career bureaucrats do not necessarily prevent them from cooperating in policy-making.[19] This system makes the bureaucrats more conscious of and responsible for working for the ministry, increases their loyalty to it, and facilitates cooperation among them in policy-making.

The high status of the financial ministry (often considered the most prestigious and the most elite bureaucracy, that is, *shōchō chū no shōchō*) further increases a sense of responsibility and loyalty to the ministry among its members. The characteristics of internal structure described above are, however, not particular to the MOF; to a lesser or larger extent they are common in Japanese bureaucratic organizations in general. Some of the characteristics may apply beyond the boundary of Japan. In Western European countries, for example, high-ranking career civil servants enjoy prestigious status, and generally have long working careers and a strong sense of mission in policy-making (Dogan 1975). These tendencies make clear differences between these countries and the U.S. case where political appointees usually occupy the highest administrative positions (Heclo 1977, 1984).

### Pursuance of the Goal: The Ministry of Finance's Control over the Budget

The MOF's activities extend from the management of the public financial system to the regulation of private financial markets. Each bureau of the MOF—that is, the budget bureau, the tax bureau, the custom and tariff bureau, the financial bureau, the securities bureau, the banking bureau, and the international finance bureau—represents one part of its broad range of administrative jobs in addition to the minister's secretariat. Among these functions, control over the budget is most crucial for the interest of the ministry as a whole. The MOF is responsible for the entire public financial system, that is, both revenue and expenditure decisions. This power makes the MOF the most powerful and informed among the ministries.

The MOF's budgetary power has a political meaning different from the decision-making power of any of its policies.[20] First, the MOF can influence all the decisions of the other ministries by examining and deciding on the budget package. Second, in the budgetary decision making, the MOF effectively promotes itself as a representative of a view beyond specific interests. Whereas politicians and the other ministries represent specific interests and push for certain programs, the MOF, unaligned with any interest groups, effectively demonstrates its technocratic neutrality as a budget examiner. To control the budget-making process is thus crucial for the MOF as a whole.[21] The conflicting interests between the budget bureau and the other bureaus are subject to this imperative.

Does the MOF show specific preferences or attitudes in making budgets? If so, what is the ultimate goal for the MOF in budget making? To answer these questions, first I will clarify how the MOF influences various spending decisions. The MOF exercises two kinds of influence over the budget.[22] One is setting the size of the total budget before the other ministries request their budgets. The other is the power to examine the budget requests of the other ministries—allowing or refusing to add new programs through hearings and negotiations with the line ministries. Before substantial request formation begins at the end of July every year, the cabinet passes the percentage ceiling on budget requests (increasing the rate compared to the previous year's budget size before implementation). This ceiling or criterion has been set annually by the MOF, and the other ministries have made this ceiling an important guide-line for their budget requests since 1961.

Besides this constraint on the aggregate size of the budget, the MOF influences each ministry's budget more substantially at the stage of examination that follows the expenditure requests. In September, immediately after the ministries submit their first budget requests, the budget bureau begins to examine them.[23] Compared to the total budget size, the adjustment of each ministry's budget request is a marginal and relatively small change, but it has a significant influence on an individual ministry's policies and programs.[24] After the examination, the MOF submits the original budget plan to the cabinet and, upon the cabinet's approval, the plan is sent to the Diet.

The MOF is ultimately interested in controlling the budget size through allocations and retrenchments at the ministry level rather than intervening in the details of a ministry's budget. The MOF budget officers scrutinize individual ministries' budgets to constrain the level of financial allocation to each of them. Alternatively, as long as the ministry retains its budget size under the level determined by the MOF, the budget officers have very few incentives for further intervention. In other words, the MOF neither wants nor actually does a thorough supervision of budget making, but rather tries to control the spending pressure in its designated range. This attitude allows the MOF room for political interventions in budget making,[25] but at the same time means that the observation of such intervention does not always harm bureaucratic interests.[26] As Campbell (1977, chap. 9) illustrates in his analysis of budgetary politics during the high economic growth period of the 1960s to the early 1970s, the MOF had a clear priority to control the budgetary size ("macrobudgeting") instead of insisting on cuts in specific expenditures ("microbudgeting").

Despite possible political intervention in some details of budget appropriation, I argue that the MOF effectively pursues its goal. Setting the budget size, if it is accompanied by the substantial leverage of examining the budget, gives the MOF the opportunity for effective control over the entire budget size, which is critical for the MOF's interests. First, the MOF, as well as the Economic Planning Agency (EPA), control the information and expertise that are necessary to guess next year's budget size. The economic statistics that are needed to justify and decide the appropriate size of the budget are not well publicized (Campbell 1977, 71–90). In addition, at this stage a good deal of information on economic conditions and tax revenue that is technically necessary for the estimate of the next year's budget size is not available. Hence, the budget estimate is based largely on the MOF's judgment. The MOF infers the next year's budgetary conditions from past experience, intuitive assessment of economic conditions, and anticipation of the political climate that will influence the budget. Third, setting the budget size relative to the previous fiscal year contributes to preventing the other ministries from adding many expensive programs at the stage of requests (Campbell 1977, 95). The MOF's estimate of the budget size could be a good target to guide budget making (Table 2.1).

The last point—which is probably the most important—is that no other governmental bureaus or branches make comprehensive budget plans. Thus the MOF budget plan is the only one on which the party government decision, as well as the Diet deliberation, depend. Article 18 of the public finance law guarantees only the minister of finance's jurisdiction of estimate, adjustment, and decision of the budget package that is handed in to the cabinet. The power to decide the government's budget is legally possessed by the minister of finance, and ultimately also by the prime minister and the cabinet. But the power to estimate, plan, and adjust the budget is substantially delegated to the budget bureau. This concentration of power in the budget bureau has been a controversial problem in the Japanese government. The LDP has attempted to take away this power from the MOF budget bureau, but these attempts have been in vain (Tanimura 1987). In this way, both the power to set the total budget size and the power to examine specific programs support the MOF's ability to keep the total budget size within the range that it wants.

The MOF is in charge of both tax revenue and budget expenditures; therefore, keeping the budget size within the bounds of expected revenue, and financing the actual budget with the revenue obtained, are important responsibilities of the MOF. Both the tax and budget bureaus carefully coordinate revenue and spending decisions when they estimate the next year's budget at the beginning of every summer, as well as when they form the government budget at the end of every calendar year. The combined responsibility for revenue and expenditure decisions helps put constraints on budget requests (Peters 1991, 320), and this responsibility is held by the MOF in Japan. Since a simple aggregation of budget requests almost always exceeds the amount available from financial sources, the interest of the MOF lies in cutting the budget. However, a question still remains: What extent of fiscal tightness does the MOF ultimately seek? This question can also be restated: What kind of public financial situation is consistent with the MOF's interests?

External economic conditions or political considerations sometimes constrain the size of the budget. These external conditions may include a huge public debt that requires a high level of interest payment, a war economy that concentrates public expenditures, and so on. Here, the MOF bureaucrats are under the same visible constraint on the size of the budget as the demanders of the budget. Under these conditions, they have neither disposal power to decide the size nor need for coordination and adjustment among the requests. Alternatively, when external political and economic conditions allow the government to make a loose budget, the MOF's control over the budget also decreases. Here, requests from all ministries and agencies are accumulated into the final budget without limiting its size. The line ministries and politicians representing the constituencies and the special-interest groups can appropriate new expenditure programs regardless of the MOF's intention.

Therefore, if the MOF rationally seeks to maintain or increase its discretionary power over budget decision making, it should avoid situations in which a loose or tight budget prevail. Except in these two extreme conditions, the MOF maintains the fiscal conditions in which it has more disposal or control over the budget size and thus can use its leverage on the requests from the ministries.

The postwar history of Japanese public finance provides several examples of the behavioral pattern of the fiscal bureaucrats described above. The MOF tries not to allow budget requests to accumulate with no significant limit. When there was a natural increase in tax revenue,[27] throughout all the years from 1961 to the mid-1970s, the MOF did not set strict limits on budget size (for example, from 1961 to 1964 it set about a 50 percent increase from the previous year's budget, and until 1974 kept to about a 20–25 percent increase). For all but a few years, the MOF could finance growing budgets under intensive spending pressure for public works and welfare programs, sometimes even at a higher pace than the national economy, without sales of deficit bonds. Given such an abundant revenue, however, the MOF continued efforts to restrict the size of the budget. It offset automatic tax increases caused by inflation or economic growth[28] by amending the income tax law almost every year. The employment of an extensive tax-cutting policy by the fiscal authority during the high-growth era contributed to keeping the ratio of total tax revenue (both at local and national levels) to national income at approximately 20 percent (Ishi 1989, 44). The policy distinguishes Japan from other advanced industrial coun-

TABLE 2.1

Increasing Rates (Percentages) of Budget Ceiling, Budget Request, and Initial Budget (to the Previous Year's Initial Budget)

| | | Ministries' Requests | | Initial Budget | |
| Fiscal Year | Ceiling on Request (%) | general account[a] (%) | general expenditures[b] (%) | general account (%) | general expenditures (%) |
|---|---|---|---|---|---|
| 1961 | 50 | 48 | | 24.4 | |
| 1962 | 50 | 40 | | 24.3 | |
| 1963 | 50 | 38 | | 17.4 | |
| 1964 | 50 | 35 | | 14.2 | |
| 1965 | 30 | 26.0 | 24.9 | 12.4 | 12.8 |
| 1966 | 30 | 25.8 | 23.6 | 17.9 | 20.4 |
| 1967 | 30 | 27.6 | 23.2 | 14.8 | 12.0 |
| 1968 | 25 | 24.2 | 22.4 | 17.5 | 14.9 |
| 1969 | 25 | 22.5 | 20.9 | 15.8 | 13.3 |
| 1970 | 25 | 22.1 | 21.5 | 18.0 | 16.9 |
| 1971 | 25 | 23.3 | — | 18.4 | 17.4 |
| 1972 | 25 | 21.5 | — | 21.8 | 25.2 |
| 1973 | 30 | 28.1 | 24.4 | 24.6 | 22.5 |
| 1974 | 25 | 22.4 | 21.8 | 19.7 | 19.0 |
| 1975 | 25 | 23.5 | 15.5 | 24.5 | 23.2 |
| 1976 | 15 | 16.8 | 10.8 | 14.1 | 18.8 |
| 1977[c] | | | | | |
| administrative expenditures | 10 | | | | |
| others | 15 | | | | |
| | 14.5 (in total) | 18.7 | 16.0 | 17.4 | 14.5 |
| 1978 | | | | | |
| administrative expenditures (excluding the research) | 0 | | | | |
| others | 13.5 | | | | |
| | 13.2 (in total) | 15.9 | 14.6 | 14.5 | 13.4 |
| 1979 | | | | | |
| administrative expenditures (excluding the research) | 0 | | | | |
| others | 13.5 | | | | |
| | 13.8 (in total) | 14.5 | 13.4 | 12.6 | 13.9 |

TABLE 2.1 *(cont.)*

| | | Ministries' Requests | | Initial Budget | |
|---|---|---|---|---|---|
| Fiscal Year | Ceiling on Request (%) | general account[a] (%) | general expenditures[b] (%) | general account (%) | general expenditures (%) |
| 1980[d] | | | | | |
| administrative expenditures | 0 | | | | |
| others | 10 | | | | |
| | 9.8 (in total) | 13.7 | 10.5 | 10.3 | 5.1 |
| 1981[e] | | | | | |
| administrative expenditures | 0 | | | | |
| others | 7.5 | | | | |
| | 7.9 (in total) | 12.5 | 8.6 | 9.9 | 4.3 |
| 1982 | | | | | |
| expenditures excluding the ones for defense, ODA, pension, measures for energy and science and technological promotion | 0 | | | | |
| | 1.9 (in total) | 5.7 | 1.8 | 6.2 | 1.8 |
| 1983 | | | | | |
| expenditures excluding aforementioned items and investment expenditures | −5 | | | | |
| | 1.46 (in total) | 0.9 | 1.5 | 1.4 | 0.0 |
| 1984 | | | | | |
| current expenditures | −10 | | | | |
| investment expenditures | −5 | | | | |
| | 1.01 (in total) | 3.8 | 1.0 | 0.5 | −0.1 |
| 1985 | | | | | |
| current expenditures | −10 | | | | |
| investment expenditures | −5 | | | | |
| | 0.86 (in total) | 8.2 | 0.9 | 3.7 | 0.0 |
| 1986 | | | | | |
| current expenditures | −10 | | | | |
| investment espenditures | −5 | | | | |
| | 1.5 (in total) | 7.4 | 1.5 | 3.0 | 0.0 |

TABLE 2.1 *(cont.)*

| | | Ministries' Requests | | Initial Budget | |
|---|---|---|---|---|---|
| Fiscal Year | Ceiling on Request (%) | general account[a] (%) | general expenditures[b] (%) | general account (%) | general expenditures (%) |
| 1987 | | | | | |
| current expenditures | −10 | | | | |
| investment expenditures | −5 | | | | |
| | 1.0 (in total) | 6.7 | 0.5 | 0.0 | 0.0 |
| 1988 | | | | | |
| current expenditures | −10 | | | | |
| investment expenditures | 0 | | | | |
| | 1.8 (in total) | 12.5 | 1.8 | 4.8 | 1.2 |
| 1989 | | | | | |
| current expenditures | −10 | | | | |
| investment expentitures | −5 | | | | |
| | 2.8 (in total) | 13.0 | 2.8 | 6.6 | 3.3 |
| 1990[f] | | | | | |
| current expenditures | −10 | | | | |
| investment expenditures | −5 | | | | |
| | 3.0 (in total) | 11.4 | 3.0 | 9.6 | 3.8 |

*Sources:* From 1961 to 1964, Campbell 1977, p. 15, Table 2; Campbell first compares the ceiling rate with the increasing rates of actual requests by the ministries and of the actual budget (general account) made at the beginning of each fiscal year. After 1964: Nihon Keizai Shimbun each year and Nakajima 1990, p. 9, Table 2.2.

[a] General account means a total amount of government expenditures except those under the special accounts that the government establishes separately for specific purposes.

[b] General expenditure means the expenditure that excludes the bond expenditures and local allocation tax from the general account.

[c] From 1977, the local allocation tax, the bond expenditures, and natural increments of pensions were exempt from the ceiling constraint. From 1977 to 1980, the ministries' requests did not include the bond expenditure.

[d] During the budget making in the 1980 fiscal year, the MOF used the term, *general expenditure* for the first time. (The general expenditure in each previous year was calculated and publicized by the MOF thereafter).

[e] From 1981, only the local allocation tax was excluded from the ministries' requests.

[f] The 1990 fiscal budget has come not to depend on special issuance of deficit bonds for the first time since the 1975 fiscal supplementary budget.

tries as a unique case that expanded the size of the public sector under natural increments of tax revenue during the same period. For example, in terms of the ratio of tax revenues to gross domestic product (GDP) as one measure of tax burdens, Japan was the second to the last among twenty-three OECD countries in 1965, 1975, and 1985 (Turkey was the last) (Ishi 1989, 7).[29]

During the period of high economic growth, even when financial resources were abundant, some MOF bureaucrats were apprehensive about the spending pressure. For example, Kōtarō Murakami, budget bureau general director in 1967 and 1968, led the "break fiscal rigidity movement" (*zaisei kōchokuka dakai undō*) and argued that the fixed expenditures would leave little room to add new programs and prevent the government from implementing effective fiscal and monetary policies.[30] The budget bureau under Murakami began to study the Public Planning Budgetary System (PPBS) developed in the United States, and sought to estimate scientifically the impact of public programs to decrease expenditures. This movement, though it ended without great impact,[31] exemplifies the budget officers' apprehension about constraints on fiscal decisions (in this case, the fixed expenditures) that decrease their control over the budget.

The MOF's tendency to strike a balance between tight and loose budgetary conditions is more apparent in its response to the budget deficits since the mid-1970s. The chronic budget deficits were precipitated by the unexpected revenue shortfalls due to the worldwide recession, but were doomed by changes in public expenditure structure caused by rapid expansion of the social security reform in the 1970s (Noguchi 1987a). This response ultimately explains the reason why the MOF chose the VAT to reform the revenue structure.

Deficit finance was likely to weaken the MOF's control over the budget size for two reasons. First, the chronic dependence of public finance on deficit bonds shifted control over the budget from the technocrats to the party in power, because issuance of deficit bonds, which was not allowed by the public finance act, required a political decision to enact a special law each year. Second, setting the budget size before the request by the other ministries would have little influence on the budgetary decision if the MOF failed to predict the tax revenue, and deficit bonds continued to finance the revenue shortfall.

After 1980, when the world economy began to recover, the MOF tried to decrease the issuance of deficit bonds to finance the general account budget[32] by ensuring the stability of tax revenue, as well as securing additional financial resources. In 1978 the MOF first proposed a tax increase through the introduction of a new tax on consumption that would provide more financial resources. After this proposal was blocked by political opposition in 1979, the MOF imposed a stricter ceiling (10 percent, in the 1980 fiscal year) on the requests from all ministries. There were few exceptions to this ceiling—for example, defense expenditures, official development assistance, and so on. Using an agenda, "fiscal reconstruction without a tax increase" (zōzeinaki zaisei saiken), set by the Second Provisional Council for Administrative Reform, the fiscal authority imposed a zero ceiling (in the 1982 fiscal year) and then a minus ceiling (in fiscal years 1983 through 1987) on almost all expenditures.[33]

Continuing the tight budget was inconsistent, however, with the MOF's interests in the long run. If the upper limit of the budget was too apparent, the line ministries voluntarily cut less urgent programs and limited their expenditures to the ceiling in order to preserve the more urgent programs. Their compliance with the ceiling left little room for the MOF to examine and cut the budget requests. Thus the MOF aimed ultimately at tax increases by the introduction of the new tax that this study employs as a case.

Instead of relating the behaviors of fiscal bureaucrats to their power interests, some readers may argue that the MOF's behavior is based on a certain ideology that the ministry has inherited from the past, or on an inherent tendency that derives from the role of fiscal bureaucrats as savers of the public money. This is often called the "balanced" or "sound budget principle," which is similar to the household financial principle—the revenue determines the expenditure and both are balanced: more revenue means more spending and less revenue means less spending.

Those who base the MOF's behavior on the "balanced budget principle" cite as evidence the existence of legal constraints on public finance and the conservative fiscal policy orientation in Japan. The postwar public finance law (zaiseihō, enacted in 1947) embodies this principle; it allows the issuance of bonds only to the amount of public work expenditures, and substantially prohibits the issuance of deficit bonds (Article 4).[34] This legislation can be attributed to the bitter experience of deficit finance for the ministry during the war economy and to the institutional ideology of fiscal bureaucrats dating back to the establishment of the modern state in the late nineteenth century. This kind of legislation that supports a sound budget principle is exceptional among the OECD countries. In 1965, when special legislation allowed the exceptional issuance of deficit bonds, the Japanese government issued them for the first time since the enactment of the public finance law in order to stimulate the economy. From the 1975 fiscal year to the present, the government continues to issue deficit bonds, but the issuance has to be legalized annually by a special law that allows an exception from the stipulation of the public finance law. This principle is often used to explain the behavior of the fiscal authority in Japan, despite the very high ratio of deficit bond issuance both to (the general account of) the national budget and to the GNP as compared to the United States and Western European countries.[35] This legal restraint is also coincident with scholarly observations that the Japanese government has rarely employed a Keynesian demand stimulus policy (Noguchi 1984, 173–221; Hadley 1989).

The illustration of public financial management in postwar Japan in this study, however, demonstrates that the "sound budget principle" argument leaves some of the facts unexplained. One example is the MOF's attempt to slow down revenue growth during the high-growth period by allowing more tax exemptions and deductions. The sound budget principle does not explain the restraint on expenditures during the natural increase of tax revenue. A more explicit counterexample is the case used here—the recent tax reform. What the MOF first intended during the period of deficit finance was not an expenditure cut as a response to decreasing tax revenue, but rather the introduction of a new tax on consumption that would change the tax revenue structure. This shows that, in order to maintain discretionary power over the budget, the MOF tries to keep the budget tight enough to use its leverage on expenditures, but also tries to make it loose enough to leave room for discretionary power over new programs.

More important, restraints on the issuance of deficit bonds by the public finance law itself cannot be equated with the sound budget principle, because the law allows issuance of bonds to pay expenditures for public works that are not financed by the revenue in that fiscal year. Based on this act, the MOF distinguishes between two bonds—construction bonds (*kensetsu kokusai*), issued within the amount of public works expenditure, and deficit bonds (*akaji kokusai*), issued beyond the amount of that expenditure. The MOF regards the former as a part of the public investment effort and the latter as a measure to finance unexpected revenue shortfall, and thus resists the issuance of the latter as much as possible. However, their distinction is largely based on the fiscal authority's interpretation of the issuance of the bonds in question (i.e., they are expected or are unexpected by the MOF) rather than on an objective definition of real economic effects of their issuance. In other words, the MOF's orientation to government bonds is indisputable with its judgment on whether their issuance is under its control or not.

Consequently, the MOF does not aim for a numerical balance between revenue and expenditure as the sound budget principle directs. Instead, the fiscal bureaucrats want a moderate amount of fiscal tightness that is closely related to their interests in increases in budgetary power.

The following section will clarify that the policy objective of tax reform is fully consistent with the MOF's goal of increasing control over the budget. The MOF chose, among several alternatives, to introduce the VAT, expecting that the stable revenue from it would not only decrease the budget deficit but that they could also count on more stable revenue from it.

### Historical and Theoretical Influences on the Value-Added Tax

Chapter 1 introduced the assumption that technocratic considerations never present one definite answer to policymakers. In the case under consideration, tax theory does not provide scientific answers to the questions about which tax system is the best or what reform should be undertaken, though it puts some constraints on the choice of alternative policies or measures. Building on this assumption, this section will show that bureaucrats choose the alternative that is most consistent with the interest of their organization, that is, increasing the organization's discretionary power. Why did the MOF decide to introduce the broad-based consumption tax from among several possible reform alternatives that were equally suitable from a technocratic point of view? How did the MOF's organizational goal relate to the introduction of the VAT, which had been its major tax policy objective since the late 1970s? Before answering these questions, the section will show that other plausible factors influenced the bureaucratic choice; but neither the heritage of the tax system nor the changing intellectual climate in tax theory explained the MOF's preference for the VAT.

The history of the tax system in postwar Japan began with the reform proposed by the Shoup Mission in 1949 during the occupation period. The reform recommendation by Shoup radically changed the existing tax system and implanted the ideal of a comprehensive income taxation that reflected the dominant tax theory in the United States (more precisely, in the Anglo-American countries) in the 1940s. The impact of this mission shaped a heritage that was quite different from the prewar one, and worked as a constraint on postwar policy changes.

Although the ideal of comprehensive income taxation has been the basis of policy discussions since then, the actual tax system has diverged from it. Thus "the reforms were only a partial success, largely because subsequent modifications gradually made the tax system more inequitable and complicated" (Ishi 1987, 246).[36] The Japanese government did not implement certain proposals by the Shoup Mission and has repealed other proposals after the occupation period. The postwar changes until the 1980s (before the tax reform examined in this study) are summarized in relation to the Shoup recommendations as follows:

1. In terms of the personal income tax, the tax system has been distorted in three ways. First, certain incomes have been exempted from the aggregate sum of the income to which the progressive tax rate is applied. For example, small amounts of savings or special accounts were exempted from the taxation; this exemption continued until the reform in 1987. Capital gains from sales of securities were exempted from the taxation (in 1953) except "continuous sales," which were repeated transactions aimed at capital gains.[37] Third, the special tax treatment of unincorporated businesses has not only advantaged unincorporated compared to incorporated businesses, but has also caused horizontal inequities between self-employed and employed people in terms of the personal income tax. Even though the tax base of the personal income tax has been narrowed, the progressivity in the personal income tax rates was nominally increased in the 1960s and 1970s, from eight brackets (ranging from 20 percent to 55 percent tax rates) to nineteen brackets (ranging from 10 percent to 75 percent). The distortion of the personal income system has been a public concern since the 1980s and an important precedent for the reform.

2. Differing from the Shoup recommendation, the corporate tax system has applied split rates on different kinds of income, for example, retained profits and dividends. Numerous tax treatments were incorporated for encouraging and increasing the incentives for savings and investment. But, in the 1980s, especially after the MOF failed to obtain passage of the new indirect tax, some special treatments were curtailed and the tax rates have increased.

3. The Shoup Mission also recommended the introduction of a value-added tax[38] (an innovative system at the time), while proposing the abolition of the existing turnover tax that accumulated the tax amount from one transaction stage to the next, and thus distorted economic activity.[39] This recommendation ultimately failed to be implemented after several postponements. Since then, and until March 1989, the Japanese government developed a system of excise taxes on selective goods and services and raised the revenue from indirect taxation by increases in tax rates and expansion of a range of taxed commodities. Japan was a unique case, for it had no broad-based consumption tax, either at the national or the local level (Ishi 1989, 304–5). Many tax experts and policymakers had concerns

about the arbitrary expansion and distortion effect of the commodity tax system as an excise on "luxury" consumption. The system also had been under criticism from abroad, especially regarding the tax on imported whisky and wine since the late 1970s.

4. Since the indirect tax system could not cover the rapidly growing sectors of the economy, for example, the service industries, the revenue share depended more on a direct tax, especially the personal and corporate income taxes. In the 1980s, the revenue share of indirect taxation was less than 30 percent and averaged approximately 25 percent.

5. As a result, the Japanese tax system around 1980, when the first government proposal was made, had several defining characteristics in comparison with other industrial countries. Tables 2.2, 2.3, and 2.4, respectively, show that taxation in Japan in terms of percentage of the GDP was lowest, its relative dependence on direct taxation was much higher than average, and, due to the absence of a general consumption tax, its share of revenue from indirect taxation was exceptionally low among eighteen OECD countries.

Theoretical development in public finance has exerted significant influence on the public discussion of tax policies in postwar Japan. The ideal advocated by the Shoup Mission undeniably contributed to increasing support for comprehensive income taxation among academics as well as policymakers who have been socialized under the postwar tax system. However, public confidence in the fairness of the actual income tax system has eroded at the same time that the intellectual climate has changed. More public financial economists in the United States, some of whom were formerly strong supporters of a comprehensive income taxation, have begun to pay attention to the tax on consumption (Bradford 1986).

Tax theory provides several criteria that are used to analyze tax systems and present alternatives to policies. Existing tax systems and policies can be analyzed positively by the theory in terms of tax incidence and the impact of tax policies on the economic system. At the same time, the theory suggests that tax policies should depend on normative principles, for example, neutrality, equity, and simplicity. The tax system is more neutral if it is less distorting of free market decisions. The principle of equity determines a "fair" tax burden on specific economic actors, persons, families, and corporations, depending on certain criteria, for example, ability to pay or benefits obtained from the public service provided by tax revenue. Simplicity means the least complexity in implementing and administering the tax system. However, tax theory, even under hypothetical conditions, leaves several alternative policies equally justified (or discredited) in terms

TABLE 2.2
Total Tax Receipts (Excluding Social Security Contributions) as Percentages of Gross Domestic Product at Market Price

| | 1955 | Ranking Order | 1960 | Ranking Order | 1965 | Ranking Order | 1970 | Ranking Order | 1975 | Ranking Order | 1980 | Ranking Order | 1980 minus 1955 (percentage points) |
|---|---|---|---|---|---|---|---|---|---|---|---|---|---|
| Norway | 27.1 | 1 | 28.4 | 1 | 29.3 | 2 | 32.9 | 3 | 36.5 | 2 | 40.2 | 2 | 13.1 |
| United Kingdom | 26.7 | 2 | 24.9 | 4 | 26.1 | 5 | 32.3 | 4 | 29.8 | 6 | 29.8 | 7 | 3.1 |
| Sweden | 25.0 | 3 | 26.0 | 2 | 31.30 | 1 | 34.8 | 2 | 35.6 | 3 | 35.6 | 3 | 10.6 |
| Finland | 24.7 | 4 | 25.8 | 3 | 27.7 | 4 | 29.3 | 5 | 32.5 | 4 | 31.5 | 6 | 6.8 |
| Germany | 23.3 | 5 | 22.7 | 11 | 23.1 | 12 | 22.8 | 14 | 23.5 | 13 | 24.5 | 13 | 1.2 |
| Austria | 22.8 | 6 | 23.1 | 8 | 26.0 | 6 | 26.6 | 8 | 27.8 | 12 | 28.5 | 11 | 5.7 |
| Australia | 22.6 | 7 | 23.5 | 6 | 23.8 | 11 | 25.5 | 11 | 29.1 | 8 | 29.8[a] | 8 | 7.2 |
| Denmark | 22.3 | 8 | 24.1 | 5 | 28.4 | 3 | 38.6 | 1 | 40.5 | 1 | 44.3 | 1 | 22.0 |
| The Netherlands | 22.1 | 9 | 22.5 | 12 | 24.6 | 7 | 25.9 | 10 | 28.2 | 9 | 28.4 | 12 | 6.3 |
| Ireland | 21.4 | 10 | 20.9 | 14 | 24.3 | 9 | 28.7 | 7 | 28.0 | 11 | 32.2 | 4 | 10.8 |
| United States | 21.0 | 11 | 22.7 | 10 | 22.2 | 13 | 24.3 | 13 | 22.8 | 14 | 22.6 | 14 | 1.6 |
| New Zealand | 20.8 | 12 | 21.7 | 13 | 24.3 | 10 | 26.4 | 9 | 30.0 | 5 | 31.7 | 5 | 10.9 |
| Canada | 20.8 | 13 | 22.8 | 9 | 24.5 | 8 | 28.9 | 6 | 29.6 | 7 | 29.3 | 10 | 8.5 |
| Italy | 20.7 | 14 | 23.2 | 7 | 17.9 | 15 | 17.4 | 17 | 15.7 | 17 | 19.0[a] | 17 | -1.7 |
| Belgium | 17.8 | 15 | 19.3 | 15 | 21.4 | 14 | 25.1 | 12 | 28.0 | 10 | 29.4 | 9 | 11.6 |
| Switzerland | 15.0 | 16 | 16.7 | 16 | 16.1 | 16 | 18.2 | 16 | 21.0 | 15 | 21.3 | 16 | 6.3 |
| Japan | 14.9 | 17 | 15.7 | 17 | 14.6 | 18 | 15.3 | 18 | 14.9 | 18 | 18.1 | 18 | 3.2 |
| Portugal | 12.7 | 18 | 13.3 | 18 | 15.0 | 17 | 18.2 | 15 | 17.1 | 16 | 21.7 | 15 | 9.0 |
| Average | 21.2 | | 22.1 | | 23.4 | | 26.2 | | 27.3 | | 28.8 | | 7.6 |

Source: Long-term trends in Tax Revenues of OECD Member Countries 1955–1980, Paris: OECD, 1981: 13.
Note: Countries have been ranked by the 1955 figures.     [a] 1979 figures.

TABLE 2.3
Tax Receipts from Incomes and Profits Tax and Social Security Contributions as Percentages of Total Tax Receipts

| | Income Tax | | | | | | | Social Security Contributions | | | | | | |
| | 1955 | 1960 | 1965 | 1970 | 1975 | 1980 | 1980 minus 1955 (percentage points) | 1955 | 1960 | 1965 | 1970 | 1975 | 1980 | 1980 minus 1955 (percentage points) |
|---|---|---|---|---|---|---|---|---|---|---|---|---|---|---|
| Australia | 48.4 | 47.2 | 50.2 | 53.7 | 55.8 | 54.6ᵃ | 5.8 | — | — | — | — | — | — | — |
| Austria | 23.6 | 23.4 | 25.6 | 25.3 | 26.1 | 26.7 | 3.1 | 23.8 | 24.3 | 25.0 | 25.5 | 27.8 | 31.5 | 7.7 |
| Belgium | 31.1 | 29.3 | 27.6 | 31.2 | 39.5 | 42.4 | 11.3 | 25.9 | 27.0 | 31.4 | 30.3 | 31.9 | 30.7 | 4.8 |
| Canada | 39.2 | 39.6 | 39.3 | 44.6 | 47.5 | 46.0 | 6.8 | 4.2 | 5.7 | 5.7 | 9.6 | 10.1 | 10.7 | 6.5 |
| Denmark | 47.5 | 44.8 | 45.9 | 51.2 | 59.0 | 54.6 | 7.1 | 4.7 | 5.0 | 5.4 | 4.0 | 1.3 | 1.8 | -2.9 |
| Finland | 42.8 | 41.1 | 44.2 | 47.4 | 52.4 | 48.5 | 5.7 | 7.9 | 6.8 | 8.2 | 9.0 | 10.8 | 8.6 | 0.7 |
| Germany | 29.0 | 31.9 | 33.8 | 32.3 | 34.5 | 35.4 | 6.4 | 24.5 | 27.6 | 26.8 | 30.4 | 34.1 | 34.1 | 9.6 |
| Ireland | 23.8 | 21.3 | 25.7 | 27.1 | 30.0 | 36.7 | 12.9 | 4.6 | 4.9 | 6.5 | 8.2 | 13.8 | 14.3 | 9.7 |
| Italy | 12.7 | 15.7 | 17.8 | 17.4 | 21.5 | 31.5ᵃ | 18.8 | 32.1 | 32.7 | 34.2 | 37.8 | 45.9 | 36.7ᵃ | 4.6 |
| Japan | 37.7 | 38.7 | 39.8 | 41.2 | 39.7 | 40.8 | 3.1 | 12.7 | 13.8 | 19.1 | 22.3 | 29.3 | 30.1 | 17.4 |
| The Netherlands | 39.6 | 39.4 | 35.6 | 33.3 | 34.8 | 32.5 | -7.1 | 16.1 | 25.4 | 30.6 | 35.0 | 38.4 | 38.5 | 22.4 |
| New Zealand | 34.1 | 36.2 | 61.1 | 61.5 | 66.5 | 69.8 | 35.7 | 22.6 | 20.7 | — | — | — | — | -22.6 |
| Norway | 46.5 | 44.2 | 43.5 | 38.5 | 40.8 | 47.2 | 0.7 | 4.5 | 8.8 | 12.0 | 16.1 | 18.5 | 15.2 | 10.7 |
| Portugal | 27.7 | 27.8 | 26.7 | 26.0 | 20.6 | 22.3 | -5.4 | 17.2 | 18.3 | 19.5 | 21.4 | 31.3 | 27.1 | 9.9 |
| Sweden | 66.9 | 61.3 | 54.4 | 54.0 | 50.4 | 43.4 | -23.5 | 2.1 | 4.3 | 12.1 | 14.9 | 19.5 | 28.7 | 26.6 |
| Switzerland | 34.9 | 35.5 | 38.2 | 40.8 | 43.8 | 41.5 | 6.6 | 21.5 | 21.6 | 22.5 | 23.4 | 29.2 | 30.8 | 9.3 |
| United Kingdom | 40.6 | 37.5 | 36.8 | 40.3 | 44.4 | 37.9 | -2.7 | 10.4 | 12.6 | 15.4 | 13.9 | 17.4 | 16.9 | 6.5 |
| United States | 53.4 | 49.9 | 46.3 | 47.9 | 43.8 | 47.0 | -6.4 | 11.0 | 14.4 | 16.4 | 19.3 | 24.5 | 26.3 | 15.3 |
| Average | 37.8 | 36.9 | 38.5 | 39.7 | 41.7 | 42.2 | 4.4 | 13.7 | 15.2 | 16.2 | 17.8 | 21.3 | 21.2 | 7.5 |

Source: Long-term Trends in Tax Revenues of OECD Member Countries 1955–1980 (Paris: OECD, 1981), 16.    ᵃ 1979 figures.

TABLE 2.4
General Consumption Tax and Taxes on Specific Goods and Services as Percentages of Total Tax Receipts

| | General Consumption Taxes | | | | | | 1980 minus 1955 (percentage points) | Taxes on Specific Goods and Services | | | | | | 1980 minus 1955 (percentage points) |
|---|---|---|---|---|---|---|---|---|---|---|---|---|---|---|
| | 1955 | 1960 | 1965 | 1970 | 1975 | 1980 | | 1955 | 1960 | 1965 | 1970 | 1975 | 1980 | |
| Australia | 9.4 | 10.1 | 7.3 | 7.4 | 6.7 | 5.5ᵃ | -3.9 | 24.8 | 23.7 | 22.6 | 20.1 | 18.7 | 22.6ᵃ | -2.2 |
| Austriaᵇ | 18.9 | 17.5 | 18.7 | 18.6 | 19.9 | 20.1 | 1.2 | 16.5 | 18.1 | 17.6 | 17.7 | 14.0 | 10.3 | -6.2 |
| Belgiumᵇ | 21.8 | 21.4 | 22.5 | 22.2 | 16.6 | 16.9 | -4.9 | 14.6 | 14.9 | 13.0 | 11.7 | 8.7 | 6.2 | -8.4 |
| Canada | 14.8 | 12.7 | 18.2 | 14.4 | 12.5 | 11.6 | -3.2 | 22.9 | 19.2 | 17.1 | 13.2 | 13.6 | 12.5 | -10.4 |
| Denmarkᶜ | — | — | 9.1 | 18.8 | 16.9 | 22.3 | 22.3 | 35.9 | 37.4 | 29.2 | 17.9 | 14.7 | 13.4 | -22.5 |
| Finland | 18.6 | 20.1 | 18.9 | 19.9 | 17.8 | 20.5 | 1.9 | 24.6 | 25.9 | 24.0 | 20.9 | 16.7 | 20.0 | -4.6 |
| Germanyᵇ | 19.8 | 17.0 | 16.5 | 17.1 | 14.7 | 16.8 | -3.0 | 14.7 | 14.1 | 14.6 | 12.9 | 10.6 | 9.0 | -5.7 |
| Irelandᵇ | — | — | 5.7 | 13.1 | 14.7 | 14.8 | 14.8 | 47.6 | 49.4 | 43.4 | 36.3 | 29.7 | 28.1 | -19.5 |
| Italyᵇ | 13.3 | 12.9 | 12.9 | 13.2 | 14.3 | 14.5ᵃ | 1.2 | 30.3 | 27.6 | 23.7 | 22.7 | 13.6 | 12.2ᵃ | -18.1 |
| Japan | — | — | — | — | — | — | — | 33.1 | 30.8 | 25.9 | 20.9 | 15.0 | 14.0 | -19.1 |
| Netherlandsᵇ | 16.3 | 13.9 | 12.3 | 14.6 | 14.4 | 16.0 | -0.3 | 15.4 | 14.0 | 14.7 | 11.5 | 7.9 | 6.8 | -8.6 |
| New Zealand | 8.8 | 6.5 | 7.7 | 8.1 | 9.0 | 10.2 | 1.4 | 15.8 | 17.8 | 18.7 | 17.5 | 13.8 | 11.2 | -4.6 |
| Norwayᶜ | 20.1 | 20.0 | 21.6 | 23.8 | 20.5 | 18.2 | -1.9 | 23.9 | 22.4 | 18.8 | 18.3 | 16.8 | 16.7 | -7.2 |
| Portugal | — | — | — | 8.3 | 11.1 | 16.4 | 16.4 | 39.8 | 38.3 | 39.9 | 32.7 | 25.2 | 23.2 | -16.6 |
| Swedenᶜ | — | 1.9 | 10.3 | 10.2 | 12.0 | 13.4 | 13.4 | 26.6 | 28.4 | 19.9 | 16.6 | 11.1 | 9.5 | -17.1 |
| Switzerland | 10.8 | 8.4 | 9.5 | 7.8 | 7.7 | 9.1 | -1.7 | 21.9 | 23.9 | 19.0 | 17.1 | 10.6 | 9.7 | -12.2 |
| United Kingdomᵇ | 6.8 | 7.3 | 5.9 | 6.5 | 8.8 | 13.8 | 7.0 | 27.5 | 25.6 | 24.9 | 19.9 | 14.8 | 13.3 | -14.2 |
| United States | 3.4 | 3.9 | 4.6 | 5.2 | 6.7 | 6.6 | 3.2 | 15.8 | 14.8 | 15.6 | 11.3 | 9.4 | 7.8 | -8.0 |
| Average | 10.2 | 9.8 | 11.2 | 12.7 | 12.5 | 13.7 | 3.5 | 25.1 | 24.8 | 22.4 | 18.8 | 14.7 | 13.7 | -11.4 |

Source: Long-term Trends in Tax Revenue of OECD Member Countries 1955–1980. Paris: OECD, 1981: 20.
ᵃ 1979 figures.    ᵇ Country with one rate of VAT only.    ᶜ Country with multirate of VAT (zero counting as a separate rate).

of the above three principles. This is because satisfying one principle sometimes interferes with the other one or two principles in the same tax system; that is, concentrating on the equity problem makes the tax administration complex and is counter to the simplicity principle.[40] In addition, how tax systems are evaluated by the normative principles depends on the interpretation of the policies that would actually be implemented. For example, tax theorists observe the same principles and come out in support of different tax systems.[41] Therefore, making tax policies and choosing policy alternatives often depend on other values or criteria that do not derive from the theoretical tax policy debate.

The idea of taxing on a base of consumption or expenditure as an alternative to income is as old as John Stuart Mill in the mid-nineteenth century,[42] and has been influential in the continental European countries. Especially since the 1970s, a direct tax on consumption expenditures has gained support among the public financial economists in the Anglo-American countries, where the idea of comprehensive income taxation was dominant (Bradford 1980). This tendency has been reflected also in the tax reports issued by Western governments.[43] One reason for the renewed interest in the consumption tax was the observation of the problems and defects in the existing income tax system that have been emerging over the last few decades in other OECD countries. To attribute these "problems" to the theoretical inferiority of income taxation is not fully appropriate, because no country, including Japan, has ever enacted a "comprehensive" income tax system as indicated by a theoretical ideal.[44]

Under this situation, the two different ideas support different directions of reform, respectively. One is to reform the existing income tax system by abolishing loopholes and exemptions, and to go back to a more comprehensive form of the income tax system. The other—which is becoming more influential—is to substitute a tax on consumption for the income tax. The latter position can be divided into two categories—an expenditure tax, which is a direct tax on consumption instead of income, and a tax system that optimally combines the taxes on consumption and income.[45]

Stimulated by the changing intellectual climate and by the introduction of the VAT in the European Community (EC) countries,[46] the Japanese MOF planned to introduce a VAT of the consumption type. This is one type of multistage tax on consumption that applies the same rate of tax on added value at all stages of transaction and exchange. First, the "firms"[47] pay the tax on the added value, that is, the difference in the value when they purchase and when they sell, which is ultimately borne by the consumers of goods and services. Because the flat rate of tax is levied regardless of the characteristics of *those who bear the tax*, as well as the other characteristics of *the filing units*, the VAT need neither to approximate the tax base of accrual income nor to integrate the personal and corporate accounts (as in the income tax). This feature significantly decreases the number of tax-filing units. Second, because the tax is determined by added value in a cash flow on the realization basis, the VAT automatically adjusts to inflation and economic growth. This is another advantage of the VAT compared to the progressive income tax that requires revision of the tax calculation method for the adjustment to these changes.[48] Theoretically, the VAT allows a simple tax calculation and causes less distortions of economic decisions if it is implemented under a uniform rate and without any substantial exclusions or exemptions.

The VAT has begun to attract academic attention as a partial substitute for income taxation. Differing from an expenditure tax, which is a direct tax on individuals, the VAT, which is proportionally levied on consumption, is regressive, and thus cannot be a perfect substitute for the progressive income taxation. In this sense, the introduction of the VAT does not ultimately aim to replace the income tax with the consumption tax. However, the compatibility of the VAT with other taxes, especially the existing income taxes, makes it easier to implement.[49]

The theoretical strength of the VAT has attracted the attention of policymakers. But this strength does not fully explain why the MOF preferred the VAT to the other reform alternatives, especially the comprehensive income tax reform. First, the strength of the VAT as a simple and neutral tax is easily lost because of its discriminatory measures, for example, applying multiple tax rates on different goods and services and exempting certain goods and services from taxation. And, actually, the EC countries most notable for adopting the VAT have complicated the system with these discriminatory measures.[50] A look at six major EC member countries (the Netherlands, the United Kingdom, Sweden, Germany, Italy, and France) shows that most countries have introduced differentiated tax rates in order to make the burdens of the VAT similar to taxes that already existed (see also Table 1.1). In addition, all of them exempted certain goods and services from the VAT (Aaron 1982). Second, the strength of the VAT as a simple and neutral taxation appears "unfair" in terms of the principle of equity because the flat rate of the tax is inevitably regressive and levies the same rate of tax on those who have different incomes. Moreover, if the poor consume a higher share of total income, they are taxed by higher average rates than the rich. The special tax exemption or deduction for necessities (e.g., foods, medicare, education, and so on) would decrease the regressivity, but, as described already, this discriminatory measure would eliminate the tax's simplicity and neutrality. All the desirable characteristics of the VAT by themselves are not strong enough to justify its introduction. In addition, shifting academic interest from a tax on income to one on consumption should not be exaggerated. For example, in the United States where more public financial economists supported the tax on consumption, the Reagan administration proposed a reform in the mid-1980s based on the comprehensive income tax system while rejecting the alternative of a consumption tax.

In addition, the history of Japanese taxation until the 1970s seemed to make a comprehensive income tax reform a more practical choice than the introduction of the VAT. First, the Japanese people were not familiar with consumption taxes; therefore, it would not be easy to accustom them to the new tax. Second, the ideal of comprehensive income taxation was deeply rooted in the minds of policymakers and tax specialists through their socialization under the tax system established by the Shoup Mission. Among the MOF bureaucrats familiar with tax policies, many supported the comprehensive income taxation.[51] Therefore, disagreement about the reform could reasonably be expected among tax experts, also even among individuals in the tax bureau. Erosion of the income tax base and increased special treatments and exemptions in the existing system may make some individuals more interested in the tax on consumption as an alternative, but may make others more conscious of the necessity to reform the income tax.

Speculating about the combined impact of developments in tax theory and the historical inertia of tax policies falls short of explaining why these bureaucrats eventually supported the VAT and why the MOF formed a strong consensus for its introduction. The analysis, then, will explore another factor that plausibly influenced bureaucratic preference for the VAT—their organizational objective of increasing their discretionary power over public finance.

How does the introduction of the VAT contribute to the achievement of the goal of maintaining control over the budget? Auxiliary characteristics of the VAT relating to revenue structure answer this question. Two such characteristics of the VAT are plausibly consistent with the MOF's interest. First, the VAT is regarded as an effective way to finance increasing public expenditures. A small change in the tax rate easily increases the tax revenue. In the EC countries, governments have continued to increase the tax rates (Aaron 1981). According to this line, the introduction of the VAT in Japan is regarded as a bureaucratic attempt to maximize revenue.

A closer examination of the case weakens this interpretation. First, the

VAT is not the only way to increase the revenue. The existing income tax system before the reform could have increased the tax revenue automatically by leaving it unadjusted to inflation and economic growth. If the MOF had wanted only to increase taxes, doing nothing would have achieved this without political costs (Noguchi 1987a, 210). Some may still argue that increasing an indirect tax is politically easier than enlarging the burden of a direct tax. The conventional wisdom among public financial economists is that taxpayers know less clearly how much they pay with an indirect tax than with a direct tax. This conventional view, however, fails to explain the present Japanese case in which the taxpayers reacted more to a 3-percent consumption tax, which was introduced in 1989, and almost neglected an accompanying tax rate decrease in the income taxation. Lastly, the ease with which tax rates can be increased cannot be equated with the ease with which revenues can be raised. For example, in Europe, evidence does not support the simple idea that the introduction of a VAT increases taxation, if measured by the ratio of total taxes to total income, or total government spending as a share of total spending, and so on (Stock-fisch 1987). Consequently, in seeking tax reform, the MOF aimed for more than raising revenues.

Another characteristic of the VAT is the stability of tax revenue. A flat rate consumption tax (with a broad tax base) does not fluctuate with economic up- and downturns as much as a progressive income tax does. Under the VAT system, which can alleviate the influence of external economic conditions on the tax revenue, the budget is less likely to be under either loose or tight constraints, which significantly decreases the MOF's discretionary power. Securing stable tax revenue was an especially urgent policy objective for the MOF at the beginning of the 1980s, since the Japanese government had accumulated debts due to a shortfall of tax revenue arising from the recession in the 1970s. The introduction of the VAT was the best policy alternative aimed at securing stable tax revenue from consumption while not interfering with economic activity. The VAT is, in this sense, closely related to the goal of the entire ministry, given the budget deficit that had persisted since the late 1970s.

The MOF's strong interest in acquiring a stable revenue explains its preference for the VAT. Alternatively, the ultimate policy objective in the introduction of the consumption tax for the MOF is securing the stability of the tax revenue. Clarifying this imperative for the MOF in the tax reform prepares one to understand correctly the strategy the MOF employed to introduce the new tax, especially the political maneuvering that was needed to compromise with the opposition. The next section examines the bureaucrats' strategy that led to the desired policy outcome.

PURSUANCE OF A POLICY OBJECTIVE BY A BUREAUCRATIC
ORGANIZATION: THE MINISTRY OF FINANCE IN THE
JAPANESE TAX REFORM

*Strategies*

The political feasibility of a proposed policy is especially important to consider when opposition may be sufficient to block legislative passage. Without formal decision-making power supported by a popular mandate, bureaucrats have to persuade some politicians to push for implementation of a proposed policy on their behalf. They also must compromise with special-interest groups and obtain public acceptance so that politicians are not forced to oppose the policy in their reelection bids.

The Japanese tax reform was circumscribed by certain conditions that interfered with bureaucratic influence over policy-making. First, in terms of the party system, the predominance of the LDP since 1955 until the tax reform period[52] made bureaucrats focus their efforts on obtaining approval from the unchanging incumbent party. The internal structure of the LDP enabled the bureaucrats to count on the LDP's majority support in the Diet unless the LDP leaders believe that a proposed policy would cause them to lose their majority in the Diet. The LDP demonstrated relatively strong party discipline in legislative decisions when the faction leaders agreed on a common policy. Therefore, convincing the LDP's leadership was a prerequisite for the bureaucrats to obtain the LDP's approval for their policy proposals. The LDP was primarily in charge of negotiation and bargaining with the opposition parties but the bureaucrats may have helped facilitate this process by influencing public opinion.[53]

An unchanging incumbent party, such as the LDP during this period, works both for and against bureaucrats. The existence of such a party allows bureaucrats to predict consequences of their proposals more easily than under frequent alternations of party governments. At the same time, however, bureaucrats confront better-informed party politicians backed by the party's experience of long-term governance. Thus the real question is how bureaucrats manage the relationship with such an experienced incumbent party. Highly technocratic characteristics of tax policy, which require detailed data and specialized knowledge to comprehend, result in formation of a small circle of policy specialists inside the government. The bureaucrats can take advantage of this exclusive and intensive network. This advantage, which arises from the requirement for expertise, is not the same as bureaucratic monopolization of policy information or specialized knowledge. Rather, inclusion of some incumbent politicians in this small circle is more important for bureaucrats to implement their desired policies than simple monopolization that leaves politicians ignorant or misinformed. I will elaborate this point by analyzing bureaucratic strategies in the Japanese tax reform case. The Japanese tax reform case is an appropriate one for observing the long-term strategies used by bureaucrats because the introduction of the VAT was planned for more than a decade, and failed twice before its enactment in 1989.

STRATEGY 1: DEFINING A POLICY PROBLEM AND SPECIFYING THE ALTERNATIVE

The first strategy that the bureaucrats employ serves to change the political meaning of a proposed policy and to change issue dimensions in which the policy is politicized. Especially when bureaucrats propose a policy that is expected to cause political opposition like the VAT, they need to convince the incumbent party that the proposal will lead neither to a significant decline in its popular support nor to a loss of its majority power. For this purpose, the bureaucrats try to propose a policy that would otherwise bring forth public antipathy, so that it appears acceptable or necessary in the public eyes. In order to analyze the way in which the fiscal bureaucrats put the introduction of the new tax on the political agenda, the argument first relies on a theoretical distinction between "agenda setting" and "alternative specification." According to Kingdon (1984), "An agenda setting process narrows the set of subjects that could conceivably occupy their attention to the list on which they actually do focus," while "the process of alternative specification narrows the large set of possible alternatives to that set from which choices actually are made" (205). These two processes, which Kingdon theoretically distinguished, correspond to two different stages of the strategy by which fiscal bureaucrats try to legitimate a proposed policy. The first stage consists of defining the policy problem and setting the agenda in which the proposed policy is connected to the problem as a viable solution. However, setting the agenda still leaves other alternatives as solutions for the given problem, in addition to the policy that the bureaucrats want to implement. The strategy is then used to gain support for the proposed policy at the expense of other alternatives, which would be discredited as viable solutions through policy implementation or a public relations campaign.

In the Japanese tax reform case, two failed proposals of major indirect taxes and the final introduction of the consumption tax, which was similar to ones proposed earlier, will be analyzed in terms of bureaucratic strategies of defining a policy problem and specifying policy alternatives. Since a detailed account of each reform proposal is given in the next four chapters, bureaucratic agenda setting will be explained briefly here (Table 2.5).

TABLE 2.5
Changing Agendas of Tax Reforms

| | Reason(s) Attached to the Government's Proposal | Alternative Agenda from Public Opposition |
|---|---|---|
| Proposal of general consumption tax in 1978–1979 | Necessity of a tax increase to reduce a budget deficit | Necessity of cuts in expenditures and waste in administration before a tax increase |
| Proposal of sales tax in 1986–1987 (revenue-neutral reform combined with income tax reduction) | Necessity of structural reform to alleviate heavy reliance on direct taxation (fairness, neutrality, and simplicity of the tax system emphasized by Prime Minister Nakasone) | The tax proposal as breaking an election pledge made by Prime Minister Nakasone |
| Proposal of consumption tax in 1988 (accompanied income tax reduction exceeding tax burden increase from the new indirect tax) | Rectification of tax inequity in the existing system, and securing financial sources for social security expenditures for the elderly | Latent agenda of opposition (demand for the income tax reform instead of the new indirect tax, and request for the presentation of social security programs that would necessitate the new tax revenue) |

Source: This table was prepared by the author
Notes: Underlying economic and fiscal conditions that motivated the Ministry of Finance to make the three tax proposals:
1. Inequity and ineffectiveness of the existing income tax system due to employment of special tax measures.
2. Necessity of a stable financial source under the budget deficit.
3. Distorted effects of resource allocations in the existing indirect tax system, which consisted of excise taxes on selective commodities and services.

When the MOF proposed the introduction of the new tax on consumption (called a "general consumption tax") for the first time in 1978 and 1979, the fiscal authority defined the restoration of fiscal health, that is, the elimination of the issuance of deficit bonds, as a major problem in need of a solution. Together with the prime minister at that time, the late Ōhira, the MOF asked for public acceptance of the added burden of the new tax as a viable fiscal solution. The public agreed with the goal of fiscal reconstruction advocated by the government, but demanded that it curtail waste and expenditures in the public sector instead of introducing the new tax. They regarded the government's proposal of the new tax not as an inevitable consequence of the struggle against the worldwide recession in the 1970s, but as a symptom of its lax attitude toward fiscal responsibility. In the proposal in the late 1970s, the new tax, which had been offered as a solution to finance the deficit, was eventually dominated by alternative solutions—a public expenditure cut and the rationalization of administrative organization.

This first failed proposal informs us of several important facts about bureaucratic roles in tax reform. First, the case in the 1980s shows that bureaucrats had begun to enact the major indirect tax with very little political support. This is confirmed by the fact that the only active supporter was Prime Minister Ōhira; moreover, some tax specialists inside the party, who were to become reliable cooperators with the MOF in two subsequent proposals, were reluctant to endorse the first bureaucratic proposal. Next, the failure to propose the new tax meant that a swift move by bureaucrats to put tax reform on the agenda and to present a concrete reform plan did not guarantee its passage. The bureaucratic advantage of easy access to policy information and of policy expertise may enable them to prepare the major policy change in their favor without letting the public know it, but public opinion can still block it at the last moment. Consequently, the rejected proposal of the general consumption tax in the late 1970s symbolizes political difficulties of the introduction of the broad-based consumption tax and indicates the bureaucrats' will to push such an unpopular tax proposal.

After the failed tax proposal, the administrative reform (gyōsei kaikaku) campaign, which aimed to eliminate public deficits, was implemented by the LDP government and became the major political agenda in the 1980s. Even though administrative reform was a political agenda proposed by the LDP leaders, the MOF took full advantage of it in order to restore fiscal health, and implemented a strict austerity policy. Despite the continuation of the austerity campaign, the chronic budget deficit lessened public enthusiasm for an expenditure cut. The politicians, special-interest groups, and electorate in opposition to the new consumption tax recognized that the expenditure cut as an alternative to the new tax also threatened their interests without effectively reducing the deficit. Also, the small changes in tax policy introduced by the MOF, that is, increases in corporate taxes and commodities taxes, changed the way the organized interest groups regarded the introduction of the new tax. The major business associations began to support the introduction of the VAT in order to avoid further concentration of taxes on large-scale manufacturers. This change by the large-scale manufacturers was in contrast to the continuous opposition to the new tax by small-sized businesses and distributors, whom the new tax would require to present to the tax authority more information on their business income.

Failure to restore fiscal health with an austerity policy during this period discredited expenditure cuts as a viable way to solve the budget deficit and an effective way to supplement the necessary revenue. The inadequacy of these policies enhanced the fiscal authority's position, strengthened the argument for the necessity of both an expenditure cut and a revenue increase, and drew public attention to the new tax as an effective means to reform the public financial structure. In other words, fiscal and tax policies implemented during this period steered the way to the proposal of the new consumption tax, which had once been eliminated from the public agenda. What is to be noted here is that implementation of these policies and their effects to impress the necessity of the new tax on the public were the results of the MOF's intentional efforts. First, taking a position fully cooperative with the administrative reform campaign, the MOF voluntarily included a scheme and procedure for cutting expenditures in the annual budget and, as a result, secured its influence over the austerity campaign. Then, implementing the austerity campaign, the MOF carefully set a range of expenditures that were subject to retrenchment, and thus were used as an indicator of the austerity policy's effect. This MOF move significantly contributed to impressing the chronic nature of budget deficits on the public during a very short period. Second, the MOF proposed ad hoc tax-increasing measures to avoid the further issuance of deficit bonds. Implementing these measures increased support for the necessity of introducing new taxation, as already described.

Public criticism of the government, however, made the MOF cease promoting the new tax as a solution for the budget deficit. Therefore, in the second proposal in 1987, the MOF proposed a new tax—a sales tax—as a part of the structural reform. The ministry argued that the heavy reliance of revenue source on direct taxation in the existing system could not catch up with the rapid change in economic activities, especially the expansion of service industries. It presented the new tax as a means of raising more revenue from indirect taxation.

At the same time, the MOF accepted Prime Minister Nakasone's offer to combine the introduction of the new tax with income and corporate tax reduction, and not to change the level of tax revenue in the reform. However, this uneasy coalition between the prime minister and the MOF resulted in the revelation of their differences, and illegitimated the proposal of tax reform as a whole. Prime Minister Nakasone, who was much more eager to implement a popular tax cut than to introduce the new tax, had once promised in an election campaign not to introduce a "large-scale indirect tax," which meant the new tax on consumption. This election pledge redefined the introduction of the new tax as breaking the prime minister's public promise, and gave the opposition a reason to reject the government's proposal of the sales tax.

This second failure of a tax proposal by the MOF shows that cooperation with incumbent politicians is a double-edged sword for bureaucrats. The incumbent party's approval enabled the bureaucrats to propose the unpopular policy, which otherwise would not have been put on the policy agenda. According to this case, however, the party's more active role may thwart bureaucratic influence if political intervention adversely affected political agendas that had been cautiously prepared. The incidence of the second public rejection of the new tax also suggests that the bureaucratic power of agenda setting hinges on contingent factors that cannot be explained by institutionalized patterns of behaviors nor predicted by decision-making routines.

In the third proposal in 1988, the MOF proposed the new tax as an effective solution for two policy problems: to rectify the tax inequity in the existing tax system and to secure financial sources for welfare expenditures for the increasing number of elderly among the population. The bureaucrats tried to convert the public feeling of tax inequity in the existing income tax system into support for the new tax. First, they emphasized that the new system would effectively tax money that might have been exempted from or evaded income taxation, and that the entire reform package would result in tax decreases. This proposal strengthened the impression that the reform would shift revenue reliance to indirect taxation without increasing the level of the tax burden. Second, they considered that proposing the new tax for securing financial resources for social security expenditures might justify the tax without stirring public antipathy. This created complications for opposing groups that tried to base their opposition to the new tax on its regressive effect on income distribution. In this way, the bureaucratic proposal of the new value-added tax dominated other alternatives, for example, comprehensive reform of income taxation, which might have become an alternative means to improve tax equity and finance the social security program. The government thus managed to pass the tax bills in the Diet and implement the unpopular new tax.

STRATEGY 2: POLITICAL COMPROMISES ON UNIMPORTANT FACTORS

A second strategy bureaucrats can employ is to modify unimportant parts of a proposed policy to obtain concessions from opposing groups. Differing from strategic maneuvering, which attempts to change the political meaning of the proposed policy, this strategy aims to alleviate the organized opposition by offering compromising measures as bargaining chips in negotiations with special-interest groups. The bureaucrats seek cooperation from incumbent politicians to intercede with the special-interest groups and learn what kind of compromise in the details of a policy weakens their opposition. At the same time, by offering compromises in some measures, it facilitates the opposition groups' acceptance of other measures with higher priorities. This in turn leads to implementation of the policy without the policy losing its minimum imperative. Because these compromises concentrate on alleviating the organized opposition, this strategy may run the risk of being perceived by other parts of constituencies, especially the unorganized public, as an indulgent submission to political pressure by the government, and result in depriving the proposal of legitimacy.

The MOF bureaucrats' behavioral pattern is consistent with the above explanation of a compromising strategy. The bureaucrats teach new members intentionally how to defend their position against political pressure. This approach, used in bargaining with others in policy-making, is often called "set the weight bases" (*jūshin jinchi o shike*). This expression originally comes from wording used in military strategy, but is used here to indicate allegedly the best way of bargaining. *Weight bases* originally meant the subsidiary bases on several concentric circles, the center of which is a home base. This lineup of bases aims to block a direct attack on the home base. In the MOF's bargaining with others, the home base is compared to the minimum imperative of the policy. Weight bases are the offers the bureaucrats make each time they concede in order to induce the bargaining partners' compromise. The analogy of military strategy suggests that the first offer should not be too compromising with political pressure (as if the subsidiary base on the largest concentric circle were far enough from the home base). It also suggests that alternative offers should be prepared so as to be presented one by one (as if each of the subsidiary bases were set to weaken the enemy at several different stages of attack).

Actually, this instruction accurately illustrates the behavioral pattern of the MOF bureaucrats who shelve one proposal if political pressure is insurmountable and offer another that is a bit more compromising than the previous one.[54]

In the tax reform, bureaucratic compromise with special-interest groups followed such a behavioral pattern. From 1979 to 1989, three times the government proposed a broad-based consumption tax that approximated the VAT system. During this process, the government continued to compromise with special interests by (1) lowering tax rates; (2) using firms' accounting books to calculate their taxes instead of relying on invoices; (3) making the tax exemption point higher; (4) allowing an optional simplified rule of tax calculation to small-scale business; and (5) decreasing the frequency of tax returns. The three proposals are summarized as follows.

THE "GENERAL CONSUMPTION TAX" DESIGNED IN 1979

1. A 5-percent tax rate levied on the amount of added value for all firms

2. Adoption of the subtraction method

3. Tax exemption point at ¥20 million (= $91 thousand; $1 = ¥219.14 in 1979) of annual sales volume

4. Application of simplified rule of tax calculation (to allow the conventional calculation of the amount of tax depending on the amount of purchase or sale) for businesses with less than ¥40 million (= $183 thousand; $1 = ¥219.14 in 1979) of annual sales volume

5. Requirement of a tax return once a year (for an incorporated business, in a business year, and for an unincorporated business, in a calendar year) and optional tax returns every three months

THE "SALES TAX" PROPOSED IN 1987

1. A 5-percent tax rate

2. Adoption of the invoice method

3. Tax exemption point at ¥100 million (= $691 thousand; $1 = ¥144.64 in 1987) of annual sales volume

4. Application of the simplified rule of tax calculation to businesses with less than ¥100 million of annual sales volume; conventionally to regard 20 percent (for retailers) or 10 percent (for wholesalers) of the amount of sales as added value, thus the tax rate could be expressed as 1 percent or 0.5 percent of sales for these firms

5. Requirement of a tax return four times a year, every three months

THE "CONSUMPTION TAX" PROPOSED IN 1988 AND INTRODUCED IN 1989

1. A 3-percent tax rate levied on the amount of added value for all firms

2. Adoption of the subtraction method

3. Tax exemption point at ¥30 million (= $217 thousand; $1 = ¥137.96 in 1989) of annual sales volume

4. Application of the simplified rule of tax calculation to businesses with less than ¥500 million (= $3,624 thousand; $1 = ¥137.96 in 1989) of annual sales volume; conventionally to regard 20 percent (for retailers) or 10 percent (for wholesalers) of the amount of sales as added value, thus the tax rate could be expressed as 0.6 percent or 0.3 percent of sales for these firms

5. Requirement of a tax return twice a year, every six months

These measures, which the MOF used to alleviate organized opposition, certainly decreased the consistency and effectiveness of the taxation. The greatest merit of the VAT from a technocratic point of view was its neutral effect on economic activity. A desirable VAT system, therefore, applies a flat tax rate on a broad tax base. More concretely, the better system has a single tax rate, a smaller number of tax-exempted goods and services, allows a lower tax exemption point with respect to a scale of business (measured by a total amount of annual sales), and uniformly applies a precise method of tax calculation, such as the invoice method used in the EC countries. The system introduced in Japan fully satisfies only one condition—a single tax rate.

The first example of a compromise that decreases the taxation's effectiveness is the use of the subtraction method instead of the invoice method. In the subtraction method, the subtraction of total purchases (or costs) from total sales is multiplied by a tax rate and the amount of applied tax is calculated. This method is sometimes called an account method because it uses only account books of individual firms in order to calculate the tax. In the invoice method, compulsory invoices show the amounts of taxes already paid by other firms (tax credit) out of the amount taxed on purchases by a firm at this stage of transaction. Since each invoice indicates the total value-added tax, that is, the input tax for a firm in question, the firm collects the invoices during a certain period determined by law, and aggregates all the input taxes on them. The invoice method, if correctly used, means a more accurate calculation of taxes based on reliable sources, though it requires more paper work from tax-filing units.

The subtraction method was used to make tax filing easier. But it was primarily interpreted as a failure to respond to public concern about the possibility of different extents of compliance with the income tax across occupational groups. Based on the experiences of other countries, the experts reported that information conveyed by invoices—that is, how much one partner sells and the other buys—would not only serve to calculate value added but would also improve business compliance with the income tax.[55] This merit of the invoice method strongly appealed to the public. A majority of taxpayers—employed people whose taxes are withheld at the source—believe that self-employed people who file tax returns benefited from a decreased burden under the pretexts of or even abuses of "necessary expenses," "salaries to their family employees," and other special tax treatments.

Second, the high tax exemption point left a significant number of business people outside the tax system. The government reduced this point from ¥100 million in the proposal of the sales tax to ¥30 million in the proposal of the consumption tax—closer to the ¥20 million in the first 1979 tax proposal. However, this level was still much higher than the points in the corresponding tax systems in the EC countries and South Korea.[56]

Third, the MOF allowed the optional use of the simplified calculation rule for small and medium-sized businesses whose share of the total number of firms far exceeded the 80-percent level. Its adoption was very likely to allow accumulation of tax amounts from one stage to another, thus making the new tax system of the VAT closer to the turnover tax in many tax-filing units. Moreover, the adoption of this measure, as well as the subtraction method, may have left room for businesses to obtain new "benefit" from this system at the consumers' expense. Tax experts and economists argued that some industrial sectors (for example, service industries) actually had a ratio of added value higher than 20 percent or 10 percent that was used in tax calculation by the simplified rule. Thus they warned that this simplified rule would provide a much smaller added value than a true figure at each stage, and bring a "benefit tax" to retailers if they imposed a 3-percent price increase on consumers under the name of the new tax. Requiring that a tax return be filed only twice a year involved a similar problem because firms might be able to invest the money that consumers paid as taxes and earn interest from it during the standard tax period of six months.

While defending the new system against public criticism,[57] the MOF has fully recognized that these compromising measures will distort the new tax system in the long run. The ministry has strong intentions to "improve" the system by bringing it closer to the theoretical ideal through reforms following its implementation.[58] Modification of the system in October 1991, about two-and-a-half years after it had been installed, seems to reflect the bureaucrats' intentions. The government has reduced, from ¥500 million to ¥400 million, the level of the total amount of annual sales at which firms can choose the simple calculation method. In addition, the government has attempted to make calculation results obtained by this method closer to business practice: it has begun to apply four different ratios of the amount of purchases out of annual sales to different industrial sectors as bases for calculation.[59] This plan also requires tax returns four times a year in order to shorten the period in which firms can use taxes for investment funds.

One may consider these compromises examined above to be bureaucratic concessions to political pressure and the decline of the bureaucratic control over policy outcomes. Bureaucratic reliance on the LDP to articulate special interest's opposition and hammer out compromise measures seems to underscore this possibility. When they compromise with special interests, MOF bureaucrats count on the cooperation of the LDP politicians, as well as the bureaucrats of the Ministry of International Trade and Industry who were better informed about special interests' conditions and intentions for compromise. To understand these compromises in terms of bureaucratic strategy, however, one needs to remember the MOF's imperative in introducing the new tax—to obtain a stable tax revenue from a broad tax base. Tax exemptions and lenient tax-filing measures as results of compromises are undesirable from a technocratic point of view, and significantly distort the taxation but do not erode much of the tax base or decrease the tax revenue. For example, with the highest tax exemption point among three reform proposals (that is, ¥100 million of annual sales volume in the previous tax year in the sales tax proposal), the total sale amount that would be taxed would decrease by only 8.8 percent, while tax exemptions would be allowed for 87.7 percent of all firms (Ozaki 1987c, 66). This is because a majority of firms in Japan are small or medium-sized.

This point is much clearer if we examine the measures on which the MOF did not compromise. The MOF resisted any measures that might lead to erosion of the tax base, especially the introduction of a wide range of tax-exempted goods, since, for them, the imperative of the new system was to secure a stable and broad tax base of consumption. In the sales tax proposal, the MOF had once attempted to make some goods that were considered essential to life—typically food—exempt from taxation, fearing that the regressive characteristics of the VAT would be a reason for public opposition. At the time, tax exemptions not only produced too many complexities but also eroded the tax base. The government's concession to tax exemptions brought intense conflicts among different industrial and commercial sectors to win exemptions, and eventually ruined the proposal itself instead of coaxing the opposition. The bureaucrats certainly learned from the failed proposal of the sales tax; they did not admit that there was a wide range of tax exemptions in the consumption tax system that was finally introduced. The MOF came to argue that the regressive characteristics of the VAT should be weakened by redistribution by social security programs and not by incorporation of exceptions and exemptions.

Another example of the MOF's successful attempt to secure the tax base was its rejection of a "zero tax rate." Zero-rated goods, like tax-exempted goods, are charged no tax but, unlike tax exemption, inputs that are used for the production of these goods can be reclaimed into the VAT system. In this system, the manufacturers and distributors of zero-rated goods are exempted from taxation with no inconvenience to their businesses; this is because their transaction partners can subtract the amount of purchases of zero-rated goods from the amount of sales when they calculate added value. Since the zero tax rate fully guarantees the advantage of tax exemption inside the VAT system, its employment is likely to narrow the tax base, not only because of the reclaim of taxes but also because of political pressure from special-interest groups that try to make their products or commodities zero rated.

The MOF successfully resisted political pressure from special-interest groups and the LDP, which sought to gain the privilege of zero tax rates. Modification after implementation added only several tax-exempted items, such as goods and services that are essential to life. Compared to the EC countries, where multiple tax rates, zero rating, and tax exemption are extensively used, the Japanese consumption tax system is closer to a theoretical ideal in this respect.

Consequently, the compromises that the MOF made were aimed at reducing opposition from organized interest groups of business and industries that might have obstructed the passage of the tax bills proposed by the government in the Diet. At the same time, the MOF insisted on rejecting measures that were likely to cause the erosion of a broad tax base, and thus to hurt their interests. The compromises with special interests were under the range of bureaucratic expectations, and did not force bureaucrats to accept the measures at the expense of their critical interests.

## THE PROCESS OF POLITICAL INTERACTION: RATIONALITIES OF BEHAVIORS OF INCUMBENT PARTY POLITICIANS, SPECIAL-INTEREST GROUPS, AND VOTERS

The preceding sections have shown that the introduction of the broad-based consumption tax was closely related to the MOF's concern for increasing its control over the budget, and the ministry pursued this policy objective throughout the reform process. Thus far, other political actors, for example, party politicians, special-interest groups, and the unorganized public, are regarded as subjects of bureaucratic strategy or manipulation to lead to the introduction of the VAT. This section explores the relationship between the rationality of these actors' behaviors and bureaucratic strategy. The discussion here will suggest that rational consideration of interests in certain situations may lead these actors to accept the bureaucratic proposal that they might otherwise have opposed.

The bureaucrats in charge of a certain policy are at an advantage in having more devoted time and allocated energy for its pursuance, but this advantage never guarantees the reflection of bureaucratic interests in policy-making. Alternatively, neither the lack of information nor ignorance of their interests solely determines the attitude of political actors other than bureaucrats, party politicians, special interests, and the unorganized public. What determines a policy outcome is to what extent and in what way the bureaucrats exploit conflicting interests inside the competing organizations and groups, that is, the political parties, special-interest groups, and the voting public.[60]

We will first consider the interaction between bureaucrats and the incumbent party, the LDP in the Japanese tax reform case. Because bureaucrats do not have an electoral mandate, fiscal bureaucrats depend on others in the political process to propose policies on their behalf and formally decide on them. Bureaucrats use the Government Tax System Research Council (GTSRC) as a political cover to define policy problems and propose specific policies as solutions. While legitimating its proposals by the use of the government tax council, the MOF must obtain cooperation from incumbent politicians to put a reform proposal on the political agenda and persuade the opposing groups to compromise. The organizational channel of the LDP used by the MOF for tax policy is the LDP Tax System Research Council (LDP TSRC).[61]

During the reform process in question, both the government and the LDP TSRC were two major decision-making bodies in tax policy-making, that is, in proposing structural reforms and revising the tax system every year.

As explained above (see note 52), the LDP one-party predominance faltered when a split in the party occurred and the non-LDP coalition government was formed in 1993, and thus the tax policy-making process explained here is also likely to change: the LDP TSRC's influence is destined to decline. But I will use the present tense in this section for consistency in explaining the policy-making process of the tax reform.

Under the LDP's majority rule, the party's proposals, which the government's policies follow, are likely to be implemented in the Diet. The

GTSRC and the LDP TSRC are considered to represent the views of the MOF and the party, respectively. What follows is a rough outline of the tax policy-making process, focusing on the roles of the government and party councils and their relationship with the MOF.

*Bureaucratic Organization and the Incumbent Party:*
*The MOF and the LDP in Tax Politics*

GOVERNMENT TAX SYSTEM RESEARCH COUNCIL: A POLITICAL
COVER FOR THE MOF

The predecessor of the present government tax council was the Provisional Tax System Committee, which existed until 1958. This commission then evolved into the Tax System Research Council (TSRC), which became a permanent advisory council in 1962. The role of this advisory council, as defined by law, is to study the existing tax system and make tax policy proposals at the prime minister's request.

The council reports on annual reform proposals in December, and on the direction of long-term reform at least once in three years. Usually, the GTSRC has a plenary session in April, and begins substantial deliberation in June when the new tax officials are annually assigned in the MOF. With the exception of one or two plenary sessions a month, the GTSRC members are divided into three special committees. The specialized tax policy fields of these committees correspond to the three divisions within the MOF tax bureau, that is, the direct tax (corporate and personal income tax), the indirect tax, and the tax on inheritance, gifts, and so on. Occasionally, a special committee is organized to study a particular policy concern at the time. Around the end of November, with extensive help from and contact with the tax bureau, a small management committee, consisting of about ten selected members, begins to prepare the report. After approval by the plenary session, the report is presented to the prime minister at the end of December.

The governments in the OECD countries frequently establish commissions to inquire into their tax systems and form recommendations for reforms, but the GTSRC differs from the task force or tax reform commissions in other industrial democracies. Ishi (1989, 11–15) summarizes this difference as follows. In the United States and European countries, the task force and commission are comprised of groups of specialists. They first review the existing tax system in general for five or six years, then recommend a structural reform. The lack of consideration of political feasibility at this deliberation stage often makes their recommendation politically unrealistic and hard to implement, but at the same time, more independent of political pressure. In Japan the government tax commission neither comprehensively reviews the whole system nor issues a reform proposal that is technically feasible. Instead, it tries to reach a compromise among various vested interests represented by commissioners. The total number of members is limited to thirty, and representation of different interests and opinions among members is quite stable.[62] About six out of thirty are representatives of industries, six represent journalism, another six represent the academic community, and three represent the opinions of local government. In addition, the commission usually includes three former government officials and three representatives of women, two labor representatives, and one tax accounting specialist. Their proposals represent a consensus among these interests, and are often ambiguous and far from resembling a concrete plan. But despite many defects in terms of theoretical clarity, these proposals are more likely to lead to policy changes (Ishi 1989, 13).

The reason why the GTSRC includes a small number of specialists and is highly political lies in the MOF's active role in policy-making. The MOF tax bureau[63] is primarily in charge of recruiting the members and preparing the original draft for the council's report as a basis for the members' consensus making.[64] In addition, the tax bureau provides the commissioners with reviews or reports on the existing tax systems, recent reforms in other countries, and technical knowledge on policies. This intimate relationship makes the government council a political cover for the MOF in proposing the tax policies. Their report often expresses bureaucratic concern about the existing tax system, represents the MOF's position in the tax reform, or closely approaches the bureaucratic motive.

Especially after the LDP TSRC increases its power, as described below, the MOF tries to use the GTSRC primarily as "a screen in order to divert attention for its real motive" (Ishi 1989, 14).[65] The number of specialists in the GTSRC has decreased and, instead, more amateurs have been selected.[66] During the reform process, through activities and reports by the GTSRC, the MOF intervened in defining tax policy problems needing solutions, manifesting the necessity of structural reform, and shaping the political agenda that framed the reform proposal.

### THE LDP TAX SYSTEM RESEARCH COUNCIL: OBSTACLE TO BUREAUCRATIC AUTONOMY OR POLITICAL SPONSOR OF THE MINISTRY?

The LDP TSRC is an organization within the party's Policy Affairs Research Council and since the 1970s, many LDP Diet members have become interested in representing their constituency's interests in tax policy. For example, in 1986, the LDP TSRC had 1 chairman of council, 1 acting chairman of council, 2 consultants, 14 vice chairmen (10 from the House of Representatives [HR] and 4 from the House of Councillors [HC]), 7 secretaries (5 from the HR and 2 from the HC), and 187 registered members (116 from the HR and 71 from the HC), that is, about 60 percent of the LDP Diet members in both houses.

The history of the LDP tax council dates back to the 1950s, but party members' active involvement in policies is about two decades old. The council studying the tax system had existed even when the Liberal Democratic Party was still divided into two conservative parties, the Liberal Party and the Democratic Party. Each party had a special committee for tax reform; these committees were merged into one special committee after the two conservative parties formed the Liberal Democratic Party. This special committee became the LDP TSRC in 1959 (Murakawa 1986). Until around 1970, the LDP TSRC was not very active. Almost at the same time as the end of high economic growth and natural increase in tax revenue, however, the LDP began to be involved in tax policy-making, which the MOF, through the GTSRC, had previously dominated. Around 1970, the report by the GTSRC began to indicate only an outline of reform direction, while the LDP TSRC began to influence the details of tax policy, including special treatments and exemptions.[67]

From December 1 to around December 20, the LDP TSRC holds meetings to discuss extensively tax reform for the following year. Each afternoon, the discussion is open to all Diet members. Each day's topic is concerned with specific tax requests from various interest groups, which are printed in one book at the beginning of December. In this meeting, the so-called small committee (*shōiinkai*) participants actively represent the interests of certain organized interest groups or industries upon which they depend for electoral support.[68] Differing from the afternoon meeting, which is substantially open to all LDP Diet members, the closed meeting in the morning includes only the president, vice presidents, consultants, and secretariats. The members of this "chairman and vice chairmen meeting" (*seifuku kaichō kaigi*) are more concerned with the technical consistency or administrative feasibility of the tax system. All the substantial decisions on tax policy inside the LDP are made by this small group of people.[69]

This method of organization and procedure of the party tax council shows that two different groups of Diet members are interested in tax policy. The first group are backbenchers or line members who have shorter terms or come from competitive electoral bases. They represent special interests in order to get tax privileges and reduce the tax burden for their constituencies. These members are active participants in the small committee. The second group of members has more experience and expertise in tax policy-making; these members are interested in examining requests from special-interest groups and in shaping the major direction of reforms from a more politically neutral position as tax experts. Former bureaucrats of the MOF among the LDP Diet members belong to the latter group. Those who were not government officials also belong to this group as a result of the experiences they have accumulated and the policies they have studied in their long careers as policymakers. This group of tax experts in the LDP has a pivotal position in tax policy-making. First, the long tenures and careers of these members as policymakers give them an advantage in policy-making compared to the part-time status and short tenures of GTSRC members. Second, they often share the same view of the tax system and, as tax experts, agree with the MOF on the reform direction. Therefore, they provide the MOF crucial support by persuading other party members and special-interest groups in opposition to accept policies proposed by bureaucrats.

These policy specialists, most of whom are party leaders, ultimately cooperated in introducing the unpopular new tax. Their cooperation was critical for the bureaucrats to obtain a final acceptance of their proposal by all the LDP members. However, the possibility existed that the backbenchers, fearing the loss of the electorate's support, would thwart the proposal of the unpopular new tax. This actually materialized in the two failed proposals before the ultimate introduction of the consumption tax. In such a case, the rise of the LDP TSRC's power worked against the bureaucrats' interests.

Observing these different consequences of the unpopular tax proposals, the question of the relationship between the political activism of the LDP TSRC and MOF interests thus remains unanswered. For example, in what way does the incumbent party's increasing intervention relate to bureaucratic interests? Does political intervention by incumbent politicians always thwart bureaucratic interests? If not, under what conditions do the bureaucrats take advantage of politicians' increasing role in policy-making? I will answer these questions by referring to recent studies of the relationship between bureaucrats and politicians in Japanese politics.

THE ROLE OF *ZOKU GIIN*

The incumbent politicians' role in policy-making has been of special interest to students of Japanese politics. Since the resurgence of popular support for the conservatives that appeared in the 1980 election results, academic attention has focused on the policy-making ability that the incumbent party developed during its long-term predominance. Many scholarly works have studied a group of policy experts among the LDP members (*zoku giin*;

literally, "tribe dietmen"), who attempt to modify or block the government's proposals in the LDP Policy Affairs Research Council (PARC) at the pre-Diet stage (Satō and Matsuzaki 1986; Inoguchi and Iwai 1987; Muramatsu and Krauss 1987; Schoppa 1991).

After the demise of the LDP's one-party predominance in 1993, *zoku giin*'s political interventions, which were effective only under the LDP's strong governing power, may no longer be of particular interest to Japan specialists. But the analysis of political and bureaucratic interaction under one-party predominance has interesting implications for the understanding of political influence over bureaucratic policy-making. I will discuss the issues related to the LDP *zoku giin* in this context, and again will use the present tense for consistency.

According to Satō and Matsuzaki (1986, 264–65), *zoku giin* may be defined as LDP dietmen who satisfy the following two conditions: those who have continued to exercise strong influence over a policy area that is categorized by the jurisdiction of a specific ministry or agency and who have been appointed in the cabinet for one term, or are to receive such an appointment. *Zoku giin* exist in areas of finance, foreign affairs, commerce and industry, agriculture and forestry, fisheries, education, social welfare, labor, transportation, post- and telecommunications, construction, and national defense. Each of the areas corresponds to a specific division of the LDP TSRC and standing committees in the Diet, as well as a particular ministry or agency.[70]

Tax experts among LDP dietmen are called the "public finance tribe" (*zaisei zoku*) and, more specifically, the "tax tribe" (*zeisei zoku*) when they are involved in tax policies. The LDP Tax System Research Council, which is one of the special committees of the LDP PARC, is a center for activities for tax experts among the LDP Diet members. It has attracted scholarly and journalistic attention and has become a notable example of the shift in policy-making power from the bureaucracy to the LDP. The dominance of the party council over the Government Tax System Research Council in tax policy-making often leads to the conclusion that the power of tax experts in the LDP has grown at the expense of the MOF as a secretariat of the government council (Kishiro 1985).

Satō and Matsuzaki (1986, 112–13) provide some important facts which confirm that the LDP TSRC has increased its influence over tax policy-making in absolute and relative terms. First, the number of interest groups that presents requests to the LDP TSRC for annual tax revisions has rapidly increased since the 1970s. The number of groups, which was 43 in 1966, began to exceed 100 in the 1970s, and reached as many as 358 in 1986.

This rapid increase in numbers reflects the growing power of the LDP TSRC as recognized by the interest groups that demand special tax treatment or tax reductions.

Second, the timing of the issuance of reports by both councils for annual revision symbolizes a shift in the power balance from the government council to the party council. The LDP TSRC, which began to issue reports for annual revisions in 1962 after the reports issued by the government council, has, since 1968, issued reports on the same day or one day before the government council's report. In the proposal of major reforms, especially the present case of the introduction of the VAT, the LDP TSRC always formulates a concrete final plan. The GTSRC, which proposes several alternatives in its interim reports, issues its final report in coordination with the LDP's report. Considering the close relationship between the LDP and the GTSRC, this means that the MOF is beginning to pay more attention to the LDP TSRC as it increases its expertise and influence.

This observation seems to run counter to the present argument, which explains the introduction of the new consumption tax by the persistent influence of bureaucrats in the political process. If the LDP's role is taken seriously, the ultimate introduction of the new tax may be the result of political maneuvering of tax experts among the LDP Diet members who had agreed with the MOF on the introduction of the new tax.

The converging interests of the party and bureaucracy under long-term, one-party predominance could also explain their agreement to the introduction of the new tax without predicating bureaucratic influence over politicians. Collusion of their interests is often exemplified by the frequent political entry of retired bureaucrats (especially of the MOF) into the LDP.[71] Aside from a blurred line of bureaucratic and political careers, there exists another possibility of collusion between the LDP and the bureaucracy. The bureaucrats may have a vested interest in the status quo. If the LDP loses power, they may need reconsider what kind of party government will be formed and what the best action is in order to get their proposed policies implemented under a new government. In addition to the costs of adjusting to a new situation, a new system may impose more costs on the bureaucrats in terms of the time and energy needed to implement policies. In this sense, Japanese bureaucrats may have an interest in maintaining the LDP majority regardless of their ideological affinity to the party.

These arguments are, however, not entirely convincing. These views fail to answer why the incumbent party often pushes the policy that it has every right to expect would place its political fate at stake—exactly as in the case of the tax reform under discussion. More specifically, neither collusion of interests nor political control arguments explain why the incumbent party leaders took a risk to support the unpopular new tax that their subordinates opposed.

To answer this question, it is worth examining the potentials of conflicting interests inside the political party. Some empirical studies in American politics show that congressmen seek to promote their influence in the legislature and the party, as well as to secure their reelection (Cain, Ferejohn, and Fiorina 1987; Fenno 1977). Turning to the Japanese LDP, a half-institutionalized pattern of promotion inside the party further encourages members to augment influence by demonstrating distinct policy expertise. As they have increased their policy expertise and experience in policy-making and gained the respect of party members and bureaucrats, LDP politicians have been promoted to more influential positions in the committees of the Diet and in the LDP PARC, and eventually have obtained position as ministers (Satō and Matsuzaki 1986, 39–42; Inoguchi and Iwai 1987, 120–21).

Under strong party discipline the party leadership has the means to control line members who depend on the party and party connections for electoral funding and nominations. At the same time, line members know the risk of insisting on representing their constituency's interest against the decisions of the party leadership. Their persistence in opposition adversely influences their future promotion to party positions, because party leaders regard such opposition as a lack of ability to consider policy-making from a general standpoint. Therefore, line members often face a trade-off between serving their constituencies' interests and maintaining a good reputation inside the party, while experienced members are more likely to lean toward increasing their influence within a small circle of policymakers.

These conflicting interests among LDP politicians allow bureaucrats more room to implement their desired policies. What factors or conditions are critical to facilitate bureaucratic influence? Some existing studies on *zoku giin* provide important keys to answer this. Inoguchi and Iwai (1987, 257–73) present an insightful distinction in the roles of *zoku giin* in policy-making, that is, between the "guard dogs" (*banken*) type, which represents the ministries' interests, and the "hunting dogs (*ryōken*)" type, which exercises influence over policies at the expense of or regardless of the ministries' interests.

The question here is when do LDP members act as "guard dogs" rather than "hunting dogs"?[72] I argue that LDP members behave differently according to which type of behaviors will benefit them more. When policies in question require specialized knowledge and expertise, for example, more experienced members tend to work for the interests of their ministries. This is not because the bureaucrats can afford to outwit politicians by using their expertise. The reason for the politicians' volunteering cooperation with bureaucrats lies in their desire to promote their own influence in policy-making circles. If bureaucrats defend their policy proposal using technocratic reasoning and ideas, endorsing the approval for them is in the interest of incumbent politicians who want to demonstrate their understanding on technical matters and thus increase their credibility and influence as policy experts. Only when politicians can identify an equally justified but distinct technocratic point of view, and make a policy proposal based on it, is the opposition to the bureaucratic proposal in their interest. Since the incumbent politicians have developed their expertise by extracting policy information from bureaucrats and making them explain more about specialized knowledge, it is unlikely that they have come to a position sharply opposed to bureaucrats.

Alternatively, if endorsing specialized knowledge or the demonstration of expertise does not benefit some members, they are more likely to oppose the bureaucratic proposal. This tendency corresponds precisely to the observation presented by Inoguchi and Iwai (1987, 258–61); in the "guard dog" type of policy-making, there exists intensive interaction between bureaucrats and politicians who form a small circle of policy experts, and in the "hunting dog" type of policy-making, many backbenchers without specialized knowledge actively represent special interests. The final introduction of the major indirect tax in the recent tax reform is explained by focusing on the relationship between policy expertise and LDP politicians' interests in cooperation with bureaucrats.

In this way, the analysis of *zoku giin* Diet members provides an important implication for the understanding of the political and bureaucratic relationship. Politicians' expertise in policy-making does not necessarily increase their independence from bureaucrats, especially when politicians rely on the bureaucracy for policy staff, and when a highly specialized subject, such as tax policy, tends to create a small circle of specialists.

## Opposition Parties

Japanese party politics long involved the interaction between the incumbent LDP and several opposition parties, the Japan Socialist Party (JSP), the Clean Government Party (CGP), the Democratic Socialist Party (DSP), and the Japan Communist Party (JCP) from the 1960s to the 1980s.[73] Though the LDP retained a majority of both houses and had a substantial power to pass government bills from 1955 to 1989,[74] it often spent enormous time and political resources (for example, formal and informal meetings on numerous occasions accompanied by step-by-step concessions) to coax the opposition parties into letting the government bills pass.

Managing the relationship with the opposition camp was a hard task even for the perennial incumbent party. The LDP needed to obtain implicit consent from the opposition parties to avoid their physical protest, that is, filibuster, boycotting of deliberation, and so on (see the first section of this chapter, "Studies of the Japanese Bureaucracy"). Outright protest by the opposition parties and the LDP's offensive response to it were likely to promote an image of the incumbent party as an abuser of majority power, and thus deprive the bills passed under such a confrontation of their legitimacy. Moreover, opposition parties rarely endorsed government bills without conditions. Opposition parties, even when they allowed the passage of the government's proposed policy, often required modifications of the bill and came to support it after bargainings and negotiations with the incumbent LDP (Mochizuki 1982). In the public debate, the opposition parties tried to keep as much distance as possible from the LDP. Ōtake (1984) explored the opposition parties' attitude in terms of the gap between the position alleged in the public debate and the policies actually presented. According to him, party politics tended to be bipolarized between the governing party and the opposition parties, although this bipolarized conflict did not necessarily correspond to the policy alternatives presented by the two camps.

A simple party competition model can explain why it was rational for the opposition parties to oppose the policies proposed by the government (Kato 1991a, 117–18).[75] The unequal size of the predominant LDP and several opposition parties in the Japanese predominant party system is the reason for the peculiar dynamics that modify the pattern of partisan competition in a multiparty system. According to Downs (1957), parties in a multiparty system try to remain as ideologically distinct from one another as possible. If the predominant LDP lost an absolute majority, the fragmented opposition camp would cause the system to be defined as polarized (Sartori 1976, 200). Under the LDP's predominance, however, unequal sizes of the incumbent party and the opposition parties results in encouraging the opposition parties to distinguish themselves from the LDP more than from other opposition parties; therefore, party politics is expected to be bipolarized between a big incumbent party, such as the LDP, and the opposition camp.

The dynamics of the Japanese one-party predominance system, according to a simple Downsian formulation, has two other consequences. The necessity to keep a distance from the incumbent party may impose problems on the smaller opposition parties that are located, on a horizontal scale representing policy positions, between the predominant party and the largest opposition party. The best strategy for the largest opposition party is simply to keep a distance from the predominant party, but the smaller opposition parties, sandwiched between two giants, must choose from whom to maintain the most distance.

Until recently, Japan's smaller opposition parties faced a dilemma because the largest opposition party was the JSP whose alleged ideological orientation toward economic and security policies was most opposed (except for those of the JCP[76]) to the predominant LDP's in the party system. Thus small middle-of-the-road parties, especially the CGP (Kōmeito) and the DSP, faced a choice between compromising more with the LDP so as not to become junior partners with the JSP or allying themselves with the JSP in order to keep their distance from the LDP. The CGP has constituted an important pivotal point in party dynamics since the 1980s[77]; this is because the DSP, which was formed from the ex-right wing of the JSP in 1960, needed to rely on the CGP as an intermediary to form a coalition with the JSP.

The choice of a coalition partner by the middle-of-the-road parties, a choice that would change the political dynamics, was influenced by personal relationships between parties and leaders but hinged largely on public attitude. The middle-of-the-road parties were relatively flexible in their ideological and policy orientation compared to the JSP, which had long been connected with the organizational support of Japan's biggest labor association, the General Council of Japanese Trade Unions (Sōhyō),[78] and with the influences of the ideological sects inside the party organization.[79] If the public regarded its approach to the incumbent party as collusion, the middle-of-the-road party shifted away from the LDP, as far as its own ideological orientation or policy attitude allowed. If the public required a more flexible attitude rather than uncompromising opposition to the LDP, the middle-of-the-road party would seek compromises. Also, if their gains for opposition to the LDP were lost as a result of support for the JSP, the middle-of-road party was likely to sever its relationship with this largest opposition coalition member.

In this sense, the opposition coalition was vulnerable to contingencies. The LDP might intervene to lure the middle-of-the-road parties into compromises. Also, the timing of the rise of public opposition determined the effectiveness of the opposition parties' coalition against the LDP government. This vulnerability of the opposition coalition explained why the

VAT was finally passed in 1988 after the breaking-up of the middle-of-the-road parties' coalition with the JSP. Bureaucratic agenda setting prevented the public apprehension about the new tax from organizing into an active opposition movement. Public opinion was generally critical of the opposition parties' refusal to participate in deliberation of the tax bills; thus the middle-of-the-road parties quit the coalition with the JSP, which insisted on absolute opposition, and allowed the LDP majority to pass the tax bills. The details of this process are explained in chapter 6.

## Special-Interest Groups

The introduction of the VAT was one of the rare examples of policies that no interest groups pushed. Many industrial sectors were worried about additional paperwork for filing the VAT. This paperwork for tax filing was considered especially costly for small and medium-sized businesses. Though, in theory, the tax burden is ultimately shifted to consumers, there was still a suspicion among tax-filing firms—especially among distributors—that they might need to pay taxes at the expense of their profits. They were overtly concerned that the new tax would discourage the consumers' purchase of goods and services. Their opposition continued to be strong until the last moment's compromise with the government. Many compromising tax-filing measures were introduced to coax special-interest opposition into acceptance of the new tax.

Observing the government's concessions, some may argue that these lenient tax-filing measures were aimed to give new privileges to special-interest groups and that the creation of these privileged groups was the critical reason for the passage of the new tax. But these measures, which both bureaucrats and the LDP leaders supported, had little to do with changing opposition groups into promoters of the new tax. They served only to prevent the special interests' opposition from blocking the passage of tax bills. This explained why many groups of small and medium-sized businesses joined the consumers' opposition after the new tax was actually implemented. This was so even though consumers opposed the new tax for reasons contradictory to theirs: consumers opposed it because they believed that its lenient tax-filing measures would benefit businesses (and criticized the regressive characteristics of the new tax), whereas the self-employed businesses argued that the consumption tax actually hurt their businesses. The strange alliance between small and medium-sized businesses and consumers showed that the new tax was not in the best interests of the small and medium-sized businesses, even with its special tax measures. The final section of chapter 6 elaborates this point.

The only special-interest groups that accepted the VAT at an earlier stage of the reform process were major business associations that represented the interests of large-scale manufacturers. They supported it immediately, before the second proposal of the VAT. However, the business associations were far from active and voluntary support groups; rather, they behaved as political realists to cope with bureaucratic strategy. Their approval of the new tax was supporting a second-best solution to avoid the concentration of tax burdens on large-scale corporations, which the MOF bureaucrats had actively implemented in the first half of the 1980s. Chapter 4 explains the fiscal and tax policies implemented by the ministry, which steered the way to the second and third proposals of the VAT.

### The Unorganized Public

During the reform process some policymakers, as well as some public financial economists, regarded the unorganized public as potential supporters of the VAT. A majority of the unorganized, especially salaried workers, were considered potential supporters in the public debate. This was because some tax specialists argued that the VAT would indirectly facilitate income tax compliance among self-employed people by requiring more information about their business incomes: salaried workers complained that tax withholding of salaried income was more strictly implemented than taxation on self-employed business income (filed by tax returns). Policymakers could appeal to the salaried workers by saying that the new tax would serve to increase income tax compliance of self-employed people.

Obviously, however, the emphasis on this merit of the VAT ran counter to efforts to alleviate opposition from special-interest groups who preferred easy tax-filing measures. Thus the bureaucrats continued to use ambiguous words like *rectification of tax inequity* to appeal to the unorganized public. Their incorporation of more compromising tax-filing measures further discredited this claim. The use of special tax measures fed opposition from the unorganized public, who regarded this divergence from an ideal system as another of the government's authorization of tax privileges for self-employed businesses. This perception was the major reason why these measures led to the opposition of the unorganized public who would bear the tax burden as consumers after the new tax system became effective in April 1989.

Insensitivity to the potential of the unorganized public's support, as well as overt concern with special-interest groups, reflect the limitation of the bureaucratic strategy. This limitation derives from the fact that the bureaucrats needed to cooperate with the incumbent LDP.

Organized interest was more important for the reelections of line members of the LDP. Thus the party paid more attention to interest groups than to the unorganized public in policy-making. If party politicians, who were closely tied to special interests, miscalculated the potential of the opposition coming from the unorganized public, the bureaucrats who relied on the politicians to compromise with special interests had no way to predict it correctly. This biased attention was reflected in the political maneuvering of bureaucrats and explains why the bureaucrats were once under intense criticism from the unorganized public.

To make the present argument on bureaucratic influence and strategy in tax reform convincing, the last half of this chapter has clarified four points. First, the introduction of the broad-based consumption tax is closely related to the MOF's primary interest—to maintain control over budget making. Internal structures (i.e., systems of employment, training, socialization, and promotion) of an organization contribute to the effective pursuance of policy objectives for organizational interests. Second, the MOF initiated the tax proposal despite opposition from every segment of society. Then, it tried to politicize the necessity of tax reform to favor the introduction of the new tax. It not only changed the advocated aims of the tax proposals but also used other fiscal and tax policies to impress on politicians and the electorate the need for the new tax on consumption. Third, the MOF made many compromises with opposing groups in seeking the introduction of the new tax. The LDP played a major role in representing special interests and informing the MOF of viable measures to alleviate the opposition. However, these political compromises were not the bureaucrats' concessions to insurmountable political pressure but rather constituted bureaucratic strategy used to implement the new tax. The bureaucrats accepted only measures to which they had attached lower priorities and left untouched the minimum imperative of the policy, which was critical to their organizational interest. Fourth, politicians' increased policy expertise and intervention in bureaucratic proposals generally preclude bureaucratic dominance over policy-making, which is based on the monopolization of policy information and expertise. But bureaucrats are able to obtain support for proposed policies by adjusting to new situations and taking advantage of the shared knowledge and expertise of experienced incumbent politicians. The tax reform is such an example of bureaucratic adjustment to new situations that successfully led to the ministries' desired policy outcome.

In concluding this chapter, however, I would like to qualify my argument so as not to overextend it. In this study I do not attribute bureaucratic influence to an institutionalized pattern in Japanese policy-making in general. Bureaucratic influence observed in the tax reform case is based on contingent factors that may be absent or weak in other cases of policy-making. Such a change in the contingent factors could have altered the entire political process and policy outcome. This qualification distinguishes the present approach from one that associates an observed pattern of policy-making with specific political institutions, for example, the "strong state" approach. The following discussion will clarify the subtle conditions under which bureaucratic influence works.

First, the bureaucratic organization can devise systems that facilitate members' pursuance of organizational interests through policy-making. But the systems do not necessarily work well. For example, in a newly developing policy field that responds to socioeconomic and technological changes in society, it is not easy to determine what alternative solution is best for organizational interests. A case in point would be a policy that involves a conflict of interests between more than one division or bureau of an organization. Conflicts between sections or bureaus at the same horizontal level within the same ministry, as well as between ministries, require a more hierarchical and highly organized decision-making mechanism than presented here.

The Japanese bureaucratic organization is generally weak in devising coordination mechanisms to resolve conflicting interests between organizational divisions on the same horizontal level. In most cases the solution is ultimately delegated to the leadership inside the organization, although it is sometimes delegated to the incumbent party leadership. Journalists often call this notorious tendency a "vertically divided administration" (*tatewari gyōsei*). Such an organization, relying on systems that nurture similar preferences and attitudes, is effective for reaching consensus among members under specific conditions: those in which members of a bureaucratic organization are familiar enough with policies to understand their relationship to the interests of the organization, and in which policies do not span the jurisdictions of different organizational divisions.

The potential for conflicts inside the bureaucracy often absorbs much of the bureaucrats' energy and time in policy-making before they face incumbent politicians. In this sense some rational choice theorists, who try to

107

identify institutionalized means to guarantee bureaucratic compliance with politicians, may go overboard to demonstrate political control over the bureaucracy. If bureaucrats' primary concern is coping with other ministries' influence rather than thwarting political intervention, the incumbent politicians can take advantage of conflicts inside the bureaucracy to lead to policy outcomes they favor. The problem for the incumbent party seeking to increase its influence over policy-making instead lies in its internal organization, that is, how to maintain the consistency and control of policy-making at the party level while reflecting members' interests in policy decisions that increase or maintain electoral support.[80]

In the case of the Japanese tax reform, the absence of conflicts between bureaucratic organizations lessens the opportunity for political intervention, and thus facilitates bureaucratic influence. The MOF was primarily in charge of tax reform, but other ministries also had vested interests in the existing tax system, and thus, opposition or support of these ministries were critical factors in determining the consequence of the tax reform. The Ministry of Home Affairs, representing the interests of prefectural and municipal governments, was concerned with how much revenue from the new tax on consumption would be allocated to local autonomies—an understandable concern since the existing excise tax on specific commodities and services had constituted an important revenue source for local governments. The Ministry of International Trade and Industry was afraid that the new tax on consumption would threaten the interests of businesses and industries. Both these ministries believed that the introduction of the new tax on consumption would hurt the interests they represented, and they opposed the MOF's proposal of it in the late 1970s. But the MOF and these ministries resolved their conflicts without substantial intervention by the LDP during the ten years of the reform process. The next four chapters will illuminate this conflict resolution between the ministries.

Second, the bureaucrats' ability to successfully persuade politicians depends on subtle conditions under which politicians share with the bureaucrats specialized knowledge and expertise about policies. Politicians may come up with different technocratic ideas and thus support different policies. In Japan, where the incumbent party politicians rely on bureaucrats as policy staff, this possibility is slim but it still exists, because politicians may seek opinions from specialists outside the bureaucracy or endorse the technocratic ideas of academics or other experts.

At the same time, strong party discipline is an important factor facilitating bureaucratic influence over the party, because bureaucrats can concentrate on persuading those whose decisions are likely to influence other members and thus influence a formal party decision. When party discipline is weak, bureaucrats need to pay attention to all incumbent politicians, and are less likely to succeed in obtaining the approval of the entire party for their proposal. The MOF's advantage in the tax reform case was that influential party members shared a technocratic point of view with the ministry.

One limitation of the bureaucratic strategy is the ministry's dependence on politicians for bargaining with opposing groups. In the Japanese tax reform case, bureaucrats obtained cooperation with the incumbent party in introducing lenient and compromising tax measures. These measures contributed to alleviating organized opposition and passing the new tax, but led to the opposition of the less organized consumers after the introduction of the consumption tax in 1989. The unorganized public regarded the use of special tax measures as another authorization by the government of tax privileges for business. This neglect of consumers and underestimation of unorganized opposition imposed a political cost primarily on the LDP, that is, it caused the LDP its biggest electoral loss since its formation in 1955. Although the MOF had also been exposed to unexpected and intense public criticism, the criticism waned rapidly without presenting a viable reform alternative to the new tax.

Admitting the limitations of bureaucratic strategy as described above, I focus on conditions in which bureaucratic influence is exercised through interaction between party politicians and the electorate. In this study, bureaucratic influence over policy does not refer to an agenda-setting power to make take-it-or-leave-it proposals, as in some rational (or social) choice literature. There, agenda-setting power means "no communication at all occurs between those who set agendas and those who vote on the proposals contained within them" (Altfeld and Miller 1984, 707) and requires bureaucrats to dominate policy agendas or to be insulated and autonomous from political pressure. The analysis of the Japanese tax reform shows that bureaucrats rely on the cooperation of incumbent politicians to articulate politically important interests and make compromises with opposing groups. Bureaucrats' adaptive behavior to the political process is critical in understanding bureaucratic influence in a new situation where the roles of bureaucrats and politicians converge.

Having clarified in this chapter the conditions that possibly facilitate bureaucratic influence, I will explain the process by which the bureaucratic influence was actually exercised. The next four chapters describe the ten years of the reform process, focusing on the question of how the fiscal bureaucrats changed their proposals for new taxes in order to cultivate the incumbent party and opposition groups.

# Lessons for Bureaucrats: From the Proposal for a Tax Increase in the Late 1970s to Fiscal Reconstruction without a Tax Increase in the Early 1980s

THE BUREAUCRATS of Japan's Ministry of Finance, who had planned to introduce a broad-based consumption tax since the early 1970s, had to wait until the political leaders were willing to propose the reform. From 1979 to 1989, three prime ministers of the incumbent Liberal Democratic Party tried to introduce the new tax. Four subsequent chapters elaborate the political processes of tax reform under the different prime ministers in 1978–79, 1986–87, and 1988–89, as well as the austerity campaign between the first and second proposals. Chapter 3 reviews the process by which opposition from society blocked the proposal for the value-added tax (VAT), a general consumption tax, and the first of three consecutive proposals for the new consumption tax. The analysis here will reveal what the MOF bureaucrats learned from this failed proposal. It will also examine how these lessons influenced the MOF's strategic maneuvering to implement a sales tax and a consumption tax, which were proposed later in the 1980s.

This chapter will clarify the following points. First, the proposal of the general consumption tax was, in retrospect, an ill-prepared attempt to introduce the unpopular new tax. The MOF expressed straightforwardly its intention to introduce the new tax to stop accumulating a budget deficit. The MOF might have taken a more cautious approach instead of one that intensified public opposition. However, they were encouraged to pursue their proposal by the enthusiastic sponsorship of a prominent political leader. Prime Minister Masayoshi Ōhira at the time wholeheartedly accepted the MOF's proposal and began to engage in an active public relations campaign for himself. The MOF simply followed the prime minister's initiative and became as reckless as Ōhira in facing public opposition to the new tax.

Second, the LDP as a whole did not support the new tax despite its prime minister's commitment to it. Even the incumbent dietmen who were familiar with tax issues and close to the MOF did not take the initiative in proposing the general consumption tax. While the party was indifferent to it, the MOF tried to make a formal proposal of the new tax through a report by the Government Tax System Research Council. In this sense, the proposal of the general consumption tax was different from two subsequent proposals of similar new taxes that obtained the active support of some incumbent politicians. The support of the incumbent party's leadership for the tax proposals in the 1980s came after the MOF alone had attempted to introduce the new tax to the policy agenda in the late 1970s.

Third, the failure of the proposal of the general consumption tax led to the so-called administrative reform campaign, which aimed at fiscal reconstruction without a tax increase, that is, attempting to get out of a deficit finance situation without increasing the tax burden. The meaning of this campaign in Japanese politics in the 1980s cannot be defined simply. But as far as tax issues are concerned, this austerity campaign was a political consequence of the government's precipitate attempt to introduce the new tax. This campaign prevented the MOF from implementing the new tax on consumption during the first half of the 1980s.

Lastly, the tax reform process in the late 1970s shows that bureaucratic swift action and early preparation for the tax reform plan did not necessarily lead to implementation of the proposed policy. The bureaucrats might have gone ahead in proposing and planning the policy while party politicians and the electorate paid scant attention, but public opposition could block the bureaucratic proposal at the last moment. Therefore, this case demonstrates that the institutionalized power of bureaucrats does not guarantee their influence, and thus refutes the view that bureaucratic influence is associated with institutional settings or the political resources they possess.

## Two Undercurrents of the Proposal for the General Consumption Tax

In December 1978 both the GTSRC and the LDP TSRC decided to propose the enactment of a general consumption tax in the 1980 fiscal year. The unpopularity of the new tax, which would place increased burdens on the public, became the major reason for the LDP's loss in the general election in September 1979. To the public, the new tax had appeared on the political agenda without advance notice. However, the consumption tax was not a new policy problem for the MOF bureaucrats, tax specialists, and

some LDP leaders, including Prime Minister Ōhira. The MOF had prepared for the installation of the new tax, and Ōhira had nurtured a sense of
mission to propose it after the Japanese public finances had fallen into the
red.

*Inside the Administration*

In no country had indirect taxes been less important than in Japan before
April 1989 when the consumption tax system was instituted. The main
reasons for the dependence on direct taxes were the Shoup Mission's recommendation and a subsequent reform to establish a system relying on
income taxation. "Had there been no Shoup Mission, Japan's tax system
might have moved toward a different type of system with a great share of
indirect taxation" (Ishi 1989, 28). One possible direction for the Japanese
postwar tax system to take was toward more dependence on indirect taxes.
Immediately after the 1950s, the GTSRC began to suggest a shifting balance of revenue sharing from direct taxation to indirect taxation. This
report certainly reflected the MOF's intention, which was to work as a
secretariat of the council. In 1956 the Government Provisional Tax System
Research Council reported that the introduction of the sales tax was a long-
term policy problem to be studied.[1] However, at the time, the MOF did not
intend to institute immediately a broad-based tax on consumption and services. A continuing natural increase from income and corporate tax revenue during a period of high economic growth had provided enough financial resources for growing expenditures, and had given the government less
incentive to change the revenue structure. In the "Long-Term Proposal on
Tax Reform" (*Chōki Tōshin*) in 1964, the GTSRC recommended that the
government need not plan the introduction of a (general) sales tax or a
VAT.

Two factors emerged in the 1970s that contributed to increasing the
MOF's interests in the broad-based tax on consumption in the 1970s. The
first was related to the introduction of the VAT around 1970 by the EC
countries. In autumn 1970 the MOF organized a research group of three
scholars and one bureaucrat[2] to study the VAT systems that had already
been or were supposed to be introduced soon in five EC countries,[3] and
published a report about their study. Although a small number of the LDP
dietmen group also went to the EC countries twice to study the VAT,[4] the
party's interest in the new tax remained low in general.

The MOF bureaucrats were interested in the VAT as a new source of revenue and, at the same time, as an effective means of reforming the tax system. In July 1971 the GTSRC submitted the "Long-Term Proposal on the Tax System," which emphasized the necessity for planning a broad-based tax on consumption for the purpose of increasing revenue shares from indirect taxation. This report called for this new tax to be a general consumption tax. It also rated the VAT system highly among possible alternative plans for a general consumption tax.[5] At the time, however, the introduction of the new tax was not an imminent task for the MOF.

The second factor that increased the MOF's interest in the new tax was explained by a sudden tax revenue shortfall in the 1974 fiscal year and the subsequent issuance of a deficit bond in the 1975 supplementary budget. The fiscal crisis in the mid-1970s completely changed the Japanese government's financial condition. Since revenue in the 1974 fiscal year was partly financed by tax revenue in the following year, the revenue shortfall in the 1975 fiscal year amounted to ¥3.879 trillion (= $13.07 billion; $1 = ¥296.79 in 1975), which was equal to 22.3 percent of the estimated tax revenue in the initial budget. The government had to finance ¥3.48 trillion (= $11.73 billion; $1 = ¥296.79 in 1975) by the issuance of bonds (¥2.29 trillion [= $7.72 billion] were financed by the issuance of deficit bonds). The bond dependency ratio increased from 9.4 percent in the initial budget to 25.3 percent in the supplementary one of the 1975 fiscal year.[6] For the MOF, the increasing budget deficit, together with the necessity for structural tax reform, made the introduction of a major indirect tax an urgent problem.

The government's intention to introduce a general consumption tax was expressed formally in the "Middle-Term Proposal on Tax Reform" (Chūki Zeisei Tōshin) by the GTSRC in October 1977. In December of that year, in the report on the 1978 fiscal year's tax reform, the GTSRC suggested that the government should make a definite plan for a general consumption tax as soon as possible.

Shortly after the GTSRC's recommendation at the end of 1978, the government publicized the plan for the new tax and decided to introduce the general consumption tax in 1980. The prompt response to the GTSRC report in the form of the government proposal can be attributed to the leadership of Masayoshi Ōhira, who had formed his cabinet in November 1978. Ōhira was the first prime minister to give full support to the MOF's intention to institute the new tax. Two prime ministers in the period from 1974 to 1978, Takeo Miki and Takeo Fukuda, were not eager to introduce the general consumption tax during their terms even though the MOF continued to suggest it to them. The next section explores the process by which the Japanese government ran into deficit finance in the 1970s, while considering the reason why Prime Minister Ōhira gave ready consent to the MOF's proposal of the new tax.

## Prime Minister Ōhira: Statesmanship or Political Naïveté

Why did Prime Minister Ōhira propose the same general consumption tax that two prime ministers of the same LDP had avoided due to its unpopularity? Some may answer that he believed that the general political climate was favorable enough for the LDP government to make up for the loss in popularity that would result from the proposal for a tax increase. In terms of the Jiji Tsūshinsha opinion polls, popular support for the LDP, which had been as low as about 25 or 26 percent from 1973 to 1976, rose to 28.2 percent on a monthly average in 1977.[7] This resurgence in popular support for the LDP was actually confirmed by the victory of candidates supported or nominated by the LDP in all elections of fifteen prefectural governors in April 1979. In addition, the Tokyo Economic Summit, held in June 1979, brought increased esteem to Ōhira's cabinet. However, even with these favorable conditions, Prime Minister Ōhira's new tax proposal ran counter to conventional political wisdom: he tried to persuade the public to accept a tax increase before the general election of the House of Representatives (HR), and believed that people would eventually accept it.

Ōhira's commitment to the new tax could be attributed to his political role in the mid-1970s—a crucial period in Japanese public finance. During this period, the Japanese government's budget, which had thus far experienced easy expansion thanks to a high rate of economic growth, began to accumulate deficits. The fiscal crisis, which was precipitated by a worldwide recession and doomed by welfare expansion in the 1970s,[8] made Ōhira, as well as the MOF, eager to implement the general consumption tax. Ōhira had a key role in the financial decision to allow the issuance of deficit bonds during this period, and consequently developed his sense of responsibility to restore the fiscal health independently of the MOF.

By the 1960s, Japanese welfare expenditures were about half of those of the United States and about a third of those of former West Germany in terms of the GNP share. At the beginning of the 1970s, public demand for an improved quality of life replaced the demand for economic growth, which had been the government's first priority in the 1960s; social welfare and environmental pollution issues had also become major public concerns. The predominant LDP, which had responded to these new demands more slowly than opposition parties, began to suffer from losses in both its popular support and numerical strength in the Diet (see chapter 2). Once the LDP government perceived this political crisis, it became an important reason for the subsequent expansion of welfare programs. Around the beginning of 1973, immediately before the Japanese economy began to be influenced by the recession that resulted from the oil price shock, the government pushed for an active fiscal policy in the supplementary budget of the 1972 fiscal year and the budget of the 1973 fiscal year. This budget expansion, represented by the enormous 1973 budget of ¥14.28 trillion (= $52.46 billion; $1 = ¥272.2),—up 24.6 percent even from the 1972 anti-recession budget—was moved ahead by Prime Minister Kakuei Tanaka (July 1972 to December 1974). A 30 percent increase in social security expenditures from the previous year caused the 1973 fiscal year to be labeled "the first year of the age of social welfare." The 32.2 percent increase in public works[9] reflected Prime Minister Tanaka's "Plan for Remodeling the Japanese Archipelago" (*Nihon Rettō Kaizōron*) to develop and industrialize, especially the rural areas, by distributing public money.

The MOF's acceptance and cooperation with the prime minister's expansive fiscal orientation during this period were different from its fiscal conservatism before and after it. The fiscal bureaucrats had a special reason to cooperate: they wanted to decrease a surplus in the international account by increasing domestic demands. This surplus had brought international pressure for revaluation of the yen[10] since the declaration by U.S. President Nixon to suspend the convertibility of dollars into gold ("dollar shock") in August 1971. A majority of Japanese policymakers especially feared the economic downturn and believed that decreased international competitiveness would be caused by a change in the exchange rate from 360 yen to 308 yen per dollar in December 1971. Though, in retrospect, this change did not shrink a large surplus in the international account, and the Japanese yen proved still to be underestimated, the MOF bureaucrats believed at the time that the further appreciation of the yen would damage the Japanese economy. This was why they allowed the expansion of fiscal policy to continue despite increases in both consumer prices and wholesale prices from 1972.[11] The MOF had resisted international pressure to revalue the yen until February 1973 when its exchange rate began to fluctuate.[12]

By the summer of 1973, the rate of increase in the wholesale price was more than 15 percent. Since journalists called this trend "fiscal inflation" and blamed it on the budget expansion, Minister of Finance Aichi and Prime Minister Tanaka began to restrain public expenditures. After March monetary policy was restrained, and after May the implementation of pub-

115

lic works was postponed. But because of the oil shock in October of that year, consumer prices and wholesale prices skyrocketed. They were finally recorded as high as 24.3 percent and 31.3 percent, respectively, in 1974. Immediately after Aichi's sudden death in November 1973, Tanaka appointed Fukuda, a former budget officer and advocate of fiscal conservatism, as minister of finance. Fukuda reduced the rate of increase in the 1974 fiscal budget to 19.7 percent, and held public works expenditures to the same amount as the previous year. However, he acceded to the prime minister's request for a ¥2 trillion (= $6.8 billion; $1 = ¥292.08 in 1974) income tax decrease.

While hyperinflation from late 1972 to mid-1974 and the accompanying recession increased criticism of Tanaka's expansionary budget, revelation of a money scandal forced him to resign in November 1974. A subsequent cabinet was formed by Takeo Miki (December 1974 to December 1976). Masayoshi Ōhira, who was appointed minister of finance, had to face a tax revenue shortfall in the 1974 fiscal year. In a speech entitled "The Present Situation of Government Finance," popularly known as "The Declaration of Fiscal Crisis," which was delivered at the HR finance committee of the Seventy-fifth Ordinary Diet on April 15, 1975, he officially stated that the revenue shortfall in the 1974 fiscal year amounted to almost ¥800 billion (= $2738.98 million; $1 = ¥292.08 in 1974). At the same time, representing the view of fiscal authority, he emphasized that this revenue shortfall was caused by a structural change in the Japanese economy, and that natural increments of revenue, such as had occurred in earlier years, should no longer be expected. With his experience in public finance as a former MOF bureaucrat and party politician, Ōhira took the critical financial situation very seriously (Satō, Kōyama, and Kumon 1990, 346). His interpretation of financial conditions meant that the government needed both to cut expenditures and to change its revenue structure by a new means of tax revenue.

Despite this critical sense of the budgetary condition, however, continuing revenue shortfalls forced Minister of Finance Ōhira to issue an enormous number of deficit bonds thereafter. He proposed to the Diet the "special" issuance of deficit bonds to finance the 1975 fiscal year budget. This practice continued until the 1989 fiscal year. For two years after December 1976, as the LDP secretary general he was in charge of the growing budget debt and the issuance of bonds. His responsibility for making exceptions in bond issuance, as well as his recognition of the need for restructuring fiscal policy during this period, were important reasons why Ōhira promoted the introduction of the general consumption tax as a fiscal solution when he became prime minister. The next section illustrates the political process of the first proposal of the general consumption tax, which followed the emergence of the budget deficit.

## THE POLITICIZATION OF THE GENERAL CONSUMPTION TAX

### The Ministry of Finance's Initiative Through the Government Tax System Research Council

From 1976 on, the MOF annually presented an "Estimate of Revenue and Expenditure of the General Account of the Government (*Zaisei Shūshi Shisan*)."[13] This kind of public presentation by the fiscal authority had been rare because the MOF had revealed as little information and data on public finances as possible. The MOF needed to attach some importance to this estimate so that it would influence public debate over the budget. But at the same time it did not want to make any precommitment to the budget making that might constrain its future decision. Thus the MOF defined the meaning of this estimate ambiguously, that is, not as a concrete "plan" (*keikaku*) but as a "key" (*tegakari* ) for planning public financial management.[14]

The estimate had a different formulation and emphasis from year to year, but in each estimate the MOF decided on a fiscal year in the near future when the government aimed to eliminate the special issuance of deficit bonds.[15] Then, it assessed a certain increase of expenditures and computed the needed tax increases to finance such expenditures without the special issuance of deficit bonds.

According to the MOF, too much dependence on the issuance of bonds was not good for three reasons: (1) increasing interest payments on bonds would repress the other items of expenditures and distort resource allocation; (2) easy dependence on the issuance of bonds would tend to cause public service to be inefficient and would force future generations to pay for the present public service; (3) increasing government bonds in the market might cause inflation or squeeze the fund demanded by the private sector as the economy recovered ("crowding out").

This formulation implied the MOF-held view that a new tax burden, as well as the economization of expenditures, were inevitable in order to restore financial health. For example, the estimate for the 1976 fiscal year budget reported that financing the estimated expenditures from 1976 to 1980 would require 20.9 percent of the average annual increase in tax revenue during the same period.[16] Because the estimated rate of increase in the nominal GNP in this period was about 13 percent,[17] a 20.9 percent increase in tax revenue required 1.62 of elasticity of tax revenue to GNP as an annual average. Judging from the tax revenue elasticity in the past (1.39 as annual average from 1970 to 1974 and 1.35 as annual average from 1965 to 1974), it was impossible to expect as high a tax revenue elasticity as 1.62 in the coming five years. The estimate suggested, then, that financial resources would fall short of expected expenditures without a tax increase. The MOF's strong orientation toward tax revenue enhancement presented a sharp contrast with those of the other advanced capitalist governments that put first priority on expenditure cuts at the time (Mizuno 1988, 48).

While emphasizing the difficulty in obtaining enough financial sources under the present revenue structure and economic condition, the MOF began to suggest the broad-based tax on consumption as a new means of tax revenue. In August 1975, immediately after his appointment, the general director of the tax bureau, Masataka Ōkura, delivered to GTSRC members the so-called Ōkura memo in order to facilitate the council's deliberations on tax reform.[18] The memo argued that Japan could not expect a large natural increment of tax revenue caused by economic recovery that would automatically guarantee financial solvency. Moreover, it contended that the estimated revenue shortfall in the near future was too large to be financed by the issuance of bonds (because of the risk of inflation). According to this position, which clearly paralleled the "Declaration of Fiscal Crisis" by Prime Minister Ōhira, financing the budget deficit required not only a large expenditure cut but also a tax increase. Though this memo cautioned against a hasty proposal for a tax increase, it also expressed the tax bureau's strong intention to introduce the new tax in the near future.[19]

About a year after the "Ōkura memo," in June 1976, the GTSRC began to deliberate on a middle-term proposal for tax reform in the 1980 fiscal year. In July the MOF set up two special divisions in the GTSRC in charge, respectively, of individual and corporate income taxes, and indirect taxes and taxes on assets.[20] The division in charge of indirect taxes decided to propose a new tax—specifically a general consumption tax (*Nihon Keizai Shimbun* [hereinafter, *NK*], a national newspaper that focuses especially on economic affairs, October 20, 1976). As a basis for figuring the form of a new tax, the MOF presented a list to the GTSRC of eight kinds of taxes, for example, the VAT as in the EC countries and the manufacturer's sales tax (*NK*, November 3, 1976).

On June 28, 1977, the GTSRC resumed the deliberations that had been suspended since the end of 1976. The GTSRC's "Middle-Term Proposal on Tax Reform" (*Chūki Zeisei Tōshin*) on October 4 explicitly proposed that a new broad-based tax on consumption would be inevitable in the future.[21] This report clearly concurred with the fiscal authority on the need to introduce the new tax as a fiscal solution. First, the report contended that, as soon as possible, the government had to solve the budget deficit and decrease the bond dependency ratio, which had amounted to about 30 percent of revenue[22] for the last three fiscal years. Second, it attributed the current budget deficit to a structural change in Japanese public finance, and hence concluded that the natural increment in tax revenue could not finance the deficit budget.[23] Third, while emphasizing the need for expenditure cuts, the report suggested that the nation should not depend only on expenditure cuts as a solution for restoring sound budget finance. Fourth, though it argued for the abolishment of unfair or unequal tax treatments in the existing tax system,[24] it stated that public expenditures would not be fully financed by additional tax revenues that would be expected from the rationalization of these treatments. Finally, considering the lower ratio of tax and social security payments to the GDP in Japan as compared to that in other OECD countries,[25] the report proposed to increase the levels of social security contributions and taxation. It concluded that introducing a broad-based tax on consumption was the best means of raising more tax revenue for two reasons: first, people already felt that the income tax was heavy, and, second, Japan had a lower share of indirect tax to total tax revenue than the other advanced capitalist countries.[26]

The MOF had first wanted to introduce the new tax in the 1978 fiscal year.[27] However, in the continuing recession and under Prime Minister Miki and, subsequently, Prime Minister Fukuda, the MOF's proposal for the new tax could get no political support. Miki's strong social welfare orientation was incompatible with both tax increases and expenditure cuts.[28] With no prospect for reforming the public financial system, the government implemented an ad hoc policy in the 1976 fiscal year to stop the annual income tax cut that had been in effect for the last sixteen years. Despite the MOF's concern with deficit finance, the political pressure further expanded the budget. In the 1977 fiscal year, the opposition parties' request to amend the government budget bill in the Diet resulted in refunding taxes amounting to ¥300 billion (= $1,117.28 million; $1 = ¥268.51 in 1977), and transferring ¥63 billion (= $234.63 million) for welfare expenditures from a reserve fund. Since the budget bill was rarely amended in the Diet in such a substantial way, this amendment was a significant shock to the MOF.[29]

Though a subsequent prime minister, Takeo Fukuda (December 1976 to

December 1978), was a renowned advocate of a sound or balanced budget, he also could not resist political pressures for government expenditures which this time came from both outside and inside the country. Since Japan's economic performance was relatively better than that in the other OECD countries in terms of inflation, economic growth, and balance of payments in the international account, these countries pressed Japan to increase domestic demands and contribute to the recovery of the world economy. A sudden rise in the exchange value of the yen from the spring of 1977 to the fall of 1978 also increased domestic pressure to demand the expansion of fiscal policy from major business associations. In the initial budget of the 1978 fiscal year, the expenditures for public works increased by 34.5 percent from the previous year. The bond dependency ratio of the initial budget was 32 percent, even though tax revenue was used to finance the budget until the end of May in the next 1979 fiscal year.[30] Without the additional tax revenue from the next fiscal year, which amounted to ¥2 trillion (= $9.5 billion; $1 = ¥210.44 in 1978), the bond dependency ratio was 37 percent. This ratio was far beyond the 30 percent that the MOF had set as the upper limit for the issuance of special bonds. Moreover, Prime Minister Fukuda had to add ¥2.5 trillion (= $11.88 billion) to the supplementary budget in the fall in order to achieve the 7 percent economic growth promised with the other advanced capitalist countries at the Bonn Summit in July 1978.

In August 1977, immediately before the GTSRC's "Middle-Term Proposal on Tax Reform," the general director of the tax bureau, Masataka Ōkura, explained to Prime Minister Fukuda that the "Proposal" would include the introduction of a general consumption tax. Prime Minister Fukuda accepted the proposal, but asked the tax officer not to politicize the general consumption tax as an issue in the general election of the HR, which was expected in the near future. Fukuda, with his long experience in public finance as an able budget compiler and a minister of finance, approved the necessity of tax increases but was not eager to take responsibility for them during his term (Yanagisawa 1985, 27).

The MOF could get no strong support from tax specialists inside the LDP either. For example, in a newspaper interview, nine out of ten leading members[31] of the LDP TSRC admitted the need for a tax increase (by means of the general consumption tax) for fiscal reconstruction. But, among them, eight were reluctant about its introduction in the next (1978) fiscal year because of the recession and the lack of administrative preparation for and public understanding of the new tax (*NK*, September 25, 1977). Thus, at the time, the LDP members familiar with the tax policy were far from taking the initiative in the tax reform. This point clearly distinguishes the proposal of the general consumption tax in the late 1970s from the subsequent proposals of the sales tax and the consumption tax in the 1980s, which some LDP tax expert members actively supported.

Opposition to the new tax from consumer groups, retailers, wholesalers, labor unions, and big business underscored the LDP's reluctance about it. Even before the "Middle-Term Proposal," a group called *Fukōheina Zeisei o Tadasukai*(literally, "a group of people who sought to reform the unfair tax system"), which included fifty-three groups representing labor, women, and so on,[32] criticized the GTSRC for accepting the MOF view. Eleven groups of wholesalers[33] passed resolutions to oppose a general consumption tax, and began to petition Prime Minister Fukuda, the MOF, and the MITI for the withdrawal of the new tax. Four Retailers' Labor Unions (*Kourigyō Rōdō Kumiai 4 Dantai*) also submitted to the government resolutions against the general consumption tax. The labor union of national civil servants began actively to express its opposition to the general consumption tax. Major business associations, the Federation of Economic Groups (*Keizai Dantai Rengōkai*, hereinafter, Keidanren) and the Japan Committees for Economic Development (*Keizai Dōyūkai*, hereinafter, Dōyūkai) opposed the tax increase for the following year because they expected it to influence the economy adversely. Though admitting its necessity in the future, they demanded an expansionary fiscal policy at that time.

Encouraged by the strong public opposition to the new tax, the opposition parties utilized tax issues to attack the government. The tax increase became the major issue in an extraordinary session of the Diet, which began on October 6 immediately after the "Middle-Term Proposal." Three opposition parties—the Japan Socialist Party, the Japan Communist Party, and the Clean Government Party—expressed strong opposition to the new tax. The reasons for the parties' opposition paralleled those of special-interest groups—the tax's regressive effect on income distribution, the anticipated increased paperwork for small distributors in filing the tax, and the expected negative effect on consumption. Besides these three parties, the Democratic Socialist Party argued against further consideration of the new tax, and only the New Liberal Club (NLC), a splinter of the LDP, agreed with its introduction (*NK*, October 19, 1977).

Despite the opposition, the MOF continued to advance the plan for the new tax. From the beginning of 1978, the MOF began to formulate a concrete plan for the new tax system—a tax rate and the point of tax exemption—and to compute the estimated tax revenue and the transition from existing excise taxes on commodities (*NK*, January 11, 1978). At the same time, the GTSRC began deliberations on the proposal in June. After meeting only six times, the Special Commission of the General Consumption Tax, which had been established within the GTSRC in August, submitted a report to Prime Minister Fukuda in September. The VAT, a multistage tax on consumption applied in principle to the net value added of all exchanges (except exports) of firms, was officially proposed for the first time in Japan and was named the general consumption tax (*ippan shōhizei*).

This tentative plan for the general consumption tax by the GTSRC tried to make the new tax more politically acceptable. First, in order to avoid criticism that the general consumption tax was regressive, the proposed system exempted taxes on food, social insurance medical fees, and education fees. Second, the plan proposed an easy method for filing the tax— a subtraction method, also called the cost credit method (*shiirekōjo*)— instead of a tax credit method with invoices. The subtraction method required reporting less information on business income than the invoice method, and thus the government considered it more acceptable for small and medium-sized businesses.

Each of these measures was supposed to weaken opposition, respectively, from the unorganized public who would pay the tax and the manufacturers and distributors who would file the tax. But neither measure was useful to coax the opposition. According to the results of an opinion poll in mid-October in *Asahi Shimbun* (hereinafter, *Asahi*, one of the most popular national newspapers), many respondents expressed a negative view of "a tax on all commodities except food." That is, 44 percent of them believed that the new tax would increase prices and adversely affect people's lives; 20 percent wanted to abolish existing special tax measures before introducing the new tax (in order to raise more revenue); and 11 percent pointed out the regressivity of the new tax (*Asahi*, November 4, 1978). All commercial and service sectors and almost all manufacturing industries continued to exhibit strong apprehension about the new tax. They were worried that it would discourage consumption and that they might not be able to shift the tax to the price and would thus be forced to pay it for themselves at the expense of their profits.[34]

In addition, the new tax encountered opposition inside the bureaucracy. The Economic Planning Agency (EPA) and the MITI did not support the introduction of the general consumption tax. The EPA was worried that the new tax would have an adverse influence on business performance in general.

## The Ministry of Finance and Prime Minister Ōhira

Without the advent of Ōhira, the prime minister newly elected in December 1978, the LDP government might not have formally proposed the general consumption tax. More than a year before becoming prime minister (in August 1977), Ōhira, who had been a secretary general of the LDP at the time, supported the new tax and had given his consent to the MOF's proposal.[35] Though Ōhira again postponed the planned introduction of the new tax from the 1979 to the 1980 fiscal year,[36] he had already decided on the new tax. The "Mainlines of the 1979 Fiscal Year Tax Reform," issued by the LDP on December 26, made clear that the new tax would be introduced in the 1980 fiscal year. The following day the GTSRC made a similar proposal in the "Mainline of the General Consumption Tax." The introduction of the general consumption tax was then endorsed by the cabinet in January 1979. In the new tax system, a uniform 5 percent tax rate was to be applied to the net added value (the difference between sales and purchases) of all firms, and a tax-exemption level was to be at ¥20 million (= $91.27 thousand; $1 = ¥219.14 in 1979) in sales volume. From the beginning of 1979, Prime Minister Ōhira had shown a strong inclination to introduce the general consumption tax in April 1980 (*NK*, January 5, 1979).

From that point on, the political process of the tax reform turned into a clear-cut conflict between a support group for the new tax, consisting of the MOF, Prime Minister Ōhira, and a very small number of the LDP leaders close to Ōhira who supported the new tax, and all others who opposed its introduction. Backbenchers and LDP line members, who had not thus far understood the significance of the party decision on the new tax, gradually increased their opposition to this hasty decision by a small circle of leaders.[37] They formed an opposition movement inside the party and joined the opposition movement formerly consisting of opposition parties, special-interest groups, and the unorganized public. Meanwhile, some LDP leaders who had reluctantly come to support or accept the general consumption tax began to express reservations or to join the opposition.

For the MOF, the prime minister's strong support should have been a good sign to implement the new tax. However, Ōhira's isolation from his party and his determination to introduce the tax intensified the political conflict surrounding the tax issue, which was beyond the MOF's control.

It was clear that the tax issue was causing the prime minister to feud with his party. Election politics exacerbated the intraparty opposition to the new tax. A majority of the LDP members of the House of Councillors (HC) who expected reelection the following summer opposed the general consumption tax. Sixty-five members of the HC asked the prime minister to be circumspect in proposing the new tax, and the House executive committee recommended against its introduction (*NK*, May 16, 1979). The prospect of the general election in the near future made the LDP members of the HR join in opposition to the new tax. In July, after the media reported the prime minister's decision to convene an extraordinary session in September, many began to suspect that Ōhira would dissolve the HR at the beginning of the session and call a general election. By winning the general election, Prime Minister Ōhira wanted to increase the number of seats held by the LDP in the HR of the Diet so as to restore a stable majority.[38]

The LDP members were increasingly frustrated by Ōhira's insistence on a tax increase. A Dietmen's Conference on Fiscal Reconstruction (*Zaisei Saiken Giin Kondankai*), led by Jun Shiozaki[39] and Kabun Mutō, organized the opposition inside the LDP, and included more than two hundred members, that is, a majority of the LDP Diet members. This conference involved interest groups from small and medium-sized businesses, retailers, and wholesalers.[40] Some LDP leaders also expressed opposition. For example, Toshio Kōmoto, chairman of the LDP Policy Affairs Research Council (PARC), advocating a positive fiscal policy, argued that the natural tax revenue increase that would result from good economic management would be large enough for fiscal reconstruction. Yasuhiro Nakasone, former chairman of the LDP executive committee, expressed a negative view of the general consumption tax and criticized Ōhira's proposal to raise the tax on lower- and medium-level incomes.

In the spring and summer of 1978 Prime Minister Ōhira and the MOF made efforts to convince people of the benefits of the tax reform. Since public opinion demanded that the government reduce inefficiency and waste in the administration before the introduction of the new tax,[41] the government tried to review the necessity of each item or program of the budget.[42] Responding to public displeasure with the existing tax system,[43] the MOF publicized the fact that it also intended to rectify the existing income tax system.[44] Both actions by the fiscal authority, however, attracted little public attention.

On August 30, the eighty-eighth extraordinary session of the Diet was convened. A general election after the dissolution of the HR was expected a few months later. In the LDP executive committee on August 31, many members asked the prime minister not to talk about tax increases until the election. The apprehension of the opposition inside the LDP, activated by members' concerns about the tax issue adversely affecting the election, was no longer groundless. In many election districts, candidates on opposition party tickets attacked the government's proposal of the general consumption tax. The wholesalers, retailers, and small and medium-sized businesses began to ask the LDP candidates whether they opposed or supported the general consumption tax. The Dietmen's Conference on Fiscal Reconstruction, in order to secure for their members the support of special-interest groups, delivered commercial and industrial groups a list of 220 signatures of LDP Diet members who opposed the general consumption tax (*NK*, September 4, 1979).

According to an opinion poll taken in the Tokyo metropolitan area (*NK*, September 22, 1979), those who supported a tax increase, even including those whose support carried certain conditions (e.g., the government's effort to reduce inefficiency in the administration), amounted to a total of only 19.3 percent. The general consumption tax was unpopular even among supporters of tax increases, and only 13.6 percent of these supporters chose it as a means of increasing taxes. The public felt the need to eliminate the issuance of deficit bonds but insisted it be done without a tax increase. Thus, although 64.3 percent of respondents answered that fiscal reconstruction was necessary, 61.1 percent of these supporters opposed the tax increase.

## The Demise of the General Consumption Tax Proposal

On September 7 the Diet was dissolved; a cabinet meeting set September 17 as the formal first day of the thirty-fifth general election campaign, and October 7 as the day of voting. The LDP ticketed 322 candidates.

As election day approached, Ōhira became more cautious about maintaining the possibility of a tax increase. What made Ōhira more prudent was not the unpopularity of the new tax but a political scandal unrelated to the tax issue—the misuse of public funds by high-ranking employees of the Japan Railway Construction Public Corporation (*Nihon Tetsudō Kensetsu Kōdan*). The media reported the scandal immediately after the dissolution of the Diet. These public employees reported fictitious business trips and used large sums of money to receive guests from supervising ministries, including the MOF. Further investigations by the Board of Audit found that this kind of wasteful expenditure had also occurred in the Environmental Agency, the Ministry of Posts and Telecommunications, the MOF, and the Prime Minister's office. The mass media sensationalized the misuse of public money as "a heaven of public money (*kōhi tengoku*)" for high-ranking bureaucrats. The media coverage focused especially on the

MOF at the top of the bureaucracy with discretionary power over the budget.[45] This scandal contributed to impressing on the public that reducing waste in the public sector was a much more urgent task than implementing a tax increase.

In order not to provoke ill feeling among the electorate, the words *tax increase* were not used in the LDP's public promises for the election. Accordingly, in the early stages of the election campaign, Ōhira gradually began to change his statements. On September 17, in his first campaign speech at Ueno Park in Tokyo, he stated that he would not necessarily insist on introducing the general consumption tax. On September 22, in an interview in Osaka, he emphasized that an important precondition for financial reconstruction was the simplification of the administrative apparatus: reduction of personnel, reorganization of special public corporations (*tokushu hōjin*), readjustment and borrowing of subsidies, revision of special tax measures, and rectification of the unfair tax system. On September 24, on a stumping tour in downtown Tokyo where many self-employed commercial and industrial people lived, Ōhira stated that the government was seeking ways to restore financial health without depending on a tax increase, especially a general consumption tax (*NK Evening* [hereinafter, *NKE*], September 25, 1979).

The other LDP leaders apparently began to deny the tax increase. The LDP secretary general, Kunikichi Saitō, said that the LDP candidates would be allowed to express opposition to the general consumption tax in the election campaign (*NKE*, September 11, 1979). The LDP PARC chairman, Toshio Kōmoto, asserted that to introduce the general consumption tax in the 1980 fiscal year was impossible, considering the opposition of most of the LDP Diet members (*NK*, September 21 and 23, 1979). A major business association, Keidanren, which had once given a grudging consent to the introduction of the general consumption tax in the 1980 fiscal year (*NKE*, August 22, 1979), now decided against it because of persistent opposition from industries and the electorate (*NK*, September 26, 1979).

Meanwhile, Ōhira finally confirmed the withdrawal of his new tax proposal. In Niigata on September 26, he promised to do his best for fiscal reconstruction without the general consumption tax, and reiterated this from the middle to final stages of the electoral campaign. But it was too late. The opposition camps began to accuse the government of concealing the tax increase until the election. The LDP appeared to be especially hurt by these accusations.

Newspaper opinion polls predicted that the LDP would recover a majority in the election. For example, an *Asahi Shimbun* opinion poll at the end

TABLE 3.1

General Election Results in 1979

|  | 1976 | 1979 |
|---|---|---|
| Liberal Democratic Party | 249 | 248 |
| Japan Socialist Party | 123 | 107 |
| Clean Government Party | 55 | 57 |
| Japan Communist Party | 17 | 39 |
| Democratic Socialist Party | 29 | 35 |
| New Liberal Club | 17 | 4 |
| Association of Social Democrats | 0 | 2 |
| Independents | 21 | 19 |
| Total | 511 | 511 |

of August reported that the LDP popular support had increased to 52 percent in contrast with 47 percent in June of the same year (*Asahi*, September 3, 1979). The LDP's lead, as predicted in newspapers, failed to materialize in the thirty-fifth general election. One unfortunate factor for the LDP was rain. Heavy rain from a typhoon in almost all parts of Japan on October 7 prevented many people from going to the polls. The turnout rate was 68 percent, the second-lowest rate for a general election since the end of World War II. In a lower turnout, unorganized or independent voters who are not loyal party supporters are generally less likely to vote. Since the number of independents,[46] in terms of party support, had increased throughout the 1970s, the LDP had to get these floating votes, in addition to organized votes, in order to maintain a majority. Thus more abstentions among these "floating" voters tended to decrease the LDP's share of votes.[47]

The election results have been compared to those of the previous general election in December 1976, when the LDP loss brought about the resignation of Prime Minister Takeo Miki. A breakdown by party of the 511 seats of the HR is shown in Table 3.1.

The election result was an apparent loss for the LDP. Immediately after the election, the LDP maintained a bare majority in the Diet because of the entry to the party of ten conservative independents who had won the HR seats in the election (as the LDP had done after the 1976 election).

Unexpected factors, like the scandal of the Railway Construction Public Corporation and the weather on election day, contributed to the LDP's loss. However, the politicization of the general consumption tax by Ōhira in the election campaign undeniably placed the LDP at a disadvantage in the election. Despite the surge of popular support for the LDP, for example, the rate of popular support for the Ōhira cabinet, 30 percent, was exceeded by the rate of nonsupport, 35 percent (*Asahi*, September 3, 1979). Thus, although Ōhira wanted to remain in office, other party leaders, especially two former prime ministers, Miki and Fukuda, argued that he should resign in order to claim responsibility that the electoral loss was a result of his dissolution of the HR.

The electoral loss initiated an even more intense conflict among several factions inside the LDP than had been the case before Ōhira took office.[48] This conflict, which was known as the forty days' conflict (*yonjūnichi kōsō*), brought much turmoil and uncertainty to Japanese politics.[49] On November 6, a month after the election, a special session was held in order to nominate the next prime minister.[50] The LDP mainstream factions (headed, respectively, by Masayoshi, Ōhira, and Kakuei Tanaka) and nonmainstream factions (headed, respectively, by Takeo Fukuda, Takeo Miki, and Yasuhiro Nakasone) could not reach a consensus on who should be the party candidate for the next election of a prime minister in the Diet. As a result, the LDP placed two candidates—Ōhira and Fukuda—in the election.

Ōhira managed to defeat Fukuda and formed a second cabinet, but the conflict inside the LDP did not wane. A motion of no-confidence against the Ōhira cabinet brought by the Japanese Socialist Party in May 1980 rekindled the rivalries within the LDP that had temporarily been mollified. Since sixty-nine members of the nonmainstream LDP factions were absent from the session in which the no-confidence motion was submitted, the motion passed with 243 votes in favor from the opposition parties and 187 votes against from the LDP. Facing a choice between the cabinet's resignation or the Diet's dissolution, Ōhira dissolved the Diet again—less than a year after the previous dissolution. The general election of the HR was held simultaneously with the election of the HC. However, Prime Minister Ōhira did not see the results of his choice because he had been hospitalized since the first day of the election campaign and died on June 12. After the autopsy, the doctor officially stated that his death was caused by spasms and constriction in a coronary artery resulting from "unimaginable mental stress."

The prime minister's sudden death quickly dispersed ill feelings among the LDP members stemming from intraparty rivalries. Candidates belonging to both mainstream and nonmainstream factions began to cooperate for elections in the name of the late Ōhira. His death also helped to divert public attention from policy issues and prolonged intraparty conflicts in the LDP that had brought a lot of disorder and had culminated in the Diet's dissolution and simultaneous elections.

Since the LDP had fought the election without selecting the next party president,[51] the opposition parties had no incumbent party leader on whom to focus their criticism. Ōhira's formal funeral, as a joint cabinet and party ceremony, moved the Japanese people. Sympathy votes resulting from Ōhira's sudden death won the LDP 284 seats in the HR and 69 seats in the HC. The simultaneous elections put an end to the close parity in numbers of the LDP and opposition parties in the Diet that had existed since the HC election in 1974 and ushered in a new era of conservative dominance that lasted until 1989.[52]

Ōhira's sudden death resulted in the confirmation of a resurgence of popular support for the LDP in opinion polls that had been reported but had not appeared in the election results until then. Cynically enough, however, the greater the impact of Ōhira's death on politics, the greater was the public's antipathy to the general consumption tax, which he had wanted to implement. The people who were politically close to him said that the MOF had persuaded the late prime minister of the value of the general consumption tax, and had driven him to his death.[53] Because no one wanted to speak ill of a person who had passed away, the public accepted this interpretation presented through the mass media.[54] The MOF became the target of criticism of tax increases; the slogan "fiscal reconstruction without a tax increase" (*zōzei naki zaisei saiken*) began to attract public attention; and the MOF was forced to remain silent about the broad-based consumption tax until the mid-1980s.

## GENERAL CONSUMPTION TAX:
## LESSONS FOR THE FISCAL BUREAUCRATS

The proposal for a general consumption tax was blocked by formidable opposition from all levels of society, and the LDP government had to pay for proposing an unpopular tax with an electoral loss in 1979. The sudden death of the prime minister, who had pushed for the general consumption tax, brought a return to the stability of the LDP predominance, but at the same time impressed on the policymakers the high cost of introducing a new tax on consumption.

In retrospect, from 1977 to 1979, the MOF bureaucrats did nothing special to persuade the public of the value of a general consumption tax. They had emphasized the fiscal crisis. They had also asked the public to bear a new tax burden in order to overcome the budget deficit and proposed the general consumption tax as the most feasible way of increasing the burden in the existing system. The public was unfamiliar with the fiscal crisis, which was still a very new phenomenon in 1979. Therefore, they would perceive the budget debt merely as the result of economic mismanagement by the government, the waste of public money, and poor administrative organization. The public regarded the government's proposal for the new tax as another symptom of fiscal irresponsibility.[55] A majority of people supported the idea that the solution for the fiscal crisis should and could be the government's responsibility and was not the public's burden. Therefore, in 1979, the proposal for a general consumption tax was politicized as the government's choice of a revenue enhancement measure at the expense of the public welfare. On the other hand, the opposition legitimately claimed that the government should cut expenditures and simplify its administration before the introduction of the tax.

Despite this public opinion, the MOF continued to emphasize the necessity of the new tax to solve the fiscal crisis and to press for its implementation. After the "Middle-Term Proposal on Tax Reform" in the fall of 1977, the MOF bureaucrats argued on television and radio for the general consumption tax in order to combat the budget deficit. When the tax bureau dispatched directors to special-interest groups of retailers, wholesalers, self-employed businesses, and stores to give a practical explanation for the general consumption tax, the bureaucrats emphasized the necessity of the new tax for getting out of the deficit finance (*NK*, November 8, 1977). The reason the MOF bureaucrats did not take seriously the political unfeasibility of the general consumption tax was inseparable from Prime Minister Ōhira's ready acceptance of the new tax. The MOF bureaucrats accepted Ōhira's appeal for tax increases after he took office, and did not use more politically feasible ways of proposing tax increases that might have weakened the opposition.[56] Ironically, Ōhira's wholehearted support and enthusiasm for the new tax politicized it as a measure of tax increase, and subsequently deprived the bureaucrats of an opportunity to set a political agenda that was more politically feasible.

From the failed proposal of the general consumption tax, the MOF learned that obtaining full support from a political leader, even though he was a prime minister, was not enough to introduce the new tax. The failure to obtain the support of the entire LDP, despite Ōhira's support, taught the bureaucrats that they needed to persuade other LDP leaders of the value of the new tax. These leaders, who might have controlled the party backbenchers' opposition and helped compromise with special interests, went instead to the opposition. In this sense, the reform proposal in 1979 taught the MOF bureaucrats that they should not restrict themselves to the role of administrators when aiming to introduce the new tax.

The bureaucrats also confirmed that they could not enact a reform at the same time that they were claiming a tax increase. The fiscal authorities and Prime Minister Ōhira stated that the general consumption tax was an inevitable means to finance the budget deficit, while the opposition to the new tax supported an alternative solution for the fiscal crisis—expenditure cuts and economization of the administration. Thus the conflict over the tax issue was regarded primarily as a disagreement about a fiscal solution, that is, a conflict between cutting expenditures and increasing the tax burden. This politicization of the budget issue was unfortunate for the MOF, which considered both cutting expenditure and securing tax revenue indispensable for a fiscal solution.

The Diet resolution on December 21, 1979, substantially ended public discussion about this problem, and explicitly stated the future direction that the government should take for fiscal reconstruction.

> The general consumption tax (tentative name) could not obtain an understanding about the arrangements and structures of the system. Therefore, the government should not depend on the general consumption tax and should increase financial resources through efforts to cut administrative costs and budget expenditures by administrative reform, to guarantee the equity in sharing the tax burden, and to revise the existing tax system. From now on the government should consider fiscal reconstruction from a broad perspective in terms of expenditure and revenue, while paying enough attention to economic prosperity and employment.

Thus the opposition to the general consumption tax had turned into a consensus for reforming administrative and fiscal structures, which led to a major policy agenda in the 1980s—"fiscal reconstruction without a tax increase."

## ADMINISTRATIVE AND FISCAL REFORM:
## FISCAL RECONSTRUCTION WITHOUT A TAX INCREASE

Administrative reform in Japan, led by the Second Provisional Council for Administrative Reform (SPCAR), belonged to a political phenomenon common in other advanced capitalist countries from the late 1970s to the early 1980s—a political response to a fiscal crisis, that is, an intense austerity campaign, even though the content of policies varied from one country to another. We could include in this group of countries the United States under the Reagan administration from the year 1980, Great Britain under Prime Minister Thatcher from 1979, France under socialist Mitterand's government from 1982, former West Germany under Chancellor Kohl from 1983, Sweden under the Social Democratic cabinet from 1982, and Denmark under conservative rule from 1982, as well as Japan under Suzuki from 1980, and Nakasone from 1982.[57] The austerity orientation was dominant in the governments of these countries during most of the 1980s. This austere economic policy—so-called neoconservatism or conservative revolution—had many similarities with nineteenth-century liberalism, which advocated the importance of a sound budget and a free market. This policy change meant a revision in the expansion of the government's role after World War II, and aimed to limit the size of the public sector by reducing expenditures and public debt, lowering tax burdens, and deregulating economic activities.

The Japanese case was different in several aspects from any other country. This campaign emerged as a reaction to—more precisely, a rejection of—the tax increase that the fiscal authority proposed as a solution for the budget deficit. This background factor led to certain characteristics of the Japanese administrative reform. First, the Japanese austerity policy was not based on an economic theory such as supply-side economics and monetarism, which were employed, respectively, by Reaganomics in the United States and Thatcherism in Britain. In the Japanese administrative reform, deficit finance was presumed "bad" without referring to any particular economic theory. This attitude paralleled the MOF's fiscal orientation. The MOF pointed out that the issuance of deficit bonds would adversely influence the economy—it would cause a crowding effect on investment in the private sector, inflation, and so on. At the same time, however, the bureaucrats did not believe in the relevance of strict interpretation of economic theory in policy-making. Though public criticism of the fiscal authority fueled the administrative reform campaign, the campaign was not necessarily contradictory to the MOF's position: both positions presumed the need to eliminate budget deficits. Second, the Japanese austerity campaign was not led by the government of the predominant LDP, but rather by a blue-ribbon commission consisting of members who represented various interests. The proposed tax increase and incidental revelation of the misuse of public funds had made the public unwilling to trust the government's ability to reform itself. In order to recover public trust in administrative reform, the government chose to establish the Second Provisional Council for Administrative Reform and to give the mandate to the commission outside the public sector.

This section intends neither to present a comprehensive analysis of the Japanese "administrative reform" in the early 1980s nor to evaluate its consequences and achievements. Rather, the analysis focuses on aspects of the administrative reform that influenced the MOF's strong desire to get out of the deficit finance situation and introduce the consumption tax. The remainder of the chapter will explain that administrative reform was brought to the political agenda in the midst of strong public criticism of the government for its past attempt to finance deficits with a tax increase. It will show that the MOF had been excluded from this process, and that the austerity policy in the early 1980s had once entirely removed the proposal of the new consumption tax from the political agenda.

The LDP government's attempt to restore a budget imbalance failed completely in late 1979. In addition to withdrawing the proposal for the general consumption tax, another bill endorsed by the cabinet to raise the pensionable age from sixty to sixty-five in the Government-Managed Pension System for Corporate Employees (*Kōsei Nenkin Hoken Seido*) was also blocked by the opposition. These failures taught the LDP that public consensus lay in cutting back wastes and costs inside the government and not in sharing an additional burden for a solution to the fiscal crisis.

Zenkō Suzuki was selected from the same faction to become the prime minister after Ōhira. In his "opinion expression speech" (*shoshin hyōmei enzetsu*) in the extraordinary Diet session in October 1980, he proposed "administrative reform" as a problem awaiting an urgent solution and suggested that the government should solve the budget deficit by reforming the public sector. However, Suzuki's proposal would have had little impact without cooperation from the other LDP leaders and support from organized interest groups outside the public sector.

Suzuki's proposal actually had full support from Yasuhiro Nakasone who had been the faction leader since the 1960s, but who had not yet served as prime minister. Nakasone had expected to occupy the office after Ōhira, but had been given only a cabinet position as director general of the Administrative Management Agency (AMA) in the Suzuki cabinet. In order to strengthen his qualifications for prime minister after Suzuki, Nakasone tried to increase the political significance of his position. Administrative reform, which was gradually rising on the political agenda as a result of the political dispute over fiscal reconstruction, was the best issue to augment the political influence of his relatively minor cabinet position and to make public attention center on his leadership. As head of the AMA, he was in charge of establishing a blue-ribbon commission, the Secondary Provisional Council for Administrative Reform; the AMA became its secretariat. The administrative deputy director general of the AMA became head of the executive office of the SPCAR, which was staffed by bureaucrats dispatched mostly from the AMA.

Nakasone's expectations from administrative reform were quite different from Suzuki's. Since he was more eager to promote his own influence through the administrative reform campaign, he put high priority on implementing reform policies and impressing on the public the SPCAR's visible policy achievements. For this purpose, Nakasone asked the SPCAR to make politically feasible recommendations. Differing from Nakasone's cautious approach, Suzuki promised to carry out all the proposals made by the SPCAR unconditionally.[58] Suzuki, who had obtained the top position of prime minister contrary to his own as well as others' expectations, did not mind dedicating his cabinet's fate to a single policy goal. He made restoration of the budget imbalance by administrative reform his cabinet's primary goal and repeated that he would "stake his political fate" on it. Suzuki resigned with good grace late in 1982 when a revenue shortfall of ¥6 trillion (= $24.09 billion; $1 ¥249.08) in the 1982 fiscal year prevented him from achieving this goal.

Despite this difference in intention between these leaders, Nakasone's active cooperation made it possible for administrative reform to become the major political agenda in the Suzuki cabinet. Administrative reform continued to take precedence over any other policies until the first half of Nakasone's term.

Second, even before the Suzuki cabinet was formed, the AMA bureaucrats had intended administrative reform. This had been an important policy goal for them for more than ten years, and they had waited for the right political opportunity.[59] They began to make concrete plans for the reform in August 1980, almost at the same time that Suzuki unofficially mentioned the need for administrative reform in order to clean up the deficit-ridden budget. Immediately after his appointment as head of the AMA, Nakasone listened to the AMA bureaucrats' proposal for administrative reform and was interested in it even before Suzuki's official proposal. In this sense, the AMA bureaucrats' preparation substantiated Suzuki's intention to carry out a mission of administrative reform and Nakasone's ambition to lead in implementing influential policies.

Third, the administrative reform campaign obtained full support from major business associations. Business seized the first opportunity to participate actively in this political campaign when Toshio Dokō, one of the most influential figures in the business community, was designated chairman of the SPCAR.[60] The SPCAR attached the condition "without a tax increase" to the aim for "fiscal reconstruction," that is, elimination of the issuance of deficit bonds, in the administrative reform campaign. The business community supported the administrative reform because leaders of major business associations believed that this was the best way to avoid tax increases. The government—especially Nakasone who headed the AMA— intended to activate the administrative reform campaign by appointing a famous and influential figure such as Dokō as chairman of the SPCAR. But this appointment substantially shifted the direction and results of the administrative reform from what the political leaders and the AMA bureaucrats had expected.

### The Process

Immediately after the LDP had obtained a stable majority in both houses in the simultaneous elections and after Suzuki had formed his cabinet, the AMA began to plan administrative reform under Nakasone. The AMA administrative deputy secretary general, Kaji, as well as Secretary General Nakasone began to hear opinions on the reform from all the other ministries. As mentioned above, the AMA suggested the establishment of the Second Provisional Council for Administrative Reform. The SPCAR followed the example of the First Provisional Council for Administrative Reform in 1963, which had studied the administrative system and pointed out problems, but whose proposals had scarcely been implemented.[61] In August the general director of the MOF budget bureau, Yasuo Matsushita, was asked to cooperate with administrative reform.[62] This meant that the MOF was far from being in a position to influence the administrative reform campaign; rather, it was able only to accept the AMA's proposal for it.

In November 1980 the Diet passed the bill[63] to legislate the establishment of the SPCAR, which was supposed to work on administrative reform for two years starting in March 1981. The nature of the SPCAR became clearer when the cabinet appointed its nine commissioners. The nine appointed commissioners were regarded as prominent figures representing various interests in society—business, labor unions, academia, journalism, and bureaucracy, all of which had vested interests in administrative reform.[64] The inclusion of various interest groups indicated two different expectations about the political significance of the SPCAR proposal in pol-

135

icy-making. On the one hand, if they reached a consensus on the policies that the government needed to implement, the SPCAR proposal would be accepted by various interests and would be more likely to be implemented. On the other hand, it was highly improbable that they would agree on specific proposals because of conflicting interests.

Among the SPCAR commissioners, the business associations' view of administrative reform was most influential in shaping the major direction of the SPCAR proposal. This was because the cabinet had designated as chairman Toshio Dokō, who was a prestigious businessman and a former president of Keidanren, and had appointed two other business people with views close to Dokō. Dokō was famous for his austere life-style and industrious character, and this enabled him to obtain wide popularity among the public. His personality and character lent credibility to his demand that the government cut wasteful expenditures without increasing taxes. His opinions were based on his deep suspicion of inefficiency and waste in the public sector.[65] He successfully obtained Prime Minister Suzuki's verbal commitment to abide by his several requests, in exchange for his accepting a position of chair of the SPCAR in March 1981. In terms of the political procedures and process of the reform, Dokō asked Prime Minister Suzuki to implement all the proposals in the reports presented by the SPCAR and to exercise strong leadership over the bureaucracy and the LDP for this purpose. In terms of the content of policies, he required the prime minister to make clear that the SPCAR aimed to restore a sound budget condition without a tax increase by a comprehensive rationalization of the administrative apparatus.

From the beginning, Dokō, who was an amateur at politics, showed skillful political maneuvering: he sometimes threatened the prime minister and the LDP leaders by implying that he would resign if they did not accede to the SPCAR proposals. This threat was effective, not only because the prime minister and the LDP leaders publicized their commitment to the administrative reform, but because the SPCAR had already obtained public support. The inclusion of famous and influential figures among its commissioners, and the special legal status of the SPCAR as an advisory council, impressed on the public the high prestige of this advisory commission. The SPCAR members' intense activity and frequent deliberation, despite their assignment on a part-time basis, were covered by the press and accepted favorably by the public.[66] The members themselves were eager to announce their activities to the press and obtain public support. One commissioner from the business circle, Ryuzō Sejima, later revealed that he leaked a lot of information to the press just so it would report on the SPCAR's daily activities (*Asahi*, October 6, 1984).[67]

The SPCAR's influence also extended to the LDP. The "Headquarters of the LDP and the Government for Administrative Reform," headed by Prime Minister Suzuki and later (from November 1982 to November 1987) Prime Minister Nakasone, publicized the direction to "show maximum respect" to the SPCAR recommendations each time the SPCAR submitted a report to the cabinet.

## The Goals and Accomplishments of the Second Provisional Council for Administrative Reform

The slogan "fiscal reconstruction without a tax increase" began to attract public attention and became popular in the mass media, even though this goal was not officially stated as a guide to fiscal reconstruction until the SPCAR Third Basic Report in July 1982.[68] This goal was strategically important to unify the business community and inspire its cooperation in achieving administrative reform. Certain industrial sectors that depended on government subsidies and some public works were reluctant to give their full support to the expenditure cut. However, all the industries opposed a tax increase either by revising the existing corporate tax or by introducing the new broad-based consumption tax. The policy goal of "fiscal reconstruction without a tax increase" was derived directly from opposition to a major indirect tax on consumption within business and industries.

Judging from its reports on policy proposals, the SPCAR believed that the expansionary tendency of the public sector was the reason for the fiscal crisis. They defined the solution to the budget imbalance as a trade-off between a tax increase and expenditure cuts: if the government increased taxes, the additional financial resources would go toward expanding existing programs or to new entitled programs. Thus the government needed to "cut off (financial) supplies" in order to "drive (itself) into the institutional reform" to economize.

Two major policy goals presented by the SPCAR were to make "an active contribution to international society" (to make defense expenditure and foreign aid exceptions to an across-the-board ceiling) and to create "a dynamic welfare society" (to depend less on government welfare and more on the individual and society). The first goal indicated that the government would exempt a few areas where the international community would re-

137

quire the continuation of Japanese spending. The second goal aimed to substitute the government's role for services provided by the private sector and to reduce existing entitled programs.

Critics, however, charged that the SPCAR, resisted by special interests, was weak in cutting back particular expenditures and programs (for example, the rice subsidy program). Thus they concluded that the administrative reform left many of the most wasteful programs untouched.[69] Administrative reform brought several changes to the Japanese governmental system that may not have been possible without it. But it had not restored fiscal health, which was the intended goal. Tax revenues fell short of the expected amounts in the initial budget in the 1981 fiscal year (by more than ¥3 trillion [= $13.6 billion; $1 = ¥220.54] = 7.1 percent of the expenditure of the general account), and in the 1982 fiscal year (by more than ¥6 trillion [= $24.09 billion; $1 = ¥249.08 in 1982] = 12.9 percent of the expenditure of the general account). The government could not decrease significantly the issuance of deficit bonds during the two years of the SPCAR term. The revenue shortfall in the 1982 fiscal year made it impossible to achieve the goal of eliminating the issuance of deficit bonds in the 1984 fiscal year, and drove Suzuki to resign as prime minister.

The policies proposed by the SPCAR that began to be implemented in the 1984 fiscal year contributed little to expenditure cuts. The revision of two large social security programs—that is, benefit cuts in public pensions and health insurance—would have resulted in long-term savings. But the Ministry of Health and Welfare had planned and prepared for these reforms for several years; instead of taking the initiative in implementing these reforms, the SPCAR recommendations worked as a catalyst to provide the political opportunity for implementing them.[70] The most visible change that administrative reform brought was the reorganization of public corporations—the transformation of the public tobacco monopoly to a quasi-public corporation, the privatization of Nippon Telephone and Telegraph (NTT), and the privatization and reorganization of Japan National Railways (JNR). However, the privatization of three public corporations also saved no money except through long-term savings by the reorganization of the Japan Railway. The SPCAR proposals also led to certain personnel control, to the elimination or reorganization of agencies and offices at national and local levels, and to the reduction of earmarked subsidies from the national to local governments. These measures were also not very effective in cutting expenditures.

The SPCAR was somewhat compromising with special interests partly because the commission included former government officials who were familiar with their demands and thus were realistic about the possibility of reforms involving such interest groups. Moreover, in addition to two former government officials among the nine commissioners, the SPCAR also included former high-ranking bureaucrats who were specialists or advisers. Former vice ministers and deputy cabinet secretariats were among the seventy-seven specialist members and advisers in expert committees and working groups that were in charge of drafting the recommendations. Their inclusion helped reduce bureaucratic resistance, as well as avoid controversies and conflicts that would have had to be resolved within the limited time allowed (Masujima 1985, 12). But critics claimed that the inclusion of former government officials among the members made the reform proposals compromising to bureaucratic interests.

In terms of public financial policies, the SPCAR's major contribution was therefore more symbolic than substantial: it politicized fiscal reconstruction and laid the framework for solving the fiscal crisis. The administrative reform campaign effectively informed the public of the critical situation of public finances and activated public support for "fiscal reconstruction without a tax increase."[71] SPCAR chairman Dokō was largely responsible for shaping the initial direction of administrative reform. The MOF had no way of influencing the initiation of this austerity campaign; Dokō was especially critical of the fiscal authority.[72]

For the MOF, the administrative campaign was a double-edged sword. It gave the MOF an opportunity to engage in a campaign to cut expenditures, which the ministry believed was inevitable to stop further accumulation of budget deficits. At the same time, its slogan "no tax increase" prevented the MOF from making the proposal to introduce the new tax, which had come to be closely associated in the public mind with a tax increase. During the administrative reform campaign, the tax increase issue became a source of disagreement between the government and the SPCAR; the definition of "no tax increase" was politically controversial. The next chapter explains how the MOF responded to this political agenda of administrative reform in order to make it possible to introduce the new tax in the near future, and to lead to the government's proposal of the sales tax in 1987.

# Reframing the Tax Issue:
# The Ministry of Finance's Fiscal
# and Tax Policies in the Early 1980s

THE PREVIOUS chapter examined the process by which public opposition to the general consumption tax turned into support for an austerity policy under the guise of administrative reform. The prevailing political agenda in the early 1980s of "fiscal reconstruction without a tax increase" (*zōzei naki zaisei saiken*) made the fiscal bureaucrats withdraw a proposal for a broad-based consumption tax. This chapter will explain why the Ministry of Finance could, against all odds, propose such a new tax again in 1986. Fiscal and tax policies implemented by the MOF in the early 1980s contributed to reviving the major indirect tax that had once been eliminated from the political agenda as a viable option of public financial reform. The MOF presented a new reason for the introduction of the new tax—shifting revenue reliance from direct to indirect taxation. This new objective was also closely related to the MOF's desire to obtain a more stable revenue source than individual and corporate income taxation.

## THE MINISTRY OF FINANCE UNDER ADMINISTRATIVE REFORM

*A Framework for Expenditure Cuts: The Imposition of Ceilings*
*on Other Ministries' Budgets*

Until the end of 1984, the MOF had shelved the proposal for a major indirect tax. Instead, the fiscal bureaucrats continued to write the budget under the constraint of a zero-ceiling, while falling back on small changes in policies for marginal tax increases. These shifts in the MOF's fiscal and tax policies came from changing political situations outside the ministry. During this period, a political agenda composed of administrative reform and the elimination of budget deficits without a tax hike played a dominant role in Japanese politics. How did the MOF cope with it? Although strong criticism of the fiscal authority fueled this campaign, the MOF began to be actively involved in the austerity policy by defining the range and extent of expenditure cuts through its annual budget decision making.

This MOF behavior allows two different interpretations of the relationship between the ministry and administrative reform. First, we may assume that the interests of the MOF and the Second Provisional Council for Administrative Reform (*Rinji Gyōsei Chōsakai*) were inadvertently converging on expenditure cuts. According to this interpretation, the MOF utilized the SPCAR's initiative to achieve one of two important objectives, that is, spending cuts, while temporarily giving up another important objective, that is, tax revenue enhancement. This view correctly points out that the MOF wanted to cut spending and, at the same time, to enhance revenue. Second, we may also consider that the MOF's policies during this period were mainly shaped by the SPCAR to which the government gave the right to recommend policies for fiscal and administrative reform. That is, the MOF had no alternative but to abide by the administrative reform campaign that the SPCAR had initiated and that became an influential public agenda in the early 1980s.

Both interpretations are, however, not fully convincing. The first interpretation slights the differences in emphasis of the MOF and the SPCAR in implementing the austerity policy, as examined below. The second interpretation fails to grasp the fact that fiscal and tax policies implemented by the MOF during this period steered the way for the introduction in 1989 of the new tax broadly based on consumption, the proposal of which had been incompatible with the administrative reform campaign in the first place.

To clarify the relationship between the MOF and administrative reform, we need to investigate what the SPCAR originally intended and to what extent and in what way its intention was supported or thwarted by the MOF's involvement in the austerity campaign. The SPCAR's ultimate aim was a comprehensive revision of administrative and fiscal structures in order to adjust to ongoing international and domestic changes (a slower economic growth rate, Japan's increasing share in the world economy, technological and scientific progress, and the aging of society). It wanted to change the relationships among the ministries and the expenditure structure so as to achieve more effective allocation and redistribution of public money. The SPCAR expected that the imposition of a ceiling on the budget would eliminate the issuance of deficit bonds, which it regarded as a precondition for the reform of the administration and public finance. It regarded the austerity campaign as a means to "starve out" the government and to force it to make sincere efforts to cut wastes. In order to restructure the administrative and financial procedures so as to resist spending pressure in the future, they wanted to establish a priority order for existing programs and curtail some, while preserving others.

The fiscal bureaucrats welcomed administrative reform as long as political pressure for spending cuts in other ministries would help to extricate the government budget from a tight fiscal situation. The MOF agreed to the need to eliminate the issuance of deficit bonds, which the SPCAR had advocated, because the deficit had likely disadvantaged the MOF with respect to the other ministries, as well as incumbent politicians. First, the other ministries' budgets were under tight constraint because of the revenue shortfall, but this constraint was neither set by the MOF nor was it under its control. Moreover, easing this constraint depended on political decisions, that is, decisions by incumbent politicians, to issue deficit bonds. As explained in chapter 2, the MOF does not try to strike a numerical balance of the budget; rather, it aims to maintain a moderate fiscal tightness in order to secure its discretionary power over the budget. The MOF intended to get out of this situation and restore its power to set the upper limit on the budget size. In this respect, the interests of the MOF and the SPCAR were converging. But the MOF was not interested in reforming the public financial structure, especially in determining a priority order or allocation of public expenditures as the SPCAR had proposed. More important, it wanted to avoid allowing the SPCAR's intervention in financial decisions.

In terms of reform of the public financial structure, the actual result of the austerity campaign was that the MOF's wishes prevailed over those of the SPCAR. The austerity policy did not establish a priority order or an emphasis across various policies. The composition rates of expenditure items did not change very much between the 1980 and 1985 fiscal years before and after the administrative reform campaign (Table 4.1). Minor changes resulted from spending increases that were exempted from spending cuts instead of cuts in expenditure items. The administrative reform campaign exempted the expenditures for defense and official development assistance (ODA). And thus they increased their composition ratios compared to other items.

The MOF's policies during this period explained this failure to reshuffle spending items and programs. First, it shifted the focus of the austerity campaign from changing the composition of spending items to controlling the entire budget size. The MOF publicized the zero-ceiling in the 1982 fiscal budget, that is, the curtailment of all the items by an equal rate, and highlighted the reduction of the total budget size as major objectives of the austerity policy. This emphasis gradually decreased the importance of the structural reform of public finances that the SPCAR had intended under the

TABLE 4.1

Changes in Allocation of General Expenditure in Japan from 1965 to 1980
(percentages of total general expenditure)

| | Social security | Public works | Education and science promotion | National defense | Official development assistance | Measures for energy | Foodstuff control | Other |
|------|------|------|------|------|------|------|------|------|
| 1965 | 17.8 | 25.1 | 16.3 | 10.3 | 0.0 | 0.9 | 3.6 | 26.0 |
| 1970 | 19.0 | 23.5 | 15.0 | 9.5 | 1.5 | 0.6 | 6.4 | 24.5 |
| 1975 | 24.8 | 18.4 | 16.4 | 8.4 | 1.2 | 0.6 | 5.7 | 24.5 |
| 1980 | 26.7 | 21.7 | 14.7 | 7.3 | 1.2 | 1.4 | 3.1 | 23.9 |
| 1985 | 29.4 | 19.5 | 14.9 | 9.6 | 1.8 | 1.9 | 2.1 | 20.8 |
| 1989 | 30.8 | 21.0 | 14.0 | 11.1 | 2.1 | 1.5 | 1.2 | 18.3 |

Source: Ministry of Finance, Zaisei Kaikaku o Kangaeru, June 1989.

Note: Table is re-created from the figure in the original document.

restriction of the total amount of expenditures. During the administrative reform campaign and a few years following it, this ceiling became a most important guideline for the next year's budget. The media reported the MOF's decision for the zero- or minus-ceiling on the ministries' requests as a start in the government's annual budget making. Shifting the emphasis from cutting specific items to controlling the entire budget size, the MOF took the initiative by imposing the ceiling on the budget. In June 1986, a month before the SPCAR proposed it in its "urgent report" (kinkyū tōshin), the MOF announced officially the imposition of the ceiling in its general estimates of the budget size for the 1982 fiscal year. This first presentation in the MOF's general estimate made the imposition of the zero-ceiling closely related to the annual budget making of which the MOF is in charge.[1]

At the same time, the MOF substantially limited the imposition of the ceiling to the scope of the general account (ippan kaikei) after excluding the allocation tax to local government and bond expenditures. The MOF had begun to classify the budget requests from other ministries as categories, using the names of the general expenditures (ippan saishutsu) from the 1980 fiscal year budget.[2] Setting the ceiling on general expenditures meant that the MOF focused on cutting general expenditures, that is, the budget allocated to the particular ministries. The exclusion of the allocation tax to local autonomies and of bond expenditures from subjects under the ceiling was justified, because determinants of these expenditures—financial needs of local governments or the amount of the bonds issued in the past, respectively—were beyond the fiscal authority's control. However, this focus was also consistent with their interest in increasing their influence over other ministries' budgets.

Limiting a range of expenditure cuts to the general account, the MOF publicized the increased amount in the general account as a "result" of the government's effort to abide by the ceiling. This evaluation of the effect of expenditure cuts exempted entirely special accounts, including the government enterprises for specific purposes (i.e., printing, public pension, and so on) and the entitlement programs with their own source of revenue. This had important consequences both economically and politically. First, this exemption enabled the fiscal authority not only to push down the increasing rate of expenditure in that year, but also to conceal the fact that the government had stopped or postponed spending for certain programs and increased the future spending burden. Differing from simple suspension and postponement of the expenditures (which the MOF had also employed as a means to repress expenditures each year),[3] the transfer of the spending burden from the general account to the special account was entirely invisible.[4] Temporary expenditure cuts using the above measure do not appear as annual increasing rates in the budget publicized by the fiscal authority, and hence are sometimes called "hidden bond issuance" (*kakure kokusai*). But this exclusion of special accounts, which serve to underestimate the budget increase, does not attract as much public attention as the exempted items within the general account, for example, defense expenditures, official development aid, public pension, expenditures related to the supply of energy and scientific and technological development, and personnel expenses.

The public finance would have to pay this after attaining the goal of terminating the issuance of deficit bonds. Therefore critics pointed out that the official evaluation of the "effect" of this fiscal reconstruction was exaggerated. But this criticism was disseminated only among those who were familiar with the public financial system and could comprehend its complicated mechanism.

This measure, however, had a more important political consequence. It contributed to the reduction of the annual budget size, which appeared in publicized numbers. For example, in the supplementary budget in the 1987 fiscal year, expenditure cuts by various special measures amounted to ¥3.7 trillion (= $25.58 billion; $1 = ¥144.64 in 1987) in the general expenditure with a reduction rate of about 10 percent (Miyajima 1989b, 22). This was why the MOF maintained a zero-growth level in general expenditures in the initial budget from fiscal years 1983 to 1987. These records gave the public the impression that the government was following the guidelines for fiscal reconstruction set by the SPCAR and making efforts to cut spending. Within the framework set by the MOF, the imposition of the ceiling was identified with the "administrative reform" advocated by the SPCAR. The

MOF rarely reiterated that the SPCAR's ultimate aim was not a spending cut but rather structural reform in the public finance, even though the SPCAR repeated this point in its reports. As a result, the slower rate of decrease in the ratio of bond dependency made the LDP, the special-interest groups, and the general public suspicious of the effect of the expenditure cuts on fiscal reconstruction under the name of administrative reform. The bond dependency ratio of the general account decreased very little from 26.2 percent in the 1981 fiscal initial budget to 25.0 percent in 1984. The negligible effects of the ceiling to reduce issuance of deficit bonds— especially until the 1984 fiscal year—discredited the effectiveness of administrative reform as a means of fiscal reconstruction. Public enthusiasm waned rapidly with no serious attempt to find alternative ways of cutting expenditures and little patience to wait for the ceiling to bring positive returns.[5]

All MOF budgetary policies during this period were aimed at across-the-board spending cuts, while avoiding the SPCAR's intervention into public financial decisions. The MOF clearly defined the meaning of *ceiling*—on what expenditures and in what way it would be imposed and how they evaluated its effects on expenditure cuts through its jurisdiction in the annual budget making.[6] In retrospect, under the economic conditions in the early 1980s, the Japanese government could not eliminate issuance of deficit bonds without a more drastic cut, which was far from politically feasible (i.e., abolition of some basic welfare programs, a 50 percent cut in defense expenditures as the Japan Communist Party proposed, and so on). But the difficulty of terminating the dependence on deficit bonds would not have been impressed on the public as swiftly as it actually was had the MOF, through the annual budget making, not called public attention to the ongoing austerity policy and its ineffectiveness.

### *A Tax Increase despite "Fiscal Reconstruction without a Tax Increase"*

Imposing a ceiling not only symbolized the government's efforts to retrench on the budget, but also gave the MOF a good excuse for a tax increase on corporations. First, the MOF narrowly interpreted Dokō's premise of "without a tax increase" to mean that the government would not increase the tax in the 1982 fiscal year (Andō 1987b, 210–16). The MOF also successfully demonstrated that the government had repressed the budget level by its imposition of an across-the-board ceiling; a tax increase necessary to finance this retrenched budget appeared even more inevitable. Then, the MOF cautiously interpreted the meaning of "without a tax in-

145

crease" as the absence of structural reform to increase tax revenue. This MOF strategy worked well. Facing the "inevitable" issuance of deficit bonds in the 1982 fiscal year, Dokō ended by accepting the MOF's interpretation of "without a tax increase," which substantially allowed for both the rationalization of existing special tax measures and for marginal increases in rates of existing taxes (*NK*, December 22, 1981).

The MOF continued to abolish tax privileges for corporations and to raise the statutory corporate tax rates from the 1982 to the 1984 fiscal year tax system revision. For the 1982 fiscal year revision, the MOF proposed the abolishment or reduction of various special corporate tax measures and new taxes on gambling and advertisements. Though the 1981 fiscal year revision provoked the organized opposition of business associations against the tax increase, the 1982 fiscal year revision resulted in the abolishment of four special tax measures, reduced the benefits given by twenty measures, and increased the tax by ¥350 billion (= $1,405.17 million; $1 = ¥249.08 in 1982) together with the other measures. For the 1983 fiscal year revision, the MOF also proposed the rationalization and abolishment of several special measures in the existing corporate tax system which expected more than ¥200 to ¥300 billion (= $842.1 to $1,263.1 million; $1 = ¥237.51 in 1983) of new tax revenue. The MOF explained that these changes would not run counter to the Nakasone cabinet's major policy aim—"fiscal reconstruction without a tax increase"—because all of the changes aimed at rectifying the inequity and unfairness of the tax burden in the existing system. After reports by both the GTSRC and the LDP TSRC, the tax increase went down to a level of ¥33 billion (= $138.94 million; $1 = ¥237.51 in 1983), the lowest since the 1976 fiscal year, which had been due to strong opposition from business and industries.

In the summer of 1983, both the LDP and the opposition parties began to argue for a significant reduction in income and inhabitant taxes that had been suspended since the 1977 fiscal year. Expenditure cuts under the ceiling and the accumulation of minor tax increases for the last few years had caused ill will toward the LDP government. In addition, all of the parties wanted to implement the popular tax policy. They expected the dissolution of the House of Representatives and a general election, possibly in the winter after a court sentencing of former Prime Minister Tanaka because of his relationship with the Lockheed Aircraft Company.[7] Taking advantage of the parties' demands for an income tax reduction, the MOF planned an indirect tax increase in order to supplement the revenue decreased by an income tax cut. The MOF and Minister of Finance Takeshita began to suggest the possibility of increases in the indirect tax in the 1984 fiscal year.

The Middle-Term Proposal (*Chūki Tōshin*) of the GTSRC recommended, also indirectly, increases in commodity, liquor, and service taxes in order to reduce income taxes.

After the election at the beginning of December, the LDP managed to maintain a majority (268 out of 512) by allying with members of the conservative splinter group, the New Liberal Club, and by accepting the successful conservative independents as party members.[8] At the time, an increase in indirect taxes in the 1984 fiscal year was a fait accompli. The LDP's policy promise of a general election emphasized an income tax reduction for that year (1983) and for the next fiscal year. In the election campaign, all the opposition parties also promised a reduction. The LDP and the government had agreed on an income tax reduction of about ¥1 trillion (= $4.21 billion; $1 = ¥237.52 in 1984) before any substantial discussion of the 1984 fiscal year revision. The MOF revealed the possibility of a revenue shortfall in the 1983 fiscal year, and stated in a meeting of the GTSRC that the government could not expect a natural tax increase in the 1984 fiscal year (*NK*, December 29, 1983). This prospect as presented by the MOF assumed the need for a tax increase in order to decrease the burdens of the income and inhabitant taxes. As a result, finding a new revenue source became a focus in discussions about tax system revision. The MOF tried to implement not only a substantial tax increase of ¥8 to ¥10 billion (= $33.68 to $42.1 million; $1 = ¥237.52 in 1984) by revising the special tax measures for corporations, but also tried to increase the corporate tax rate and to effect a new tax on commodities that had not yet been taxed.

The MOF's proposal to increase the tax burden on corporations surprised business associations, especially Keidanren (the Federation of Economic Organizations) whose president, Inayama, had maintained informal contact with the LDP leaders and had asked for no tax increase. The major business associations were especially opposed to the 1.3 percent increase in the corporate tax rate, the decrease in the deductible ratio of reserve for a retirement allowance, and the increased rate in the petroleum tax. The MOF compressed the tax increases on liquor and commodities to about ¥350 billion (= $1.47 billion; $1 = ¥237.52 in 1984) and the additional corporate tax burden to ¥450 billion (= $1.89 billion).[9] But the business associations were not satisfied with these concessions, and negotiated directly with three top LDP leaders (the so-called *sanyaku*—the two chairmen of the Policy Affairs Research Council and executive committee, and the Secretary General for the withdrawal of the tax increases. The LDP government finally compromised with the businessmen by making the 1.3

percent corporate tax increase a temporary measure for two years, and by rejecting the MOF's proposal for a new commodity tax on office automation electric machines.

The final amount of revenue from tax increases in the 1984 fiscal year was about ¥800 billion (= $3.37 billion; $1 = ¥237.52 in 1984), the second largest amount under the postwar tax system, but still quite moderate when compared to the MOF's original proposal. The 1984 fiscal year revision consisted of tax increase measures that were politically more feasible and technically easier under the existing system.

The 1984 fiscal year revision also included elements of reform trends in many countries at the time: compressing a number of tax brackets and decreasing tax rates. The income tax revision lowered the maximum rate of the progressive structure (by 5 percent) for the first time since the Shoup recommendation in 1949, and pushed up its minimum rate (by 0.5 percent) for the first time since the 1969 fiscal year. The government justified the former measure by comparing the high level of the maximum rate to rates of the United States and European countries. While raising the minimum tax rate in order to secure a financial source to curb the tax burden on middle-level income earners, the MOF avoided a tax increase at all income levels and in all households by increasing various tax exemptions. But these changes benefited the middle- and higher-income classes more than the lower-income classes. This unequal benefit of the revision, as well as the low level of the tax reduction, failed to dispel increased public opposition to a heavy income tax burden.

### Political Consequences of Fiscal and Tax Policies

At first glance, the MOF's budgetary and tax policies during this period appeared to run counter to its interests. The application of a uniform rate of ceiling on the budget requests of other ministries seemed to weaken its control over the budget. First, the ceiling on budget making politically symbolized the SPCAR's power to force the government to cut expenditures. In addition, expenditure cuts resulting from the ceiling increased the other ministries' role in the total budget-making process. The other ministries attempted to preserve more important programs at the expense of less urgent expenditures and volunteered to cut budgets beneath the ceiling imposed on expenditures before the MOF's examination of the ministries' budgets. This situation left the MOF little room to intervene in the budget requests accumulated by the ministries.

In terms of tax policies, the "without a tax increase" campaign prevented the MOF from increasing taxes by reforming the tax system. In order to raise tax revenues, the MOF increased the rates of existing taxes on liquor, stamp duties, and selective excise taxes on commodities,[10] and added new commodities and services on which the selective excise tax would be applied from the 1981 to the 1984 fiscal years. But these policies were not what the MOF had intended. One of the important reasons for the MOF proposal of a general consumption tax was the reformation of the existing indirect tax system, which the MOF regarded as inconsistent. Because of rapidly changing economic activities at the time, the MOF felt that the existing indirect tax was based on an arbitrary rather than objective or justified criterion for choosing commodities and services to be taxed. In this sense, the "fiscal reconstruction without tax increase" campaign seemed to force the MOF to employ measures of tax increase that were counter to its policy aim of consistency in taxation.

In spite of this impression, however, these policies provided better conditions for the MOF to propose the broad-based tax on consumption in the near future. First, the imposition of a ceiling on almost all expenditures impressed upon all politicians and interest groups the shortage of financial resources. The LDP, the opposition parties, and the special-interest groups began to worry that continued spending cuts not only prevented them from asking for new public services, but also threatened their or their constituency's vested interests in existing programs. The proposal to cut expenditures by a uniform rate of ceiling actually transformed public criticism of waste and inefficiency in the administration into apprehension about the possible reduction or elimination of specific programs.

A 5 percent ceiling on public works from fiscal year 1984 (to fiscal year 1987) especially irritated the LDP politicians. For example, in July 1984 Chairman of the LDP PARC, Masayuki Fujio asked Prime Minister Nakasone to change the name of the MOF's general estimate of the budget size from a "ceiling" on the budget requests (*gaisan yōkyū waku*) to a "criterion" for the budget requests (*gaisan yōkyū kijun*). Fujio, who was a strong supporter of public works and related interest groups, did not like the idea that the MOF could set such a strict upper limit on budget requests regardless of the politicians' will. This change of name had no significant effect on budget making, but it triggered the LDP leaders' active support for a tax increase, including a new consumption tax to finance investment expenditures.[11] These LDP leaders' support for the broad-based consumption tax derived from their resentment of the MOF which had strictly ap-

149

plied a ceiling on the budget under the pretext of "fiscal reconstruction." The demand for increasing public works expenditures was widespread among the LDP politicians.[12]

An alternative measure to a tax increase for financing the programs was active fiscal expansion through the issuance of deficit bonds, which some LDP leaders, including Toshio Kōmoto, advocated.[13] The research committee, chaired by Tatsuo Murayama, had an important role in weakening the demands within the LDP for expansionary fiscal orientation. This committee, so-called the Murayama research committee,[14] issued the first report on fiscal reconstruction in the fall of 1984. It rejected an active fiscal policy and easy tax reduction and proposed a tax increase as a solution for fiscal crisis. Tatsuo Murayama, a former MOF bureaucrat who had served as general director of the tax bureau and whose views were very close to those of the MOF, was thus a strong supporter for the MOF within the LDP.[15] Since the chairman of the PARC, Fujio, had promised that three top LDP leaders would respect its report, this committee also contributed to legitimating the tax increase as a measure to finance the budget.

As the LDP was beginning to accept a tax increase, the growing tax burden on corporations that the MOF justified as "inevitable" irritated the business associations that had given the most enthusiastic and influential support to "the fiscal reconstruction without a tax increase" campaign. From the spring to the summer of 1984, Keidanren started an active campaign that accused the government's tax policy of imposing a greater tax burden on enterprises in Japan than in other advanced countries. Keidanren calculated the tax burden on Japanese enterprises under the current tax system, compared this result to cases in other countries, and demonstrated the higher burden of corporate taxes in Japan (Kubouchi 1984). The Federation argued that maintaining the high taxation on corporations would reduce the international competitiveness of Japanese industries, and tried to dissuade the LDP from further corporate tax increases. The MOF, however, argued against Keidanren and pointed out that several of its calculations were inappropriate. The debate about the international comparison of the corporate tax burden involved not only the MOF tax bureau and Keidanren but also economists. While the MOF estimate of actual tax burdens included only statutory tax rates at national and local levels, Keidanren emphasized the inclusion of the effects of special tax measures (tax exemption, credits, and tax deferrals, for example, accelerated depreciation and tax-free reserves) to calculate the effective tax burden on corporations.[16] A cross-national comparison of the tax burden on corporations was difficult because an evaluation of the corporate tax burden depends also on the practice of tax filement and the situation of tax incidence.[17] In any case, this debate showed that Keidanren was concerned that the MOF had concentrated tax increases on business and industries under the administrative reform campaign. Despite Keidanren's antipathy to a major indirect tax in the past, it now worried that the rapidly accumulating burden of corporate and commodity taxes might influence economic activity more adversely than the new tax.

By 1984, there had been no explicit decrease in the budget deficit. Therefore public expectations for administrative reform and expenditure cuts to recover fiscal health also diminished. During this process, the public had reached no consensus on the size of the government.[18] The accumulation of minor tinkering with the tax system in order to supplement the revenue added to public criticism of the tax policy. At the same time, the public began to think that a broad-based consumption tax might be inevitable in the future under tight budgetary conditions. The opinion poll by Jiji Tsūshinsha showed a significant gap between December 1982 and December 1983 in terms of the public perspective on the introduction of a major indirect tax. In 1982, 29.0 percent of respondents expected its introduction in the next year, almost equaling the number (27.0 percent) who did not expect it. However, in 1983, 42.2 percent of respondents expected it and exceeded those who did not (23.3 percent). These results showed the rapidly increasing public attention given the tax question (*Jiji Yoron Tokuhō*, January 1983 and January 1984, respectively). The introduction of a broad-based consumption tax redefined itself as a measure for changing a revenue structure that had impaired the public financial system.

The political consequences of fiscal and tax policies are summarized as follows. The LDP politicians could no longer put up with a shortage of financial resources for public works that would directly benefit their constituencies. The business associations wanted to exchange the concentrated tax burden on industries for other financial resources. If expenditure cuts failed to provide enough resources to prevent added burdens on them, they had no reason to oppose the government's proposal of a new tax. This change of feeling by large-scale manufacturers was in contrast to the continuous opposition to the new tax by small businesses and distributors who feared that the tax would require them to present more information to the tax authority on their business income. As criticism and complaints about the MOF's policy increased, the MOF reiterated that their proposed policy was based on the goal of "fiscal reconstruction without a tax increase." This

151

deflected the censure to the administrative reform campaign, which imposed the ceiling on expenditures without decreasing the issuance of deficit bonds. During this process, with no explicit *political* move, the MOF's policies indirectly and implicitly contributed to discrediting the SPCAR's claim on the fiscal reconstruction.

The above analysis shows that the MOF bureaucrats were far from exercising full control of the political agenda; the major aim of "fiscal reconstruction without a tax increase" during the administrative reform campaign was set by the SPCAR. However, it also demonstrates that the fiscal bureaucrats still had room to influence the political agenda and redefine policy issues to lead to favorable policy outcomes. Fiscal and tax policies that had been authorized by the administrative reform campaign stretched out the MOF's plan to introduce a broad-based consumption tax, but at the same time gradually changed the attitude of the LDP leaders and business associations in favor of the new tax. The MOF's behavior in the early 1980s provides a good example of bureaucratic adaptation to political agendas that were initially out of the bureaucrats' control.

## NEW AGENDA: SHIFTING THE REVENUE RELIANCE FROM DIRECT TO INDIRECT TAXATION

After the 1984 fiscal year revision, Ogura, chairman of the GTSRC, pointed out that the government would no longer finance the income and inhabitant tax reduction by means of an increase in other existing taxes, and argued for the need to introduce a broad-based consumption tax. The GTSRC's critical evaluation of its own proposed policy for the past three years indicated a subtle change in the focus of the tax policy debate. In 1981 the dominant political agenda of "fiscal reconstruction without a tax increase" prevented the GTSRC from even deliberating or studying a new tax on consumption. In 1984 the continuing budget deficit and waning public enthusiasm enabled Ogura to frankly suggest the possibility of introducing the new tax in the future.

The MOF cleared the first obstacle for the proposal of the new consumption tax because of waning public support for a spending cut. It now needed a more positive reason for its proposal. The new agenda set by the MOF was "shifting the revenue reliance from direct to indirect taxation." This was first officially presented when the 1985 Fiscal Year Tax System Revision by the GTSRC proposed the need for a "structural reform including revisions of both direct and indirect taxation" in the near future. During the reform process, the MOF repeatedly cited the revenue statistics of other OECD countries and argued that a composition ratio of direct taxation in Japan's total tax revenue (including the national and local levels) was next to the highest and the ratio of indirect taxation was lowest among the OECD countries.[19]

As early as the beginning of 1983, the MOF also had a vague plan to introduce a new consumption tax with an income tax reduction.[20] Then, the MOF began to admit that feelings of a heavy and unfair income tax burden were widespread among taxpayers. More specifically, the ministry accepted the salaried workers' feelings about heavy income taxation and the business associations' complaint of high corporate taxation compared to other countries. This was the biggest change in the MOF's response to public antipathy to the existing income tax system. The ministry had thus far contended that widespread feelings of tax inequity and heavy burdens among salaried workers were groundless.[21] As already shown, until the mid-1980s, it had also resisted the protests from business associations about a heavy corporate tax burden compared to other countries.[22] But now the MOF began to argue that introduction of the new consumption tax would provide financial resources to reduce individual and corporate income taxation and thus rectify the heavy reliance on direct taxation.[23]

The MOF's new agenda seems very different from its proposal of the general consumption tax in 1979, which was politicized as a tax increase. In this second proposal, however, the MOF's interest in obtaining a stable revenue source did not change. First, the MOF's new proposal to decrease the income tax burden did not mean weakening its concern about securing financial resources. By the income tax reduction, the MOF intended lowering the progressive tax rates, which become nominally high on salaried income taxed at the source: maintaining a high progressive structure was meaningless without comprehending incomes from sources other than salaries and wages as a tax base. While proposing the new tax, the ministry continued to emphasize the tight budgetary condition and repeated warnings of revenue scarcity. Fiscal bureaucrats tried to avoid situations in which the acquisition of financial resources from the introduction of the new tax gave justification for an easy tax reduction and spending pressure, which would overturn the austerity policy set by the administrative reform campaign. In this sense, the MOF's new agenda for the tax reform had an ambivalent relationship with the administrative campaign: while it utilized the administrative reform campaign for illuminating the continuing need

153

for spending cuts, the new tax proposal was certainly against its "without a tax increase" slogan that precluded a structural change of the tax system leading to a tax increase.

Second, the MOF's new aim of shifting revenue reliance from direct to indirect taxation directly underpinned its interest in securing a stable revenue source. Though the MOF presented this shift in revenue reliance as necessary and inevitable, there was no tax theory to support balancing a revenue source between direct and indirect taxation. Miyajima (1989a, 263–64) called this opinion to support more equal revenue reliance between direct and indirect taxations "a view to rectify the composition ratios between direct and indirect taxation in tax revenue (*chokkan hiritsu zeseiron*)," and he showed that it had no support from tax theory. To advocate the need for shifting revenue reliance, the MOF also cited data that showed Japan's exceptionally high reliance on direct taxation. Nor did instances of more dependence on indirect taxation in other countries necessarily provide a compelling reason for Japan to shift the tax burden to indirect taxation.

Consequently, the MOF's emphasis on the need for structural reform derived from some other motive. When a comparison is made between direct and indirect taxation, especially a progressive income taxation and the flat rate of a broad-based consumption tax, the latter provides a more stable revenue source than the former, as already elaborated in chapter 2. In this sense, the new reform aim to shift revenue reliance to indirect taxation was consistent with the MOF's interests.

By the mid-1980s, in two different ways, the MOF influenced the political agenda in favor of the new consumption tax. First, the fiscal bureaucrats effectively demonstrated the continuing budget deficits under the austerity campaign; they discredited the dependence on spending cuts as the only viable fiscal solution. The proposal of the general consumption tax in 1979 failed because it was associated with a tax increase to finance the budget deficit, and cutting expenditures was proposed as a more viable alternative to eliminate the issuance of deficit bonds. Revealing the ineffectiveness of spending cuts as a fiscal solution certainly contributed to the acceptance of the new tax as an effective way to secure tax revenue.

The MOF, however, cautiously avoided politicizing the new tax as a measure for a tax increase. Its alternative political agenda was to shift revenue reliance from direct to indirect taxation to ease a heavy income tax burden. This new agenda situated the new consumption tax as one part of structural reform. The MOF tried to take advantage of political pressures

154

for income tax reduction, but at the same time prevented the tax cut from materializing without the financial means for it. Shifting revenue reliance from indirect to direct taxation was consistent with its interest in obtaining more secure tax revenue in the long run.

The next chapter explains how the MOF's new agenda was transformed by Prime Minister Nakasone's active exercise of political leadership. Exploring this process, it also explains why the second proposal for the new consumption tax was again blocked by public opposition.

# The Tax Reform Proposal in
# the mid-1980s: Uneasy Cooperation
# between Prime Minister Nakasone
# and the Ministry of Finance

As CHAPTER 4 has shown, in the early 1980s the Ministry of Finance implemented fiscal and tax policies that influenced the public attitude to the budget deficit. The continuing budget deficit and the ad hoc tax increase to finance it led to a loss of public confidence in the effectiveness of expenditure cuts as a fiscal solution. The political impact of these policies steered the way for the future proposal of the major indirect tax, which had once been eliminated from the political agenda. The MOF capitalized on the political opportunity to propose the new tax, the so-called sales tax, during Nakasone's administration in the mid-1980s. Despite the MOF's cautious handling of tax issues, however, this second attempt to introduce the new tax was blocked by public opposition. The major reason for this failure was that the tax proposal was regarded as breaking a public promise made by Prime Minister Nakasone at the time: the prime minister had pledged that he would not introduce the major indirect tax during the election campaign.

This chapter interprets this consequence as a result of the unsuccessful coordination of interests in tax reform inside the administration between Prime Minister Nakasone and the MOF. The first section will show that, as a prime minister, Nakasone remained exceptionally aloof from bureaucrats, and that his strong desire to achieve a popular income tax cut worked against the MOF's effort to influence the public agenda in favor of the introduction of the new tax. At the same time, the argument shows that this failed proposal made the MOF prepare for effective compromises with special interests, and that this preparation became the impetus for a swift proposal of a similar new tax, the so-called consumption tax, in the subsequent year.

156

## COORDINATION OF INTERESTS INSIDE THE ADMINISTRATION:

## THE MOF AND PRIME MINISTER NAKASONE

### Different Emphases on Tax Reform by Bureaucrats and Nakasone

In the 1985 fiscal year tax system revision, the MOF proposed to abolish the tax exemption system on savings and to levy a commodity tax on office automation equipment. The opposition from special-interest groups blocked both proposals, but the tax increase, mainly on corporations, amounted to ¥300 billion (= $1.26 billion; $1 = ¥238.54 in 1985) in the 1985 fiscal year revision, which recorded the largest increase since the 1982 fiscal year.

Though the LDP did not support the MOF's attempt to introduce the new excise taxes on commodities, the result of the 1985 fiscal year revision was not necessarily objectionable for the MOF. The revision demonstrated the need for a tax increase despite the upheaval of opposition, and thus prepared the way for the MOF to propose the new broad-based consumption tax as an alternative measure to enhance the revenue.

While the MOF was cautiously moving toward the new tax proposal, another movement for tax reform was brewing inside the administration. At the beginning of December, before the heated debates on the 1985 fiscal year revision, Prime Minister Nakasone proposed structural tax reform for the first time. This proposal was made independently of those made by both the GTSRC and the LDP TSRC, which cited the necessity for such a reform almost at the same time.

Nakasone became the first LDP president since 1970 to win a second term, and he needed a political agenda after administrative reform. Inside the LDP, his faction was not large enough to stabilize his leadership.[1] The declining number of seats in the House of Representatives after the general election in 1983 and Tanaka's great influence inside the LDP also impaired Nakasone's rule. As head of a small faction, Nakasone always attempted to augment his influence inside the LDP by obtaining public support for his proposed agenda. In this sense, his style of leadership—he referred to himself as a "presidential type of prime minister"—was different from that of his predecessors who were attentive to the process inside the LDP and the bureaucracy, and appreciated the importance of consensus making from the bottom up.[2] He actively set a policy agenda, established an advisory council for policy recommendations, and attempted to take the initiative in various policies. This pattern of leadership was popularly called "advisory

157

council politics" (*shingikai seiji*) and "brain-trust politics" (*burēn seiji*). Administrative reform was a prototype of this style:[3] he succeeded in increasing his political influence and becoming a prime minister, even though he had begun to commit to this campaign as a minor cabinet member. Nakasone chose structural tax reform for his last big policy campaign and selected it as one of the "final accounts of postwar politics" (*sengo seiji no sōkessan*).[4]

A structural tax reform had not been enacted after the Shoup Recommendation in 1949, and public criticism of the existing tax system had been growing since the 1970s. The attempt to tackle this problem satisfied Nakasone's political ambition. In proposing the tax reform, he followed the *political* style of Ronald Reagan whose friendship he had often flaunted. At that time the United States under Reagan was planning a drastic simplification of income taxation by compressing the number of tax brackets. Reagan's tax reform advocated the attractive ideals of "fairness," "simplicity," and "neutrality"—and later "growth." Nakasone modified the slogan so as to respond to the Japanese public's demand for tax reform, and advocated "fairness," "justice," and "simplicity," instead. "Fairness" and "justice" were important in order to emphasize that the reform would provide the solution to more than a decade-long public concern about tax inequity. "Simplicity" meant that the reform would reduce the income tax burden by lowering tax rates and decreasing the number of tax brackets as in the U.S. reform.

In this way, aside from the MOF's intention to reintroduce the new tax proposal, Prime Minister Nakasone initiated a tax reform from 1986 to 1987. His proposal was aimed at income tax reduction and supported "revenue neutrality," that is, equal amounts of tax reduction and tax increase in the same reform package. The MOF wished to introduce the broad-based consumption tax at the same time as a reform of income taxation, and decided to join Nakasone's initiative. Although the progressive income tax system had many supporters in the tax bureau,[5] these bureaucrats did not oppose lowering the maximum tax rate and compressing brackets because the existing system had applied the statutory income tax rate effectively only on withheld income. The high progressive structure of the Japanese income tax system before the reforms in the 1980s had been nominal in the sense that incomes from various assets, land, savings, and capital gains had evaded taxation. The bureaucrats became more conscious of this problem as salaried workers became increasingly dissatisfied with the income tax system.

Because the taxes of most salaried workers in Japan are withheld at the source, they felt that a tax inequity existed between them and self-employed workers who submitted their own tax returns. This tax inequity of salaried workers is popularly described as the "9-6-4 (*kuroyon*) problem" in which the three numbers (9, 6, and 4) are regarded as ratios of the taxed incomes to what taxpayers are actually earning (10). This expression illustrates the tax inequity across occupational groups as follows: salaried workers pay taxes on nine-tenths of their actual incomes, self-employed businessmen and farmers pay taxes on six-tenths and four-tenths of their actual incomes, respectively. The criticism is based on suspicions of "legal" tax evasion by self-employed people who determine their own tax exemptions and deductions based on their own assessments of their incomes and those of working family members and of their necessary expenses. Suspicions of tax inequity seem to be verified by the special tax measure legislated in 1973, which allowed small business entrepreneurs to become "quasi-corporations" (*minashi hōjin*) and deduct their own salaries as "deemed salaries" from the net incomes of corporations.[6] The verdict of the supreme court on "the salaried workers' tax suit" in March 1985 confirms that the tax authority could comprehend the income of self-employed people less accurately than those of salaried workers; the verdict also states that efforts to rectify this were necessary for tax equity.[7] Even though no valid analysis exists to prove this vertical inequity,[8] the less accurate understanding of business income of self-employed people was reason enough for the feelings of "unfairness" and "inequity" among salaried workers. Various opinion polls show that, under the existing system, most people felt that the tax burden was heavy and the tax system unfair; that salaried workers were most disadvantaged; and that self-employed people were privileged.[9]

Nakasone tried to use this deeply rooted feeling of tax inequity to formulate a core support group for the tax reform as a whole. Nakasone's emphasis paralleled the MOF's belief that the income tax burden on salaried workers was heavy. The MOF wanted to compress the number of brackets in income tax rates. But it had not planned on such flat income tax rates with few tax brackets, as had been introduced in the U.S. reform that Nakasone supported. In this sense, Nakasone's approach was more aggressive in order to obtain the support of urban salaried workers who now made up a rapidly growing group of voters.[10]

This marriage of convenience between Nakasone and the MOF was therefore built on a fragile base. What was most important for the MOF was the introduction of a broad-based consumption tax to shift dependence on tax revenue from direct to indirect taxes. The income tax reduction remained a secondary part of the ministry's reform design. On the other hand, Nakasone considered the income tax reduction a reform imperative. He did not mind giving up the new consumption tax or was ready to compromise in introducing a more incomplete form of tax on consumption with a narrower tax base. This was why Nakasone often ignored the intentions of the fiscal authority and the tax specialists within the LDP[11] who gave precedence to the introduction of the new broad-based tax on consumption. Despite these differences between the prime minister and the MOF, the tax reform was proposed by the LDP government in the mid-1980s.

### Politicization of Tax Issues and Conflicting Interests

In the 102d Diet session, which resumed in January 1985, the LDP government officially expressed that it would work on a comprehensive tax reform including the revisions of indirect and direct taxes. This statement substantially admitted plans to introduce a broad-based consumption tax. High-ranking MOF bureaucrats also stated that the ministry would present a major plan for tax reform by the next fall and implied the introduction of the broad-based consumption tax in the 1987 fiscal year (*NK*, January 8, 1985). The MOF began to show its support for the VAT as part of the reform (*NK*, January 28, 1985).

At the same time, the MOF formulated several measures for income tax reduction in the 1987 fiscal year: lowering the maximum rate of income tax, decreasing the number of tax brackets, and increasing both the minimum tax rate and the minimum amount of income to be taxed (*NK*, March 23, 1985). But the ministry tried not to arouse public expectations for tax reform because it feared that the income tax reduction would be politicized with no measure to finance it, that is, the new broad-based consumption tax.

Despite the fiscal authority's cautious attitude, Prime Minister Nakasone was eager to appeal to the public by using tax issues. As mentioned above, he announced attractive ideals of tax reform—"fairness, simplicity, and justice"[12]—ideals similar to the Reagan tax reform. Nakasone announced that his proposal for tax reform had been stimulated by the simplification of the income tax structure in the U.S. Treasury's reform proposal the previous fall.[13] He even clarified his plan on the income tax reduction: it would hold down the maximum tax rate (70 percent at a national level at the time) and loosen the progressivity curve in order to decrease the tax rates of middle-aged salaried workers (with an annual income between ¥3 and ¥8 million [= between $12.58 and $33.55 thousand; $1 = ¥238.54 in 1985]).[14]

While Nakasone also stated that he did not intend to introduce "a general consumption tax that would be like a casting net on every stage of transaction," Minister of Finance Takeshita represented the fiscal authority's intention to introduce the broad-based consumption tax. This contradiction in tax reform visions between the prime minister and the fiscal authority became the subject of criticism by opposition parties.[15] High-ranking MOF tax officials asked Prime Minister Nakasone not to reject the VAT as a viable reform alternative. Nakasone qualified his answer later, saying that he did not mean to exclude the VAT from consideration.[16] But Nakasone's subsequent statements involved the same contradiction (Kishiro 1985, 169–72). He continued to say that he did not intend to introduce "a large-scale, comprehensive, inclusive general tax on consumption of multiple-stages like casting a net over the amount of sales." For those who were familiar with tax policies, his definition of a tax that would not be introduced meant precisely the EC-type VAT.

The MOF and the LDP were also in disagreement. Instead of the VAT, which the bureaucrats favored, many LDP members, except those familiar with the tax issue, supported the manufacturers' sales tax, that is, a single-stage consumption tax instead of the VAT. Their support for the manufacturers' sales tax was closely related to opposition by special-interest groups to the VAT. Small and medium-sized businesses, as well as distribution industries, absolutely opposed the VAT because they considered that any tax on consumption would not only increase their tax-filing burden but would also discourage consumption and decrease their profits. In addition, they were worried that the tax authority would investigate their business accounts through the detailed transaction records that the new tax system would require, and this would enhance their compliance with the income tax. The manufacturers' sales tax, which a majority of the LDP dietmen preferred, would apply only to manufacturers and would not influence retailers and wholesalers, many of whom were self-employed small and medium-sized businesses.

Rising opposition from these groups made the business leaders reserve their previously expressed support for the new tax. For example, Noboru Gotō, the president of Nisshō (Japan Chamber of Commerce and Industry), with small and medium-sized businesses among its members, went from acceptance to opposition of the new tax within less than a month (*NK*, January 10, 1985). Nor did Keidanren (the Federation of Economic Organization) agree with the MOF and the LDP in terms of a system design for the new tax. Keidanren, which was the most enthusiastic supporter of the new tax in the business community, preferred the retailers' sales tax, which would have the least influence on manufacturing industries.

Reflecting the sensitive responses of special-interest groups to tax reform expected in the near future, the tax issue gradually became politicized. Certain factors outside the country also fostered politicization of tax reform. The media reported often on President Reagan's tax reform proposal in May. This media attention activated debate on income tax reform, including a simplification of the system such as in the United States. In addition, foreign pressure, especially from the United States, to expand domestic demands, continued and contributed to promoting discussion about a tax reduction, as well as an active fiscal policy.[17] According to an opinion poll by the Management and Coordination Agency (from May to June), the tax issue became the issue of most concern to the public, replacing price policy which had been at the top since 1958 (NK, August 12, 1985).

### A Proposal for "Structural Reform"

The 1986 fiscal year tax revision included only minor changes.[18] Meanwhile, the MOF began to formulate a consensual plan. In 1985 Masaru Mizuno became the general director (kyokuchō) of the tax bureau. This appointment showed that the MOF was beginning to prepare for structural reform that included the introduction of the new consumption tax. Mizuno had planned the general consumption tax six years before. Tsunaaki Ōyama and Mamoru Ozaki had been assigned as secretaries (shingikan) under him.[19] Immediately after the new leadership came to the bureau, the second tax section of the tax bureau in charge of the indirect tax began to deliberate on the details of the reform, and decided the EC-type VAT was the strongest candidate for the new tax (Asahi, December 6, 1986).

During the summer of the same year, the MOF tax bureau formally arrived at a consensus on the major direction of the reform for the 1987 fiscal year, that is, revenue neutrality (equal amounts of direct tax reduction and tax increase achieved by the introduction of a large-scale indirect tax). This decision meant that the MOF began to plan the tax reform under Nakasone's leadership, and accepted his idea for revenue neutrality for the reform package. They no longer resisted a tax reduction if the reform would introduce a new broad-based consumption tax from which they could expect stable revenue in the future.

The tax experts inside the LDP also agreed on the MOF's plan. The Murayama research committee reported that the VAT would be the most appropriate among various types of large-scale indirect taxes. The Ministry of Home Affairs (MHA), whose jurisdiction of supervising local autonomies would be related to tax reform,[20] also reacted positively to the plan.

During this process, the MOF also tried to close the gap between the ministry and the prime minister, but Nakasone showed no signs of cooperating with the MOF on the tax proposal. First, he ordered new GTSRC members to be chosen from the private sector rather than from the official world for deliberation in September. Ten new special members were selected under the prime minister's close supervision. [21] He decided that the GTSRC should propose a tax reduction only in the interim report for the spring, and recommend the tax increase in the final report in the fall. Because the election of the HC would be held in the summer, this procedure meant that the report on tax reduction was arranged to precede the election and the report on the tax increase was to follow the election.

The MOF feared that Nakasone's strategy to highlight the tax reduction would result in a failure to introduce the VAT. The bureaucrats felt that the revenue neutral reform would be difficult if the electoral campaign were to increase public expectation for a tax reduction.[22] Some LDP members familiar with fiscal policies concurred with the MOF's position.

Resisting Nakasone's promotion for a tax reduction, the MOF displayed a pessimistic estimate of future financial conditions and reiterated the impossibility of implementing a reduction only, without an increase to finance it. Before the 1986 fiscal revision, the MOF publicized, in an unusual statement in the GTSRC, that the tax revenue in the 1985 fiscal year would be smaller than estimated (by ¥300 to ¥500 billion [= $1.26 to $2.1 billion; $1 = ¥238.54 in 1985]) (*NK*, December 3, 1986).[23] In the "Interim Prospect of the Public Finance" (*Zaisei no Chūki Tenbō*), which was submitted to the Diet on January 31, 1986, the MOF stated its estimate that maintaining the current level of expenditure would produce a revenue shortfall of ¥6.08 trillion (= $36.08 billion; $1 = ¥168.52 in 1986). It pointed out that to achieve the government goal of eliminating the issuance of deficit bonds in the 1990 fiscal year would require choosing either to decrease public services or to increase taxes.

The GTSRC's interim report on April 25, 1986, symbolized the government's ill preparation for the tax reform; the prime minister and the MOF's new broad-based consumption tax continued to differ in their emphases on tax reduction. The content of the report was ambiguous. First, following an order from the prime minister, the report did not mention financial measures of tax reduction—the new consumption tax and the tax on savings, that is, the revision of the "Maruyū" system—both of which the GTSRC had already begun to deliberate. This incomplete report on financial measures led directly to ambiguity in the expected size of the tax reduction. Though the MOF accepted the prime minister's order to put more emphasis

163

on tax reduction, it refrained from showing its expected size in order to prevent public expectation from growing. In February, well before the report, the MOF made a detailed plan for direct tax reform[24] and the plan was reported to and accepted by Prime Minister Nakasone (*NK*, February 5, 1986). But the GTSRC report did not include any implication of the size of the tax reduction. In order to avoid making the reduction a fait accompli with no way to finance it, the MOF tax bureau, as a secretariat of the GTSRC, excluded the size of the tax reduction from the interim report.[25] The LDP TSRC's report was similar to that of the GTSRC.

Because of the ambiguity of the reform plan, the interim report failed to raise public expectation as Nakasone had intended. According to an opinion poll by *Asahi Shimbun* in May 1986, only 9 percent of respondents expected that the tax system would improve by the reform under consideration. Twenty-three percent of respondents answered that they did not expect it, and 13 percent regarded it as simply a measure by the governing party to obtain more electoral support (*Asahi*, May 31, 1986). Judging from this opinion poll immediately after the interim report, the public did not expect that tax inequity would be rectified by "the first fundamental reform since the Shoup mission," as the Prime Minister had called it. One more result to be noted in the opinion polls was a decreasing rate of opposition to the so-called large-scale indirect tax. The same poll by *Asahi Shimbun* reported 57 percent opposition to and 25 percent support for a large-scale indirect tax. Twenty-five percent of the support rate meant a significant increase when compared to the less than 10 percent acceptance rate at the time of the proposal for a general consumption tax in October 1978.[26]

After serving as a host in the Tokyo summit in May, Prime Minister Nakasone dissolved the House of Representatives on June 2. Simultaneous elections of both houses, the HR and the House of Councillors, were scheduled for July 6. Popular support for the LDP had increased steadily since December 1983 when Nakasone decreased his party's seats in the HR, immediately after the former prime minister Tanaka was pronounced guilty of his involvement in the Lockheed scandal (see above, chap. 4, n. 7). To extend his term as LDP president,[27] Nakasone needed his party's victory in the elections. The simultaneous elections were considered an advantage for the LDP, which could finance the elections of both houses. A big gain by the LDP in the elections in the summer of 1980 seemed to have proven this.

As the elections approached, the tax reform became one of the big issues in the campaign,[28] even though the LDP did not include tax reduction as a policy promise. One reason was that the opposition parties, pointing out the ambiguity of the financial measures of tax reduction being presented, began to accuse the LDP of hiding a tax increase behind the tax reduction plans. The opposition parties mistook the disagreement the prime minister was having with the MOF and related LDP members as the government's conspiracy to conceal its intent to increase the tax until winning the election by promoting the income tax cut.

With disagreement inside its own government, the LDP was far from adept at responding to the opposition's criticism. Some LDP leaders drove Nakasone into a difficult situation by expressing overt support for a tax increase that contradicted the prime minister's emphasis on tax reduction. The LDP PARC chairman, Fujio, who had argued for the necessity of a tax increase, expressed strong support for the abolition of the Maruyū system (another major aim of tax reform) and showed positive views about the large-scale indirect tax (*NK*, June 6, 1986).[29] Even though Fujio later modified his statement, the opposition parties picked up Fujio's words as an expression of the government's support for the tax increase, and began to require that the LDP hold public discussions on the tax issue. Nakasone tried to quell public suspicions by saying that he would "not introduce a 'large-scale indirect tax' that the people and the party opposed." This repeated verbal commitment temporarily extricated him from trouble, but was destined to work as a severe constraint on the government to propose the new broad-based consumption tax, as the next section explains.

### The MOF's Efforts to Persuade the Prime Minister

The election result was an overwhelming victory for the LDP. The LDP obtained 300 of 512 seats in the HR, and 72 of 126 seats in the HC. All the national newspapers (*Asahi*, *Mainichi*, *Yomiuri*, and *Sankei*) had anticipated the LDP's majority in the elections, but the LDP's win far exceeded their predictions. The politicization of the tax reform had had no direct adverse effect on the election for the LDP.

Before the third Nakasone cabinet began on July 22 with Diet nominations, three new LDP leaders—Abe, Takeshita, and Miyazawa, who intended to take office after Nakasone—decided to extend Nakasone's second term, at least until the passage of a bill to reform the national railway in an extraordinary session in the fall. In his extended term, tax reform became an important political issue. Nakasone also wanted to obtain consent to extend his term by using the tax reform, since it would be a big enough job to require another term for his cabinet.[30]

Nakasone tried to secure cooperation for the tax reform from all the leaders in his new cabinet and the newly selected LDP leadership. He assigned

165

them to positions closely related to the tax reform, that is, Abe as chairman of the LDP executive committee, Takeshita as LDP secretary general, and Miyazawa as minister of finance. The LDP formally decided, on September 11, on a one-year extension of Nakasone's term, and the following day in a policy speech at the beginning of the extraordinary session, the prime minister announced his intent to reform the tax system. The prime minister's strategy of putting a tax issue on the political agenda had achieved one of his important objectives—to stay in office. His next objective was to enact a large, popular tax reform under his leadership.

During the election campaign, Nakasone highly praised the U.S. tax reform as a drastic policy change, and, at the same time, stated that such a decision would not result from bureaucratic decision making (*NK*, June 29, 1986). Three days after the election, Nakasone asked the MOF to abide by his election pledge not to introduce a large-scale indirect tax (*NK*, July 10, 1986). He also asked Masayoshi Itō, chairman of the LDP PARC, to assign Sadanori Yamanaka, a member of Nakasone's faction, a chair in the LDP TSRC. Yamanaka was known to have a strong political arm, with influence over the MOF as a tax expert, even though he had not been very close to Nakasone. Even though chairmen of the LDP TSRC usually came from the same faction as the head of the PARC, Nakasone had avoided asking for a tax council chairmanship for one other candidate, Tatsuo Murayama, who was a member of the same Miyazawa faction as Itō and was a former bureaucrat.[31] This selection demonstrated Nakasone's intention to weaken bureaucratic influence in the tax reform.

Immediately after the election, on July 18, the small expert committee of the GTSRC reported on three alternative plans for the proposal of new indirect taxes. These alternatives included a system that the special-interest groups were more likely to accept, as well as the plan the MOF supported. They were (1) a manufacturers' sales tax that would apply to sales of all manufactured goods except the transaction of raw materials, other goods in the production process, and machinery; (2) a sales tax with exemptions for interfirm transactions, which was similar in principle to a retail sales tax; (3) a Japanese-style value-added tax that would be similar to the EC-type VAT taxed on the added value of goods and services at every stage of a transaction. The adjective "Japanese-style" was added to the third alternative plan in order to show that consideration for Japanese commercial customs was being included in the system. Concrete measures had not yet been specified.

The GTSRC's final report, which was submitted to the prime minister on October 28, clarified for the first time the amount of tax reduction—¥2.7

trillion (= $16.02 billion; $1 = ¥168.52 in 1986) of inhabitant and income tax reduction by decreasing the tax brackets and ¥1.8 trillion (= $10.68 billion) of corporate tax reduction by lowering the effective tax rate below 50 percent. But the report still remained unclear about a tax increase. It listed two alternative plans for about a ¥1 trillion (= $5.93 billion; $1 = ¥168.52 in 1986) increase by the abolition of tax exemptions for small-lot savings. In terms of a new indirect tax, yielding about ¥4 trillion (= $23.74 billion) of revenue increase, the report did not decide the type of tax that should be introduced; it showed a preference only for the Japanese-style VAT. The MOF had already known that only the Japanese-style VAT could raise as much revenue as ¥4 trillion, but had not been eager to include in the GTSRC report the crucial decision on the type of system. This procedure was quite different from the proposal of a general consumption tax in 1979 when the GTSRC took the initiative in the proposal.

The MOF bureaucrats could not reflect their preference for the VAT in the GTSRC report for two reasons. First, Prime Minister Nakasone's repeated promise and the pledge of many LDP candidates not to introduce "a large-scale indirect tax" made it difficult for the MOF to propose a multistage consumption tax such as the VAT. Prime Minister Nakasone supported the manufacturers' sales tax in order to maintain consistency between the tax reform plan and his past pledges and statements that had explicitly denied the introduction of a multistage consumption tax such as the VAT.

Second, special-interest groups strongly opposed the new broad-based consumption tax, although different industrial sectors and groups targeted their opposition to different types of the broad-based consumption tax. Conflicting interests among them became apparent when the GTSRC heard the testimonies of nine people on August 22. Eiji Suzuki, chairman of Keidanren, expressed support for the Japanese-style VAT and opposition to the manufacturers' sales tax. Keidanren's support meant that large-scale manufacturers, especially several industries (auto, electricity, and so on) whose products were taxed, accepted the VAT. They shelved the retail sales tax, which was better for their interests, and decided to cooperate with the MOF in order to avoid the worst alternative for their interests, the manufacturers' sales tax. However, Noboru Gotō, the head of the other major business association, Nisshō, opposed the Japanese-style VAT in the interests of the small and medium-sized businesses among its members. The representatives from the distribution industries not only opposed the new tax but also criticized Keidanren for presuming the introduction of a large-scale indirect tax and pushing the Japanese-style VAT. Even within the

GTSRC, the third special commission split into two groups—one supporting the manufacturers' sales tax, the other the Japanese-style VAT.

The tax bureau quickly responded to this situation and began a "five hundred people pilgrimage"—bureaucrats, from the level of assistant director and up, visited as many as five hundred persons, including all the LDP Diet members, important members of the opposition parties, executives of four major business associations, and top leaders of the distribution industries who had shown stiff opposition to the new tax. Even though the tax bureau's general director, Masaru Mizuno, emphasized that they were going to listen to people's views on tax reform, the bureaucrats actually tried to persuade others of the value of the Japanese-style VAT and to get an informal consent for it. They began their mission with a visit to the prime minister immediately after the simultaneous election (*NK*, July 15, 1986).

Until the GTSRC's final report, the leaders in the LDP TSRC leaned toward the introduction of a Japanese-style VAT, which most tax experts had already supported (*NK*, October 16,1986). Also, the MOF had already obtained support for this plan from LDP leaders Takeshita and Fujio. Therefore, the MOF's immediate task at this stage was to persuade Nakasone to accept it.[32] The prime minister was still going his own way on tax reform. On September 4 he ordered the MOF administrative vice minister, Akira Nishigaki, and the general director of the tax bureau, Masaru Mizuno, to "study further his statement made during the election campaign," that is, his election pledge not to introduce a large-scale indirect tax (*NK*, September 5, 1986). On October 7 Shunpei Kumon, one of the special members elected by Nakasone, told the press that support for the manufacturers' sales tax was most dominant in the GTSRC. Even though he withdrew this statement the next day, the mass media reported that the government had begun to incline toward the introduction of a manufacturers' sales tax. When Nakasone talked about the tax reform with three leaders of the LDP TSRC (the chairman, Sadanori Yamanaka; the acting chairman, Tatsuo Murayama; and chairman of the small committee, Ganri Yamashita) on October 18, he asked them to abide by his election pledge (*NK*, October 19, 1986). On the twenty-seventh, in a video-taping for a television broadcast, he indicated that he could be in charge of the final decision on the large-scale indirect tax were the LDP TSRC not to reach a consensus on it (*NKE*, October 27, 1986). In a meeting with the newly elected LDP Diet members on the twenty-eighth, he repeated his original idea that tax reduction would precede a tax increase. He stated: "Thus far, the MOF has taken the lead in policies; as a result, the politicians have been killed." He quoted examples of Ōhira's sudden death in the political turmoil after the LDP's electoral loss, which could be attributed to the proposal of the general consumption tax. He also mentioned Suzuki's resignation, which followed his cabinet's broken promise to eliminate the deficit bonds in the 1984 fiscal year under the MOF's austerity policy. He emphasized that he would not be killed and instead would exercise political leadership (*NK*, October 29,1986).

*How Nakasone Backed Down*

From the beginning of November, however, Nakasone began to change his attitude and to indicate that the Japanese-style VAT would not be counter to his election pledge. He made his first formal statement about this in his answer to a question posed by the JSP in the Diet. He qualified his past statement by saying that it left open the possibility of introducing a Japanese-style VAT that would exempt some distributors.[33] There were three reasons for his change of attitude. First, the Japanese-style VAT was the only measure among the three alternatives of the broad-based consumption tax to raise enough revenue for an income tax cut as large as Nakasone desired. According to the MOF's reform plan from the 1986 to the 1989 fiscal year, which had already been made in late September and officially shown in the GTSRC report,[34] the new indirect tax would have to provide financial resources for a tax reduction that would amount to about ¥4 trillion (= $23.74 billion; $1 = ¥168.52 in 1986). A manufacturers' sales tax that would be levied on the sales of manufactured products at one stage could not raise as much revenue.

Second, the chairman of the LDP TSRC, Yamanaka, supported the Japanese-style VAT. Nakasone expected that his strong political ally would be impervious to the MOF's influence and the special interests' pressure, but Yamanaka acted independently of the prime minister himself. Yamanaka turned out to be a more ardent supporter for financing the deficit-ridden budget by a tax increase than the MOF.[35] Proud of his tax expertise,[36] Yamanaka could not support the manufacturers' sales tax which he believed was a less consistent indirect tax system than the Japanese-style VAT. He had wanted to increase the tax revenue as a solution for fiscal deficits, but he had already compromised with Nakasone by making the reform revenue neutral. Therefore, Nakasone could no longer urge Yamanaka to support the manufacturers' sales tax, which might lead to a net tax reduction.

Politically, a more important reason was that some LDP leaders attempted to reinterpret the prime minister's election pledge as being consistent with the introduction of the VAT. New leaders, who were the prime minister's heirs-apparent, were especially eager to help Nakasone evade censure for the breaking of his election pledge even if he were to accept the Japanese-style VAT. They wanted to complete both a tax reduction and an increase under his leadership. They were afraid that Nakasone's insistence on a tax reduction before a tax increase would result in leaving only the latter to a future cabinet. In his statement in a press interview, Takeshita, the LDP secretary general, said that Nakasone would not abide by this election pledge if the party decided on the Japanese-style VAT (*NK*, October 22, 1986). Miyazawa, the minister of finance, contended in the Diet that the new tax would be consistent with the prime minister's election pledge if it had a limited influence over the people by restricting the number of tax-filing units and the range of transactions on which the tax would be applied (*NK*, November 6, 1986).

Fourth, there was stiff business opposition to the manufacturers' sales tax that Nakasone supported instead of the VAT. Major business associations, especially from Keidanren and Dōyūkai, increased pressure on the prime minister. Newspapers reported direct negotiations on this issue between the prime minister and the leaders of Keidanren.[37]

After Nakasone changed his mind on December 5, the LDP TSRC managed to reach a decision on the direction of major reform. This included the introduction in January 1988 of a Japanese-style VAT, which was named a "sales tax," the abolition of a tax-exemption system on small-lot savings (Maruyū system) in October 1987, as well as corporate and income tax reductions.[38] These results meant that the MOF succeeded in obtaining formal approval from the LDP government on two policy objectives that had been sought for almost a decade, that is, the introduction of the broad-based tax on consumption and services, and the abolition of the tax-exemption of savings' interest (Maruyō system).

### Background of the LDP Decision on the Sales Tax: Latent Opposition

In retrospect, especially considering the public uproar against the sales tax that occurred later, it was curious that the LDP had made the formal decision to introduce it without much difficulty. A majority of 244 members of the LDP TSRC[39] preferred the manufacturers' sales tax because the small and medium-sized businesses and distributors in general formidably opposed the Japanese-style VAT.[40] There were several reasons why, at this stage, the LDP decided on the sales tax that was to be blocked ultimately by the opposition inside as well as outside the party. First, the abolition of the Maruyū system (the system that allowed tax exemption of interests on small amounts of savings) attracted more attention from the LDP members. Conflicting interests in both the private and public sectors had politicized the abolition of the Maruyū system for the past several years.[41]

This time, the leading politicians specializing in postal policies—the so called postal tribe (*yūsei zoku*), especially Shin Kanemaru in the Takeshita (previously, Tanaka) faction[42]—came to support the abolition of the Maruyū system. In addition, the banking industries, which had previously opposed it, now accepted the abolition of the tax-exemption system with the condition that they receive equal treatment with the post offices. The MOF showed the Ministry of Posts and Telecommunications (MPT) the direction its compromise would take: it would give a part of the right to invest funds in securities to the MPT instead of abolishing the system. Then, joined by the LDP postal tribe (including Takeshita, Keizō Obuchi, and Ichirō Ozawa), both ministries formulated a compromise plan. However, backbenchers and junior members of the postal tribe[43] resisted the opposition until the final decision reached by the three party leaders.[44] Thus, at this stage, the Maruyū issue absorbed a lot of energy for the reform inside the party.

The second important factor that contributed to repressing opposition to the sales tax was the exclusion of junior members from discussion in the LDP TSRC small committee. Yamanaka held deliberations within a small circle of people until the plenary session of the council on October 30. A small number of leaders participated in the discussion of the small committee on tax reform headed by Ganri Yamashita, which was usually open to all the members. These leaders included Yamanaka and Murayama as chairman and acting chairman of the LDP TSRC, respectively, fifteen vice chairmen[45] including Yamashita, two secretaries,[46] seventeen chairmen of all the division committees, and two chairmen of the special committees of the PARC. Even though the members of the small committee included the major figures of the opposition groups to the new tax, for example, Ken Harada and Jun Shiozaki as vice chairmen, the closed discussion helped decrease interruption in the formulation of the reform plan which otherwise came from the opposition side. Growing pressure from the backbenchers to participate[47] forced Yamanaka in November to open the deliberations of the small committee to all the LDP TSRC members. The committee met quite intensively twice a week in November and every day in December until the decision on the fifth, but during this period, supporting opinion for the tax reform dominated opposition.

Third, disciplined behavior on the part of the LDP leaders temporarily quelled existing opposition inside the party. Two opposition groups had begun to study an alternative to the tax reform in order to oppose the new tax proposed by the MOF. One was the "Study Group on the New Tax System" (*Shinzei Kenkyūkai*), made up of forty members of first- to third-term dietmen of the HR and those who were members of the HC since 1980. The other was the "Dietmen's Study Group on Fiscal Reconstruction" (President Ken Harada, *Zaisei Saiken Giin Kenkyūkai*)—a reorganization of the "Dietmen's Conference on Fiscal Reconstruction," which had been organized at the time of the proposal of the general consumption tax (*Asahi*, October 22, 1986). This organization had already recruited more than 300 members from both Houses, 153 of them having attended the meeting on November 21 which passed a resolution that the LDP should keep President Nakasone's election pledge and oppose "the large-scale indirect tax"[48] (*NKE*, November 21, 1986). In addition, the Federation of Diet Members in the Big Cities (*Daitoshi Giin Renmei*) voted in the party head-quarters on the opposition to the new tax, and emphasized that they would have to abide by LDP President Nakasone's election pledge (*NK*, December 3, 1986). To repress these opposition movements inside the LDP, the leaders of each faction met individually with members who opposed the reform, and held meetings on the tax reform (*NKE*, December 2, 1986) in order to prevent them from expressing stiff opposition in the LDP TSRC meetings.

Fifth, the opposition parties that had already been allied against the LDP could not focus their criticism on the sales tax. In mid-December, the Clean Government Party worked to make an alliance bridging the Japan Socialist Party and the Democratic Socialist Party. They were also joined by the Social Democratic League (SDL). The opposition parties had learned from the fact that their numerical weakness and lack of cooperation had allowed the LDP to enact several important bills in the past Diet session, and decided to strengthen their cooperation.[49] However, they did not recognize that they could get the biggest political gain from concentrating their opposition to the sales tax rather than the abolition of the Maruyū system. They had not yet realized that the opposition to the sales tax would obtain the most public support.[50]

Sixth, special-interest groups that had formerly provided active opposition became more interested in winning special tax measures and exemptions for their industries and businesses instead of blocking the new tax itself. This process will be described later.

Elaboration of the process thus far showed that the MOF spent much time and energy during the early stages of tax reform to persuade the prime minister to agree to the sales tax and to reach a consensus on abolition of the Maruyū system which was first politicized. These conditions were more likely to make the MOF bureaucrats underestimate public opposition to the sales tax. Several contingent factors described above seemed to confirm their optimism at the time, and the LDP leaders who supported the introduction of the new tax were far from cautious about the potential opposition. This situation was to change as the government publicized the formal tax reform plan.

### The Proposal of the Sales Tax: Ineffective Compromise

"The Major Line of the Tax Reform" by the LDP and the "Report on the 1987 Fiscal Year Tax System Revision" by the GTSRC were publicized on December 23, and based on them, the LDP government formally decided the "Major Line of the Tax System Revision" (*Zeisei Kaisei Taikō*). The content of the reform was as follows. First, the reform would reduce the income and corporate taxes by ¥4.6 trillion (= $27.30 billion; $1 = ¥168.52 in 1986) for three years. The income tax reduction of about ¥2.7 trillion (= $16.02 billion) would be implemented for the two fiscal years of 1987 and 1988. The minimum amount of taxed income would be raised from ¥500 thousand to ¥1.2 million (= $2.97 to $7.12 thousand; $1 = ¥168.52 in 1986), tax brackets would be reduced from fifteen (with a range of 10.5 percent to 70 percent) to six (with a range of 10 percent to 50 percent). The basic rate of corporate tax would be reduced from 43.3 percent to 37.5 percent for three years from the 1987 to the 1989 fiscal year, and would result in about ¥1.8 trillion (= $10.68 billion in 1986; $1 = ¥168.52 in 1986; or = $13.05 billion in 1989; $1 = ¥137.96 in 1989) of reduction. In 1987, the first fiscal year of the reform, the income and inhabitant tax reduction would be about ¥1 trillion, and the corporate tax reduction about ¥400 billion. Tax increases by the introduction of the sales tax, as well as the abolition of the Maruyū system, would be the same amount as the reduction. The reform would abolish the tax-exemption system of small-lot savings and the tax on savings interest by 20 percent (15 percent at the national level and 5 percent at local levels) except the savings of the aged above sixty-five, single-parent (mother-child) families, and the disabled. Lastly, a 5 percent sales tax would be levied on almost all the added values of goods and services at every stage of transaction and exchange.

The MOF made two important political compromises for the LDP "Major Line" and the next government's proposal of tax reform, especially in the design of the sales tax. About 87 percent of corporations and distributors whose annual sales would be less than ¥100 million (= $593.4 thousand; $1 = ¥168.52 in 1986) would not need to file taxes, and would also have an option of paying taxes based on much simpler calculations in order not to exclude the tax-filing corporations from the transaction.[51] This measure could be regarded as "special consideration" in order to alleviate their opposition. The MITI and a group of Diet members representing their industries' interests, together with the politicians familiar with commercial policies—the so called commercial tribe (*shōkō zoku*), emphasized special consideration for small and medium-sized businesses. Employing a high tax-exemption point was also important within the LDP as a measure to show that the sales tax was not "the large-scale indirect tax" that Nakasone had promised not to introduce. Nakasone himself reiterated that the new tax did not run counter to the election pledge because of this high tax-exemption point (*NK*, December 8, and *NKE*, December 10, 1986).

In addition to setting a tax-exemption point according to the amount of total sales, the MOF suggested seven fields of goods and services to be exempted from the tax. These seven fields were categorized into three groups for tax exemption. Transactions concerning capital goods (lands and securities) and transactions of interest and security fees were exempted because levying the tax on their "consumption" was inappropriate. Food and drinks, and services and goods concerned with medicare, education, and social welfare, were tax exempt because they were goods and services basic and necessary for life. Finally, the goods that were already taxed under the existing excise tax were excluded in order to coordinate the existing indirect tax system with the new system.

Tax-exemption of specific items became the target of the special-interest groups' pressure through hearings by the MOF and discussions in the LDP PARC. Shelving their absolute opposition to the new tax, industries and businesses began to press their LDP ally in order to evade taxation on the goods and services of their sectors. With especially strong pressure from industries and LDP tribes, seven fields increased into forty-three items of exemptions in the LDP's "Major Line." The MOF justified their addition as a result of the specification of the previous seven fields. But some items were pushed into the given fields of tax exemption (for example, fishing boats were classified in the field of food and drinks!). In addition, the exemption spread substantially into items and services, which had not been included before, that is, those connected with transportation, housing and real estate, and cultural activities. At the stage of the bill's formation in the following year, the number of exemptions increased again to fifty-one items. However, while attempts to quell their pressure left special-interest groups dissatisfied, the dispute over tax exemption increased the impression that the new tax system would be the product of political pressure, and thus arbitrary and inconsistent.

Aside from the compromises made in the sales tax system, the MOF gave up implementing several measures they had proposed for the "rectification of tax inequity." In December, increasing business pressure on the LDP blocked the proposal to rationalize two special measures of the corporate tax (the reduction of two tax-free reserves for retirement allowances and bad debts). The LDP also rejected the reduction of a special measure in the quasi-corporation tax system—allowing self-employed people only half the amount of income tax deduction. At the same time, the reform limited the tax deduction of necessary expenses for salaried workers to a few items that would make very little difference. Since the quasi-corporation system had been infamous for tax inequity between salaried workers and self-employed people, failing to include this measure made salaried workers' lose confidence in the reform's appeal for tax equity.

The lack of direct measures to rectify alleged "tax inequity" confirmed the MOF's failure to obtain the salaried workers' support for the tax reform. Since the summer of 1986, the MOF had begun to issue pamphlets, make posters, and appear on television shows to explain the tax reform in the following year. While explaining the tax increase measures (*NK*, November 26, 1986), the MOF tried to emphasize that the tax reform would lower the tax burden on middle-aged salaried workers with spouses and children. The MOF, however, could not convincingly persuade the public to accept the benefits of the tax reduction, because some tax specialists raised doubts about the validity of the MOF's estimates of taxes after the proposed reform. A group of scholars calculated the estimate of taxes that would result from the reform, and showed results that differed from the MOF's predictions. In mid-September, a Policy Planning Forum (*Seisaku Kōsō Hōramu*) estimated the influence of the tax reform, assuming it would contain the same measures as those in the package that the MOF was planning and about which the GTSRC was deliberating.[52] These results were quite different from the MOF's. According to this group, the reform would put more of a tax burden on members of the middle-income class with an annual income of less than ¥5 million (= $29.67 thousand; $1 –¥168.52 in 1986). More than 80 percent of the salaried workers (except civil servants) belonged to this group. It would significantly lower the burden on those in the higher-income group with an annual income of more than ¥6 million (= $35.6 thousand; $1 = ¥168.52 in 1986).

Disagreeing with these results, in mid-October, the MOF presented the GTSRC with its own estimate, which showed a tax reduction for almost all age groups. The conflicting results between the Forum and the MOF came from different assumptions of tax incidence. Masaaki Homma in the Forum, argued that the MOF's estimates were based on unrealistic and unacceptable assumptions, for example, that all corporate tax reduction would quickly benefit households; that about 40 percent of the new indirect tax would become an additional burden on corporations without being shifted to consumers through pricing; that the amount of households' consumption was underestimated and contributed to lowering the burden of the indirect tax (*NK*, October 15, 1986). Almost all the calculations and estimates by the other groups of tax experts, special-interest groups, and journalists were counter to the MOF's calculations and closer to the Forum's in the sense that the reform would not benefit middle-income groups. Immediately before the LDP's formal decision on the tax revision, the Policy Planning Forum again presented the estimate of the reform based on the government's plan. They showed a resulting tax increase for salaried workers' households with an income below ¥6.5 million (= $38.6 thousand; $1 = ¥168.52 in 1986). This result discredited the government's claim of a tax reduction for all salaried workers. Consequently, the public remained suspect about the effect of tax reduction by reform.

## RISING OPPOSITION AND THE DEMISE OF PROPOSED TAX BILLS

Until February 4, 1987, seven bills for tax reform, including the introduction of the sales tax and the income tax revision, were submitted to the Diet. From February to March, an opposition coalition was formed between the opposition parties and retailers, wholesalers, and small and medium-sized businesses who had been traditional LDP supporters. Opposition also came from consumers' groups; further, the government's attempt to obtain the support of salaried workers' households also failed. As local elections approached, the number of LDP local branches that passed resolutions opposing the new tax was growing, and LDP Diet members began to participate on the side of the opposition despite their party leaders' repeated warnings and persuasions.

The first shock came when the socialist candidate won a seat in a by-election of the HC in Iwate Prefecture. The seat had been vacated by the death of Michiyuki Isurugi on March 8. As the first national election after the simultaneous elections the previous summer, this election was regarded as an opportunity to judge public support for tax reform. The LDP had continued to hold this seat in Iwate—the so called heaven for conservatives, and their candidate, Rei Isurugi, was considered likely to receive sympathy votes as the widow of the late Michiyuki Isurugi. Therefore, the record-breaking number of votes for Jin'ichi Ogawa, the socialist candidate (twice as many as for Rei Isurugi) was totally unexpected and was labeled the "Iwate shock." Since Ogawa had emphasized the opposition to the sales tax and won, the "Iwate shock" activated the opposition side.

On April 12, thirteen gubernatorial elections, two mayoral elections, and elections of forty-four prefectural assemblies and nine municipal assemblies were held. The LDP did not win back two crucial gubernatorial seats in Fukuoka and Hokkaidō, and also decreased the total number of seats in prefectural and municipal assemblies by about 10 percent.[53] The opposition parties, encouraged by the results of the unified local elections, delayed the Diet's deliberation by taking their time to cast votes ("cow-walking tactics"), and the tax bills were finally dropped.

The remainder of this section describes the process by which rising opposition killed the tax bills submitted to the Diet.

## Threatening Opposition from Traditional Supporters and Consumers

Starting in January 1987, the LDP government began to make efforts to explain the new tax to the public. The Japanese had been totally unfamiliar with a broad-based consumption tax in general; therefore, a lengthy explanation was needed about the practices of the system. The LDP published a booklet, "Tax Reform (*Zeisei Kaikaku*) Q&A" that concentrated half its pages on the sales tax and also justified the tax reform as not "breaking the election pledge." The LDP reprinted this booklet because fifteen thousand issues of the first printing had been distributed immediately through party connections. This demand was extraordinary for a party publication, and showed that a wide range of people was concerned about the new tax. The JSP published a corresponding booklet, entitled "Big Tax Increase by the Ultimate Means" (*Kyūkyoku no Daizōzei*), which criticized the tax reform and sold 110 thousand issues by the end of January (*NK*, January 30, 1987).

The MOF began to make serious efforts to explain to corporations and distributors the details of the system, the characteristics of the VAT, the use of invoices, and the "shift" (*tenka*) of taxes to consumers through pricing. From mid-January to mid-April, the MOF visited forty-four commercial and industrial organizations in the country for this purpose (*Asahi*, April 14, 1987). The MOF believed that the opposition to the sales tax derived from a lack of public understanding and expected that further explanations about the new tax would weaken the public opposition. However, too little

177

time remained to solve this "misunderstanding." First, the bureaucrats were betrayed by unexpected opposition to the use of invoices. The use of invoices had not been highlighted in discussions either of the GTSRC or the LDP TSRC.[54] The major controversy inside both tax councils had been a choice between two single-stage taxes (the manufacturers' sales tax and the retailers' sales tax) and the VAT, which represented a multistage tax. Public discussion covered by the media had also focused on such a choice. As a result, a majority of self-employed businesses became acquainted with the use of invoices for the first time immediately before the submission of tax bills to the Diet. They were rapidly becoming concerned about the sales tax, which would not only give them more paperwork in filing their taxes but would also increase the possibility of the tax authority's investigation of their compliance with their business income through invoices.

Another unexpected opposition came from the distributors' concern about the tax-shifting problem. The discussion among policymakers thus far had centered on the possibility of an unwarranted price increase that would take advantage of the introduction of the new tax. However, many retailers of various sizes were worried that they could neither levy the tax on prices nor shift it to consumers because of competition in lowering prices. Failing to shift the tax to consumers meant that the retailers would have to pay it at the expense of their profits. The MOF had been totally unprepared for this concern among retailers.[55]

Moreover, two methods of tax exemption resulted in intensifying opposition from manufacturers and distributors. First, the special interests, who had been eager to exempt taxation on their produced goods and services, began to recognize that obtaining tax exemptions did not necessarily guarantee that they were free from the influence of the sales tax. For example, a canned fruit was exempted from the tax but the tax was applied to its container. The manufacturers or distributors might not be able to shift the tax on the container to the price of the canned fruit that was claimed for exemption from taxation. Since the number of tax-exempted goods and services had been enlarged by political pressure, this kind of concern was more salient than before. In this way, even the industries and sectors that had won the tax exemption for their businesses felt betrayed by the government, and were afraid of losing profits.

The tax exemption of distributors whose annual amount of sales in the previous year had been lower than ¥100 million caused a more serious problem. This exemption point was very high compared to the European countries' VAT system.[56] The MOF intentionally set such a tax-exemption point in order to protect many smaller-sized intermediaries within the complicated network of distribution that the introduction of the sales tax might "rationalize." This was a cheap bargaining chip for the MOF because this high tax-exemption point would put a significant number of firms outside the sales tax system, while decreasing revenue very little. Even though 87.7 percent of businesses were exempted from the tax, the revenue loss from this exemption was considered to be only 8.8 percent. However, these smaller-sized wholesalers and manufacturers began to worry about their exclusion from transactions with the larger-sized manufacturers and distributors in a hierarchical and stable transaction relationship (so-called *keiretsu*). The taxed manufacturers and distributors might avoid buying from tax-exempted businesses because the buyers could neither calculate nor subtract the taxes on goods and services at earlier stages of transaction without invoices issued by the sellers. In order to solve this problem, the MOF left for the small and medium-sized businesses the option of filing taxes, and prepared a very generous (actually too compromising) method of simple taxation for tax-filing purposes. Under this system, fixed rates of 20 percent for retailers and 10 percent for wholesalers of the total sales amount would be deemed added values, which would be subject to a 5 percent tax rate. In retrospect, this system was supposed to benefit the small and medium-sized businesses, but at the time they did not understand this, and regarded this procedure as harmful for their businesses.

In this way, while the MOF's efforts to persuade the related interests failed, the opposition become activated. Arguing that the introduction of the sales tax ignored the election pledge, seventy-seven groups of distributors and manufacturers began to appeal to the public through newspaper advertisements (*Asahi*, December 11, 1986). On November 21, in Osaka, the Japan Association of Department Stores (*Nihon Hyakkaten Kyōkai*) decided to oppose any type of large-scale indirect tax, especially the Japanese-style VAT; in Tokyo, the Japan Association of Chain Stores (*Nihon Chain Store Kyōkai*) also expressed absolute opposition (*NK*, November 22, 1986). On the twenty-seventh, the Center Organization for Opposition to the Large-Scale Indirect Tax (*Ōgata Kansetsuzei Hantai Chūō Renraku Kaigi*; hereinafter, Chūōrenrakukaigi),[57] including eleven distributors and textile and clothing industry groups, decided that they would try to obtain 150 signatures from the LDP Diet members opposing the new tax (*NK*, November 28, 1986). This organization, with about six million members and influencing more than twenty million votes, had pushed the LDP candidates to sign an opposition petition.

The opposing groups began to ally with the opposition parties and withdraw their political support for the LDP. On January 26, Chūōrenrakukaigi held an opposition meeting with four opposition parties—the JSP, the CGP, the DSP, and the SDL. In mid-January, cooperation between the opposition parties and the five labor groups was achieved. Moreover, the distributors' group, which had been the LDP's traditional supporter, approached the opposition parties. Many individual distributors' organizations at the levels of prefectures, cities, and towns began to secede from the LDP's local organizations and to decline the recommendation for candidates on the LDP ticket in the upcoming unified local elections. The president of the Association of Chain Stores, Shinji Kiyomizu, a prominent figure on the opposition side, stated on January 20 that he was no longer contributing political funds to the LDP. On the same day, the Association of Department Stores presented a report on the expected influence the sales tax would have on management, and concluded that all department stores of any size would be forced into deficit-ridden management because of the increasing costs of tax filing and the difficulty of shifting all the taxes to consumers through pricing (*NK*, January 21, 1987). About a month later, on February 24, the Association of Department Stores also decided to freeze its contribution to the LDP.

The crucial element in the opposition movement was to achieve unity among distributors, manufacturers, consumers, and labor unions in late February. The Japan Federation of Textile Industries (*Nihon Sen'i Sangyō Renmei*)—including many small and medium-sized manufacturers, the Association of Department Stores, and the Association of Chain Stores—took the initiative and organized the People's Conference on the Tax System (*Zeisei Kokumin Kaigi*) with about four hundred groups of distributors, small and medium-sized businesses, industries, consumers,[58] and labor unions (*NK*, February 25, 1987).

To cope with the deepening opposition of special interests relating to the above three problems, the Chief Cabinet Secretary, Masaharu Gotōda, in a meeting of administrative vice ministers, asked the ministries and agencies to persuade the related interest groups and organizations to accept the sales tax. Nakasone also asked the MITI to persuade the distribution industries to accept the sales tax at the end of January. But the special interest's opposition was already beyond the administration's control.

The prolonged recession due to the rapid acceleration in the exchange rate of the yen also adversely influenced the tax reform. Since late September 1985, following the G-5 conference which had intended to correct the value of the dollar, the yen had sharply appreciated from the level of $1 equaling ¥240 to a level of ¥210. The rapid upward correction of the yen stopped once in the autumn of 1986 at the level of ¥150–¥160, but climbed again to as high a level as ¥130 against the dollar in the spring of 1987. Japan's economy hit bottom in November 1986, then gradually showed signs of recovery at the beginning of 1987, but soon the resumption of the yen's valuation again slowed its pace. The stagnation of exports was a devastating blow to related industries. Among business associations, there had been a disagreement on tax reform. For example, Keidanren principally supported the sales tax and Nisshō opposed it.[59] But at the time, both positions agreed to implement the tax reduction immediately and postpone the introduction of the new tax. They requested these moves of the LDP leaders in late January 1987 (*NKE*, January 27, 1987). The tax reform was also accused of thwarting the expansion of domestic demand, which foreign pressure encouraged by the further appreciation of the yen.[60]

*Revolt of Local Governments and Elements of the Liberal
Democratic Party: The Influence of Unified Local Elections*

The proposed tax reform would decrease income and corporate taxes at the national level; in addition, a liquor tax, the revenue of which financed local allocation taxes, would be decreased and thus the revenue from the new indirect tax would be allocated to the local autonomies. The Ministry of Home Affairs, which had agreed with the MOF on this issue, also had a vested interest in the introduction of the new tax. Observing the active public opposition to the sales tax, the MHA warned against such a movement at the local level through six groups of local governments (the National Organization of Governors, that of mayors, and so on). For example, in a meeting of the National Association of Chairmen of City Legislatures (*Zenkoku Shigikai Gichōkai*), the administrative vice minister of the MHA stated that the local governments could not obtain financial resources from local taxes if they opposed the tax reform (*NK*, August 22, 1986).

The MHA's persuasion turned out to be ineffective in the face of the unexpected refusal of some local autonomies to comply with the national government's tax policy decision. As the local unified elections were approaching, rising opposition among special-interest groups and consumers was gradually pushing the local governments toward opposition, and some of them began to resist including revenue from the sales tax in their budgets. In February, among thirteen prefectures that were waiting for gubernatorial elections, seven began to exclude their revenue allocated from the sales tax in their budget plans for the next fiscal year. Four of these prefectures' governors had been supported by the LDP in the previous elections (*Asahi*, February 11, 1987). By mid-March, forty-two prefectural assemblies had already formed their attitude to the sales tax; among them thirteen passed the opposition resolution and twenty of them required "careful consideration of the introduction" (*NK,*, March 15, 1987).

The LDP's local branches also began to "require careful reconsideration of tax reform" to their national headquarters. In the upcoming unified local elections, they had to rely on the organized support of self-employed people. The most radical opposition came from the Tokyo branch, which had already resolved its opposition to the sales tax the previous fall. In the National Assembly to Promote the Tax Reform (*Zeisei Kaikaku Suishin Kaigi*) on February 10, which the LDP held in order to obtain cooperation from the local party organizations, several representatives of the prefectural branches expressed outright opposition.

Fearing that the local opposition would shatter the fragile consensus among the LDP dietmen, the leadership began to strengthen party discipline. On January 21, the LDP executives confirmed that they would make no concessions to the request to modify the bills. Under the names of the secretary general, Takeshita, and the chairman of the PARC, Itō, the party issued the extraordinary notification that party members, abiding by the party resolution, should neither answer inquiries about the tax reform from the mass media nor sign for the opposition. However, some LDP members who were more vulnerable to pressure from opposing groups expressed noncompliance with the party decision. On February 12, two LDP Diet members participated in an opposition meeting of retailers from their election district in downtown Tokyo, and they expressed their opposition to the tax. In their election district, the organized support of the self-employed was crucial. On the same day, two vice chairmen of the LDP TSRC (Kabun Mutō and Jun Shiozaki)[61] hinted at the modification of the sales tax bill in a meeting with representatives of the national retailers' organization. In a meeting held the following day, the party leaders managed to agree on persuasion instead of immediate punishment for the vice chairmen.

*Opposition Parties*

The Diet session resumed on January 26, 1987. The MOF had no other choice except to entrust the passage of the bill to the LDP leadership as public opposition increased. Besides the bills involved with the tax reform, the ministry included a bill to remove the 1 percent ceiling of the GNP on defense expenditures, as well as a budget bill that aimed both to help the Japanese economy recover from the recession and to expand the domestic demand. Facing the termination of his extended term in October, Nakasone was anxious to pass all the cabinet-sponsored bills. The LDP leaders, including new leaders and their mentors, wanted to decide on these policies as well as the unpopular tax reform under Nakasone's cabinet. However, the LDP was slow in working out a compromise with the opposition parties. The Takeshita (previously, Tanaka) faction, which usually managed to compromise through their strong connections with the opposition parties, did not move until the last moment; they were worried that the tax issue would hurt Takeshita's political fate as a candidate for their faction for the next prime minister.

In the 108th session, the opposition parties effectively maintained their solidarity in opposition to the government, while the incumbent LDP was suffering from intraparty opposition. Several reasons accounted for the opposition parties' solidarity. First, they could concentrate on the tax bills that they opposed. Although they could not agree on one important issue—the removal of the 1 percent ceiling on defense expenditures, this issue was assigned secondary importance to the tax issue.[62] They opposed the abolition of the tax exemption on savings and the introduction of the sales tax, and supported the income tax reduction.[63]

Second, the opposition parties could resort to boycotting deliberations to drive the LDP to give up the tax bills. The Diet stopped functioning at the beginning. Once again, the opposition parties refused to participate in the Diet deliberations after the LDP's majority decided to open the budget committee of the HR without obtaining the opposition parties' acceptance. Their boycott continued for one month after the beginning of February. The opposition parties' refusal to attend the Diet involved some risk of arousing public criticism that boycotting deliberations constituted irresponsible behavior on the part of representatives. But at the time, rising opposition outside the Diet considered the opposition parties' behavior an effective strategy for resisting the LDP's numerical strength. The opposition movement inside the LDP also encouraged these parties to continue boycotting the Diet deliberations.

Third, the opposition parties could use the passage of the government's budget bill to induce the LDP to compromise on tax issues; the LDP government needed to pass the budget bill in the HR before Nakasone's visit to the United States on April 29 in order to show "Japan's effort to expand domestic demands by public expenditure." The "Iwate shock" in March confirmed that the opposition parties were on the right track.

The last factor that fostered the opposition parties' solidarity was timing. In the unified local elections on April 12, the LDP's loss was apparent; so, in this sense, the opposition's strategy was working. This loss also proved that the resistance to the LDP's tax reform benefited the socialists much more than the others. The CGP and the DSP began to reconsider the effect of the opposition's cooperation on their electoral fortunes.[64] However, they continued their solidarity because they were about to make a big political gain by killing the cabinet-sponsored tax bills.

### Compromise after Political Turmoil

In retrospect, the special-interest groups' strong opposition movement was not necessarily attributed to one clear disadvantage expected under the new system, nor did they share consistent criticism of the government's proposal. However, these various opposition movements could agree on the censure of Nakasone's election pledge. This was also why the opposition parties effectively attacked the government. This criticism became a strong driving force for the opposition because it was the most easily understood way to illegitimate an unfamiliar new tax.

Among the postwar cabinets, Nakasone's cabinet had thus far enjoyed record-breaking popularity in terms of its continuity and level, but the tax issue destroyed this popularity. According to a Jiji Tsūshinsha opinion poll, the popular support rate for Nakasone's cabinet dropped sharply from 43.4 percent in July 1986, around the time of the simultaneous elections, to 25.9 percent in March 1987, immediately before the decision to drop the proposal of the sales tax, while the nonsupport rate was rapidly rising from 33.0 percent to 53.3 percent during the same period. An opinion poll by *Asahi Shimbun* in late March showed that 82 percent of the people opposed the sales tax and 74 percent felt that the tax was counter to the prime minister's public promise. Nakasone could not go on a stumping tour for the unified local elections because no local branches of the LDP welcomed him as a result of his cabinet's great unpopularity.

While many LDP leaders began to consider a "flexible" response to the opposition, that is, amending or killing the tax bills in this Diet, Nakasone became one of the few hardliners for the sales tax.[65] Reflecting on the prime minister's intentions, at a meeting on March 19, six LDP leaders,[66] Minister of Finance Miyazawa, and Chief Cabinet Secretary Gotōda continued to take a resolute attitude toward the passage of both the budget and tax bills.

To break up the impasse caused by the opposition parties' persistent refusal to attend the deliberations, the LDP requested of HR Chairman Kenzaburō Hara, as a compromise with the opposition parties, that the sales tax bill be entrusted to his care.[67] In the Japanese Diet system, the chairmanship was considered a neutral post: a newly elected chairman selected from the incumbent party (the LDP) would secede from that party and a vice chairman would usually be selected from the largest opposition party (at the time Shinnen Tagaya from the JSP). The opposition parties therefore welcomed the LDP's action as a sign of compromise. After the LDP took a vote on the budget bill in the HR budget committee on April 16, they began to seek a compromise plan. On the twentieth, after meetings of the chairmen of the party Diet affairs committees, the secretaries general of the LDP and opposition parties deliberated on a plan for mediation by Hara. Even though the LDP secretary general, Takeshita, once decided to accept the opposition parties' request to "drop" the sales tax bills, he was resisted by the prime minister and Chief Cabinet Secretary Gotōda. Thus the compromise failed between the LDP, which tried to save face by "freezing" the bill, and the opposition parties, which had argued for "dropping" the bill. Nakasone accepted the "flexible" response to the bill, but resisted dropping it. The next day, Chairman Hara and Vice Chairman Tagaya also failed to fill the gap between the LDP and the opposition parties. The Diet then went through two days of disorder. On April 21 the opposition parties resisted the LDP's attempt to pass the budget bill in a plenary session of the HR by a majority power. They used the strategy of "cow-walking tactics" for the first time in ten years. The Diet had two all-night deliberation sessions until April 23 with several recess periods, but voted only for two among five motions.

Meanwhile, Kanemaru and Takeshita began to revive the compromise plan that accepted the "dropping" of the sales tax bill, and asked Vice Chairman Tagaya to help put together a compromise with the opposition parties. Many LDP leaders and ministers decided to give full support to dropping the bills after the two-day Diet session. They managed to persuade Nakasone and Yamanaka, while the opposition parties agreed to the concession. Nakasone finally gave up the tax bills. He wanted to have the budget bill pass at least in the HR before his visit to the United States, and thus he needed to compromise with the opposition to the tax reform to achieve his purpose. The 1987 fiscal year budget was alleged to include measures for the expansion of domestic demand, which had been requested by other industrialized countries including the United States.

The points of the final mediation plan that Chairman Hara formally showed to Takeshita, to the secretary general (*kanjichō*) of the LDP, and to the secretary general (*shokichō*) of the opposition parties on April 23 were as follows: (1) all the parties would make a maximum effort for tax reform, including the revision of the revenue share of direct and indirect taxes; (2) a deliberative body represented by all the parties would be established; (3) this body would decide on how to deal with the tax bills in this Diet. The third point was essentially interpreted to mean that the tax bills would be dropped if the parties could not reach agreement during this session. The MOF had been alienated from the whole process of party politics, and the partisan compromise meant that the MOF could do nothing more for the tax bills.

*Aftermath*

The budget bill was finally passed in the Diet on May 21, after the government's finances had depended for fifty days on a provisional budget. On May 27, the 108th Diet session was closed, and all the tax bills were killed with no deliberation on them. This meant that the 1987 fiscal budget was to start without securing about 80 percent of the revenue. Two days before, the Deliberative Body of Tax Reform (*Zeisei Kaikaku Kyōgikai*), chaired by Masayoshi Itō, had been established with representatives of the LDP and the opposition parties—the JSP, the CGP, and the DSP, but not the Japanese Communist Party. Since many bills failed to pass in the 108th Diet, the LDP government decided to convene an extraordinary session for sixty-five days from July 6 to September 8. The prime minister wanted to submit some parts of the tax reform bills in this session and to complete even a smaller scale of the reform before the termination of his extended term. In the interim report of the deliberative body on July 25, the LDP and the opposition parties agreed to implement an income tax reduction before the tax increase. However, they still disagreed on the amount of the reduction and on the measures to finance the tax reduction. After the report the government submitted the tax bills, including a further income and inhabitant tax reduction, a more modest corporate tax reduction in the 1987 fiscal year, and the abolition of the Maruyū system (tax exemption of interests on small amounts of savings). The MOF wanted to include in the bill the final amount of income and corporate tax reduction (¥4.5 trillion [= $31.11 billion; $1 = ¥144.64 in 1987]) in the next two fiscal years to preserve the possibility of a future proposal of the new broad-based consumption tax: such a large tax reduction required a new tax as a financing means. But the LDP thought that the introduction of a new tax in the near future would be difficult, and decided to exclude this final goal from the tax reform bill. The possibility of the introduction of the broad-based consumption tax was getting smaller and smaller during the process of political compromise, and the fiscal bureaucrats were growing more disappointed.

The LDP tried to compromise with the opposition parties with an additional income tax reduction and a special tax exemption for the aged after the abolition of the Maruyū system. On August 26 the opposition parties finally accepted the LDP's offer of ¥1.54 trillion (= $10.65 billion; $1 – ¥144.64 in 1987) of income tax cuts in exchange for the abolition of the Maruyū system. The amount of reduction increased from ¥1 trillion in the previous tax reform bill to ¥1.3 trillion (= $6.91 to $8.99 billion) in the revised bill, and ¥240 billion (= $1.66 billion) was further added as a modification in the Diet. The government made the opposition parties accept the tax reform package by increasing the amount of income tax reduction more than they had previously proposed. In this plan, the minimum taxable income was raised from ¥1.2 million to ¥1.5 million (= $8.3 to $10.4 thousand) and the number of tax brackets was reduced from fifteen to twelve. These modifications changed the income tax structure so that the burden on salaried workers with an annual income of ¥5 million to ¥6 million would decrease more significantly, and the reduction for those earning more than ¥7 million (= $48.40 thousand) would be smaller than the previous government's proposal. In the extended session, the modified tax bills passed in the HC and became law on September 25. The 1987 fiscal year tax system revision was completed, but the introduction of the sales tax had been totally erased from the original plan.

While the proposal of the general consumption tax had been supported only by the Prime Minister Ōhira several years earlier, the MOF enlisted support for the sales tax from LDP leaders and business associations. The MOF successfully led the LDP government to the proposal of the sales tax, but this proposal was blocked by the opposition parties in the Diet backed by public opposition.

Two issues need to be clarified in this case in terms of bureaucratic influence. The first one concerns the role of the LDP politicians who were familiar with tax issues and cooperated with the MOF to negotiate with special interests. For the proposal of the sales tax, the cooperation of leading incumbent politicians was critical, but their role did not overshadow bureaucratic influence. The MOF still retained much control over public discourse over tax reform, which such politicians lacked. For example, the MOF left unclear how much revenue would be obtained from the new tax and in what way the new revenue would be offset by the income tax reduction.[68] This was mainly because of the difficulty in estimating the amount of revenue from a new tax; in the case of the proposed tax reform, the introduction of the sales tax involved merging the existing excise tax on commodities into the new sales tax system (which meant lowering the rates

187

of excise taxes on commodities until they reached the level of the sales tax rate) and then using the sales tax revenue to finance the income tax reduction. Because estimating the effects of such a complicated tax reform on households was so difficult, the MOF feared that the presentation of unreliable data would make the public suspect an increased tax burden after the introduction of the new tax.

This point distinguished the MOF and the LDP politicians who were eager to introduce the sales tax. Whereas the MOF recognized the subjective nature of estimates and the data of the tax reform and thus the uncertainty inherent in the revenue neutrality proposal, many LDP leaders were more positive about the reliability of such estimates and the idea of revenue neutrality. Only after various estimates of the reform's influence on households in the private sector (against the MOF's estimate) raised doubts about an increased tax burden on lower- and middle-income classes did the LDP begin to criticize the MOF for inducing the party and the prime minister to follow the bureaucratic proposal for a new tax by "distorting" the evidence of revenue neutrality.[69]

The second issue is the ultimate reason why the sales tax proposal was forced to be withdrawn. The analysis of the process has shown that the disagreement inside the administration consistently thwarted the MOF bureaucrats' attention from the public opposition, which was a direct reason for the withdrawal of the new tax. The failure to coordinate the interests in tax reform between the MOF and Nakasone was symbolized in Nakasone's repeated statements, including the fatal election pledge not to introduce the "large-scale indirect tax." Alternatively, the disclosure of this disagreement fed the opposition among industrial and consumer groups with conflicting interests in taxation. The prime minister's election pledge provided a consensual reason for opposition to the sales tax. Opposition groups could commonly reject the government's proposal as breaking the prime minister's election pledge.

The MOF's imperative was the introduction of the sales tax. Its new agenda of "shifting revenue reliance from direct to indirect taxation" was advocated for establishing a broad tax base on consumption. The MOF's proposal to reform income taxation was a part of this revision of the composition ratios between direct and indirect taxes in the long run, and was not aimed at income tax reduction in the first place. The fiscal bureaucrats accepted Nakasone's suggestion of an income tax reduction as long as the sales tax would finance income taxation. For Prime Minister Nakasone, however, a drastic income tax reduction was most important in the reform package. Prime Minister Nakasone, motivated by political ambition, wanted to imitate the successful U.S. tax reform under the Reagan administration in 1986. He employed the same idea of revenue neutrality as in the U.S. case, and made a tax cut compatible with his cabinet's public promise of the "elimination of the issuance of deficit bonds." But originally he had not been very interested in a measure to finance a tax cut, especially the broad-based consumption tax. Nakasone had stated explicitly from the beginning of 1985 that he would not introduce "a large-scale indirect tax levied on every stage of transaction like a casting net," which precisely meant the VAT.

These differences within the administration first appeared to the public as the government's attempts to conceal the subsequent introduction of the new tax by preceding it by an income tax reduction, even though the prime minister, the LDP, and the MOF had no such unified political strategy. This impression intensified because Nakasone prevented the MOF from straightforwardly proposing the new tax, while the MOF did not reveal prematurely the range and extent of tax reduction. Initially, the disagreement within the administration left the public confused about the government's intentions at an early stage of reform. When the disagreement became apparent with the prime minister's promise not to introduce "a large-scale indirect tax" amid the electoral politics, it was destined to kill the proposal of the new tax.

In order to arrive at a formal proposal for tax reform, the MOF was concerned with how to persuade Nakasone to introduce the new tax and how to make the new tax compatible with his election promise. The MOF had little time to pay attention to the opposition of special-interest groups represented by the LDP members. The MOF ran out of time before it could explain the plan and persuade the special-interest groups and the public to accept it. As a result, various measures designed to alleviate opposition from distributors and manufacturers instead confused them, and eventually increased their resistance and opposition to the new system. The MOF, as well as tax experts inside the LDP, learned a valuable lesson about compromising with special interests in exchange for the withdrawal of the sales tax proposal.

The ultimate withdrawal of the sales tax proposal showed that the bureaucrats did not have full control of the policy agenda. Nakasone's election promise provided a legitimate complaint for opposing groups whose interests in tax reform and policy were conflicting and who otherwise might not have formed an effective opposition coalition. Because bureau-

189

crats rely on politicians to sponsor their proposed policies, failing to obtain their cooperation, especially from high-ranking political leaders, could thwart efforts to implement a policy. In other words, if Prime Minister Nakasone had been more cooperative with the MOF, the proposal for the sales tax might have had a different consequence. The next chapter describes the process of the enactment of the consumption tax under Prime Minister Takeshita, who served as the MOF's close political sponsor.[70]

# The Third Attempt: Introduction of
# the Consumption Tax and
# the Securities Trading Scandal

TWO IMPORTANT points distinguished the proposal of the sales tax in 1987 from that of the general consumption tax in 1979. First, this time, while the government's failed attempt to introduce the general consumption tax several years before had forced the MOF to shelve any tax reform proposal in the near future, tax reform itself was regarded as an important policy problem even after the sales tax proposal was dropped. Different reasons for opposition to tax reform explained contrasting consequences in the two cases. The general consumption tax had been criticized as a tax increase that the public regarded as a symptom of the government's fiscal irresponsibility. In the case of the sales tax, however, an issue not directly related to tax policies, that is, that the proposal would break Prime Minister Nakasone's promise to the public, became a major reason to refuse the government's tax proposal. This reason for opposition, which concerned the credibility of the political leader's word rather than the tax policy, was destined to be short-lived.

Second, the major indirect tax, which had not won powerful political or organized sponsors in the late 1970s, enlisted firm support from leaders of the LDP and the business community in the mid-1980s. The party's support for the unpopular tax could be attributed to the demand for the financial resources that were expected from the new tax. Business associations wanted to avoid the further concentration of a tax burden and turned their opposition to support for the new tax. In this sense, the MOF's tax and fiscal policies in the early 1980s were still effective by securing support for the new tax from the incumbent party and the business community (see chapter 4).

In fact, those MOF policies are what prompted the LDP government immediately to work for another proposal of a broad-based consumption tax. In mid-October, one month after the passage of the 1987 fiscal year tax revision, the LDP TSRC formulated a tax reform plan similar to the failed proposal of the previous April, and the LDP and cabinet formally agreed to

191

implement it. In early November, Takeshita, the newly elected LDP president who was to be the next prime minister, showed a strong inclination to introduce a new broad-based consumption tax. The make-up of the new cabinet and the party leadership was also favorable for proceeding with the tax reform. The assignment of two new leaders, either of whom was likely to be the next prime minister—Miyazawa as Minister of Finance and Abe as LDP Secretary General—guaranteed the cooperation of different faction leaders. Michio Watanabe, who was familiar with fiscal and tax policies and close to the MOF, became chairman of the LDP PARC. Itō, who had been the former PARC chairman and a strong supporter for the introduction of the new tax, became chairman of the executive committee of the party. Yamanaka, who had pushed for the proposal of the sales tax, remained as chairman of the LDP TSRC. Under the above leadership, as early as November 26, only seven months after the withdrawal of the sales tax proposal, the prime minister and the LDP agreed to legislate for the tax reform the following fall.

The new prime minister, Takeshita, certainly contributed to such a quick response from the LDP government. As a typical party politician, Takeshita had had a close look at the MOF by serving as minister of finance in five terms (four terms covering about five years in the Nakasone cabinet). He was a more sympathetic cooperator for the MOF than Nakasone, and respected the intentions of the MOF as well as the LDP TSRC in the tax reform. His style of political maneuvering also differed from Nakasone's. Takeshita focused on weakening the organized opposition to a policy rather than setting the policy agenda to appeal to the public. Takeshita's approach was more effective in leading to the implementation of such an unpopular policy as the new tax.

The close cooperation between the MOF and the party under Takeshita led to a unified tax reform agenda; the government explained that the tax reform would serve to rectify the tax inequity and secure financial resources for increasing the welfare expenditures of an aging society. The MOF bureaucrats connected the new tax with the reform aims that curried public favor. Though the new tax was not necessarily the only means to achieve these aims, the popular aims were closely associated with tax reform. The difficulty in finding an alternative way to finance the accompanying income tax cut prevented public apprehension about the new tax from evolving into opposition immediately. In terms of special interests' opposition, the government became more compromising in employing measures that would gain more political feasibility at the expense of consistency and the efficiency of the taxation.

This chapter first shows that the MOF bureaucrats decided on the above major reform directions shortly after the sales tax was dropped from the political agenda. I will argue that the MOF formulated the new agenda for the tax reform through close cooperation with the LDP politicians, but did not lose its control over the agenda nor compromise in terms of its critical interests. Then, the chapter introduces the reform process.

Because of the new reform agenda and the use of compromising measures in the new system, the government's proposal of the consumption tax first met with less opposition than that of the sales tax. However, the government's persuasion began to reveal its weaknesses when an originally unrelated political problem became entangled with the tax issue. In this "Recruit" problem, many incumbent party leaders and government officials were suspected of insider trading of securities of a company called Recruit. The public and the media accused politicians and government officials of benefiting from tax-exempted capital gains from sales of securities. Ineffective taxation on capital gains, which was not part of the reform, became a symbol of tax inequity in the public's eyes, and the government's claim that it was rectifying tax inequity lost credibility.

Helped by the timing of the politicization of this problem, the government managed to pass tax bills before public opposition culminated. As the implementation date for the new tax approached, however, public mistrust of the LDP government rapidly changed to stiff opposition to the new consumption tax. The lost credibility of the LDP government, brought about by the Recruit problem, gave a legitimate reason for public opposition to the new tax. The LDP had to pay a high political price for the new tax that the MOF had planned for a decade: heavy losses in the election of the House of Councillors three months after the introduction of the consumption tax.

The final section of the chapter describes the period after the LDP's electoral loss when public opposition to the new tax rapidly waned. It examines the whole reform process, focusing on the rapid rise and fall of the opposition movement.

## Seeking a Compromise for the Introduction of the New Tax

### A New Agenda: Rectification of Tax Inequity and Preparation for the Aging of Society

The MOF had started a new public relations campaign in the summer of 1988 with a newsletter for the general public about the tax system. The MOF began to pay more attention to the political feasibility of the proposal. The change in the MOF's approach appeared for the first time as early as November 1987 in a book, *Current Conditions of the Indirect Tax System* (*Kansetuszei no Genjō*), written by a director in the tax bureau in charge of the indirect tax, Nobuaki Usui. In addition to a detailed explanation of the system and practice of the current indirect taxation system, this book included a section called "Perspective for Considering Tax Reform." Even though Usui stipulated that all the views and opinions expressed were his own, the book, which was published as a separate volume of the MOF's public relations journal *Fainansu* (Finance), conveyed the reformulation of the tax bureau's approach to the introduction of the new tax.[1] The new aims of the reform—the rectification of tax inequity and preparation for an aging society—which the reform proposal supported later in the GTSRC reports and in the LDP's "Major Line," had already been presented in this book. It emphasized the necessity of taxes that would be levied more evenly on income, consumption, and assets, and suggested the reform (Usui 1987, 533–58).

Using the new tax as a measure to improve the whole tax system went far beyond the MOF's previous argument. In the proposal for the sales tax, the MOF had advocated shifting the revenue dependence from direct to indirect taxation, but it was not clear how and why this shift in the revenue source would improve the whole system. The MOF explained, rather indirectly, that the new tax broadly based on consumption would cover the new economic activities that evaded current taxation and would improve the existing indirect tax system.

This time, the MOF accepted the public's complaints of a heavy tax burden and inequity in the existing income tax system. Though it cautiously avoided answering whether the tax inequity *actually* existed, the MOF assigned directly to the new consumption tax the role of responding to the public "feeling" of a heavy tax burden and tax inequity under a system that relied heavily on direct taxation. Then, it pointed out the difficulty of taxing incomes from different sources equally, and suggested a reform that would result in a more equitable tax on income, consumption, and assets, that is, the new indirect tax broadly based on consumption.[2]

Another important change was in the MOF's approach to a tax reduction. In proposing the sales tax, the MOF had been reluctant to use Nakasone's strategy of deflecting public attention away from the new tax by tax reduction. Previously, the ministry had been afraid that expectations for a tax cut might keep the government from proposing a new indirect tax and threaten the framework of the revenue neutrality of the reform. This time, the MOF was willing to offer a net tax reduction in the same reform package in order to sell the new indirect tax. As a result, there was no disagreement between the MOF and the LDP politicians who were eager to see an income tax cut. The LDP government set a unified agenda to highlight the major indirect tax as a measure for lowering the burden of the tax withheld from incomes of salaried workers who suffered from a "feeling" of tax inequity in the existing system.

As a new reason for the reform, the MOF also raised the issue of the aging of society. The MOF attempted to demonstrate that the burden of taxation as well as of social security fees on salaried workers would be intolerably heavy without a tax reform to decrease revenue reliance on income taxation. However, the fiscal bureaucrats neither committed themselves to a concrete financial program of social security expenditures nor tried to work with the Ministry of Health and Welfare (MHW) for the establishment of a new financial plan of welfare programs by expected revenue from the new tax.[3]

The MOF's new approach was converging with the LDP politicians' idea for increasing the political feasibility of the reform. Its active political involvement in the agenda setting of tax reform, however, did not mean that the LDP dominated in decisions about the reform. Bureaucratic influence was persistent in some critical issues. A typical example of such issues involved the use of the revenue from the new tax for welfare expenditures. With some exceptions,[4] the LDP politicians seriously considered a plan to use the new tax revenue exclusively for social security expenditures. For example, the new chairman of the executive committee, Itō, confirmed his positive view of it (*NK*, November 5, 1987). Even the new prime minister, Takeshita, immediately before he was to take office as the newly elected LDP president, suggested the introduction of the new indirect tax for securing stable revenue for public welfare.

Responding to requests by some LDP leaders, as well as members of opposition parties in the Diet, Minister of Finance Miyazawa promised to show in March 1988 the government's view of the relationship between an aging society and the tax reform in the Diet. This promise appeared in a report by the MOF and the Ministry of Home Affairs as the "Perspective on Social Security Benefits and Contributions at the Beginning of the Twenty-first Century." This report included an estimate of the ratio of the burden of social security contributions and taxation to the national income, which would reach a level above 50 percent in 2020, up from 36.6 percent in 1988. The report also picked up the estimated ratios of the tax burden to the salaried income, which would increase to a level of 8.2 percent in 2000 and 13.1 percent in 2010, assuming a nominal economic growth rate of 5.5

percent (*NK*, March 12, 1988). But, while emphasizing rapidly increasing social security contributions and expenditures in the near future, the report fell short of explaining the relationship between the new tax and the social security program. This was because the MOF was reluctant to predetermine the appropriation of revenue from the new tax for social security programs, even though the ministry had extensively used financial preparation for an aging society as a reason to make the new tax more acceptable to the public.

Generally speaking, the MOF did not like to earmark tax revenue because this would decrease available funds whose usage the MOF influences. There were several additional reasons why the MOF avoided connecting the new tax revenue to social security programs. First, the claim that the new tax would finance increasing social security expenditures was inconsistent with the aim of administrative reform to limit the size of the government. At the same time, the MOF was more concerned that new revenue from the broad-based consumption tax would trigger irresistible spending pressure from the incumbent party. Many LDP leaders, tired of a tight fiscal constraint on expenditures under the austerity campaign, wanted more budget allocation, and welcomed the revenue enhancement for public welfare.[5]

Financing social security expenditures with a new broad-based consumption tax also would involve several problems in policy implementation. Earmarking the new tax for welfare expenditures would prevent the national government from allocating revenue to local governments that would need to supplement the revenue from the excise tax integrated into the new system. More important, as the ratio of the number of elderly people to the total population grew, financing public pensions and health insurance with a broad-based consumption tax would lead to redistribution among the aged. Without an accompanying revenue enhancement of income taxes from younger generations or, assuming a significant gap between the wealthy aged and the poor aged,[6] taxation for social security expenditures, at best, would become a circulation of public money between the aged and the administration. Indexed pension benefits and inflated welfare costs would necessitate a rapid upsurge in the tax rate, which would substantially decrease pension benefits through a tax increase, unless social security expenditures obtained appropriation from revenue besides the consumption tax.[7]

While the government attempted to propose a major indirect tax with these new aims, the opposition parties clung to their previous strategy, arguing that the government's proposal broke Nakasone's public promise of

1986 and also violated the Diet resolution of 1979. The former reason for opposition was less effective because of Nakasone's resignation as prime minister. The Diet resolution on fiscal reconstruction began to lose relevance after about ten years, including the period of the austerity campaign.

*Deliberation in the Diet: Demands for an Income Tax*
*Reduction by Opposition Parties and the Prime*
*Minister's Initiative for a Reform Proposal*

The 112th ordinary session of the Diet resumed on January 25, 1988. In his policy speech in the plenary meeting of the HC, the prime minister clarified the government's intention to introduce the new indirect tax. The government had delegated the proposal to the GTSRC, which conducted public hearings throughout the country from February to March. During the Diet deliberation focusing on the 1988 budget, therefore, Prime Minister Takeshita showed a concrete plan for reform but initiated a discussion on the new tax in general by pointing out "six concerns about the large-scale indirect tax." This list included all the undesirable consequences of the new tax that the opposition parties had criticized, that is, the regressive character of the new tax, the increased burden of tax filing, the possibility of inflation, and so on. Takeshita said that solving these concerns was a precondition for the introduction of the new tax.

Differing from his predecessor, Nakasone, Prime Minister Takeshita's new initiative relied fully on tax experts inside the administration. The prime minister's secretary, who was a former MOF bureaucrat, made the original draft of the list of six concerns. The MOF was ready to answer these concerns in order to defend the new tax when Takeshita publicized them. For example, the regressive effect and the heavier burden on the low-income classes could be alleviated by the other measures in the tax system (e.g., by raising the minimum taxed income) and by welfare policies and expenditures: special considerations and devices in the system would lower the burden of tax filing for businesses. With the prime minister's cooperation, the MOF intended to justify the introduction of the new tax by demonstrating that it would be free of all the problems the opposition parties presented as reasons for their opposition.

Instead of being involved in the discussion on tax reform initiated by Takeshita, the opposition parties first concentrated on the request for a tax cut. After the HC budget committee had begun their deliberations in February, three opposition parties—the Japan Socialist Party, the Clean Government Party, and the Democratic Socialist Party—made a common request to include a ¥3 trillion (= $23.41 billion; $1 = ¥128.15 in 1988) reduction in inhabitant, income, inheritance, and corporate taxes in the 1988 fiscal budget. The opposition parties used the request for a tax reduction each year both to appeal to the public and to modify the government budget. This time, however, their request meant more than an attractive appeal to the public for tax reduction or a tactic to delay the Diet's deliberations. Using their request for an income tax cut, they tried to induce the Takeshita administration to make a verbal commitment to the new tax.

The opposition parties demanded the tax cut without the introduction of the new tax; they delayed deliberations on the 1988 fiscal budget by refusing to attend the session. On March 20, immediately before the end of the session, the LDP promised that that year's tax cut would not be financed by the new tax. The LDP and the opposition parties agreed to legislate the tax cut in an extraordinary session scheduled for July. This agreement was the beginning of the opposition parties' strategic mistake. First, the promise not to finance the next fiscal year's tax cut involved neither a decision about the future proposal of the new tax nor a concession on the government's side. Though the opposition parties failed to recognize it, the government was able to finance the tax cut in that year by using the natural increment of revenue, that is, without the new tax. Second, using the agreement, the government could link the demands for the tax cut to a structural tax reform as it had planned. The opposition parties, though they had requested a continuous tax reduction after the 1988 fiscal year, presented an abstract plan to finance their proposed tax cut. They listed several measures for the rectification of tax inequity and expected a natural increment in tax revenue.[8] This incomplete specification of financial measures gave the government a good reason for proposing the new tax as an effective financial measure.

Consequently, the agreement between the LDP and the opposition parties affirmed a tax cut without the introduction of a new tax in 1988, but left room for the government to propose the introduction of a new tax after 1988. In this sense, by agreeing to this tax cut, all the opposition parties except the JCP[9] committed themselves to a tax reform leading to the introduction of a new indirect tax.

*Slow but Steady Progress*

While negotiations between the LDP and the opposition parties on the problem of a tax cut in the 1988 fiscal year postponed substantial discussion on the new indirect tax, some changes appeared in the groups that were opposed to the new tax. The People's Conference on Tax Reform, which had been the most unified alliance including almost all the opposition groups since 1986, held an executive committee meeting on March 26, but the discussion was not very active. After three days, the Conference affirmed its opposition in alliance with the JSP, the CGP, and the DSP against legislation to introduce the new indirect tax in the upcoming fall. However, the weakening of the opposition movement was undeniable.

One reason for this was the change in leadership of the major opposition organizations. The President of the Association of Chain Stores, Shimizu, who had been one of the main organizers of the opposition coalition, was to terminate his term as president the following May. Despite Shimizu's intention to serve the next term, many members wanted to elect a new president. The Association, which had once broken relations with the LDP due to its stiff opposition to the sales tax, came to terms with the party in December 1987. But many members thought that Shimizu's resignation was necessary to restore completely their relationship with the incumbent party and avoid the adverse influence their stiff opposition to the sales tax might have in future discussions of tax reform. Thus Takaoka, the president of Seibu, a large-scale chain store, obtained the members' support and became the new president of the Association. Shimizu subsequently resigned.[10] Shimizu remained as chairman of the major opposition coalition, People's Conference on Tax Reform, after his resignation, but lost significant influence.

The leadership also changed in Nisshō, which had been the only opposition organization among major business associations. Noboru Gotō, as head of Nisshō, had implied support for the new indirect tax, but each time he did so, pressure from members of small and medium-sized businesses compelled him to withdraw his statement. His failing health caused him to resign in the middle of his term in December 1987, and Rokurō Ishikawa succeeded him in his post. Ishikawa established the tax system special committee in January 1989 to make a consensual view on tax reform inside Nisshō. Establishing this kind of organization in Nisshō was quite exceptional (*NK*, January 22, 1988). In March 1988, only four months after Ishikawa became its head, the Nisshō leadership published the results of opinion polls by members, which showed a majority's acceptance of the new indirect tax.[11] Ishikawa's patient persuasion of the members contributed to weakening the opposition to the new indirect tax (*Asahi*, April 15, 1988).

The government's procedure for proposing the new tax contributed further to weakening the opposition. First, the government tried to activate

199

public discussion of tax reform in general. As the case of the sales tax showed, various groups that had been dissatisfied with or against the different parts of the government's proposal had allied in opposition to the introduction of the new tax. In order to avoid that situation from recurring, the MOF scheduled public hearings immediately after the GTSRC published "the basic problems to be solved in the tax reform" and tried to activate public discussion of tax reform in general. Public hearings were held at twenty sites throughout Japan from February 8 to March 3. Compared to only four hearings at the time of the sales tax proposal, this increase showed the MOF's recognition of the importance of public opinion.

In public hearings, the MOF as a secretariat did not mind that the opposition to the new tax prevailed over the opinions supporting it (*Asahi*, March 11, 1988). Instead of persuading the public to accept the new tax, the MOF endeavored to make the public more conscious of conflicting interests and different views. They expected that the public would be more likely to accept the new indirect tax if it recognized the difficulty of forming a consensus for an alternative reform measure that would satisfy different interests.

A second important factor that weakened the opposition was the way in which the government initiated discussion of the new indirect tax. The subcommittee of the GTSRC in charge of the indirect tax began to deliberate on different kinds of a new indirect tax to be introduced at the beginning of March (*NK*, March 3, 1988). The MOF influenced the deliberation agendas of the GTSRC by working as its secretariat. First, it focused on an EC-type VAT, a turnover tax, a manufacturers' sales tax, and a retailers' sales tax. However, in the final stages of deliberations, the general consumption tax appeared as a subject for discussion, and two single-stage taxes—the manufacturers' sales tax and the retailers' sales tax—were dropped from the proposed alternatives. On March 22 the GTSRC finally proposed three multistage taxes in its tentative plan: an EC-type VAT, a general consumption tax, and a turnover tax. The VAT-type tax would be levied on the added values of commodities and services, that is, the difference between what firms purchase and what they sell at each stage. Two ways of subtracting the tax amounts in the earlier stage of transaction—by issuing invoices and by basing the tax on business accounting books—distinguished the EC-type VAT and the general consumption tax, respectively.

There was a subtle political calculation in the exclusion of the two single-stage taxes—the retailers' and manufacturers' sales taxes—and the inclusion of the turnover tax as an alternative tax type. When the GTSRC had prepared for the proposal of the sales tax in the fall of 1986, the GTSRC and the MOF had to include two single-stage taxes even though they had not seriously considered proposing them. Prime Minister Nakasone had supported the single-stage taxes, especially the manufacturers' sales tax at that time. However, the inclusion of single-stage taxes had increased the opposition to the Japanese-type VAT from the distribution industries, which had increased their expectations for a manufacturers' sales tax as an acceptable alternative. Learning from this bitter past experience, the GTSRC and the MOF excluded the two single-stage taxes.

Inclusion of the turnover tax in the GTSRC report had a reason. The MOF and the GTSRC were determined to reject this as a final choice because this tax accumulates tax amounts as the stages of transaction increase and is inferior from a technocratic point of view. But they left it as an alternative in order to demonstrate that the government intended to give special contributions to businesses to simplify the compilation of the new tax as much as the turnover tax. The government wanted to emphasize that combining the accounting method of the general consumption tax with the simple taxation method[12] would have as little influence on small and medium-sized businesses as the turnover tax. Presenting three alternatives was therefore a result of careful consideration aimed at alleviating opposition from special-interest groups.

In April the GTSRC conducted public hearings at five places in the country in order to listen to the public's response to their March report. More than half the respondents supported the new indirect tax, although many of them still demanded administrative reform and further rectification of tax inequity.

At the end of the hearings the GTSRC started to work on the interim report on the tax reform, which was issued on April 28. It proposed to introduce a "new consumption tax," which would be either the EC-type VAT with invoices or the subtraction-method VAT with an accounting method.

The GTSRC report also suggested an income tax reduction by decreasing the number of brackets in the tax rate structure from twelve (ranging from 10.5 percent to 60 percent) to six (from 10 percent to 50 percent). In addition, it suggested raising the maximum limit of the minimum tax rate to ¥2 million (= $15.61 thousand; $1 = ¥128.15 in 1988) of taxed income, taxation on capital gains from securities' transactions, and a decreasing corporate tax rate. But the new indirect tax was the focus of the policy discussion. The interim report emphasized that easing the feelings of tax inequity and of a heavy tax burden by more revenue reliance on indirect taxation was the most important aim of the tax reform. Securing financial resources for the aging of society was a second reason for reform in the report.[13]

The tax bureau could influence the selection of alternatives in the interim report. Hiroshi Katō, the new chairman of the special committee in charge of the indirect tax, contributed to the GTSRC's close cooperation with the MOF. Katō had changed his opposition to the sales tax to support for the new tax on consumption in general, and became a member of the GTSRC upon the MOF's request.[14] During the deliberations on the new tax to find the best compromising measure, Katō, with Chief Cabinet Secretary Keizō Obuchi as an intermediary, met and listened to the LDP members who had opposed the sales tax.

With Katō's cooperation, the MOF prevented the GTSRC report from showing a preference for the EC-type VAT with invoices. Chairman Ogura and many council members continued to prefer the EC-type VAT, which had also been supported in the public hearings. For example, when GTSRC chairman Ogura frankly expressed his support for the EC-type VAT at a public hearing in February, saying that the other taxes were "inferior types" (*darakugata*), the MOF made every effort to deny that the new tax would be the EC-type VAT.[15] Without showing an order of preference for one or the other, the MOF insisted on listing the general consumption tax using an accounting method together with the VAT with invoices.

Previously, the tax bureau had agreed with the GTSRC that the EC-type VAT with invoices was superior, but this time it guided the council's deliberation into the use of the accounting method, which the LDP supported. The MOF and the LDP had an implicit agreement to compromise with the special interests by choosing the VAT without invoices: both the LDP and the MOF learned that much of the opposition to the sales tax from special interests was concerned with the use of invoices. The MOF was now ready to make the new tax system more acceptable to the special-interest groups.

Another part of the report reflected the MOF's intention to increase the reform's political feasibility. In order to sell the new indirect tax, the MOF tried to impress on the public a capital gains tax on the sale of securities as a measure for the rectification of tax inequities. While a majority of GTSRC members had been worried about the disagreement in public opinion of how to tax securities, the MOF pushed the proposal for a "taxation to be principally levied on capital gains from securities." This was because the MOF had already planned for the taxation of "quasi-gains" (*minashi baikyaku eki*) as a compromising measure, as will be explained in the following section.

The details of the design of the new tax system were left to the LDP TSRC's decision, and the further decline in the GTSRC's influence was apparent. This procedure served to weaken opposition inside the LDP and organized interests. The LDP TSRC began deliberations on the new indirect tax in a small committee on March 23. On April 5 the LDP TSRC began two weeks of hearings on the new indirect tax with representatives of more than three hundred related organizations and groups. Attendees ranged from major business associations to an organization representing the interests of new kinds of businesses, and also covered various industrial sectors. The focus of the hearings was on groups of small and medium-sized businesses and self-employed people and distributors' organizations, which had shown stiff opposition to the sales tax proposal the previous year. As described above, Nisshō, representing the interests of small and medium-sized businesses, had turned its opposition to the sales tax to support for the new indirect tax, but its representatives were cautious about expressing their own positions in the hearings. This was because five out of eleven groups of small and medium-sized businesses still opposed the introduction of a new indirect tax. Representatives from the distribution and textile industries expressed opposition or required that careful consideration be given to the introduction of the new tax.

When the hearings ended, the LDP TSRC began to plan the major line of the reform. On April 28 the chairman and vice chairmen of the LDP TSRC decided on a draft for the basic direction of the structural tax reform that formally affirmed the introduction of a new indirect tax. But in the following plenary session, the junior members of the LDP TSRC rejected the draft as a "hasty" decision. Most of them were the same members who had opposed the sales tax. They also criticized the leadership's decision to publicize a major party line on the tax reform on May 20. Yamanaka, who listened more patiently to the members' opinions than he had the previous year, postponed the formulation of the major line of the reform until late May. Yamanaka further suspended it until mid-June when Prime Minister Takeshita and LDP Secretary General Shintarō Abe agreed on the submission of the bills for the tax reform to the extraordinary session scheduled in July.

While the leadership had to take considerable time until the formal decision, the opposition to the sales tax inside the LDP was not as strong as it had been, and the opposition from local branches of the party was insignificant. The LDP TSRC members who had opposed the sales tax claimed they needed more time for deliberation, but they no longer opposed the new consumption tax itself.[16] On May 24, in an executive meeting of the chairman and vice chairmen of the LDP TSRC and all the chairmen of division committees in the LDP PARC, it was decided to use the general consumption type of VAT. This decision was also accepted easily by line members in the small committee.

As the discussion focused on details, a consensus was reached among the LDP leaders and members familiar with tax issues to narrow the range of tax exemptions. Pressure from special-interest groups for tax exemption, which had been one of the reasons for the failure of the sales tax proposal, was not as intense as in the previous year. The LDP members had learned that allowing the special-interest groups to press for tax exemption had impaired the new system. Various industrial sectors were more cautious about pressing for tax exemption for their products and merchandise. Businesses and industries understood that tax exemption was not necessarily advantageous because taxed manufacturers and distributors would avoid doing business with tax-exempted parties whose added values in sales could not be subtracted from the tax amount levied on them.

The LDP's "Major Line of the Tax Reform," publicized on June 14, followed the major direction of the reform discussed thus far inside the government. In terms of direct tax reduction, the party attempted to highlight the income tax reduction, which would amount to about ¥2.3 trillion (= $17.95 billion; $1 = ¥128.15 in 1988). Following the GTSRC suggestion, the "Major Line" further decreased the number of tax brackets from six to five with the same range of 10–50 percent. At the same time, a 10 percent minimum tax rate would be applied to households with higher income than before, and various measures would be used to raise basic and special personal tax deductions. These measures significantly lowered the income tax burden. In correspondence with the decreased number of income tax brackets, the inhabitant taxation would also be simplified and lowered. Corporate tax reduction was also included in the reform package.

Having learned from the previous year's proposal, which had aroused public suspicion about the effect of the tax reduction, the government aimed to secure the support of salaried workers for this income tax reduction. According to this reform plan, the MOF predicted a low tax burden for almost all households. Private research groups and opposition parties did not come to exactly the same conclusions as the MOF, but the disagreement was much smaller than in the previous year. The results of research groups and interest organizations were similar to the MOF's in terms of average households with one couple and children, but they differed from the MOF in predicting an increased tax burden on single persons, working couples, and the aged.[17] But these differences were too small to fuel public opposition to the tax reform. The main reason for closing the gap between the official estimate and the estimates by private groups was a much more explicit orientation to an income tax cut in the government's proposal. An individual income tax cut of more than ¥3 trillion (= $23.41 billion; $1 = ¥128.15 in 1988) was expected to exceed the tax increase from the introduction of the new tax.[18]

In terms of the proposal for a broad-based indirect tax named the "consumption tax," the "Major Line" affirmed the usage of the accounting method on which the MOF and the LDP agreed. This method would not significantly change the corporations' tax filing method, while the invoice method would require businesses to give the tax authority more information on corporate income through a written record of exchanges and transactions.

The second important point was narrowing the scope and range of tax exemption. Despite pressure for tax exemption from various sectors, it was confined to services concerned with medical care, education, and welfare. The LDP TSRC agreed to push the tax exemption point down from ¥100 million to ¥30 million (from $780.34 thousand to $234.1 thousand; $1 = ¥128.15 in 1988) of annual sales. The lower tax-exemption point avoided the complicated problem of the exchange between taxed corporations and tax-exempt distributors and manufacturers. More important, however, this exemption point was still high enough to exclude from taxation almost all farmers who had pressed the LDP for tax exemption of food.

The new compromise introduced at this stage was to enlarge the range of corporations that could use the simple taxation method. This method was designed to decrease the task of tax filing for smaller-scale businesses by allowing them to regard 10 (20) percent of sales as added values for wholesalers (retailers) for easier tax calculation. Under the sales tax, a corporation with ¥100 million (= $0.78 million; $1 = ¥128.15 in 1988) of annual sales could choose this taxation method, but the consumption tax would allow corporations with up to ¥500 million (= $3.9 million) of annual sales to use this method. The corporations could file taxes once in six months, while the proposal for the sales tax had required a tax return every three months. In addition, the firms whose annual sales are between ¥60 million and ¥30 million can use the vanishing exemption method, which allows them to reduce tax gradually as their sales decrease and thus gives them tax credit. The MOF basically agreed with the LDP on these measures. The tax rate was lowered to 3 percent from a previous 5 percent because of the party's consideration of political feasibility.

## The Waning Technocratic Idea and Political Compromise

For the sake of political feasibility, the government was now more willing to sacrifice the effectiveness and consistency of the tax system than it had been in the proposal of the sales tax. The GTSRC final report indicated dissatisfaction with this political compromise from a technocratic point of view. On June 14, the day after the LDP's proposal for the consumption tax in the "Major Line," the GTSRC issued the "Report on the Tax Reform," which concluded their deliberation on the tax reform. Usually, the GTSRC report followed the LDP's formal decision and affirmed the party decision. But this time it recommended that the future government should change from using the accounting method (that is, the general consumption type VAT) to a new system with invoices (that is, the EC-type VAT). The MOF accepted the inclusion of this unusual requirement in the final report made by the council members to the incumbent party: the MOF also aimed ultimately to establish a VAT system based on the invoice method in the future. The MOF's strong inclination to reform the new tax system by adopting the invoice method differed greatly from the LDP as well as another bureaucratic organization, the MITI, which worked with the LDP to articulate interests of small and medium-sized businesses and to decide on compromising measures.[19]

The special-interest groups' response to the LDP's "Major Line" was much more favorable than before. The executive committee of the People's Conference on the Tax System unanimously passed a resolution that they would oppose the new consumption tax, but the members did not necessarily agree on such absolute opposition to the new tax. The biggest change appeared inside the distribution industry, which had been the core of the opposition alliance. The small and medium-sized distributors and specialty shops continued to display firm opposition. But the large-scale distributors, for example, the Association of Chain Stores and the Association of Department Stores, said that they would go along with the new tax if they could ensure that the proposed system would not adversely affect their businesses. A majority of manufacturing industries came to accept the new tax and praised the lower tax rate.

Except for these groups, the policymakers paid special attention to the Union of Japan Private Labor Unions (*Zennihon Minkan Rōdō Kumiai Rengōkai*; hereinafter, Rengō), which had been the biggest organization representing employed people in the private sector since its formation in November 1987. It was a major organized group that could represent salaried workers whose support the government had tried to win by stressing the rectification of tax inequity. Rengō's approval was important also because some member unions provided important organized support for the DSP, whose acceptance of the reform was crucial for the passage of the tax bills in the Diet. The reform plan, however, fell short of the expectations of about a third of the member unions of Rengō that had previously shown some understanding of the new consumption tax. They regarded the LDP's decision on the new tax as too compromising to special interests and as not responding to their request for tax equity between salaried workers and self-employed people. Rengō tried to make the new tax system less compromising to business interests and to induce more measures for income tax equity, though it was more compromising than it had been to the sales tax proposal.

In this way, the consumption tax proposal evolved from close cooperation between the prime minister, the LDP (especially its leaders and dietmen familiar with tax issues), and the MOF. This process was quite different from the proposals of the general consumption tax and the sales tax, which had lacked critical support from the LDP leaders and the prime minister, respectively. Observing this close cooperation, journalists and the media reported the incumbent party's influence over the government's proposal at the expense of the MOF. For example, newspapers covering the disagreement between the LDP and the MOF on the tax rate reported that the lower rate of 3 percent, supported by the LDP, had prevailed over the 5 percent rate pushed by the MOF. However, this decision on the tax rate was not a big concession for the MOF. The reason the fiscal bureaucrats had insisted on 5 percent was based on their estimate of public finances; it had shown that tax revenues under 5 percent would be necessary to achieve the government's promise to eliminate the issuance of deficit bonds in the 1990 fiscal year.[20] If the LDP decided on the lower tax rate and accepted the delay in the elimination of deficit bonds expected under that tax rate, the MOF had no reason to resist it.[21] The bureaucrats regarded this as a highly political decision.

Even though the media coverage focused on the intense political pressure from the LDP and interest groups to win more compromising tax filing measures, the MOF rejected several critical measures pushed by special-interest groups and supported by incumbent politicians. A notable example was the MOF's successful refusal to adopt a "zero tax rate." This system would apply a zero tax rate to tax-exempt transactions, and allow the tax-exempt corporations reimbursement of the taxes included in their purchases. In a system of zero tax rates, a tax-exempt business need not pay, at the expense of its profits, the taxes that have crept into prices on services

207

or commodities that it has purchased. Some industries, for example, the food industry, which asked that its products be exempted, argued the use of this measure in an LDP hearing, and some LDP members showed a positive attitude toward it. The MOF resisted. Because the measure would solve the disadvantages of tax exemption, the bureaucrats were worried that special-interest pressure for tax exemptions would get out of control if this protective measure were incorporated into the system. The MOF pointed out that employing a zero tax rate would narrow the tax base and cause the complicated problem of tax refunds. It succeeded in dissuading the LDP from using the system.

Close examination of the compromising measures leads to two conclusions about the bureaucrats' influence over the design of the consumption tax. First, the inclusion of various special tax measures in the system was a result of bureaucrats' willing concessions in order to make the proposal more politically feasible. Actually, these same measures had already appeared in the MOF's tentative plan in January that year: lowering the tax rate, pushing down the tax-exemption point, and allowing more corporations to employ the simple taxation method.[22] This tentative plan, which might have been a *ballon d'essai* by the MOF, showed that the bureaucrats had been ready to sacrifice the consistency and efficiency of the system in order to increase the political feasibility of the reform before the LDP politicians intervened in making a tax reform plan.

Second, despite intense political pressure, the MOF rejected the compromising measures that ran counter to its interests. All possible compromising measures were scrutinized, and any that might erode the broad tax base were rejected. Optional tax exemptions and generous tax filing measures for small and medium-sized businesses were encouraged because they weakened opposition from these groups without decreasing tax revenue significantly. The zero tax rate and expansion of tax-exempted items were regarded as primary causes for narrowing the tax base and were resisted by the MOF. The LDP politicians contributed to making the final plan, but the MOF's bottom line for compromises remained untouched, even though the special-interest groups pressed the politicians to go beyond it.

Though the MOF's compromises with special interests were effective without thwarting its aim of establishing a broad tax base, these measures risked discrediting the reform's professed aim, "the rectification of tax inequity." Several measures were actually perceived as the government's attempt to preserve special tax (filing) treatments for special interests by consumers and salaried workers. First, the use of an accounting method nudged the feeling of tax inequity by a majority of salaried workers. Using invoices is the most accurate method for determining the added value, and thus the amount of tax. This system also guarantees an open relationship between the tax authority, the consumers, and the distributors in terms of filing taxes and of shifting the tax to prices. Many salaried workers believed that the existing system of taxation on self-employed businesses allowed them to give the tax authority less information about their incomes than the salaried workers. They expected the tax authority to be able to ascertain such information by checking invoices. Compared to the invoice method, the accounting method permitted more opportunities for tax evasion by corporations. The use of the accounting method therefore appeared to reassure tax privileges for self-employed people.

Relating to this point, the labor unions, especially Rengō, began to suspect that the new consumption tax system could produce a new kind of tax inequity. Under the new system without invoices, Rengō argued, it was difficult for the tax authority to ascertain if distributors were manipulating transaction records or keeping inaccurate records in their accounting books and not filing the taxes that the consumers paid.[23] In order to justify use of the accounting method, the MOF explained that in most EC countries, the invoice method had been substantially replaced by the accounting method because distributors were issuing invoices based on their accounting books rather than making the accounting books depend on invoices. But when this problem was politicized, this explanation proved to be too weak to respond to public criticism.

Expanding the range for applying the simple taxation method involved a more serious problem than use of the accounting method. The simple taxation method would allow the calculation of the amount of taxation by considering 20 percent (for retailers) or 10 percent (for wholesalers) of the sales amount as added values through exchange or transaction without subtracting the tax levied on the previous stages. The number of corporations with annual sales of less than ¥500 million (= $3.9 million; $1 = ¥128.15 in 1988) that the government permitted to use the simple taxation method amounted to 96.7 percent of the total number of firms.[24] In terms of the number of tax units,[25] therefore, the new tax, which was supposed to be a multistage tax of the subtraction type, would be closer to the turnover tax of the accumulative type. In terms of share of tax base, with which the MOF was most concerned, this measure may have had little impact because the small and medium-sized firms' share in total amount of sales and exchanges as a tax base was expected to be well under 10 percent. But this problem could not be slighted. Aside from this technical problem, the method may allow to collect a "subsidy" or "profit tax" (*ekizei*) from consumers. This could be given to the distributors if the taxed commodities and services had a higher rate of added value than the statutory 20 percent or 10 percent with a 3 percent tax shift to price. Service industries certainly have a higher rate of marginal profit than 20 percent. This "profit tax" became one of the primary subjects for "revision" (*minaoshi*) of the consumption tax after its introduction.

In addition to the compromising measures included in the consumption tax, various revisions in direct taxation in the reform package came under public criticism. Growing public concern and mass media coverage politicized several measures as examples of tax inequity. These included the absence of taxation on capital gains from the sale of securities, the "quasi-corporation" taxation for self-employed businesses, and the special tax measures for medical doctors.[26] The MOF wanted ultimately to rectify these measures, but this time it proposed incomplete measures for the purpose of reforming direct taxation. It feared that drastic changes to enhance income tax revenue and abolish special tax treatments would trigger the resistance of vested interests and lead to the third failure to implement a consumption tax.

This cautious attitude of the MOF was observed in its proposal for new taxation on capital gains. From an earlier stage of tax reform, the MOF had planned a system that would allow taxpayers an option between a tax based on a tax return and a tax on "quasi-capital gains" (*minashi baikyaku eki*) from the sale of securities.[27] The MOF emphasized this as a measure to "tax all capital gains in principle" (*gensoku kazei*), and persuaded the GTSRC and the LDP TSRC to present this as a response to the public's demand for tax equity.

The apparent compromise with special-interest groups at the expense of the effectiveness of the new tax, coupled with the incomplete revisions in direct taxation, made the reform package unattractive to the public. The opinion polls reported low public expectation for the rectification of tax inequity through the reform.[28] But this public disappointment did not evolve immediately into significant opposition. Initial opposition to the reform was much less salient than in the previous year. The unorganized public could not articulate its criticism of the complicated reform package, and opposition was little more than an expression of concern about the unfamiliar new tax and disappointment with the direct tax reform. Another stated aim of the reform—preparation for an aging society—further complicated public opposition which took seriously the regressive effect of the consumption tax on income distribution.[29]

The cabinet endorsed the "Major Line of the Tax Reform" on June 28. At

the same time, the government publicized the estimates of the net tax reduction—about ¥2.4 trillion (= $18.73 billion; $1 = ¥128.15 in 1988)—
from the reform package. The revenue from the consumption tax—about
¥5.4 trillion (= $42.14 billion; $1 = ¥128.15 in 1988)—would be offset
easily by the income tax cut (about ¥3.1 trillion), the retrenchment of existing excise taxes on commodities (about ¥3.4 trillion), the corporate tax cut
(about ¥1.8 trillion), the inheritance tax cut, and so on.[30]

## AN UNEXPECTED OBSTACLE: UNCOVERING
## POLITICAL SCANDAL IN SECURITIES TRADING

In 1988, in light of the weakened opposition from special-interest groups,
the government could have expected easy passage of the consumption tax.
The unorganized public gave no active support for the new tax but, at the
same time, it had not yet found a reason to organize opposition to it. An
extraordinary session convened on July 19 with seventy days left in the
term. The demand for a tax reduction by the opposition parties gave the
government a good excuse to open the extraordinary session where it could
concentrate its energy on the passage of the tax bills. This time the opposition parties could not use the budget bill as a bargaining chip for opposition
to the tax bills as they had done by boycotting the budget deliberation in the
Diet when the sales tax bills had been submitted.

On May 29 (the same day as the passage of the bill for an income tax
reduction in the 1988 fiscal year), the cabinet endorsed six tax reform bills
and submitted them to the Diet. However, the Diet could not begin deliberations until four days before the end of the term because of the opposition
parties' resistance. An emerging political scandal provided the opposition
parties with a reason to refuse to deliberate on the tax bills.

The "Recruit problem" had originated from one newspaper's coverage
of the bribery of a deputy mayor by a real estate company, Recruit Cosmos.
It developed into a nationwide political problem involving a wide range of
politicians, including many LDP leaders and members of the major opposition parties (except the JCP), businessmen, journalists, and so on. The Recruit Cosmos, one of the affiliated companies of the Recruit, offered these
politicians opportunities to buy their stocks before offering them to the
public in the winter of 1984 and the fall of 1986. Since the recipients expected (or were believed to expect) a big surge in the price of the stocks
after they would be offered to the public, and since some of the recipients
obtained loans from the Recruit for their purchases, this was regarded as

211

insider trading and was investigated because of the suspicion of bribery. During the same period, the Recruit, which was rapidly expanding its business as a small company providing job information, also made large financial contributions to a wide range of politicians. The opposition movement, which had been relatively quiescent at earlier stages of the reform process, became active as the Recruit problem was politicized and was connected with the tax reform issue. The next section describes this process.

*A Split inside the Opposition Camp*

The Recruit problem began to be politicized around May, but it was not connected with tax reform immediately. Thus the opposition movement was not very active at first. For example, the result of the gubernatorial election in Fukushima Prefecture on September 4 showed that the public did not want absolute opposition to the new tax. The conservative candidate, who had refrained from revealing his position on the consumption tax, defeated both conservative and progressive candidates who had focused on the consumption tax as an electoral issue. The People's Conference had tried in the election campaign to activate the opposition movement against the new tax and had planned opposition meetings immediately before the election in Fukushima. However, this plan had been blocked by self-employed people who had supported the conservative candidate. The victory of this candidate contrasted well with the supplementary election in the Diet and the unified local elections of the previous year that had augmented the opposition movement to the sales tax. The election result in Fukushima showed that the self-employed people's opposition to the consumption tax was not strong enough to determine electoral results as their opposition to the sales tax had done.

The inability to link the tax issue with this election result impaired the solidarity of three opposition parties—the JSP, the CGP, and the DSP—in their resistance to the government's tax bills. The middle-of-the-road parties had already been concerned that in this three-party alliance, the JSP could appeal to the public most effectively. The CGP especially had tried to distinguish itself in the opposition camp by making a viable policy appeal for negotiations with the LDP rather than by expressing absolute opposition to the government's proposal. It now began to seek another strategy for increasing its influence over the tax issue. At the same time, the LDP attempted to force the CGP to leave the opposition alliance. Since the CGP served as a mediator between the JSP and the DSP, its removal would mean the collapse of the alliance.[31]

Besides some contingent factors concerning intraparty politics, public opinion discouraged the opposition parties' insistence on boycotting the Diet deliberations. A majority of the public was critical of the opposition parties' refusal to participate in the Diet deliberations. Opinion polls by *Nihon Keizai Shimbun* reported that, although about 30 percent of respondents accepted the boycotting of the deliberations by the opposition parties, more than 50 percent were critical of it (*NK*, September 26, 1988). The absence of popular support for the opposition parties' resistance reflected a weaker opposition movement to reform outside the Diet than when the sales tax had been proposed. If the public did not sensitively respond to the tax issue, the two middle-of-the-road parties found little meaning in their alliance with the JSP.

In early September, the Diet decided to establish the special research committee on the problem of the tax system (*zeisei mondaitō chōsa tokubetsu iinkai*), the purposes of which were to deliberate on the tax issue and investigate the Recruit problem. In order to obtain agreement for this committee, the LDP first compromised with the CGP and the DSP. The JSP, excluded from this bargaining, joined with the CGP and the DSP in hopes of maintaining the opposition alliance. The establishment of this special committee meant that the Recruit problem was beginning to be linked with the tax issue.

The deliberation on the tax bills began in the plenary session of the House of Representatives on September 22, and the bills were sent to the special committee on the same day. The JSP, the CGP, the DSP, and the SDL cooperated to publicize the "Basic Plan on the Tax System" as an alternative to the tax reform package proposed by the government on October 18. But, until November 16, when a majority of the LDP passed the tax bills in a plenary session of the HR attended by the CGP and the DSP, the opposition alliance was difficult to maintain; the socialists were absolutely opposed to the tax bills and uncompromising toward the Recruit problem, while the CGP was more flexible about both issues.

The tax bills finally passed the Diet in December after the CGP and the DSP agreed to attend the session. Before the enactment of the tax bills, the Diet had extended its session twice; this 163-day session was longer than any other extraordinary session in postwar history. The LDP spent a lot of time persuading the middle-of-the-road parties to attend the sessions in order to avoid deliberation by only the majority party, which the public would view as an abuse of numerical power.

Since the tax issue was intertwined with the Recruit problem, the middle-of-the-road parties—the CGP and the DSP—that had argued for an

213

investigation of this problem could not easily compromise on the tax bills whose passage they did not absolutely oppose. The LDP's reluctance to investigate the Recruit problem in the Diet exacerbated their dilemma. This was why the middle-of-the-road parties resisted voting on the tax bills in the special committees of both houses and why the LDP forced the votes and passed the bills by itself without the opposition parties' consent. But, reflecting public opinion critical of their boycotts, the CGP and the DSP helped the LDP open the following plenary sessions of the HR and the HC by attending them and let the incumbent party pass the tax bills. The attendance of both parties made the passage of the tax bills legitimate, though only the LDP voted on them. In this sense, they showed implicit consent to the bills' passage while maintaining their opposition to the tax reform in public. The JSP and the JCP had not attended the plenary session of the HR and prolonged the voting on the tax bills by "cow-walking" in the plenary session of the HC. Without major modifications, the tax bills passed in the HR on November 16 and were enacted on December 24 after passage in the HC.

### The Tax Issue Becomes Intertwined with Political Scandal

The Recruit problem was gradually politicized during the Diet's deliberations on the tax reform and became closely intertwined with the new tax after the passage of the bills. The politicization of this problem encouraged public opposition to the tax reform.[32] This problem, to which the tax issues had not been directly related, became linked in the public's mind with the new tax for three reasons. First, many LDP politicians, who were deeply involved in the tax reform, were found to have obtained stocks under their own names or the names of their secretaries and relatives and to have received contributions from the Recruit. The list of politicians included Prime Minister Takeshita; the former prime minister, Nakasone; Minister of Finance Miyazawa; the LDP secretary general, Abe; and chairman of the LDP PARC, Michio Watanabe. Minister of Finance Miyazawa was forced to resign after the opposition parties concentrated their attack on his vague explanation of his relationship with the Recruit, and later Prime Minister Takeshita served as minister of finance as well. In addition, Recruit appeared to have a close political connection with the LDP. For example, the president of Recruit, Hiromasa Ezoe, was also one of the special members appointed to the GTSRC at Nakasone's request.[33] Though three members of the opposition parties—one each from the JSP, the CGP, and the DSP— and the chairman of the DSP had also obtained the stocks, they resigned as

Diet members, and the DSP chairman resigned his party position. Their resignations provided a reason for public criticism to center on the LDP, which had not taken the same actions as the opposition parties.

Second, the public seemed to find the same kind of inequity and unfairness in the tax system as in this "problem." Since this kind of insider trading itself had not been illegal, those who gained large profits would not be prosecuted unless bribery was proven. In the public's eyes, the acquisition of big profits by privileged people without legal punishment bore a close parallel with tax privileges which they believed to be legally permitted in the existing system. In this sense, the Recruit problem reminded the voters of their discontent with the tax reform, especially in terms of rectification of tax inequity, and stirred up their resentment of the government.

Finally, this problem shed light on the imperfect taxation on capital gains as well as the lax regulation of securities trading. The media began to pay more attention to the "principal" taxation on capital gains in the reform package, and reported extensively that this measure fell short of their expectations for the rectification of tax inequity. The illumination of incomplete taxation on capital gains seemed to confirm that the incumbent party had not made sincere efforts to rectify tax inequity, while preserving tax privileges for prominent figures among the LDP politicians. Consequently, the Recruit problem provided a common reason for opposition among various social and occupational groups with different interests in taxation, and the consumption tax became a major target of opposition to the tax reform.

## The Rise and Fall of Public Opposition to the Consumption Tax

Public opposition outside the Diet had not been strong enough to support the alliance of the opposition parties, and had allowed the government to pass the tax bills. Ironically, it grew rapidly immediately after the enactment of the bills. With the introduction of the tax due in April, the public began to worry about the added burdens that might be imposed on them by the new system. In addition to apprehension about the unfamiliar tax, new facts concerning the Recruit problem contributed to the public's ability to articulate its opposition to the consumption tax and its mistrust of the government that had proposed it.

The consumption tax, now intertwined with the Recruit problem, became the major election issue for the first time in a supplementary election of the HC in Fukuoka on February 12, 1989. The candidate who had the support of the JSP and Rengō defeated his opponent on the LDP ticket. The next day, four businessmen, including the former president of the Recruit Corporation, Hiromasa Ezoe, were arrested on suspicion of bribery, and the Recruit problem became a criminal case. In March, the former president of Nippon Telephone and Telecommunication (NTT) and two former vice ministers (of the Ministry of Labor and the Ministry of Education) were also arrested on suspicion of bribery, that is, of acquiring securities as a reward for special business favors for Recruit.

Two middle-of-the-road parties that had cooperated with the LDP to pass the tax bills began to be threatened by rising public criticism of the new tax and the Recruit problem. Because some members of these parties were also involved in the Recruit problem, they were afraid that they were now associated with the LDP. These parties thus came to express absolute opposition to the new tax, as well as demand a thorough investigation of the Recruit problem. The leaders of the CGP and the DSP were forced to resign because of the Recruit scandal. Chairman of the DSP Saburō Tsukamoto, who had acquired securities from Recruit Cosmos, stepped down in early February, immediately before his second term as party chairman was to end.[34] In mid-May, Chairman of the CGP Junya Yano also resigned in order to take responsibility for one party member's acquisition of Recruit Cosmos stock and the party's involvement in another securities trading scandal.

At the same time, these parties began to distance themselves from the LDP and to ally with the JSP, which was obtaining public support for its consistent resistance to the consumption tax. The approval rate of the LDP cabinet dropped rapidly to a record-breaking low after the tax bills were passed in the HR, as journalists reported new relationships between the LDP and the Recruit.[35] Prime Minister Takeshita, who had hinted at resignation since the previous fall, finally left office in June.

Faced with public dissatisfaction with the new tax system, the GTSRC began to deliberate on "revision" at the end of June, less than three months after the system was installed. In the election campaign, the LDP tried to alleviate the public's negative feelings about the new tax by promising "revision" even though the MOF was reluctant to make a hasty revision. The LDP also criticized the alternative financial plan proposed by the opposition parties that argued for the "abolition" of the new tax system. But public support continued to side with the opposition camp, especially with the JSP which had not conceded to the government at all and whose leftist ideology was easier for a wider range of the electorate to accept than the JCP's.

The elections of half the seats in the HC resulted in an ignominious defeat for the LDP and a marvelous gain for the JSP. It was apparent that the consumption tax was a major reason for this result.[36] The LDP had had 69 contested seats out of 126, but won only 36 seats in the election. The socialists went from 22 to 46 seats, and 10 candidates supported by Rengō also obtained seats. The LDP lost a majority in the House in the Diet for the first time since its party formation in 1955. The number of LDP seats, combined with the remaining 73 seats which were not contested, was 109 and far from 50 percent of 252 total seats. Prime Minister Sōsuke Uno, who had hurt the LDP further by his own personal scandal in the election, resigned about three months after he entered office following Takeshita. Toshiki Kaifu was then elected prime minister. In the four short months after the consumption tax was introduced, there had already been three prime ministers.

In the general election in March 1990, however, about eight months after the election of the HC, the LDP won 275 seats out of 512. The JSP increased its number of seats, but the other opposition parties reduced their number of members. Waning public enthusiasm toward the tax issue explained the rapid resurgence of electoral support for the LDP. Before the general election, support for "the revision" of the consumption tax had begun to increase.[37] This change coincided with public disappointment with the opposition parties that had presented no attractive alternative proposal.[38]

Neither the government nor the Diet had made serious efforts to revise or repeal the system for two years after its implementation. In 1989 the government proposed a revision plan, but because the LDP lacked a majority in the HC, the opposition's support was needed to pass the bills. The opposition parties still argued for the abolition of the system and avoided a compromise with the LDP to revise it. In 1990, as public criticism of the consumption tax waned, the opposition parties began to propose a comprehensive revision focusing on decreasing the regressive characteristics of taxation. This time, the LDP and the opposition parties could agree on solving the "benefit tax" problem by improving the simple tax calculation method. However, their attempt to compromise collapsed in December 1990 because of a disagreement on tax exemption of food. While the opposition parties argued for tax exemption of all transactions and sales of food, the LDP proposed a tax exemption at the retail stage but a lower tax rate at the wholesale stage. Neither the LDP nor the opposition parties was eager to narrow substantially the range of tax exemption by retracting special tax filing measures. They expected a unified local election the following spring, and did not want to trigger antipathy from distributors and the self-employed by a revision of tax filing measures.

This failure to compromise, however, shifted public criticism from the LDP government to the opposition parties that insisted on tax exemption for food and refused to accept a government plan that would certainly improve the system. For example, Rengō criticized the JSP's uncompromising attitude. The opposition parties had hoped that their opposition would help them in the elections, but the results of the unified local elections betrayed their expectations.

Immediately after the elections, the LDP and the opposition parties agreed on a revision of the consumption tax system. First, the government restricted the number of firms that can employ the simple taxation method: only those with total annual sales of ¥400 million (previously ¥500 million) would have it as an option. The maximum level of the total sales amount was pushed down to ¥50 million from ¥60 million. The government also set four "quasi-ratios of purchases to total sales" that were more appropriate for different industrial sectors and businesses: these were 90 percent for wholesalers and 80 percent for retailers; two new ratios were applied to manufacturing, construction, mining, agriculture, and fishery (70 percent), and to services, transportation, telecommunications, and real estate (60 percent). This revision also required tax returns four times a year in order to shorten the period in which firms could use taxes for investment funds. The expansion of tax exemption was limited to a small range of services and commodities—house rents and more service fees in education, welfare, and medical care—and tax exemption of food was avoided. This revision was far from making the tax system consistent and effective from a technocratic point of view, but was still an improvement in the sense that it reduced distortions and discrimination by small tax measures. More important, the revision of the consumption tax was consistent with the MOF's intention not to increase the range of tax exemption and tax discrimination.

The bill to introduce the consumption tax had passed in the Diet with no significant modification; the opposition parties' strategy to resist the bill's passage had failed because of weak public opposition to the consumption tax at that stage. Public mistrust of the government as a result of the political scandal had yet to be linked with the tax issue. In the election three months after the installation of the new tax system, public criticism of the new tax caused the LDP's drastic loss of seats. Opposition to the consumption tax once demanded its abolition. This opposition movement, however, waned rapidly, and the consumption tax took root in Japanese society even though it had once been under intense criticism. Why had public opposition not increased until after the passage of the tax bills? Also, why did the opposition, which had once demanded the repeal of the new tax, quickly lose power?

The quiescence of opposition before the passage of the tax bills could be attributed to the various compromising measures in the new system that benefited special-interest groups, as well as the government's efforts to shape the agenda that served to justify its reform proposal. Even though the new tax had apparently been unpopular, public opinion could find no reason for the opposition that was as strong as "breaking the public promise" had been for the proposal of the sales tax. The opposition to the new tax neither articulated a criticism of the complicated government package nor came up with a viable alternative to the proposal. In addition, the new goal of securing financial resources for the aged contributed to the defense of the new tax against criticism of its regressive character. Financing social security expenditures, especially old-age pensions, by the consumption tax was expected to decrease social security benefits substantially through price increases. The complexity of tax incidence, however, was beyond the public's understanding. Thus the government's appeal to finance welfare expenditures with the new tax was effective in preventing the opposition from becoming active during the early stages of tax reform.

The MOF bureaucrats were conscious that the attractive reform aims were used *politically*—to weaken the opposition to the new tax—and that these aims were not fully justified from a technocratic point of view. They recognized that the introduction of the new tax could not lead *directly* to achievement of the advocated aims—rectification of tax inequity and provision of financial resources for increasing welfare expenditures. The LDP politicians who supported the new tax were less conscious of the existing gap between their sponsored proposal and the advocated aims. For example, many LDP leaders who gave critical support for the new tax were eager to make a new financial plan to allocate revenue from the consumption tax for welfare programs. Here, the MOF bureaucrats were more "political" than the incumbent politicians in the sense that they adopted the attractive aim purely as a means to appeal to the public. The bureaucrats fully recognized the political nature of the tax proposal.

At the same time, there existed an explicit limitation for the bureaucrats in influencing the political agenda: the bureaucrats depended on the incumbent politicians to articulate the interests of the opposing groups and to seek compromises with them. This was why the MOF bureaucrats adopted many compromising measures suggested by the incumbent politicians in so far as these measures did not contradict their minimum imperative—establishing a broad tax based on consumption. In this sense, the fiscal bureaucrats profited from cooperation with incumbent politicians (as well as other ministries, i.e., the MITI) to cultivate the opposition of special-interest groups: they did not concede to the compromising measures that would narrow the tax base even though the political pressure was intense. Because of their dependence on the incumbent party, however, the bureaucrats failed to pay attention to the less organized interests, which were not well represented by the incumbent party—consumers and salaried workers. Their indifference to these unorganized interests explained the rise of opposition that threatened the newly introduced consumption tax.

The government's persuasion faltered when the unorganized public, which had been alienated from making the final plan, could change their dissatisfaction with the new tax to a concrete reason for opposition. The emerging Recruit problem uncovered the acquisition of big profits in securities' trading by privileged and well-informed people involved in policy-making. The public found in this scandal a basis for opposition to the new tax—its mistrust of the government. Despite the seemingly active public discussion of tax issues for one year after the introduction of the new tax, however, the opposition failed to reach a consensus on a concrete reform proposal that could have repealed it. The opposition consisted of a wide range of social groups—from consumers and salaried workers who resented the government's special consideration of organized interests, to self-employed people who reverted to opposing the consumption tax even with its generous tax-filing measures. Though all of them were dissatisfied with the tax reform, they had conflicting interests. Thus the movement inevitably faded when the political scandal ended with the prosecution of several people. The MOF ultimately succeeded in introducing the broad-based tax on consumption, while imposing a massive political cost on the incumbent LDP.

# Conclusion: Bureaucracy, Party, and the Power of Rationality

IN JUNE 1991 the chairman of the Japan Socialist Party, Takako Doi, resigned in order to take responsibility for her party's defeat in the unified local elections in the spring. In 1986 she had become the first female party head in Japan. Her steadfast opposition to the new consumption tax won public support and led the JSP to the biggest victory in its history in the election of the House of Councillors in 1989. Thereafter, she continued to insist on abolishing the new consumption tax, expecting this strategy to augment her party's popularity. Her leadership had prevented the party from agreeing with the government to revise the new system, even though some party members had begun to support compromises with the incumbent Liberal Democratic Party in revising the new system. Therefore, despite her personal popularity, her failure to win the election while using the tax issue forced her to resign.[1] Her resignation, as well as the passage of the bill to revise the consumption tax system (the previous May), symbolized the end of a period in which opposition to the consumption tax was the issue used to determine public support for the parties. As the tax issue became less salient and public opposition to the consumption tax decreased, the Ministry of Finance became more confident that the consumption tax had taken root in Japanese society.

The present study has regarded the ultimate establishment of an unpopular new tax in Japanese society as the result of successful political maneuvering by bureaucrats. It has examined the interests of fiscal bureaucrats and observed how they pursue these interests in a democratic polity. Building on the tax reform case, the analysis has first shown that fiscal bureaucrats expressed their interest in power through their efforts to control the budget. Next, the study has explored the possibility that fiscal bureaucrats attempt to achieve their desired policy outcomes by strategic maneuverings.

The MOF's concern for maintaining discretionary power over the budget was apparent in its response to the fiscal crisis in the 1970s. The most significant manifestation was its persistent attempt to introduce a new indirect tax broadly based on consumption. Faced with an unexpected revenue shortfall since the mid-1970s, the MOF endeavored to ensure the stability of tax revenue, as well as to secure more financial resources. When this revenue shortfall led to chronic dependence on deficit bonds, the MOF took up the new consumption tax as an important policy objective. The tax was expected to yield more stable revenue than the income tax with progressive rates. Among various types of consumption taxes, the MOF preferred the value-added tax as the most consistent system from a technocratic point of view.

This study examines how the bureaucrats attempted to achieve their policy objectives by strategic manipulation of the policy-making process, namely, by enlisting support from the incumbent party, shaping the political agenda, and compromising with special-interest groups. This study is especially concerned with the relationship between bureaucrats and party politicians. I start from the assumption that bureaucrats need to obtain cooperation from the incumbent politicians in their attempt to implement a favored policy; I consider the possibility of bureaucratic influence under intensive interactions with or interventions by the politicians. More specifically, to implement an unpopular policy, in this case the new tax, the bureaucrats need to identify and utilize conflicting interests of party politicians—especially between those who are mostly concerned with reelection and those who wish to promote their reputation inside the policy-making circle—and to enlist the latter's support. While utilizing dividing interests in the party organization, the bureaucratic organization needs to maintain its consensual decision making and coordination of behaviors by informing members of organizational interests, as well as appropriate behaviors to pursue them. Using the Japanese tax reform case, the study argues and shows that the (bureaucratic) organization can provide a good internal mechanism that organizes individual behaviors to pursue rationally common objectives.

This chapter first shows that the introduction of a new consumption tax was especially difficult in Japan, if one considers the accompanying political and policy conditions. I introduce several comparative cases of other countries that recently introduced the VAT. Next, my argument is compared to other possible explanations for the same case. In the final section, recent changes in Japanese politics are examined, especially the LDP's split and a subsequent demise of LDP rule. I explain the LDP's split as a result of the party's failure to coordinate members' different interests, which was also recurrently observed in the tax-reform process. At the same time, I show a prospect of bureaucratic influence on policy-making in a situation where party governments are undergoing changes. This chapter then concludes by suggesting the general implications of bureaucratic influence and the power of rationality in politics.

## JAPANESE TAX REFORM IN A COMPARATIVE PERSPECTIVE: INTRODUCTION OF THE VALUE-ADDED TAX

In the Japanese tax reform case, the importance of bureaucratic influence was further underscored by the marked political difficulty in the enactment of the VAT. A comparison of Japan with other countries that have enacted a VAT will clarify Japan's difficult passage of this reform. For example, the EC countries that introduced the VAT in the 1970s attached more political meaning to tax reforms than to usual domestic policies. The new tax system was mandated for the harmonization of European markets among the twelve EC countries.

Japan had no special political reason, as the EC countries had, to incorporate a new VAT into its tax reform plan. On the contrary, because it differed from the U.S. income tax reform under the Reagan administration, which had great influence on tax reforms in other countries at the time, the Japanese government's proposal of the new tax was more vulnerable to criticism. In 1986 the U.S. reform had initiated a new direction for the reform of income taxation by simplifying its structure—compressing the number of tax brackets and decreasing the tax rate while broadening the tax base. In Japan, the mass media and tax specialists, as well as Prime Minister Nakasone and the MOF, lauded the U.S. reform. Although the reform ideals proposed by the government resembled those of the U.S. reform, the Japanese reform itself was not modeled exactly on this predecessor. The Japanese tax reform simplified the income tax structure, but at the same time introduced the VAT, which the American policymakers at the time had rejected because of its regressive characteristics.

Moreover, all the countries that had introduced a VAT before Japan had used it to replace an inferior indirect tax system. France, Italy, Germany, and the Netherlands had used turnover or production taxes that accumulate the tax amount from one stage to the next, and Britain had had a wholesale sales tax (Aaron 1981, 7). Many other countries, for example, Canada, Denmark, Greece, Ireland, New Zealand, Norway, Portugal, and Sweden also had implemented single-stage general consumption taxes before the introduction of the VAT.[2] In these countries people were familiar with taxes on consumption, and administering the VAT was similar to, although

223

not the same as, the existing consumption tax. At the same time, the governments used a convincing justification, that is, the replacement of an inferior single-stage general consumption tax with a superior multistage tax on consumption; public financial economists unanimously support the latter if compared to the former.

The OECD data in 1985[3] shows that Japan was a peculiar case in that it lacked a general consumption tax of any form (that is, it had nothing like a broad-based consumption tax, including a single-stage tax) before the introduction of the consumption tax in 1989. In Japan, the excise tax on specific commodities and services was regarded as an incomplete form of the general consumption tax; however, the existing indirect tax system covered a much narrower range of consumption items and services. Therefore, the Japanese were totally unfamiliar with a consumption tax, and the introduction of the new tax required additional administrative actions to manage the system. In addition, most Japanese people supported the existing commodity taxes that were levied on "luxury" goods in spite of the fact that these taxes are considered inferior to the broad-based consumption tax in terms of simplicity and effectiveness of taxation, as well as the distorted effect they have on markets.

The peculiar situations in Japan that made the VAT's introduction difficult are more illuminated when viewed in comparison with other countries that recently introduced it. East Asian countries, Taiwan (in 1986) and South Korea (in 1977), also used the VAT to improve their existing indirect tax systems that included a turnover tax. For example, in South Korea, before the tax reform in 1976, there existed both excise and turnover taxes with more than fifty different rates, ranging from 0.5 percent to 300 percent (Kwack and Lee 1992, 120). It is not hard to imagine that the ordinary public, as well as the tax specialists, were conscious of distortions and adverse effects of the complicated tax system. Taiwan also had a turnover tax that was called the business tax before the reform in the mid-1980s (Lin 1992), and the introduction of the VAT meant a clear improvement of this inferior multistage tax that accumulated the tax amount from one stage to another. In addition, at the time of the VAT's introduction, political opposition was not very strong in either country.

Among advanced industrial countries, Canada (in 1991) and New Zealand (in 1986) introduced the VAT almost at the same time as Japan. Canada had as difficult a time as Japan in introducing an invoice-type VAT, though Canada's conditions were much more advantageous for its introduction—existing inferior major indirect taxes. Before the introduction of the VAT, called the Goods and Services Tax (GST), Canadians had a system of three different taxes on consumption—a manufacturers' sales tax (MST) at the federal level, a retail sales tax (RST) at the providential level, and some excise taxes on selective commodities at both the federal and providential levels. The GST was proposed as a replacement of the MST at the federal level; the MST caused serious distortions—exemptions of all services and certain goods, multiple tax rates, promotion of incentives to push costs and distribution functions as far forward as possible in the transaction process (to decrease tax at the level of manufacturing), and an advantage to imported goods over domestic products (Kitchen 1987, 381). Though major indirect taxes on consumption, both at the federal and providential levels, were a special problem for the Canadian introduction of the VAT, the very existence of the MST should have been reason enough for the government's proposal of the VAT as a measure to replace it. For example, public discussion tended to concentrate on the superiority of the GST to the MST, and did not focus on other alternatives to the MST (Dungan, Mintz, and Wilson 1990, 647). Despite this seemingly favorable condition, the Progressive Conservative administration under Prime Minister Brian Mulroney not only encountered fierce opposition, which postponed the introduction of 7 percent of the GST, but also suffered from the decline of Mulroney's approval rating until he stepped down in June 1993:[4] the tax was blamed for contributing to Canada's prolonged recession.

New Zealand may be a more interesting case than Canada for comparison with Japan. The labor government in New Zealand, which also employed a tax mix strategy of income tax reduction and enhancement of consumption tax, used almost the same reasons as the Japanese government to propose tax reform in the 1980s. First, it used the existence of deficits as a reason for the introduction of the VAT (called the GST).[5] This was the exact reason given by the Japanese government, more precisely, the MOF and Prime Minister Ōhira, in the late 1970s. Second, the New Zealand government argued that the introduction of the VAT was the only way to improve the existing income tax system by effectively applying a consumption tax on the rich, who might have evaded their income taxation (New Zealand Government 1984, 9–10; New Zealand Government 1985, 3). This reasoning was also used by Japanese who supported the introduction of the VAT. The MOF regarded the new tax as more effectively applied than income tax. It aimed at shifting revenue reliance from direct to indirect taxation in the second proposal of the sales tax in the mid-1980s, and rectifying tax inequity in the proposal of the consumption tax which was finally introduced in 1989. In public debates, some economists and opinion leaders argued that the VAT was a convenient way to decrease distortions and evasions in the existing income taxation, and tried to justify the Japanese government's proposal.[6]

Despite these inherent similarities of the tax proposals between the two countries, however, the New Zealand government met with much less political opposition than the Japanese did. The New Zealand government used similar reasoning much more effectively to obtain public support than did the Japanese fiscal authority. The question here is whether this difference was due to political reasons or whether it derived from more skillful maneuvering by policymakers in New Zealand?

An important difference in partisan politics existed between Japan and New Zealand in the 1980s when both governments grappled with the introduction of the VAT. In New Zealand, the labor government came to office virtually without political commitments. The labor party had made no public promises about economic policies because it won in a snap election (Groenewegen 1988, 102). Moreover, the labor government inherited budget deficits from the conservative government which was in office during most of the 1960s and 1970s; it also had to deal with a tax system that it criticized as distorted in the tax reform proposal. In other words, the labor government in New Zealand had a free hand to propose and change policies. Contrary to this situation, in Japan the LDP had been in office since 1955 and was responsible for all the economic policies. This was why the public did not accept the government's proposal for the VAT as a measure to finance the budget deficit in the late 1970s. This was also why the fiscal authority, aware of the distortions of the income taxation and the erosion of the tax base, could not use these factors as direct reasons for the introduction of the VAT.

At the same time, since the 1970s, the ideal of a comprehensive income taxation in New Zealand had eroded in the public's mind, but such an ideal was still viable in Japan in the 1980s. For example, in New Zealand the rate-scale simplification in the 1970s (clearly counter to the ideal of progressive taxation) preceded the further rate simplification from a five-step scale to a three-step scale of 15, 30, and 48 percent in the mid-1980s (New Zealand Government 1985, 13). The idea of simple, effective taxation was dominant among policymakers who advocated a free-market ideology.[7] The existence of consensus on simple taxation in New Zealand contrasted markedly with the persistent Japanese allegiance to the progressivity of income taxation. While the public showed continuous support for progressivity, the MOF bureaucrats themselves were ambivalent about it: they did not completely give up reforming the income tax system itself, that is, broadening the income tax base, but they supported the introduction of the VAT as an indirect measure to rectify tax inequity.

The last point concerns the existence of a wholesale tax in New Zealand. This tax was introduced in the 1930s with a fairly broad tax base, but this base was eroded to the level at which only a quarter or a third of the total private expenditure on consumption was covered in the 1980s (Groenewegen 1988, 94). The wholesale tax in New Zealand was getting closer to an excise tax on selective commodities, such as existed in Japan, than to the general consumption tax that it should have been. In this sense, the New Zealanders, as well as the Japanese, were unfamiliar with a broad-based tax on consumption. However, there was still an important difference. The complex system of the wholesale tax in New Zealand had some visible disadvantages for consumers, that is, the retail price increase in addition to the amount of the wholesale tax levied on the previous transaction stage[8] (New Zealand Government 1984, 10–11). The Japanese excise tax on selective commodities (i.e., eighty-five kinds of commodities in 1987) and services was considered distorted and complex by policymakers and tax specialists. But Japanese consumers supported this system without noticing tax burdens that were usually included in the price.[9] In this way, while the introduction of the VAT was considered consistent with consumers' interests in New Zealand, in Japan it appeared pitted against them.

The preceding comparison shows that Japanese policymakers took an approach to the introduction of the VAT similar to their counterparts in New Zealand, but encountered more difficulty in implementing it because of several differences in political and policy conditions. The New Zealand case implies that the Japanese MOF might have implemented the broad-based tax on consumption more easily if conditions had been similar to those available to the New Zealand policymakers.

## JAPANESE TAX REFORM IN A BROADER POLITICAL CONTEXT: THE RELATIONSHIP BETWEEN BUREAUCRATS AND POLITICIANS

The previous section showed that the introduction of the VAT in Japan was exceptionally difficult compared to countries that recently introduced similar major indirect taxes. This section examines possible explanations for the uniqueness of Japan's tax reform case by using existing views of Japanese politics under the LDP's one-party predominance. These explanations include, respectively, the statist approach, the pluralist approach, the social coalition analysis, and the rational choice approach.

As reviewed at the beginning of chapter 2, the two existing approaches for studying Japanese politics—the statist and the pluralist positions—evaluate the power balance between bureaucrats and politicians differently.

227

Whereas the former accepts the persistence of bureaucratic influence, the latter points out that the incumbent LDP has increased its influence at the expense of bureaucrats. At the same time, however, both statist and pluralist approaches shed light on the more complex relationship between the two groups of policymakers. As discussed in chapter 2, the statist position has come to pay much attention to the role of politicians in policy-making (Okimoto 1989). Pluralist theorists also admit the influence of bureaucrats, in spite of politicians' increasing interference in policy-making (Satō and Matsuzaki 1986; Inoguchi and Iwai 1987; Muramatsu and Krauss 1987). But neither of these approaches directly addresses the question of why bureaucratic influence persisted as the LDP's policy-making ability increased. Each approach is concerned with generalizing the policy-making process in terms of the power relationship between bureaucrats and politicians.

The Japanese tax reform in the 1980s is an interesting but controversial case for considering the relationship between the LDP and the bureaucracy in terms of existing views. First, the reform process since the late 1970s corresponded exactly with the period in which the LDP's influence over tax policy-making increased significantly (see the final section in chapter 2). Tax policy was considered the best example of a policy field in which the LDP gained influence at the expense of the monopolistic policy-making power that bureaucrats once enjoyed. Journalists and scholars often referred to the LDP Tax System Research Council (one of the subcommittees of the Policy Affairs Research Council) to show incumbent politicians' growing interest and increasing interference in the details of policy-making.

Second, this case provides evidence for two contradictory explanations for the power relationship between the LDP and the MOF. Despite much opposition from society in general, the MOF had intended to introduce the new consumption tax for more than a decade. The statist view, therefore, would use the introduction of the new tax as a manifestation of strong bureaucratic power embedded in the Japanese political system. The pluralist view, however, attaches more importance to the LDP's role in the introduction of the new tax by emphasizing that the LDP was mainly in charge of alleviating opposition to the new tax from special-interest groups.

Neither view provides a consistent explanation of the entire reform process. First, the statist view falls short of explaining the failures of the two MOF proposals for new consumption taxes in 1979 and 1987. That the MOF needed a decade-long effort to finally introduce the consumption tax in 1989 runs counter to the statist view of strong bureaucrats who are autonomous and insulated from political pressure. Some pluralists provide excellent accounts of the two tax reforms in the 1980s, that is, the proposals of the sales tax (in 1987) and the consumption tax (in 1988) from their viewpoint (Inoguchi and Iwai 1987, 256–72). The pluralist view, however, still does not adequately explain why the LDP leaders, many of whom had opposed the introduction of the new tax in the late 1970s, came to support its introduction in the late 1980s. Nor does it consistently explain why incumbent politicians with specialized knowledge and power to intervene in policy decisions supported such an unpopular policy as the consumption tax.

The weaknesses of both views in explaining the recent tax reform process derive from their common assumption about the power of technocratic bureaucrats. Both approaches implicitly assume that bureaucrats' monopolization of policy information and expertise ensures their dominant influence over policy-making. Thus the pluralist position, which regards the LDP's increasing policy-making power as a significant change in the Japanese policy-making process in the 1980s, concludes that bureaucratic influence had declined. Observing the same change, the statist position argues that bureaucratic dominance in policy-making persisted despite the LDP's increasing ability. Both positions, therefore, find it difficult to provide a consistent explanation for the tax reform case in which bureaucrats ultimately won, but only after two defeated attempts.

The argument presented here appreciates the importance of policy information and expertise for bureaucrats to exercise influence over policy-making. But it attributes bureaucratic influence to *the strategic use of policy information and technocratic expertise*, not simply to controlling information and taking advantage of the relative ignorance of party politicians and the electorate.

The alternative explanation, which regards Japanese politics as a "conservative social coalition" of the LDP, bureaucrats, and major business associations, may still challenge this study's account of the tax reform. Differing from the focus on policymakers seen in both the statist and pluralist views, this view pays more attention to one consequence of policymaking, that is, the low salience of "popular" representation (McCormack and Sugimoto 1986). According to this view, the tax reform in the 1980s is a good example of collusive interests of the predominant LDP, the bureaucracy, and major business associations. It is a result of the underrepresentation of the will of the unorganized public, particularly consumers and salaried workers (Yamaguchi 1989, 221–58; Shindō 1989, 179–235). The rising consumer opposition to the new tax *after its introduction*, as well as the lack of consumers' effective representation during the tax-reform process, seem to support this view. However, this explanation assumes more coherent interests within the ruling conservative coalition and among the unorganized public than actually existed. First, it presumes that the ruling conservative coalition had given constant support to the introduction of the major indirect tax. It pays little attention to the fact that many of the LDP leaders and major business associations of large-scale manufacturers[10] had changed their opposition to support for the new tax in the early 1980s.

Second, the introduction of the new tax did not repress a certain reform alternative that had the support of the unorganized public.[11] Rather, the major reason for the passage of the new consumption tax was that opposing groups could not come up with a viable reform alternative to the government's proposal, despite the seemingly active public debate on the tax reform. After the public agreed to restructure the existing tax system in the mid-1980s, a reform alternative was needed to oppose effectively the introduction of the new tax that the MOF had presented as an inevitable part of that structural reform. Academicians, economists, and tax specialists in the private sector frequently corrected the statements and data presented by the government that they felt overemphasized the merit of the new tax. But their policy suggestions showed academic accuracy rather than political clarity. They failed to give the public a clear idea about tax problems that might have generated an alternative to the government's proposal. The failed attempt to make a viable alternative can be attributed to contradictory public claims about the tax reform instead of a lack of competent policy staff on the opposition side. The unorganized public supported a slogan of "comprehensive income tax reform." At the same time it opposed the introduction of the identification number system, which is crucial for comprehending individuals' income as a tax base. This was an important reason why the opposition parties could not make a viable alternative plan to the new tax even when the public gave its strong support to their proposal for abolition of the new tax system (see chapter 6).

The rational choice perspective is of special interest to examine here. Though its general conclusion of the incumbent LDP's larger role in policy-making resembles the pluralist one, the rational choice perspective's emphasis on reelection incentives of backbenchers and their representation of constituencies' interests further clarifies an important aspect of political intervention. Among many cases of such political interventions in tax policies motivated by special-interest representations, the most notable example in the 1980s was the failure of a "green-card" system. In 1979 the MOF proposed to introduce the "green card," an identification card (like a social security card in the United States) that would aim to comprehend total amounts of individuals' interests from five specific kinds of investment and savings exempted from taxation under a certain limit.[12] The tax authority decided to employ this card system in order to accurately assess the income individuals derived from interest. The government planned to tax the interest in conjunction with other income from the 1984 fiscal year. The government bill for this reform was passed by the LDP's support in the Diet in April 1980.

In the fall of 1981 a sudden rising opposition from the LDP, special interests, and opposition parties against the green-card system forced the MOF to promise the "flexible" (as opposed to strict) implementation of this system. Several different reasons accounted for the opposition.[13] First, the banking industries were worried about the disincentive to savings—especially a flow of funds from deposit accounts to other assets or bonds with more tax privileges.[14] Second, the Ministry of Posts and Telecommunications and the post offices were worried about the MOF's increasing control over the funds in postal saving accounts. The postal service and banking industries began to increase pressure on the LDP politicians who were connected with their interests. Finally, the opposition parties began to oppose this system formidably as a threat to the general public and a violation of privacy. The Diet decided to suspend the implementation of the system in April 1983.

The green-card system was a typical case of political influence over tax policy-making that clearly was against the interests of fiscal bureaucrats. The green-card problem involved complicated conflicts between the MOF and the MPT, and between the postal service and the private financial industry, as well as competition between the LDP politicians, who were close to the MOF and represented the MPT's interest, and the financial institutions. Inoguchi and Iwai (1987, 237–42) explained this as a case in which even a powerful bureaucratic organization such as the MOF was forced to change its policies in the face of LDP politicians connected with special interests. In their view, a special weakness of the MOF, which became apparent in this case, was that the MOF's allies inside the LDP (leaders of the public finance tribe; ōkura zoku) did not adequately represent the interests of fiscal bureaucrats. Rather, these politicians accepted a majority of backbenchers' opposition and acted as their agents to block the policy against special interests. In this sense, the green-card case fully supported the rational choice perspective's major argument—that backbenchers' reelection incentives, not bureaucratic intentions, determine the major consequences of policy-making.

Although both cases—the introduction of the VAT and the failure to establish the green-card system—involved the more active role of the LDP politicians and the MOF's critical interests in policy-making, the consequences were quite different. In the green-card case, representation of special interests by the LDP politicians—especially backbenchers—dominated the policy-making, and experienced politicians and policy specialists simply followed the majority opinion, that is, the opinion of line members. In the case of the introduction of the VAT, the party leaders repressed backbenchers' opposition to the new tax and allowed the biggest loss in elections, while implementing the policy that was of interest to the MOF.[15] Why were the two cases, in the same policy field during the same period, so different?

As the rational choice perspective argues, reelection is the most important concern for party politicians in general. In many policy-making cases, the LDP politicians' concern for reelection is an essential factor in explaining policy outcomes. But as politicians have long tenures, they are more likely to come up with a very different kind of interest. As the role of the LDP PARC in policy-making is institutionalized, the incumbent politicians who have organized their electoral support have an incentive to increase their influence inside the party. This new incentive motivates the party members with longer tenures to be aloof to specific-interest pressure and works as a constraint on backbenchers whose major concern is reelection. While an overemphasis on specific interests often obstructs their promotion within the party and into legislative positions, effective demonstration of a "general" concern for policies increases their reputation and promotes their intraparty influence. Thus the incumbent politicians must choose between, or at least balance out, the necessity of constituency service and their interest in promotion within the party and legislature.

Experienced politicians' desire to promote their reputation gives the bureaucrats the opportunity to persuade them to accept policies about which they share understanding or specialized knowledge. The tax reform case provides excellent evidence for this argument that the bureaucrats coped with incumbent politicians who had two different incentives in policy-making. In the tax-reform case, support for the introduction of the VAT was considered a qualification to understand complicated tax policies and a sign of expertise among party politicians. Thus the bureaucrats could obtain the support of experienced politicians. In the green-card case, on the other hand, the bureaucrats could not promote the interest of experienced politicians: the green-card system was so simple that politicians' understanding of the system could not be considered a sign of their policy expertise. This difference requires a special attention because it explains a reason why the LDP leaders who were familiar with tax issues repressed backbenchers' opposition to defend the bureaucratic proposal in one case but not in another.

## BUREAUCRATIC INFLUENCE AND THE POWER OF
## RATIONALITY IN POLITICS

### Extensions of the Case: Intraparty Dynamics of the LDP and Changes in Party Governments

As I have explained in the previous section, bureaucratic influence hinged on whether bureaucrats found ways to exploit different interests of politicians in the same incumbent party in the Japanese tax reform case. As I emphasized in the introduction, the LDP's one-party predominance is used as an idealistic condition in which the interaction between the bureaucratic organization and the same incumbent party can be observed without considering the factors involving alterations of party governments or formations of party coalitions. At the same time, stability of partisan politics encourages bureaucrats to become more politically involved. While uncertainty and the impossibility of predicting future political conditions decrease the meaning of the strategic behaviors of bureaucrats, bureaucrats can form expectations about future conditions under stable partisan politics and pursue certain policy objectives in the long run. The political party itself is also likely to organize and institutionalize the pattern of governing after being in office for a long time. This is why the study also pays attention to intraparty dynamics inside the LDP.

As I have shown by using the tax reform case, coordinating members' interests is indispensable for maintaining the party's coherence. This problem of interest coordination is also related to the recent major change in Japanese party politics—the split of the LDP in June 1993. Different interests of party members brought several crises during the LDP's long-term governance, but the most recent crisis in 1993 finally resulted in the breakup of the party.

On June 18, 1993, a nonconfidance motion against Miyazawa's cabinet presented by the JSP, the CGP, and the DSP, was passed in the House of Representatives. A total of 255 members, including 39 from the LDP, voted for this motion against 217 LDP members and 3 conservative independents. Most of these LDP dissidents and some of 18[16] members who

233

abstained from voting, subsequently quit the party and formed two new conservative parties—the Renewal Party (*Shinseitō*), consisting of the previous Hata faction members, and the Harbinger (*Shintō Sakigake*), consisting of 9 junior members headed by Masayoshi Takemura as an experienced politician.

Since the formation of the LDP in 1955, this was only the second time a nonconfidence motion was passed. The first one was in 1980, when the late Prime Minister Ōhira was trapped in an intraparty conflict after the proposal of the unpopular general consumption tax. However, the passage of the nonconfidence motion in 1993 was different from the previous one. First, almost a sixth of the LDP members in the HR voted for it and sixteen members were intentionally absent, while the previous passage was mainly caused by the chaotic situation resulting from factional conflict. Second, this time the line dividing the members of the LDP for and against the cabinet did not necessarily correspond to a difference in factions, whereas the hardship of the Ōhira cabinet in 1980 resulted from animosities between different factions.

The LDP's split in 1993 dated back to a breakup of the Takeshita faction (*Keiseikai*) in December 1992, which had long been most influential inside the LDP. Resulting from intense strife involving the next leadership of the biggest faction inside the LDP, it caused Tsutomu Hata to declare that he would leave the faction with forty-four members from both houses of the Diet and support Ichirō Ozawa, who was isolated from some influential members because of his strong-armed management of the faction. This group was named "Forum 21" and competed with the remaining part of the Keiseikai faction. The latter subsequently formed a faction headed by Keizō Obuchi (Obuchi faction), with Seiroku Kajiyama and Ryūtarō Hashimoto, who had been rivals of Ozawa.[17]

In the meantime, a scandal involving a truck company, Sagawa Kyūbin was disclosed: a small mob had been reportedly involved in the selection of Takeshita as the LDP president. This developed into a money scandal involving the LDP vice president, Shin Kanemaru. This new scandal further illuminated the importance of the reforms of the political fund-control system, as well as the HR election system,[18] which were attempted but failed to succeed under the Kaifu cabinet. The animosity between the two groups of the former Keiseikai revolved around these issues. The Hata faction became an enthusiastic supporter of political reform, although Ozawa had been closely tied with Kanemaru as a mentor. This was partially a result of the group's antipathy toward the Obuchi faction, which had retained important party positions in the Miyazawa cabinet and thus maintained a cautious attitude about these issues. More important, however, a positive attitude about political reforms was likely to strengthen the Hata faction's intraparty position, which had been inferior to that of the Obuchi faction. This issue could attract backbenchers across factions.

Political reforms had been important since the Recruit problem. Junior members, especially those who had only one or two terms, came to be irritated by the factions and party leadership that failed to carry out reforms of the electoral and political fund-control systems. For example, in December 1991, after an attempt at political reform was defeated under the Kaifu cabinet, largely by the intraparty opposition, fifty-eight members, mainly backbenchers, formed the Association of Junior Members for Political Reform (*Seiji Kaikaku o Jitsugensuru Wakate Giin no Kai*). Throughout 1992, the LDP junior members even began to form study groups and associations with backbenchers of the opposition parties aiming at reforms of the political fund control and electoral systems. This movement constituted an important part of the transition in Japanese party politics in that year. It was also facilitated by the split of the biggest LDP faction, Keiseikai (as described above) and the formation of another conservative party, the Japan New Party.

As discussed in chapter 2, backbenchers of the LDP were more concerned with reelections than experienced members, but at the same time they needed to abide by the party and faction leadership decisions often against constituencies' interests. The HR election system of multimember (mostly 3–5 seats) districts with single nontransferable votes had contributed to their dilemma. Since they were likely to pit themselves against other conservative candidates, to advantage themselves in competitions with similar candidates they needed party nominations as well as financial and personal back-ups, which depended on the good will of the party and faction leadership. In this sense, compliance with their bosses was important for junior members but it could cost them the loss of constituencies' support when the party leadership decision was against their interests. Alternatively, if they were faithful to their constituencies against the leadership's will, they would be punished—by being deprived of nominations, by having financial or personal support cut, or by being assigned unfavorable positions in the party as well as in the Diet.[19]

Obviously, junior members who had established neither a strong organizational base inside the party nor a solid electoral base inside their district were interested in changing the electoral system. The experienced and leading members, in general, had vested interests in the present system in which they retained more controls over their electoral base, as well as faction subordinates. This difference in interests between junior and senior members became apparent in intraparty discussions on political reform before the LDP's split in 1993. Many junior members were more eager to compromise with the opposition parties in incorporating into a new electoral system elements of the proportional representation that were believed to give smaller parties an advantage. On the other hand, many leaders, except those in the Hata faction as well as the traditionally reform-oriented Kōmoto faction,[20] maintained a cautious attitude and clung to the former party decision to establish a single-member district system. Opinion polls among the LDP members by the LDP secretary general, Seiroku Kajiyama, in May confirmed these divided opinions inside the LDP, as well as inside each faction. All the major factions—headed by Mitsuzuka (formerly, Abe), Miyazawa, Watanabe (formerly, Nakasone), and Obuchi—split between the members who supported flexible compromises with the opposition parties and those who clung to a single-member district system that was believed to give the LDP an advantage. All the members of the Hata faction and a majority of those in the Kōmoto faction supported the compromise plan that was likely to obtain the opposition parties' approval, and the Katō group, a splinter of the former Abe faction, primarily supported some kind of compromise (*Asahi*, June 3, 1993).

The frustration of junior members reached a peak when the LDP leadership decided to cling to a single-member district system, which the opposition parties could not accept. They expressed their noncompliance with the leadership in their attitude toward a nonconfidence motion against the Miyazawa cabinet submitted by the opposition parties. Three out of five who voted for the motion outside the Hata faction were junior members with one and two terms: ten out of sixteen members who did not attend the voting were also such juniors. The Harbinger (*Sakigake*), which was subsequently formed, consisted of nine junior members with one or two terms, headed by a senior leader. It was rare that backbenchers or junior members acted against the leadership in voting on such an important issue.

The LDP's thirty-eight-year-long one-party predominance was interrupted by the party's split without having to wait for an electoral defeat. Although it remains to be seen which direction the Japanese party system will take, this split shows that the intragenerational conflict inside the party, which factional rivalries overshadowed, is an important factor in the analysis of the LDP's past dominance. In the proposal of the consumption tax in 1988, seniors and party leaders finally succeeded in repressing the revolts of backbenchers. Five years after that, junior members became the power that precipitated the LDP's breakup.

The political change in Japan in 1993 also provides a new insight into the relationship between bureaucratic power and party politics. The passage of a nonconfidence motion in the LDP cabinet was followed by general elections in which the LDP could not restore the majority that had been lost by the pre-election exit of dissident party members. Seven parties and one legislative group formed the new coalition government, while leaving the LDP and the JCP as opposition parties. A new prime minister, Hosokawa, came from the Japan New Party, which had been formed about a year earlier. With this first non-LDP government since 1955, many observers of Japanese politics believe there will be a decline of political control over the bureaucracy. According to them, now that the LDP, which has many policy specialists, has lost its predominance and the future governments are expected to be formed by parties with little experience in policy-making, bureaucrats are more likely to dominate policy-making than before.

I disagree with the above interpretation of bureaucratic influence under the new partisan situation. I argue that bureaucrats may not be able to implement as major a policy change as occurred under the LDP rule, especially if the policy is unpopular. The view that attributes bureaucratic influence to the lack of policy expertise of incumbent politicians is also found in the explanations of Japanese politics before the LDP's loss of power. As I have already shown in chapter 2, the existing explanations assume that bureaucratic power lies in the monopolization of policy information and expertise. The difference between the conclusions of bureaucratic dominance and effective political control over bureaucracy derives from whether the scholars consider that bureaucrats monopolize the policy expertise or that the politicians effectively intervene in bureaucratic policy-making. In this book, using the recent tax reform case, I dispute the above assumption itself and contend that bureaucratic influence in democratic policy-making hinges on more subtle characteristics of bureaucratic organizations and intraparty politics.

Since I have already described the intraorganizational dynamics of bureaucracy in chapters 1 and 2, I would like to explore the conditions on the side of incumbent politicians that facilitate bureaucratic influence. Because of the LDP's need, as an incumbent party, to allocate legislative and governmental positions to its members, the party developed a sophisticated system of promotion for its members, one based on seniority as well as achieving a career as a policy specialist (*zoku giin*). When the LDP was in

237

office, therefore, its members had to show their policy expertise in order to promote their influence inside the governing party. Thus they supported an unpopular policy, such as the consumption tax, so that their support would be regarded as a sign of their expertise.

The above explanation shows that the LDP politicians often supported an unpopular policy proposed by bureaucrats not because they were tricked by bureaucrats but because they believed that such support would advance their intraparty influence. In other words, if policy expertise were not an advantage for influence inside the party government, the incumbent politicians would have little reason to support the policy that placed their own or their party's electoral fortune at stake. In such a scenario, bureaucrats would not be able to find incumbent politicians who voluntarily support an unpopular policy, and thus they would have a harder time implementing such a policy.

For example, under the non-LDP coalition government, the MOF's proposal to raise the consumption tax rate in early 1994 was thwarted by political pressure from the parties inside the governing coalition. The MOF, with the cooperation of some incumbent politicians (most of them former LDP members), had persuaded Prime Minister Hosokawa to propose an income tax reduction that was financed by raising the consumption tax rate from 3 percent to 7 percent after three years. This tax increase proposal was sweetened by changing the name from "consumption tax" to "people's welfare tax" (*kokumin fukushizei*), though only a part of "the welfare tax" revenue was to finance the welfare program. Hosokawa's proposal was withdrawn on the same day he first publicized it. The members and parties inside the coalition government, especially the JSP, as well as the electorate's antipathy, led to this immediate withdrawal. After several days of turmoil, the incumbent parties compromised with the prime minister. It was decided that there would be a tax reduction only for the next fiscal year, which would be financed by deficit bonds, and the consumption tax rate increase was to be abandoned. The result was especially unfavorable for MOF bureaucrats, who wanted to avoid a tax cut without the new revenue. Though a prolonged recession contributed to the final decision, which put the highest priority on the income tax cut, political opposition from the coalition government was the major reason the MOF was forced to abandon the consumption tax increase.[21]

The consequence of the Hosokawa cabinet's attempt to raise the consumption tax rate indicates that whether the incumbent politicians benefit from supporting the bureaucratic proposal is an important factor in determining bureaucratic influence. The recent change in Japanese politics further confirms that bureaucratic influence over democratic policy-making is associated with politicians' interest in policy problems rather than with politicians' indifference and unfamiliarity with policy problems.

## Implications of Bureaucratic Influence and Rational Behavior

It is a common concern among students of contemporary politics as to whether the development of democratic societies fosters an increase in bureaucratic power—a situation that runs counter to the values of representative democracy. Despite the normative claim that bureaucrats should make apolitical and impartial contributions to policy-making as technocrats, bureaucrats may violate their political neutrality and represent specific private interests. Alternatively, the complexity of policy problems, which limits participation in policy discussions to a small circle of specialists, results in the dominance of technocratic influence over interest representation in society.

In contrast to the aforementioned views, this study argues that both technocratic positions and ideas themselves have strategic values. Aside from the actual impact of specialized knowledge and expertise in policy-making, the use of technocratic ideas in a policy proposal favors the influence of technocrats. This argument is based on the assumption, made at the beginning of this study, that the support for a certain policy at the expense of other alternatives always necessitates a political decision. Technocratic considerations always leave several alternatives equally justified; thus the policy experts inevitably use another criterion or value that has nothing to do with their specialized knowledge or expertise in a policy decision. This "criterion" for bureaucrats is often the interest to promote the power of their own organizations.

Building on empirical analysis, this study explores the possibility that a bureaucratic organization reaches a consensus based on its organizational interest in the policy-making process and coordinates members' behaviors for the pursuance of policy objectives. In this context, rational pursuance of policy objectives by individual bureaucrats is closely related to the organization. The bureaucratic organization provides an artificial environment that shapes preferences and organizes behaviors among its members who would otherwise have a truncated view on their circumstances bounded by their limited information and perceptional capability. At the same time, the argument supports the usefulness of the rationality assumption for reasons other than theoretical clarity (Elster 1989, 26–35) and "positive value," that is, "approximation of real processes" (Tsebelis 1990, 38). In

239

this sense, the present study shows the validity of political analysis that uses the concept of rationality which serves to analyze individual behaviors in the organization.

Faced with the possibility of bureaucratic influence, we may need to seek alternatives to bureaucratic administration or measures to cope with this influence. What kind of political force in a democratic system, if any, can effectively keep bureaucrats from exercising excessive influence? How can a democratic society take advantage of specialized knowledge and incorporate the merits of technocratic ideas into policy-making without hurting democratic values? As emphasized earlier, no scientific answer perfectly solves policy problems and no purely technocratic choice of policy exists. If we seek the assistance of technocrats in policy-making, their political influence becomes a potential threat to a representative democracy. One might suggest replacing the function of the bureaucratic organization with a group of policy specialists organized on an ad hoc basis for a short tenure. Unlike the semipermanent bureaucratic organization,[22] this kind of a group would rarely have a power interest. Such an ad hoc group, however, would certainly be more vulnerable to pressure from the party in power whose government would be in charge of assigning its members and deciding the range of its decision-making power. Therefore, it would risk overrepresenting the electoral mandate given to the incumbent party and sacrificing its freedom from external political pressure.

At the same time, it is important to note that bureaucratic influence may not be a prevalent threat to a democratic policy if it heavily depends on contingent factors, and if it cannot be guaranteed by stable elements embedded in specific institutions—decision-making procedures, distribution of policy information, and so on. For example, in the Japanese tax reform case, aside from the unity of the bureaucratic organization, that is, the MOF, the voluntary cooperation of some incumbent politicians who had a closer view of the fiscal bureaucrats proved critically important for the final introduction of the new tax. Encouraging cooperation of such politicians as policy experts constitutes another important base for bureaucratic influence. At the same time, however, the incumbent politicians will not cooperate with bureaucrats if such cooperation cannot be used to promote their influence inside the party. Therefore, whether bureaucrats attain a favored policy outcome is determined by conditions both inside the party and in the bureaucracy.

Therefore, I conclude this study by pointing out an additional consequence of bureaucrats' active political influence. The threat to democratic society lies not only in the persistence of bureaucratic influence at the expense of the electoral mandate, but also in the concessions of bureaucrats to political pressure. The analysis of this case points to the possibility that, under current conditions where political and administrative roles are converging, the influence of bureaucrats is associated with a more active involvement in politics. Faced with resistance from special-interest groups and public opposition, they come to regard concessions as necessary for the implementation of a proposed policy. The bureaucrats give up measures to which they attach a low priority as they try to reach the objectives to which they assign a high priority. Such compromises tend to hurt the consistency and effectiveness of a policy that the bureaucrats may otherwise have claimed. The resulting reform in the present case shows that stable revenue from a tax broadly based on consumption was established, but that the application of equal and effective taxation was sacrificed because of the special consideration given to tax-filing measures.

This study concludes by pointing out the contradictory consequences of bureaucratic influence. In order to reflect technocratic considerations in policy-making, bureaucrats have to increase their political influence over policy-making. Coping with political pressure, however, requires them to be more sensitive to political realities. They have to modify policies to make them politically feasible at the expense of technocratic considerations. Consequently, they cannot introduce their desired policies unless they are ready to abandon their allegiance to the consistency and effectiveness of a policy and accept political reality.

# Notes

INTRODUCTION

1. There are two different kinds of general consumption tax: a multistage tax and a single-stage tax. The VAT is a multistage tax; another multistage tax, the turnover tax, does not subtract the tax applied at previous stages of transaction. Several single-stage taxes are based on the stage of transaction that is taxed, for example, the manufacturers' sales tax, the wholesale sales tax, the retail sales tax, and so on.

2. For example, Aberbach et al. (1981), Arnold (1979), Dogan (1975), Muramatsu and Krauss (1984), Suleiman (1974), and Page (1985).

3. This argument is common in two different schools of bureaucratic studies. One is the sociological study of bureaucrats dating back to Weber (1978); the other is the economic study of bureaucracy represented by Niskanen (1971). Both variants are discussed in chapter 1.

4. The former position corresponds to the one taken by sociological studies of bureaucracy and the latter to that of economic studies.

5. I return to this point later in the introduction; it is elaborated fully in chapter 1.

6. For a more precise understanding of this concept, refer to Simon's formal presentation of bounded rationality (1955, 1956a).

7. In this sense, this study is similar to Arnold's analysis of bureaucratic decision making in the U.S. context. His analysis extends the behavioral model of bureaucrats so that it includes congressional influence on the bureaucrats' decision (Arnold 1979).

8. In this study, because of the predominant party system in Japan since 1955 to the 1980s, the bureaucratic organization is assumed to face a single incumbent party. This setting enables one to avoid the complex problems arising from coordination among parties in the governing coalition.

9. The ideal type is a key component of the social scientific methodology formulated and used by Max Weber (1958, 1978). This term "refers to the construction of certain elements of reality into a logically precise conception" and "the term 'ideal' has nothing to do with evaluations of any sort" (Gerth and Mills 1958, 59).

10. They surveyed the social backgrounds of bureaucrats and politicians in Japan, and used other data on the bureaucrats' perceptions of pluralist policy and social conflict for comparison with the cross-national data presented by Aberbach et al. (1981).

11. The recent work by Silberman (1993) explains a strong organizational orientation of the Japanese bureaucracy through the comparative analysis of a process in which the bureaucratic organization emerged in the nineteenth century. According to him, the revolutionary origin of modern Japanese political elites (at the time of the Meiji restoration) is a reason for the development of a strong organization of

bureaucracy as a response to uncertainty of the leadership succession. Silberman's work, though it is a historical analysis, shares with my work both the interest in the intraorganizational dynamics of bureaucracy and the concern with the influence of political process over the bureaucratic organization.

12. Pempel (1990, 4) defines the meaning of party "dominance" as follows: "The dominant party must dominate the electorate, other political parties, the formation of governments and the public policy agenda." As a clear-cut case, he presents the Liberal Democratic Party in Japan which "held unambiguous majorities in both houses of parliament, providing all the prime ministers and virtually all the cabinet ministers, from its formation in 1955 until 1989." In July 1989, immediately after the introduction of the new tax on consumption, which is the subject of this study, the LDP lost a majority in the election of the House of Councillors of the Diet. The LDP dropped from the category of a clear-cut case of one-party predominance. In June 1993 two splinter groups, as well as some individual members, quit the party because of disagreements over reforms of electoral system and political finance, as well as intrafactional animosity. This split in the party confirmed that the LDP was no longer a predominant party; the electoral defeat in 1989, on the other hand, was regarded mainly as a temporal phenomenon that impaired the party's one-party predominance. The implication of this event is described in the final chapter.

13. In this study, the terms *VAT, broad-based tax on consumption*, and *large-scale indirect tax* all will be used for the new tax that the MOF wanted to implement. The value-added tax (VAT) indicates the MOF's original intent and is the most precise name. (However, the consumption tax that was effective in April 1989 was not exactly the same as the ideal VAT system because of the MOF's compromise with special-interest groups.) The government proposed the new tax calling it a broad-based tax on consumption, and then chose the system of the value-added tax among several alternatives. Journalists and the media used the term *large-scale indirect tax*, and this name was most popular among the public.

14. In order to answer these questions, I conducted field research in Japan during the summers of 1989 and 1990 (for a period of approximately seven months). This research included an extensive search of several newspapers, related periodicals, and government and Diet documents written during the reform process, as well as interviews with former and present government officials, public financial economists, journalists, and Diet staff who were deeply involved in or well informed about tax policy-making.

CHAPTER ONE
BUREAUCRATIC RATIONALITY AND STRATEGIC BEHAVIOR: THE FRAMEWORK

1. Weber regards the process of modernization of a state as that of bureaucratization "characterized by formal employment, salary, pension, promotion, specialized training and functional division of labor, well-defined areas of jurisdiction, documentary procedures, hierarchical sub- and super-ordination." Thus, "the democratic

state no less than the absolute state eliminates administration by feudal, patrimonial, patrician or other notables holding office in honorary or hereditary fashion, in favor of employed civil servants" (Weber 1978, 1393). He argues that bureaucratization progresses even within the political party as well as in the public administration, but bureaucratic officialdom still retains its strength as the most efficient organization. According to Weber, "as long as a parliament can support the complaints of the citizens against the administration only by rejecting appropriations [of the budget] and other legislation or by introducing unenforceable motions, it is excluded from positive participation in the *direction* of political affairs" (1408).

2. Whereas value rationality depends on a "clearly conscious formulation of the ultimate values governing the action and the consistently planned orientation of its detailed course to these values" (Weber 1978, 25), instrumental rationality as a characteristic of bureaucratic behavior "involves rational consideration of alternative means to the end, of the relations of the end to secondary consequences, and finally of the relative importance of different possible ends" (26).

3. Weber gives one answer as to why the modern state has come to provide such an order:

> The universal predominance of the market consociation requires on the one hand a legal system the functioning of which is *calculable* in accordance with rational rules. On the other hand, the constant expansion of the market . . . has favored the monopolization and regulation of all "legitimate" coercive power by one universalist coercive institution through disintegration of all particularist status-determined and other coercive structures which have been resting mainly on economic monopolies. (Weber 1978, 337)

4. Welfare economics shares this interest, but it has a different approach from public-choice theory. Welfare economics aims at the normative defense of the market mechanism and justification of government intervention when a market fails.

5. Buchanan and Wagner (1977) argue that, as the Keynesian idea has diffused, this premise, called by his bibliographers "presuppositions of Harvey Road," has contributed to expanding government expenditures and deficits in democratic politics.

6. These goals include power, income, prestige, security, convenience, loyalty (to an idea, an institution, or the nation), pride in excellent work, and desire to serve the public interest.

7. Using technical words, the bureau maximizes the budget whose size is positively and monotonically associated with almost all the possible goals of bureaucrats, "salary, prerequisites of the office, public reputation, power, patronage and output of the bureau" (Niskanen 1971, 38) until it recaptures the consumer surplus on its monopolized service.

8. Recently, Niskanen himself modified his assumption so that bureaucrats act to maximize their *discretionary* budgets (Niskanen 1991). However, the assumption

still relates bureaucratic power to the size of the bureaucrats' discretionary budgets without paying attention to the specific political and institutional context.

9. This point is clearly presented by Buchanan. He attributes the expanding tendency of government expenditure to the effect on democratic politics of Keynesian economics, which replaced the orthodox principle of a balanced budget. He argues that "elected politicians enjoy spending public monies on projects that yield some demonstrable benefits to their constituents" and do "not enjoy imposing taxes on these same constituencies" (Buchanan and Wagner 1977, 93–94). If the government runs a budget deficit, the politicians can expand expenditures without tax increases.

10. In chapter 14, Niskanen (1971) modifies this assumption, but shows almost the same result of budget maximization.

11. A more detailed discussion of different views of the state in public-choice literature is found in Mueller (1989, chap. 17).

12. McCubbins and Schwartz (1984) demonstrate this point clearly. Congress prefers decentralized and incentive-based "fire-alarm" oversight to centralized and interventionist "policy-patrol" oversight of administrative compliance. This is because the former is more effective (in the sense that it requires less time and less opportunity costs) to take as much credit as possible for the net benefits of a congressman's potential supporters.

13. For a review of economists' perspectives on the structure of firms, see Milgrom and Roberts (1988) and Williamson (1988). For a recent survey of the literature on the principal-agent relationship, see Hart and Holmstrom (1987). For the possibility of its application to political science, see Moe (1984).

14. More concretely, in a firm's production decisions, a professional manager (agent) has information about production and profit that an owner (principal) does not have, and is assumed to choose actions seeking a goal other than profits, which is hard for the owner to observe.

15. The voters here include the constituency in their own election districts, as well as interest groups that are likely to support financially congressman whom they favor; they are capable of threatening the reelections of unfavorable candidates.

16. This assumption does not require that every voter responds rationally to congressmen's behavior, and that she or he has effective means to reward and punish them. Elaborating on this point, Weingast and Marshall (1988) argue that rational ignorance among voters "does not imply that the interests of constituents are irrelevant for representatives or that the latter are free to pursue their own interests" (136). According to them, this prevalence instead benefits interest groups. This is because "interest groups . . . monitor congressmen and provide them with information. Groups also mobilize their members in support of friendly congressmen" (136). Thus "legislators are advantaged in attracting support from interest groups located in their district" (136–37). The roll-call vote system in Congress creates a specific voting pattern associated with each member, and certainly increases the sensitivity of congressmen to their constituency's reaction to certain policies.

17. Some rational choice theorists, however, have begun to incorporate the effect

of individual congressmen's ideology on voting into the so-called capture theory, which explains regulatory outcomes by a power balance between the related interest groups. This literature utilizes the concept of "slack" in principal-agent theory, and argues that the electorate's spare knowledge about the substance of legislation allows congressmen to vote according to their ideology at the expense of the electorate's economic interests (Kalt and Zupan 1984, 1990).

18. In early literature, lack of party discipline is critical with regard to congressmen as rational individuals who maximize their chance of reelections because strong party discipline is likely to constrain legislators' policy decisions in a way quite different from their desire for constituencies' service. For example, Weingast and Marshall (1988), assuming that "parties place no constraints on the behavior of individual representatives," explicitly state that they therefore "treat the individual as the decision-making unit" in Congress (137).

19. This possibility is related to a problem of corruption in the bureaucracy. See, for example, Rose-Ackerman (1978).

20. This tendency to slight bureaucratic organizations in the economic approach may be attributed to peculiarities of the bureaucratic organizations in the United States to which the theorists implicitly and explicitly refer to construct their models and refine their perspectives. In the United States, there are two kinds of administrators: bureaucrats in the formal civil service system and political appointees in specific administrations. The United States has a double-career system to "accommodate twin tasks in any higher civil service system," that is, "overall supervision of the administrative machinery below and personal advisory relations with political ministers above" (Heclo 1984, 10). Most other Western democracies, including Japan, have two different kinds of groups in the formal civil service system: high-ranking bureaucrats with frequent exposure to politics and others engaging in more administrative work (Heclo 1984, 10). The U.S. dual-career system works to discourage members inside the administration from seeking organizational goals when compared to the system of formal career service. Political executives enter office by quitting their private career temporarily and serving briefly in a political office (Heclo 1977, 100–103; Wilson 1989, 198). Political appointees with short tenures are less likely to pursue organizational interests or personal interests related to the assigned office than careerists; fewer possibilities for reward during short tenures may decrease commitment to a job, or they may not be able to obtain cooperation from their careerist colleagues or subjects. Civil servants who stay long in specific administrative bureaus or institutions are more likely to have interests related to their own organizations; the expansion of the discretionary power of the organization will reward them, for example, by obtaining more privileged positions or work assigned to members, increased job security, and so on. The failure to emphasize this difference in incentives between political executives and career civil servants was one important criticism of the economic model of regulation with its focus on the competition of social interests (Hirshleifer 1976, 242).

21. Simon (1987b) explains more about the differences between them: "In its

treatment of rationality, neoclassical economics differs from the other social sciences in three main respects: (a) in its salience about the content of goals and values; (b) in its postulating global consistency of behavior; and (c) in its postulating 'one world'—that behavior is objectively rational in relation to its total environment, including both present and future environment as the actor moves through time. In contrast, the other social sciences, in their treatment of rationality, (a) seek to determine empirically the nature and origins of values and their changes with time and experiences; (b) seek to determine the processes, individual and social, whereby selected aspects of reality are noticed and postulated as the 'givens' (factual bases) for reasoning about action; (c) seek to determine the computational strategies that are used in reasoning, so that very limited information-processing capabilities can cope with complex realities; and (d) seek to describe and explain the ways in which nonrational processes (e.g., motivations, emotions, and sensory stimuli) influence the focus of attention and the definition of the situation that set the factual givens for rational processes" (26).

22. In more technical words, transitivity and completeness of preferences permit consistent maximization.

23. The minimax rule in a game theory situation has the same premise but applies a different rule of choosing alternative means from a maximization rule, which chooses an alternative so as to maximize the worst possible pay-offs.

24. Simon uses the terms *procedural rationality* or *bounded rationality* to mean the same concept that he presents. For formal presentation of this concept, see Simon 1955 and 1956a. For an interesting contrast between the rationality concept in game theory and that in learning theory, see Simon 1956b. For further understanding of this concept, see Simon 1982, 203–495; 1987b, 196–206, 241–79. For application to political science, see Simon 1985.

25. Braybrooke and Lindblom state this relationship as follows: "While the conventional view of problem solving is that means are adjusted to ends (policies are sought that will attain certain objectives), it is a significant aspect of policy analysis as actually practiced that, in certain specific ways, the reverse adjustment also takes place. Since the reverse adjustment is superimposed on the conventionally conceived adjustment of means to ends, the net result is a reciprocal relationship between means and ends or between policies and values that is different from that envisaged in the synoptic ideal" (Braybrooke and Lindblom 1963, 93).

26. For example, Kingdon argues that clarification of goals is often counterproductive. "It could be that some individual actors in the process are fairly rational a fair amount of time, but when many actors are involved and they drift in and out of the process, the kind of rationality that might characterize a unitary decision-making structure becomes elusive" (Kingdon 1984, 82).

27. As opposed to the assumed situation in this study, if the competent policy expertise exists outside bureaucracy, that is, in the legislature or in the party, exposure to such policy staff may enable the politicians to come up with a viable alterna-

tive to a bureaucratic proposal, and the party politicians may prefer it to the bureaucratic one. But this situation is rare in many parliamentary democracies. Moreover, the advantage of politicians in this situation results from the cooperation of other expert organizations instead of effective political control over bureaucracy.

CHAPTER TWO
BUREAUCRATIC RATIONALITY AND STRATEGIC BEHAVIOR:
JAPANESE TAX REFORM

1. This poll presents options to support a particular individual party: to support the conservatives rather than progressives in general; to support the progressives rather than conservatives in general; or to choose the position of party independence.

2. Geographical movements of population and changes of industrial structures during the period of high growth decreased the rural population in primary industries such as agriculture and fishing, which were important support groups for the LDP. These movements also contributed to increasing urban population in manufacturing and service industries, which was the potential support group for the opposition camp. The influence of demographic change on elections was predicted in the 1960s (Ishida 1963). Miyake nicely summarizes the reason why demographic change, which had already begun in the 1960s, led to the electoral change, with some time lag (Miyake 1977).

3. Murakami attributes the decline and the resurgence of conservative support to the increasing "new middle mass" that emerged from the economic affluence of post industrial society, and has a different value orientation (pursuing consummatory virtues) from that predominating in industrial society (emphasizing instrumental values) (Murakami 1982, 1987).

4. An opinion poll by Jiji Tsūshinsha presented interesting evidence for the conservative resurgence around 1980, which was hard to ascertain from the election results. First, the opposition parties did not increase their popular support as much as expected from the election results in the 1970s. Second, the popular support for the LDP had already begun to increase in 1977—three years before the elections to both Houses in 1980 confirmed the conservative resurgence.

5. Krauss provides a candid explanation of "snap voting" in committees and in plenary sessions:

> The committee chairman or speaker, a senior LDP politician under orders from the prime minister, would deviate from regular procedure and use his wide powers to regulate deliberations—powers that included opening sessions and altering the agenda—to shut off debate and call for a sudden vote. The LDP members, given prior notice, would then quickly exercise their majority, and the presiding officer would declare the bill passed amid the noisy protestations of opposition members. The Japan

Socialist Party (JSP) in retaliation would then boycott Diet sessions, bringing all deliberations to a complete halt, until agreement could be reached on how to normalize the session. This was usually accomplished by the speaker taking responsibility for the disorder and resigning in a face-saving gesture to the opposition. (Krauss 1984, 249)

6. In the Japanese Diet, the legislators walk to cast votes into a voting box, thus this "cow-walking tactic" by the opposition parties can effectively delay passage of the bill supported by the LDP majority.

7. Muramatsu (1981) uses empirical data and shows the declining power of bureaucrats versus politicians and, with Krauss (1984), analyzes their relationship in a comparative perspective.

8. There are several different approaches, even among the scholars employing the pluralist view. Ōtake (1984, 1979) illustrates the power balance among the major political actors, including bureaucrats and politicians, by using several empirical cases. Yakushiji (1987) tries to measure the power balance between them quantitatively.

9. Japanese citizens between the ages of twenty-one and thirty-three can apply to take the examination by which new bureaucrats are selected.

10. Even though the selection process is highly competitive and objective, the recruitment system cannot be said to be open if graduates of the specific universities have similar social backgrounds and are similarly socialized. Koh (1989, 152–70) provides evidence to support this possibility.

11. These proportions are based on data up to the end of the 1980s. From the 1990s, there is an indication that the proportion of graduates of the University of Tokyo, especially the Faculty of Law, will decrease.

12. These characteristics of career officials, especially those in the MOF, are frequently mentioned in books written by journalists as well as former bureaucrats (Hashiguchi 1977). Some academic work also indicates this (Campbell 1977, 44–45).

13. I confirmed this tendency among fiscal bureaucrats in interviews with several of them from junior to senior positions from 1989 to 1990. This tendency is described by a former official of the MOF in Yanagisawa 1985, 2–7.

14. Even though young career officers are in top positions, they are helped and taught by the noncareer officers who know the details of tax administration. These noncareer officers are usually promoted to the same top positions of local tax offices somewhere else after they have assisted and supported the young career officers.

15. Of course, several anecdotal examples of political interventions exist (Jin 1986, 216–20). But even in these cases, the political pressure worked to support some bureaucrats among candidates who had already been selected through career advancements inside the ministry. Though both the pluralist arguments and rational choice perspectives emphasize a selection of new candidates for government officials who have positions more closely aligned with the conservative LDP's ideol-

ogy, this biased selection is too weak to be used as evidence of the incumbent party's effective control over bureaucrats. That is because this selection is also likely to be a result of bias inherited inside the bureaucratic ministries. In other words, no clear cases exist in which members who have positions more closely related to the incumbent politicians gain more advantages in their careers than those who abide by the ministry's position or interest.

16. This principle is maintained even in appointments to the highest position for career officers, an administrative vice minister. This position is usually decided more by the predecessor, with the cooperation of retired bureaucrats who held the position. For example, see Nihon Keizai Shimbunsha (1992, 168–72). This unwritten rule of nonpolitical intervention in personnel matters of bureaucracy may be broken after the demise of the LDP's long-term rule. In December, 1993, Hiroshi Kumagai, the MITI minister of the five-month-old coalition government, required Masahisa Naitō, a director of the industrial policy bureau, to resign from the ministry. Kumagai had criticized Naitō for inappropriately promoting a young bureaucrat who was about to seek a political career, and Naitō accepted the resignation "not to disturb the ministry by the political intervention." Since Naitō was considered the next administrative vice minister among the MITI bureaucrats, the minister's demand for resignation surprised the bureaucrats who presumed that politicians would not intervene in their personnel matters.

17. The noncareer officers, who usually stay in the same division or bureau and specialize in a specific policy field, have detailed knowledge of policy implementation and legislative interpretation, and help the career officers who annually change positions.

18. Only by showing much higher competence than their colleagues can the noncareer officers get higher management positions, which are usually dominated by the career officers. The possibility of promotion, even though it is quite small, provides the noncareer bureaucrats with working incentives and promotes their job morale.

19. The discussion is based on interviews with MOF bureaucrats in the summers of 1989 and 1990. Similar observations are reported by Campbell (1977, 48–49) and Rosenbluth (1989, 20).

20. Campbell and Szablowski (1979) appreciate the importance of influential and leading departments, agencies, and ministries in the Canadian policy-making process, and distinguish a "central agency" as a group of "super bureaucrats" from other bureaucratic organizations. They define the central agencies so that they often "co-ordinate the interdepartmental development of policy," "develop policies which other departments must follow," and "monitor the performance of other departments" (Campbell and Szablowski 1979, 2). They consider the financial ministry (or department) as a typical example of a central agency.

21. The bureaucrats' career path also reflects the importance of the budget for the MOF. Among thirty vice ministers, during the postwar period up to 1989, eighteen had been the general director of the budget bureau previously (among them are six

former general directors of the tax bureau), and during the same period, only three general directors of the budget bureau did not become vice ministers.

22. Campbell (1977, 71–98) and Kawakita (1989, 40—57) explain the budget-making process in greater detail.

23. The details are as follows: in September, the assistant directors (*shusa*) in the budget bureau (a total of thirty-three in 1989) start to examine the ministries' requests. Beginning in October, and for about two months afterward, three vice general directors of the budget bureau (*shukeikyoku jichō*) begin to examine the budget requests that have already been looked at by the assistant directors. The vice general directors make the final decision on the budget examination, while listening to explanations by the assistant directors who now defend the budgets of the corresponding ministries.

24. The MOF, however, cannot influence the details of the other ministries' budgets once a budget plan has been made. The planned budget is often quite different from the implemented budget (Katō 1982, 5).

25. Before the demise of the LDP rule in 1993, the incumbent politicians tried to impose certain programs on the MOF. Sometimes the MOF failed to resist before the formation of the original draft as well as a process of deliberation on the MOF's original plan inside the incumbent party. Also, in deciding defense expenditures or foreign aid, which are deeply concerned with international politics, the LDP leaders' influence was great, especially in negotiations at the final stage (Campbell 1977, 172—99).

26. In this sense, my argument does not contradict the assertion by McCubbins and Noble (forthcoming a and b), who argue for effective control over budget making by the LDP. The difference between my argument and theirs is that I set a much more modest goal for the MOF.

27. Ishi (1989, 50–51) also points out the possibility that a natural increment of tax revenue, which was partially used for tax reduction, might be intentionally created by the MOF. This is because the MOF tended to underestimate the anticipated rate of economic growth; thus the expected amount of natural tax increase was used as a financial resource at the stage of budgetary preparation, and allowed enormous natural increments of tax to materialize after the budget was implemented.

28. This effect is called "bracket creep" and occurs in a progressive income tax system if it has no measures to offset the effect of inflation or economic growth. Noguchi (1984, 30) shows that less dependence on the income tax revenue during this period (for example, in 1960, about 50 percent of tax revenue) effectively restricted the expansion of public expenditures from the revenue side. During this period, in general, the MOF's effort to restrict the size of the public sector was significant (Noguchi 1980). After the government stopped revising the income tax law since the late 1970s, the dependence ratio on the income tax increased to about 70 percent until the end of the 1980s when the tax reform was enacted.

29. Especially in 1965 and 1975, the gap between Japan, Western European countries, and the United States was wide; in 1965, the ratio for Japan was 18

percent, while the ratios for these Western countries ranged from 36 percent in Sweden to 26 percent in the United States; in 1975, the Japanese ratio was 21 percent, while ratios of other countries showed more increases ranging from 44 percent in Sweden to 30 percent in the United States (Ishi 1989, 7).

30. Murakami believed that the ongoing tendency of fiscal conditions would lead to a crisis in the future; that is, any items of the budget, once they are introduced, automatically or naturally increase the expenditures each year because of institutional and legislative obligations. These items include social security expenditures, grants-in-aid to local governments, and expenditures for issuance and interest payment of bonds (Murakami 1967). A more detailed explanation and discussion on this campaign is found in Campbell (1977, 241–51), Yamaguchi (1987, 248–79), and Hashiguchi (1977, 46–67).

31. In order to restrain the increase in fixed expenditures, this movement aimed at two practical measures: to eliminate a supplementary budget in the middle of the fiscal year and include all the expenditures in the initial budget, and to open the budgetary process by eliminating "hidden money or resources" for the MOF. These measures aimed to adopt some criteria to decide on a budget that was more objective and open. Adopting these criteria was useful for restricting expenditures, increasing the flexibility of the budget structure, and leaving more elements of the budget under the MOF's influence. But at the same time, sharing identical criteria among participants in budgetary decision making might threaten the fiscal authority's privileged position and work as a double-edged sword for the MOF. This may be why most of the budget officers ended up being uncooperative with Murakami, who initiated the movement.

32. The percentage of bond sales in total revenue reached a peak of 34.7 percent in the 1979 fiscal year and then decreased. The level in 1989 was 11.8 percent. (Both ratios include construction bonds, but the amount of construction bond issued each year has been fairly stable since 1979.)

33. Noguchi (1987a) argues that this clear orientation of the fiscal authority in Japan to decrease the deficit dependency is counter to the view Buchanan and Wagner (1977) present: that deficit finance tends to expand public expenditures.

34. The public finance law also prohibits the Bank of Japan (Japanese Central Bank) from buying the bonds (Article 5).

35. Another way of measuring the budget deficit is the saving-investment gap of the general government in the national account statistics. This measure includes the surpluses in the social security special accounts, while the revenue's bond dependence ratio is related to the issuance of long-term national bonds. The definition of *deficit* is, however, varied among countries because of differences in budgetary systems. The peculiarities of the Japanese budgetary system, according to Noguchi (1987a, 220), are as follows: the total amount of the expenditures must be equal to that of revenues at the budgetary stage (in the settlement, there could be a difference between the two) by including the bond revenue, even though the amount of the bond revenue is called the "deficit"; social security contribution is not included in

the revenues of the general account, even though the subsidies for social security programs are included in the expenditures. Thus the magnitude of the deficit would be much smaller in Japan where public pension programs currently yield surpluses, if Japan employs the same measure as in the United States where the entire account of social security programs is included in the federal budget.

36. Ishi (1987) also provides more detailed accounts of the actual system's divergence from the Mission's recommendation.

37. The MOF has intended the introduction of a tax on capital gains from sales of securities by revising the securities transaction taxes, but has yet to succeed in doing so as of 1993.

38. The tax recommended by the Shoup Mission is the income type of value-added tax, which is not the same as the consumption type of VAT which many countries now employ. This difference comes from the treatment of investments in the computation of the tax. If the system permits businesses to deduct a sum of investment from sales during the taxing period, such as purchases of inputs in production, this is the consumption type of VAT. Alternatively, if the system permits the subtraction of values of depreciation of investment goods, as well as the purchases of goods and services from the total amount of sales, this is the income type of VAT.

39. The turnover tax, which is one kind of general consumption tax, was introduced in September 1948 and repealed in December 1949. Unpopularity is one reason why it was short-lived.

40. This trade-off exists even in terms of the same principle: to increase horizontal equity among those with the same income does not necessarily go together with increasing vertical equity to transfer the wealth from the rich to the poor.

41. This kind of disagreement is especially salient when comparing income with expenditure taxes (Goode 1980; Bradford 1980).

42. Public financial economists consider this as the first clear support for the consumption tax. For example, see Kaizuka 1988, 185.

43. For example, both *Blueprints for Basic Tax Reform* by the U.S. Treasury (U.S. Treasury Department 1977) and the Meade committee report in Britain (Institute for Fiscal Studies 1978) treated the idea of a tax on expenditures as a desirable and practical alternative to income taxation.

44. "An income tax is a levy based on a particular aggregation of transactions according to a complicated set of rules laid down in statutes, regulations, rulings and court decisions, and the like. In one sense that set of rules *defines* income for tax purposes: income is what the law says it is" (Bradford 1986, 16). The widely accepted "comprehensive" definition of income is that of Haig and Simons: "personal income may be defined as the algebraic sum of (1) the market value of rights exercised in consumption and (2) the change in the value of the store of property rights between the beginning and end of the period in question" (Simons 1938, 50).

45. This classification of ideas in support of specific tax systems is based on Kaizuka (1988).

46. The research division of the tax bureau of the MOF, which is devoted to studying tax policies in general, informs colleagues inside the bureau of developments in tax theory and reforms in other countries. This information is important for achieving a consensus on the rough direction of future reforms and the bureaucrats' idea of social welfare. Since the early 1970s, when the value-added tax was introduced in the EC countries, the research division of the tax bureau has studied this new kind of tax.

47. The category of "firm" here includes not only corporations, but also individual proprietors including the owners of stores, lands, hotels, and restaurants, and professional practitioners.

48. As this sentence shows, the discussion here is a comparison of the progressive income tax with the flat-rate consumption tax.

49. Bradford (1986, 320–29) presents one of the best discussions of the theoretical strength and practical possibility of the VAT. His discussion also seriously considers its compatibility with and introduction under the existing income taxation.

50. Further discussion is found in the chapters on these countries in Pechman (1988).

51. This fact was confirmed in interviews with MOF bureaucrats and Japanese public financial economists during the summers of 1989 and 1990.

52. Pempel (1990) identifies party dominance by four dimensions: that is, the "dominant party must dominate the electorate, other political parties, the formation of governments, and the public policy agenda" (4). He concludes that Japan offers one of few clear-cut cases. As described later, however, the LDP lost its majority in the House of Councillors in the July 1989 election following the introduction of the new consumption tax. About four years after the introduction of the new tax, in June 1993, intraparty conflicts and a dissident movement put an end to thirty-eight years of the LDP's one-party predominance: two splinter groups and several individual members quit the party after the second passage of nonconfidence motion since the formation of the LDP in 1955. In this chapter, I explain the Japanese political system under the LDP's one-party predominance without mentioning later developments; these recent changes will be discussed in the final chapter.

53. The LDP-opposition bargaining and bureaucratic relationship with the interest groups is discussed in the last section of this chapter.

54. The top-ranking and retired bureaucrats with whom I conducted interviews pointed out this strategy, and emphasized that new members are taught by their bosses and made fully conscious of it. In my interviews with younger bureaucrats, this point is also confirmed. But they seem to label the same pattern of behavior differently than their seniors, as *saratori*, which is short for *sarani toraretara*, meaning "if you are overtaken in (points by your opponents)."

55. Many public financial economists in Japan expressed this view during the reform process. Bradford (1986, 328) showed the same view based on European experiences.

56. For example, Ishi (1989, 306 n. 11) reports that the ¥100 million level in the

sales tax proposal was approximately twelve to twenty times as high as the figures in these countries. Therefore, a ¥30 million level was still considerably high.

57. The MOF was especially eager to defend the use of the subtraction method because this became a key for the acceptance of the new tax by special interests. The ministry argued that the invoice method in EC countries did not facilitate audits as much as theoretically alleged, and thus was substantially similar to the subtraction method. Its reason for defense may have relevance because some tax experts report that the advantages of invoices in supplying evidence regarding tax liability are not fully realized in Europe (Aaron 1981, 3).

58. This fact was confirmed in interviews with MOF bureaucrats in the summers of 1989 and 1990.

59. New "quasi-ratios of purchases to total sales" are 90 percent for wholesalers and 80 percent for retailers; two new ratios are applied to manufacturing, construction, mining, agriculture, and fishery (70 percent) and service, transportation, telecommunication, and real estate (60 percent).

60. Of course, it is possible to consider situations in which other political actors can exploit conflicting interests and disagreements inside the bureaucracy if the bureaucratic organization fails to make a consensus or to coordinate members' behaviors. I cite the factors that lead to such situations in the concluding sections of this chapter.

61. Discussion of both tax councils in this section is based on interviews with LDP members, MOF bureaucrats, and former members of the GTSRC held in March 1985, and in the summers of 1989 and 1990 under the promise of anonymity.

62. Besides thirty members, special or supporting members can also be appointed. In 1985 Prime Minister Nakasone argued that members needed to be appointed from the private sector in order to reflect public opinion and answer the criticism that the MOF would use the GTSRC to express its own opinions. Ten more special members were appointed in addition to the eighteen existing special members at the time.

63. The main secretariat of the GTSRC is formally the Management and Coordination Agency, but actually the MOF tax bureau and (to a lesser extent) the tax bureau of the Ministry of Home Affairs are involved in its management.

64. My interviews with former members of the GTSRC strongly support the view that a membership mainly of nonspecialists allows the MOF substantial control over the council's agenda and decisions. The MOF's strong control over the GTSRC has been confirmed by several studies (Ishi 1989, 11–15; Kawakita 1989, 95–96; Kishiro 1985, 137–50), even though they vary in evaluating the relative independent influence of the GTSRC members.

65. The same view was expressed by former government tax council members in interviews conducted in the summers of 1989 and 1990.

66. "Jinjiroji," *Nihon Keizai Shimbun* (hereafter, *NK*; January 11, 1988).

67. The most noteworthy example of the LDP's intervention in tax policy, despite resistance from the MOF and the GTSRC, was the introduction of a special tax

measure in 1973. This allowed small business entrepreneurs to become quasi-corporations for tax purposes and permitted them to deduct more of their business income from taxation.

68. The political pressure on the individual Diet members from special interests is substantial. The special-interest groups often come to the LDP headquarters to ensure that their demands will be represented by their supporting politicians (Kishiro 1985, 19–20), and they are ready to switch their electoral support to other politicians if these Diet members do not do well for their interests.

69. The policy-making process inside the LDP is further discussed by Kishiro (1985, 18–25; 69–76).

70. Of course, journalistic and scholarly observers of Japanese politics identify other policy fields with specialized *zoku giin*. For example, the finance tribe who covers the MOF's jurisdiction is also called the banking, the securities, or the tax tribe (*ginkō, shōken,* or *zeisei zoku*), which corresponds to a more categorized sub-field of financial matters. A growing subpolicy field from one of the listed policy areas may give a new *zoku* name to a politician specialized in it. For example, those who are specialized in the highly technological developments of telecommunications among the posts and telecommunications tribe are called the new-media tribe (*nyūmedia zoku*) or simply the high-tech tribe (*sentan zoku*). Also, an existing policy area that had not attracted politicians' attention thus far has gained importance and has now been added to the *zoku* policy areas. This is the environment tribe (*kankyō zoku*).

71. For example, in 1986, 28.8 percent of LDP Diet members were former government officials. The ratio of the former bureaucrats to total LDP Diet members has increased since the formation of the LDP, and this increase corresponds to an observation of growth in the LDP's policy-making power (Satō and Matsuzaki 1986, 102–3). But at the same time, ex-bureaucrats now lose their past privileges, that is, prompt promotion to a political career, and thus bureaucrats who ultimately seek a political career tend to quit the administration at earlier stages of their service to ensure that they have time to step up the ladder of promotion inside the party with other members with different backgrounds.

72. Another interesting question involves the relationship between these two types of behaviors and the LDP's overall policy-making power. Schoppa (1991) argues that in the hunting-dog activities, *zoku* "contribute to 'party dominance'"; in the guard-dog activities, "they detract from it" (84–85). Satō and Matsuzaki (1986, 160–61) specify that the conflicts of interests among different groups of *zoku giin* may decrease the LDP's overall policy-making capability unless the party leaders who do not represent specific interests effectively intervene in conflicts and provide solutions for them. Satō and Matsuzaki do not use the terms *hunting dog* or *guard dog* but consider similar situations.

73. The New Liberal Club (NLC), a splinter of the LDP, existed from the mid-1970s to the mid-1980s when it merged with the LDP; the Social Democratic League (SDL) claimed its membership after the general election in 1979. The oppo-

sition camp could not prevent the LDP (sometimes with the cooperation of conservative independents) from controlling a majority in either house of the Diet until the LDP lost many seats in the House of Councillors (HC) election in July 1989. In 1992 the Japan New Party was formed and obtained four seats in the HC election that year. In June 1993 the LDP split, and two conservative parties—the Renewal Party (*Shinseitō*) and the Harbinger (*Sakigake*)—were formed by the LDP splinters, the former Hata faction (one part of the ex-Takeshita faction), and a group of junior members led by a long-tenured leader, respectively. These new conservative parties, including the Japan New Party, then opposed to LDP dominance and allied with the existing middle-of-the-road parties and the socialists in 1993. Thus the political party dynamics in Japan are destined to change. But for the purposes of this study I concentrate on the system before these changes occurred and only mention the recent changes in the final chapter of the book.

74. In the mid- to late 1970s, the LDP had to endorse the successful conservative independents after the elections to secure the number of votes needed to pass the bills (see the first section of this chapter). Except for these years when the LDP found it difficult to manage committees because of close parity with the opposition camp in the number of seats, the LDP government could count on the passage of its proposed bills because of relatively strong party discipline. As stated above, after the LDP's major loss of seats in the HC election in 1989, the LDP lost a majority in one House of the Diet. But during the reform process and until the introduction of the VAT in April 1989, the LDP had a clear-cut case of one-party predominance according to Pemple (1990). Thus in this book I treat the Japanese party system as a one-party predominant system unless I direct otherwise.

75. For more detailed accounts of the dilemma of the Japanese opposition parties, see Pempel 1975.

76. Since the 1980s, the JCP has rarely participated when other opposition parties have cooperated to make demands on the LDP about policy matters. One of the rare exceptions was the cooperation between the JSP and the JCP to oppose the introduction of the consumption tax in 1988.

77. This role of the CGP in party politics contrasted well with its limitation to extend its popular support: the CGP's ties with the religious organization, Sōkagakkai, have prevented it from expanding public support outside that group. Sōkagakkai is an organization of one variant of Buddhism in Japan that is especially strong among the urban population and is the single largest support body since the formation of the CGP in 1964. The CGP cut formal ties with Sōkagakkai in 1970, but Sōkagakkai remains the CGP's single important support group, and certainly prevents it from obtaining loyal supporters beyond the bounds of this religious organization.

78. In 1989 the General Council of Japanese Trade Unions was dissolved and merged into the National Federation of Private Sector Unions (Rengō). It sent its own candidates to the Diet with the support of some opposition parties in the House of Councillors election in 1989. After it failed to win a seat in the HC election in

July 1992, it concentrated more on forming an effective coalition with other opposition parties against the LDP, and its president, Akira Yamagishi, had an important role to make a tentative alliance between existing opposition parties and splinter conservative parties (*Shinseitō* and *Sakigake*) in 1993.

79. The JSP began to publicize its intention to revise its economic and security policies in the 1990s.

80. The recent (June 1993) split of the LDP shows that this problem really matters.

CHAPTER THREE

LESSONS FOR BUREAUCRATS: FROM THE PROPOSAL FOR A TAX INCREASE IN THE LATE 1970s TO FISCAL RECONSTRUCTION WITHOUT A TAX INCREASE IN THE EARLY 1980s

1. The GTSRC's "Long-Term Proposal on Tax Reform" (*Chōki Tōshin*) in 1968 repeated this point.

2. The three scholars were Kazuo Kinoshita, Ryuichirō Tachi, and Keimei Kaizuka; the MOF bureaucrat was Sōhei Hidaka, deputy division chief of the tax bureau.

3. These five countries were Britain, former West Germany, Italy, Belgium, and France.

4. In April 1970 five dietmen headed by chairman of the LDP Policy Affairs Research Council (PARC), Mikio Mizuta, and another group in autumn 1971 headed by chairman of the financial division of the PARC, Sōsuke Uno, went on tours of inspection of the EC countries' VAT systems. Each group published a report. However, a majority of the LDP Diet members were not yet familiar with the VAT or an indirect broad-based tax on services and consumption.

5. The term *general consumption tax* has two different meanings here. First, tax specialists used it as a generic name for various broad-based taxes on consumption, including both single- and multistage taxes. Second, the Japanese policymakers named the new tax on consumption proposed in the 1970s the "general consumption tax" (*ippan shōhizei*), which was the subtraction-method VAT. Perhaps this was a direct English translation of the generic name for the broad-based tax on consumption. In other words, the same term indicates the generic name in the first instance and the specific name in the second. To avoid confusion, hereafter, I will use this term only to refer to the tax proposed in the late 1970s; I will retain the broad-based tax on consumption or major indirect tax on consumption as the generic name.

6. Even though the government began to issue long-term bonds in the mid-1960s, the ratio of bond revenue to total revenue remained low, that is, about 10 percent until the 1974 fiscal year.

7. The Jiji Tsūshinsha opinion poll allowed respondents to identify themselves as party independents without specifying the party they supported. It also gave them an option to support the progressive rather than the conservative camp in general, or

vice versa. Therefore, the LDP's support rate, which obtained votes from party independents or unorganized voters in the elections, appeared much lower than the rates reported by other opinion polls and expected from the election results.

8. For a further explanation of this point, see Noguchi 1987a, 204–9.

9. The 32.2 percent increase in public work expenditures from 1972 to 1973 was exceptionally high compared to an annual rate of increase of 23.4 percent from 1970 to 1972.

10. The MOF's cooperation with Prime Minister Tanaka can be explained in several ways. Campbell (1977, 254) provides two interesting and plausible explanations. First, the MOF feared that resistance would bring drastic retaliation, for example, political intervention in decisions about personnel affairs and promotions within the MOF, or a reduction in the ministry's discretionary power. Second, the MOF's ideological transformation from a smaller to a larger governmental role, which had been on-going since the 1960s, was brought to bear on the budget for the first time by the advent of Tanaka. I believe both explanations are partially true. Tanaka had increased his influence over some MOF bureaucrats since 1962 when he became a minister of finance for the first time. The MOF bureaucrats were impressed by Tanaka's ability to formulate new policies—especially to find new sources of tax revenue (for example, the gasoline tax in 1954 and the motor vehicle tonnage tax in 1971). As he gained personal popularity and professional respect for his ability, MOF bureaucrats began to support his active fiscal policy. Tanaka's influence was not extended to all MOF bureaucrats. Therefore, the MOF as a whole voluntarily accepted a positive conception of public finance in order to avoid further appreciation of the yen.

11. Some political leaders even advocated the idea of an "adjustment inflation"—to increase domestic demands even at the expense of price increases and to decrease a surplus in the international account.

12. In retrospect, the Japanese policymakers had no reason to fear the revaluation of the yen except for an emotional insistence on the status quo under uncertain conditions. For a further explanation of changes in the international economy and the Japanese government's policy response from the late 1960s to the early 1970s, see Nakamura 1980, 223–41, and Kōsai 1981, 188—205.

13. This estimate was presented yearly for five years, but was subsequently replaced in 1980 by the "Interim Prospect of Public Finance" (*Zaisei no Chūki Tenbō*).

14. *Zaisei Kinyū Tōkei Geppō*, August 1976.

15. The fiscal authority carried over the target year from the 1980 fiscal year (in the first and second estimates) to the 1982 fiscal year (in the third). Moreover, they had to set a new target—the 1984 fiscal year (in the fourth and fifth estimates)—because of accumulating deficit bonds.

16. The "Middle-Term Proposal on the Tax System" in 1977 was based on the estimate of the 1977 fiscal year budget, which was similar to the one for the 1976 fiscal year discussed here.

17. The report used the estimates and data given in the "Economic Plan from 1975 to 1980" (*Shōwa 50 Nendai Zenki Keizai Keikaku*), which had been submitted by the Economic Advisory Council to the government in January 1976.

18. The content of the "Ōkura memo" is found in Andō 1987b, 120–122.

19. The memo proposed careful preparation for the introduction of the new tax for two reasons: first, the country would have to take care in timing the tax increase so that it would not adversely influence the business cycle; second, measures to cut expenditures and to decrease inequity in the existing tax systems would be needed in order to persuade the public to accept the tax increase.

20. Two divisions of the GTSRC publicized an interim report in December 1976, based on their deliberations.

21. The "Middle-Term Proposal" was made immediately before some changes in membership were made in the commission (members usually have three continuous terms of three years each). The report officially counted ninety-one meetings since October 1974 for drawing up the "Middle-Term Proposal" in 1977 when the prime minister requested it. They included thirty-seven plenary sessions, eighteen meetings of two special divisions, four meetings of a small committee on basic problems, twenty meetings of a temporary small committee for making the report, and twelve other meetings. During this period, the GTSRC also worked on making reports for the 1975, 1976, and 1977 fiscal year tax revisions.

22. When the MOF explained the "Middle-Term Proposal," it frequently cited data on the bond dependency ratio of other advanced capitalist countries compared to the Japanese rate. The data in three fiscal years from 1975 to 1977 (in the case of the United States, from 1976 to 1978), given as percentages, were as follows:

|      | Japan | United States | Britain | West Germany | France |
|------|-------|---------------|---------|--------------|--------|
| 1975 | 25.3  | —             | 18.2    | 21.2         | 12.2   |
| 1976 | 29.4  | 18.2          | 14.2    | 16.0         | 3.5    |
| 1977 | 29.7  | 11.3          | 13.2    | 13.3         | 3.2    |
| 1978 | —     | 13.3          | —       | —            | —      |

*Source:* OECD data.

23. The estimate used economic indicators from the "Economic Plan from 1975 to 1980" (*Shōwa 50 Nendai Zenki Keizai Keikaku*), which the Economic Advisory Council had submitted to the government in January 1976.

24. The "Middle-Term Proposal" distinguished two kinds of unfair tax treatments: special tax measures to achieve specific policy goals, and inadequate arrangements and practices built into the existing system of corporate taxes and income taxes.

25. Table 2.2 confirms this. See, especially, the 1975 data.

26. Table 2.4 confirms this. See, especially, the 1975 data. MOF bureaucrats often cited the OECD data on the revenue structure of member countries to justify the introduction of the new tax. For example, see Yanagisawa 1977.

27. The "Estimate of the General Account" for February 1977, aiming to stop

the issuance of deficit bonds in the 1980 fiscal year, implied the need for a tax increase by the introduction of a new tax (the general consumption tax) from the 1978 fiscal year, in addition to the economization of subsidies and social security expenditures. The top MOF bureaucrats also stated that the ministry wanted to introduce the new tax as soon as possible—in the 1978 fiscal year (*NK*, September 22, 1977).

28. In February 1975 the MOF administrative vice minister, Fumio Takagi, and directors of the budget bureau and the tax bureau, Michio Takeuchi and Keijirō Nakahashi, respectively, visited Prime Minister Miki to emphasize the necessity of instituting the VAT in order to finance increasing welfare expenditures. But the prime minister was not very interested in its introduction (Kishiro 1985, 181).

29. At the time, the finance committee in the HR was a "reversal committee" (*gyakuten iinkai*) in which the number of members from opposition parties exceeded the number from the majority LDP, excluding a chairman who did not have voting power. The close numerical strengths of the LDP and the opposition parties in the Diet increased the spending pressure from both the incumbent and the opposition parties, and resulted ultimately in the unusually significant amendment of the government bill.

30. The MOF tried to make compatible two requests, one to expand domestic demand and the other to reduce the deficit bond by using up a part of the tax revenue in the next fiscal year. But this "provisional and exceptional budget" (*rinji tokurei no zaisei*) did not work as the government had intended, and the bond dependency ratio increased.

31. The ten leading members of the LDP TSRC included Ippei Kaneko, chairman; Tsuneo Uchida, adviser; Sōichirō Itō, Seisuke Okuno, Ihei Shiseki, Tatsuo Murayama, Ganri Yamashita, Shigesada Marumo, and Tokutarō Higaki, vice chairmen; and Yoshirō Hayashi, secretary.

32. These groups who sought to reform the unfair tax system included the General Council of Trade Unions of Japan (*Nihon Rōdō Kumiai Sōhyōgikai*), the Association of Female Voters (*Fujin Yūkensha Dōmei*), the Association of Employed People of Japan (*Zenkoku Sararīman Dōmei*), and so on.

33. The groups of wholesalers included the Association of Chain Stores of Japan (*Nihon Chain Store Kyōkai*), the Association of Department Stores of Japan (*Nihon Hyakkaten Kyōkai*), and the Association of Small and Medium-sized Commercial and Industrial Groups of Japan (*Zenkoku Chūshō Shōkōgyō Dantai Rengō*).

34. Exceptional acceptance and support came from the machine and auto industries, and the food industries, respectively. This was because a 15 percent excise tax had already been levied on the products of the first two sectors, and foods would be exempted from the new tax (*NK*, September 13, 1978).

35. Ōhira's ready consent to tax increases surprised the MOF bureaucrats who expected more reluctance or resistance from him (Yanagisawa 1985, 32).

36. This decision was mainly a result of Ōhira's own party's pressure. Three top-level LDP executives—Secretary General Kunikichi Saitō, Chairman of the

Executive Committee Tadao Kuraishi, and Chairman of the PARC Toshio Kōmoto—made this decision with Ōhira.

37. In September the LDP TSRC began deliberations on the general consumption tax, as well as the 1979 fiscal year tax revision. Its small committee, consisting only of the leaders, passed the new tax quickly (*NK*, December 25, 1978). The new tax resolution was carefully prepared with the cooperation of MOF Vice Minister Ōkura, who had served as the general director of the tax bureau for three years, the LDP top executives, and the main members of the LDP TSRC (Kishiro 1985, 44).

38. In the general election in 1976, the LDP obtained only 249 seats, which fell short of half the total of 511 seats, and managed to maintain its majority by asking elected conservative independents to join the party. Ōhira had wanted to stabilize his cabinet by his party's winning a majority in the election.

39. Jun Shiozaki was a former general director of the tax bureau. He opposed the MOF's consumption tax proposal because of his administrative experience with a turnover tax in the 1940s.

40. The Dietmen's Conference on Fiscal Reconstruction not only expressed opposition to the general consumption tax, but also proposed to the prime minister a so-called added tax (*fukazei*), which meant a temporary increase in corporate and individual income taxes by a fixed rate for a certain period (*NK*, August 7, 1979).

41. In the opinion polls by *Yomiuri Shimbun*, the largest newspaper company in Japan in October 1978, 12.2 percent of respondents opposed the general consumption tax because its enormous revenue would allow fiscal irresponsibility; 12.5 percent supported it with the condition that the government would implement administrative reform (rationalization of the administration) and the rectification of tax inequity (in the existing income taxation) (*Zenkoku Yoron Chōsa no Gaikyō* 1978, 562).

42. For example, in April Prime Minister Ōhira ordered the MOF to carry out a "summer review," which required other ministries and agencies to reexamine their needs for various subsidies before their requests for the next fiscal year, though its effect was not officially reported. Makoto Nagaoka, who was the general director of the budget bureau at the time, recommended this review to Prime Minister Ōhira when Ōhira asked him about effective measures for cutting expenditures (Andō 1987b, 164).

43. According to the opinion polls by *Asahi Shimbun* in October 1978, a majority of respondents felt that the tax burden was heavy (50 percent) and that the tax system was unfair (67 percent). Most answered that medical doctors, big business, and self-employed people were privileged under the existing system (*Asahi*, November 4, 1978).

44. For example, in July the government proposed the abolishment of some special treatments in the existing tax system, that is, tax exemptions on small amounts of savings (*maruyū seido*) and the revision in August of some special tax credits for unincorporated businesses. To cope with the opposition, Prime Minister Ōhira even suggested that the introduction of the income tax increase would substitute for a part

of the revenue that would otherwise come from the new tax. On July 30, in a television interview broadcast on NHK (*Nihon Hōsō Kyōkai*), Ōhira suggested the possibility of an income tax increase at the same time as the implementation of the general consumption tax. But this suggestion was also unpopular.

45. At the end of October, the MOF issued a warning to nine top-ranking bureaucrats who were implicated in the scandal, including the vice minister.

46. According to Jiji Tsūshinsha, which conducts a monthly opinion poll on party support, the annual average rate of LDP support had decreased from 35.9 percent in 1970 to 29.6 percent in 1979, while the average rate of the independents had increased from 18.1 percent to 32.2 percent during the same period. The annual average of total support rates for all the opposition parties, including the support rate for the progressive camp in general, had even decreased from 28.2 percent to 23.7 percent during the same period (*Jiji Yoron Tokuhō*, 1970–79). Therefore, the decline of the popular support rate for the LDP was more likely to be caused by the LDP's increasing share of party independents.

47. Zen'ichirō Tanaka showed clearly that the LDP's share of votes in the total votes differed significantly between regions that had had heavy rain and those that had had no rain on election day in 1979. In the latter regions, the resurgence of popular support for the LDP in terms of voting share was as apparent as in the general election in 1980 that resulted in a landslide victory for the LDP (*Asahi*, evening edition, September 22, 1980).

48. Ōhira, as a minister in the Miki administration and a party secretary general in the Fukuda administration, prevented both prime ministers from dissolving the Diet. Thus Fukuda and Miki were especially critical of Ōhira when he dissolved the Diet and failed to obtain enough seats for a stable majority in the general election.

49. For example, when South Korea's President Park Chung Hee was assassinated on October 26, the deepening conflict among several of the factions inside the LDP prevented Prime Minister Ōhira from going to his funeral, and the former prime minister, Nobusuke Kishi, attended it instead.

50. The Japanese Constitution states that a special Diet session must be convened within thirty days after a general election, and that, in this session, a Diet resolution shall designate the (next) prime minister from among its members upon the resignation of the cabinet.

51. Masayoshi Itō became the acting prime minister.

52. All the factors worked to the LDP's advantage in this election. For example, the voter turnout rate for the HC election was the highest among the postwar HC elections, and the rate for the HR was the fourth highest among the postwar general elections.

53. All the MOF bureaucrats with whom I conducted interviews said that the LDP Diet members, even in the late 1980s, accused them of killing Ōhira by proposing the general consumption tax. Masataka Ōkura, who was responsible for the general consumption tax as a director of the tax bureau and as a vice minister, said that Masaya Itō, who worked as a political adviser to Ōhira, still accused him and the MOF of killing Ōhira (Andō 1987b, 113).

54. This interpretation slighted Prime Minister Ōhira's voluntary and strong support for the general consumption tax. Even after the mass media had reported that Prime Minister Ōhira had given up the introduction of the general consumption tax in the 1980 fiscal year, Ōhira told a certain top-ranking MOF bureaucrat that he did not mean the withdrawal of the tax proposal itself (*NKE*, October 3, 1979).

55. When the opinion poll by *Yomiuri Shimbun* in October 1978 asked respondents to choose two effective measures for decreasing the budget deficit, almost all the answers supported the curtailment of inefficiency in the administrative organization and of public expenditures, in addition to rectification of tax inequity in the existing system. Only 3.4 percent of respondents supported the tax increase as a viable solution (*Zenkoku Yoron Chōsa no Gaikyō* 1978, 562).

56. For example, after the government proposed the general consumption tax in December 1978 for the 1980 fiscal year, both budget and tax bureaus also deliberated whether the general consumption tax should be earmarked for social security under the name of a "social welfare tax" (Andō 1987b, 162). Moreover, in July 1979, the MOF planned to introduce a special tax for fiscal reconstruction. It would add a few percentages to the existing corporate and individual income tax for only one or two years before instituting the general consumption tax (Andō 1987b, 112). This temporal system of the added tax (*fukazei*) might have been useful to soften the LDP's opposition to the general consumption tax because the intraparty opposition group, Dietmen's Conference on Fiscal Reconstruction, supported the added tax rather than the general consumption tax.

57. A group of scholars, chaired by John Creighton Campbell, studied "governmental responses to budget scarcity" in the United States, Great Britain, Japan, France, Sweden, and Denmark, in *Policy Studies Journal*, vol. 13, no. 3 (1985). Campbell's two articles (1985a, 1985b) introduce the subject and discuss its relevance to Japan, respectively. A group of economists studied "the conservative revolution" in the United States, Great Britain, France, and Switzerland, in *Economic Policy*, vol. 2, no. 2 (1987) (De Menil and Portes 1987).

58. Differing from Suzuki, Nakasone qualified his commitment with the following statement, made on both formal and informal occasions: "Although the government was going to make every effort to implement the policies proposed by the SPCAR, I hope that the SPCAR will propose those policies that the government can make an effort to implement."

59. This statement was made by a bureaucrat of the Management and Coordination Agency (into which the AMA was reorganized by the SPCAR), who was deeply involved in the administrative reform campaign, in an interview with me in 1986.

60. The business community even organized support committees for administrative reform in order to assist the activities of Chairman Toshio Dokō and two other representatives of the SPCAR. The "Five Men's Committee," consisting of top leaders and presidents of the five major business associations, and the "Ten Men's Committee," consisting of vice presidents of these groups, were formulated, and special executive committees were established as their secretariats.

61. The First Provisional Council proposed forty items, but the government implemented only eleven of them.

62. Yasuo Matsushita said that he talked with Kaji about the administrative reform and the establishment of the SPCAR before Suzuki declared that such a reform was an urgent policy problem (Andō 1987b, 209–10).

63. The Provisional Council for Administrative Reform Establishment Law decided the purpose, tasks, organization, power of investigation of administrative organs and public corporations, and the two-year term. This special legislation for the establishment of the SPCAR was exceptional because most advisory councils have the legal support of one common legislation, the Advisory Council Establishment Law.

64. Eight commissioners, in addition to Chairman Toshio Dokō, were Jirō Enjyōji (adviser of a large newspaper company, *Nihon Keizai Shimbunsha*), who was considered to represent the view of journalism; Keizō Hayashi (president of the Japanese Red Cross Society and a chairman of the Local Government System Research Council), who was considered to represent the position of local government; Kagayaki Miyazaki (president of the big chemical company, *Asahi Kasei Kōgyō*), and Ryūzō Sejima (vice president of the Commerce Association of Tokyo, *Tokyo Shōkō Kaigisho*), who were businessmen having positions close to Dokō in terms of administrative reform and fiscal reconstruction; Kiyoaki Tsuji (professor at the International Christian University), who had thorough knowledge and expertise in public administration; Yutaka Tanimura (chairman of the board of trustees of the Tokyo Stock Market and a former MOF vice minister), who was well known in official circles; Hidenobu Kanesugi (vice president of the Japanese Confederation of Labor, *Zennihon Rōdō Sōdōmei*); and Yasuo Murayama (vice president of the General Council of Trade Unions of Japan, *Nihon Rōdō Kumiai Sōhyōgikai*).

65. Dokō continued to criticize the government in terms of economic management. In the late 1970s he pushed the government toward a more expansionary fiscal policy in order to overcome the recession, and was critical of a hasty and easy acceptance of tax increases as a fiscal solution.

66. The Commission's deliberations, which were usually held once a week, were held 121 times during the two-year term, and the number of meetings of the expert committees and working groups came to a total of 595 (Masujima 1985, 21–24).

67. During the 117 days from its establishment to the issue of the First Report, *Yomiuri Shimbun* (one of the biggest nationwide newspapers in Japan) reported on the SPCAR on 82 of these days (70 percent of that time), and if we include the articles mentioning the SPCAR indirectly, this figure comes to 102 days (87 percent of that time) (Masujima 1985, 34). The other popular newspaper, *Sankei Shimbun*, ran an extensive campaign to support administrative reform. *NHK* (*Nihon Hōsō Kyōkai*) telecast a program called "A Day of Mr. Dokō," in order to introduce his activity in the SPCAR; this program recorded a high audience rating.

68. The "First Urgent Report" by the SPCAR in July 1981 did not present "fiscal reconstruction without a tax increase" as a guideline for fiscal policy but assigned to

it the role of changing the public consciousness and institutionalized pattern of policies. The first report only decided not to increase taxes in the 1982 fiscal year, and officially decided nothing about the possibility of a tax increase afterward.

69. For example, SPCAR member Kiyoaki Tsuji admitted that he "felt deeply how thick the wall of vested interests was" (through his activities in the SPCAR) (*Yomiuri Shimbun*, March 15, 1982).

70. Campbell (1985b, 515) made the same point. For the reforms of public pension and health insurance systems, see Kato 1991b.

71. For example, opinion polls by Jiji Tsūshinsha in June 1982, fifteen months after the SPCAR started, showed that the public was attentive to the fiscal crisis and supported "fiscal reconstruction without a tax increase." Of the respondents, 77.2 percent knew about the enormous tax revenue shortfall and the issuance of deficit bonds; the percentage of those who did not know remained at 22.8 percent. As to what measure should supplement the revenue shortfall, 37.1 percent of respondents supported expenditure cuts; the percentage of supporters for the tax increase was as small as 2.5 percent, and even including those who supported the combined measures of expenditure cuts and the issuance of deficit bonds, the percentage was still only 14.7. Absolute opposition to the tax increase amounted to 52.9 percent. However, in terms of specific measures to cut expenditures, the public did not necessarily agree with the administrative reform campaign. For example, 51.1 percent of respondents demanded that expenditures be cut from the defense and official development assistance, which the government had exempted from the ceiling, while maintaining the level of social security and educational expenditures, which the government had put below the ceiling (*Jiji Yoron Chōsa Tokuhō*, July 21, 1982).

72. In addition to Dokō's hostility, the MOF could not influence the SPCAR through its representative. The SPCAR commissioner Yutaka Tanimura, who was a former vice minister of the MOF, seemed to have a slightly different view of a fiscal solution from his juniors within the MOF. He put more emphasis on expenditure cuts and rationalization of the administrative apparatus as a fiscal solution. He seemed fully dedicated to this goal (for example, see Tanimura 1987). Even though retired bureaucrats do not have a view that completely contradicts the interests of their home ministries and agencies in general, their view tends to be more independent of these interests after their retirement.

CHAPTER FOUR
REFRAMING THE TAX ISSUE: THE MINISTRY OF FINANCE'S
FISCAL AND TAX POLICIES IN THE EARLY 1980S

1. Yasuo Matsushita, general director of the budget bureau at the time, denied, however, that the MOF intentionally announced the ceiling before the SPCAR's report (Andō 1987b, 219).

2. Before the MOF announced fiscal reconstruction as its goal in the 1980 fiscal year, it had not distinguished general expenditures (*ippan saishutsu*) from other

items in the general account (*ippan kaikei*), that is, the allocation tax to local governments and the bond expenditure.

3. This kind of simple measure includes decreasing the appropriation to pension funds and the health insurance fund from the general account, suspension of the payment of provisional local allocation tax, and so on.

4. Miyajima (1989b, 21–22) explains the procedure that these measures follow when applied to certain itemized expenditures and programs: "(1)Part or all the spending burden of the expenditures and programs is temporarily transferred to the special account, the account of government investment, the loans program, or the local finance program; (2) the above accounts and programs finance the transferred burden by borrowing or by issuing bonds; (3) the general account pays these interests, and decreases and suspends the expenditures that would otherwise be urgent."

5. After the 1987 fiscal supplementary budget, the bond dependency ratio began to decrease substantially, due mostly to the unexpected natural increase from tax revenue. Ironically, however, public enthusiasm had already been lost by then.

6. The MOF might choose to impose a flat-rate ceiling on general expenditures instead of setting priorities among existing items and programs for another reason. The latter measure would likely trigger serious resistance from and intense political conflict among other ministries before any specific proposals for expenditure cuts were in effect. The other ministries also preferred cuts resulting from the ceiling to specific expenditure cuts, because specific expenditure cuts involved more risks for them: the fiscal authorities might cut harshly or even abolish specific programs in which they had vested interests. At the same time, expenditure cuts from structural reform required more time to go into effect. Therefore, the best way to achieve the annual goal of a budget cut was to concentrate efforts to repress the amount of general expenditures. What is to be noted here, however, is that this policy orientation helped the MOF to secure influence over the other ministries through the budget-making process, and left little room for the SPCAR to influence the entire public financial system.

7. The Lockheed scandal, in which former prime minister Kakuei Tanaka was implicated, was one of the biggest scandals in postwar Japanese politics. Tanaka was arrested and charged with accepting a bribe from the Lockheed Aircraft Company in 1976 with regard to the sale of Lockheed aircraft, but his trial was terminated in 1993 because of his death.

8. Tanaka's guilty verdict in his relation to the Lockheed Aircraft Company was a focus of public attention in the 1983 electoral campaign. This certainly contributed to the loss of thirty-four LDP seats compared to the previous general election in 1980.

9. This was possible through the withdrawal of a reduction in the deductible ratio of reserves for retirement allowance.

10. Here, the commodity tax meant an indirect tax that excluded taxes on alcoholic beverages, tobacco, and sugar, which could be justified as taxes on luxury and unhealthy consumption, and taxes on stamps and security transactions and excises

in motoring and transportation-related fields, which were earmarked for financing government services in the same fields. The selective excise tax on commodities was unique to Japan at the time, and could be regarded as an imperfect form of the general consumption tax in other countries.

11. In November 1984 the LDP leader, Shin Kanemaru, who was the most influential representative of interests relating to public works (construction, commerce, and so on), stated that the next year (1985) would represent a chance for a tax increase with revenue to finance public works. In the same month, Fujio hinted at the possibility of an indirect tax increase, including the introduction of a large-scale consumption tax that would accompany an income tax decrease after the 1986 fiscal year (*NKE*, January 29, 1984). Kanemaru and Fujio supported new leaders, Noboru Takeshita in the Tanaka faction and Shintarō Abe in the Fukuda faction, respectively, who were important candidates for future prime ministers.

12. *Nihon Keizai Shimbun* reported that about 90 percent of LDP Diet members of both Houses were against the austerity policy and desired the increase in public investment (*NK*, September 28, 1984).

13. Kōmoto, as the other faction head, criticized the Nakasone cabinet's austerity policy. He wanted to seize the chance to win the party presidential election in October 1984.

14. This committee, consisting of eleven LDP dietmen, began to prepare the report behind the scenes in order to avoid political pressure on their report in February 1984.

15. After Tatsuo Murayama entered the political world, he won respect from the LDP members because of his expertise in tax issues, even though he was not necessarily good at political maneuvering in tax politics (Kishiro 1985, 98–106).

16. At the national level, the statutory rates of corporate tax were 43.3 percent on retained profits and 33.3 percent on distributed profits at the time. Assuming the share of retained profits was 70 percent, the actual tax rate at the national level would have been 40.3 percent. At the local level, the inhabitant tax on corporations was 17.3 percent of the statutory corporate tax rate at the national level, and an enterprise tax of 12 percent was levied on all the profits. The MOF calculated the tax burden of the local and national statutory tax rates and argued that the resulting rate of 52.9 percent was similar to that in other advanced countries. Keidanren calculated the effective tax rate, including the effects of the special tax measures for corporations. According to Keidanren, in Japan, the effective tax rate was not much different from the statutory rates since the late 1970s when the government began to curtail special tax measures. The other advanced countries, however, significantly reduced the tax burden on corporations by actively using tax incentives and by having big differences between statutory and effective tax rates. Thus the Japanese corporations' actual tax burden, as indicated by the effective rate, was much larger than the corresponding rates of the other advanced countries despite a small gap in the statutory rate in comparison with the other countries.

17. A number of economists found relevance in Keidanren's view of the increas-

ing tax burden (Noguchi 1985) and of international comparison (Ishi 1989, 186–201), even though no one fully supported Keidanren against the MOF.

18. Various polls showed an ambiguous public view on the size of the government. Among them, the opinion polls by Jiji Tsūshinsha provided the annual results to the same questions for a short period from 1982 to 1984. In February 1982, 24.4 percent of the respondents supported a small government that retrenches the expenditures and 16.5 percent supported big government that spends a lot on welfare, education, and public works with a certain amount of tax increase. In the same months, in 1983 and 1984, supporters for a big government showed significant increases, respectively, of 23.1 percent and 27.9 percent, but at the same time the supporters for a small government did not decrease, and maintained 26.8 percent and 18.0 percent, respectively; about 30 percent reserved their answers. (The above results appeared in *Jiji Yoron Tokuhō*, March 1982, 1983, and 1984, respectively.)

19. Statistics confirmed this MOF claim. For example, a composition ratio of Japan's direct taxation was 65.6 percent in the 1985 fiscal year, which stood next to New Zealand's 69.0 percent among twenty-three OECD countries. A ratio of indirect taxation was 20.1 percent, the lowest among these countries. The MOF calculated the composition ratios of each OECD country. A presentation of all the MOF data is included in Ozaki 1987c, 70–71.

20. Representing the MOF's view, Minister of Finance Takeshita implied the fiscal authority's interest in the income tax reform, as well as the introduction of the new consumption tax, when he answered a question from the opposition party in the HR budget committee on March 7, 1983 (*NK*, March 8, 1983).

21. This point will be elaborated in the following chapter.

22. Although the MOF bureaucrats had not accepted this publicly until the mid-1980s, inside the ministry they had long agreed that the existing income taxation was not effective because of the many loopholes and difficulties in comprehending incomes (interviews with three MOF bureaucrats in the summer of 1989).

23. This MOF view was most clearly presented in Ozaki 1987c, 71.

CHAPTER FIVE

THE TAX REFORM PROPOSAL IN THE MID-1980s: UNEASY COOPERATION BETWEEN PRIME MINISTER NAKASONE AND THE MINISTRY OF FINANCE

1. Nakasone's faction was the fourth largest in number in the LDP following the Tanaka, Suzuki, and Fukuda factions at the time. He was threatened by a plan behind the scenes by the other faction leaders to support another candidate for the LDP presidency. The former prime ministers, Suzuki and Fukuda, once tried to support Susumu Nikaidō in the Tanaka faction in order to prevent Nakasone from serving a second term. He managed to win the second term with the assistance of Tanaka.

2. For an analysis of Nakasone's leadership style, see Muramatsu (1987) and Igarashi (1989).

3. The other policy changes that also relied on the same style of leadership were

not as "successful" as administrative reform. Some reform efforts did not lead to results as substantial as Nakasone had expected (for example, the educational reform); others led to the results he wanted but were not very popular (removing 1 percent of the GNP's constraint on the defense expenditure).

4. The other campaigns were educational reform and the privatization of the Japan National Railway.

5. This information comes from an interview I conducted in the summer of 1989 with an MOF bureaucrat who was involved in the tax reform from 1985 to 1986 as a tax officer. According to this bureaucrat, many individuals inside the tax bureau supported an income tax structure that gradually increased progressivity and calculated tax amounts from incomes by using equations, a system similar to the one in West Germany at the time.

6. This legislation was brought about by pressure from the LDP, despite opposition from the GTSRC and the MOF.

7. Professor Ōshima of Dōshisha University filed this suit, arguing that it was against the constitution to allow only self-employed people and farmers (not salaried workers) to exempt necessary expenses by reference to real expenditures. The verdict recommended the rectification of tax inequity, but did not admit that the income tax law was unconstitutional because it considered that salaried workers' necessary expenses were included in the earned income exemption by a rough estimate.

8. Some economists point out the possibility of this kind of tax inequity between different income groups or different occupational groups, but their analyses are based on data at the macro level because comprehensive tax-filing data are not publicized. The National Tax Authority also does not examine the possibility of this inequity based on the tax-filing data. However, it is true that the salaried workers' taxes are increasing more rapidly than those of the other occupational groups. For example, according to the MOF's data presented at the time of the 1986 fiscal budget making (that is, a year before the tax reform proposal at the end of 1986), the average amount of income tax on employed people increased by 30 percent for five years while those of the employed business and other entrepreneurs (lawyers, doctors, and so on) decreased, respectively, by 30 percent and 10 percent for the same period (*Asahi*, February 10, 1986).

9. For example, according to an opinion poll by *Asahi Shimbun* in May 1986, 70 percent of respondents felt that the tax burden was heavy and 71 percent felt that an "unfair" tax burden existed. Of the 71 percent who felt that the tax burden was "unfair," 29 percent believed that salaried workers were disadvantaged. This rate was far greater than the percentage of respondents (9 percent) who considered the "vertical tax inequity" between different income groups as a major problem (*Asahi*, May 31, 1986). An opinion poll by *Yomiuri Shimbun* reported similar results in April 1985, about a year before the *Asahi* poll. In that earlier poll, 37.7 percent of respondents felt that the tax burden was heavy and 46.6 percent felt it was extremely heavy; 41.2 percent believed that the current share of the tax burden was unfair and

271

32.8 percent believed that it was relatively unfair. Further, 69.8 percent of respondents felt that salaried workers were "disadvantaged," choosing among the three alternatives of "advantaged," "appropriate," and "disadvantaged," while the percentage of respondents who chose "advantaged" amounted to 49.9 percent for self-employed businessmen, 39.8 percent for farmers, 82.5 percent for practicing doctors, 79.3 percent for politicians, 58.4 percent for high-income earners and wealthy persons, and 39.8 percent for enterprises. *Yomiuri Shimbun*'s results more clearly showed that the public was more concerned with horizontal equity than vertical equity (*Zenkoku Yoron Chōsa no Gaikyō* 1985, 519).

10. After the simultaneous elections in 1986, Nakasone stated that his strategy to obtain public support was (1) to secure organized supporters, farmers, and self-employed people, and (2) to gain support from urban citizens, especially salaried workers. In his address to the LDP summer seminar on August 30, 1986, he explained that the LDP had won as many as 304 seats in the election because of the success of this strategy. The content of his address was widely reported in major national newspapers.

11. Nakasone had not served as a minister of finance, whereas other LDP leaders—Tanaka, Fukuda, and Takeshita (and also the late Ōhira)—had close personal ties with the MOF through their experiences as financial ministers.

12. Nakasone sometimes added "choice" to these ideals of the tax reform.

13. This information comes from the record of the HR budget committee in the 102d session of the Diet, January 4, 1985.

14. Middle-aged salaried workers were believed to have heavy financial burdens because of housing and educational expenditures.

15. In the HR budget committee, on February 5, 1985, the secretary general of the Clean Government Party, Junya Yano, pointed out five types of large-scale indirect taxes: the EC-type VAT, the turnover tax, the manufacturers' sales tax, the retail sales tax, and the wholesale sales tax; he asked the prime minister which tax system would he would promise not to introduce.

16. This information is from the record of the HR budget committee, February 6, 1985.

17. The government began to study income tax reduction as one of the general economic measures for the expansion of domestic demands (*NK*, July 31, 1985).

18. These minor changes in the 1986 fiscal year tax revision included tax reduction for the acquisition of houses, rationalization of special tax measures, and extension of the 1.3 percent rate increase on the corporate tax.

19. Both Mizuno and Ozaki remained in the same positions until the passage of the tax bills to introduce the consumption tax in the Diet in December 1988. Ozaki became the next general director immediately thereafter.

20. The MHA was involved in the tax reform for two reasons. First, direct tax reform was supposed to include a reduction in the inhabitant tax. Second, since the new indirect tax would replace the existing indirect tax, the local governments that

depended on commodity excise taxes for its revenue would need to share the revenue from the new tax with the national government.

21. Of the new members selected for the GTSRC, three were businessmen, two were former bureaucrats who had worked for the MOF and Japan National Bank but who were close to Nakasone, and the others were academics, novelists, journalists, and so on (Kishiro 1985, 194–95). They showed support for the prime minister's ideals (*Asahi*, September 14, 1985).

22. For example, Kiichi Miyazawa, chairman of the LDP executive committee, felt that planning a financing measure was inseparable from the discussion of a direct tax reduction (*NK*, September 29, 1985). The interim report by the Murayama research committee on October 8 also emphasized that a tax reduction and increase should be implemented at the same time in a revenue neutral reform. Prime Minister Nakasone was indifferent to this report and criticized it as only an "analysis" rather than a "policy consideration" of the tax reform. He seemed to believe that the MOF had initiated this report; Murayama, chair of the research committee, was a former MOF bureaucrat and served as general director of the tax bureau.

23. Usually, the MOF does not publicize a revenue shortfall in the current fiscal year (even if it has already found it) as early as December, because such an estimate would force the ministry to alter its estimate of the tax revenue in the next fiscal year, and would influence budget negotiations within the administration and later in the Diet.

24. This plan would lower the maximum tax rate (by combining income and inhabitant taxes) from 88 percent to about 60–70 percent, lower the effective rate of the corporate tax from 52.92 percent to less than 50 percent, and include taxation on capital gains and on formerly tax-free savings.

25. The MOF presented neither specific numbers nor tax rates in the original draft that was presented to the GTSRC as a basis for the interim report. The special members, who were as eager for tax reduction as Nakasone, insisted on including such data in the report, but the MOF permitted only the maximum income tax rate and the effective corporate tax rate whose decreases were to be recommended in the report. One special member, Shunpei Kumon, stated that the GTSRC's deliberations and its report were under the MOF's perfect control (*Asahi*, April 26, 1986.)

26. A similar result was obtained in 1985 in an opinion poll by Sōgō Kenkyū Kaihatsu Kikō, which accepted telephone calls to hear taxpayers' opinions. Opposition to a large-scale indirect tax exceeded support for it, but the difference between the two was small. Many people, especially among salaried workers, expressed the view that the introduction of the large-scale indirect tax was better than the current direct tax system which imposed a heavy burden on salaried workers (*NK*, October 17, 1985).

27. Nakasone's second term was to end in October 1986.

28. In an opinion poll by *Nihon Keizai Shimbun*, 33.8 percent of respondents

believed that taxes would be an important issue in the election; 15.1 percent felt that a countermeasure to the valuation of the yen and recession would be a big issue; and 14.8 percent believed that welfare would be an important issue. Percentages of respondents who chose as important issues education and reform of the national railway, which Nakasone considered his "closing accounts of postwar politics," remained as low as 12.0 percent and 3.2 percent, respectively (*NK*, June 27, 1986).

29. Another reason why Fujio expressed this at the expense of the LDP popularity had to do with faction politics. Fujio, a member of the Fukuda faction, supported Shintaro Abe as a future candidate for prime minister. He feared that Nakasone would end his term in the fall after implementing only the tax reduction, and that the tax increase would be left to the next prime minister. In addition, too big a victory for the LDP in the double elections would give Nakasone an advantage and a reason to extend his term as prime minister. This was in opposition to the other factions' interests. The LDP leaders from other factions had interests similar to Fujio's. For example, Kiichi Miyazawa, chairman of the LDP executive committee, who aimed to occupy the office after Nakasone, Toshio Kōmoto, head of the Kōmoto faction, Shin Kanemaru, the LDP secretary general and a mentor of Noboru Takeshita all agreed on the necessity of the tax increase.

30. The other factions that had new leaders also wanted to enact tax reform in Nakasone's term because they expected it would be politically difficult. For example, the LDP vice president Kanemaru, a mentor of Takeshita, indicated the possibility of extending Nakasone's term until the ordinary session the next year, presuming that the reform of the national railway and tax reform would be important policy problems in his term (*NK*, August 6, 1986).

31. Murayama was assigned acting chair of the LDP TSRC. To balance the representation from major factions inside the LDP, Ganri Yamashita of the Tanaka faction was assigned as chair of the small committee on tax reform.

32. Since Nakasone had already shown a positive attitude about the revision of the Maruyū system despite remaining opposition within the LDP, the MOF concentrated on persuading the prime minister to accept the broad-based tax on consumption.

33. This information is from the record of the HR budget committee, November 4, 1986.

34. In September the MOF had added an inheritance tax cut of ¥300 billion (= $1.78 billion; $1 = ¥168.52 in 1986) to the plan.

35. The MOF seemed to welcome Yamanaka as chairman of the LDP TSRC (*Asahi*, December 24, 1986).

36. He boasted that he had taught Mizuno, the general director of the tax bureau, all about taxes when Mizuno was a young bureaucrat (*Asahi*, December 24, 1986).

37. For example, *Asahi Shimbun* reported that Eishiro Saito, the president of Keidanren, visited Nakasone at night on October 21 immediately after the media reported that the manufacturers' sales tax had been picked from among three alter-

native plans in a meeting between the prime minister and Yamanaka (*Asahi*, December 24, 1986).

38. Among four plans that the MOF and the MHA presented, the LDP used the plan that would lower minimum tax rates, would not change tax exemptions, and would benefit salaried workers and self-employed people equally.

39. This number amounted to more than half the 446 LDP Diet members from both Houses at the time.

40. For backbenchers, especially those who were first elected in the simultaneous elections, the organized support of these special-interest groups in their election districts was critical.

41. For example, in the 1985 fiscal year revision, the MOF had attempted to control the huge tax-exempted funds from postal savings under the Ministry of Posts and Telecommunications (MPT). This attempt involved either the abolition of the system itself or the tax authority's investigation of the abuses of tax-free accounts. The group in alliance with the MPT within the LDP, the postal tribe (*yūsei zoku*), was highly organized, especially in the largest Tanaka faction. The national organization of postmasters increased oppositional pressure on individual Diet members in their election districts; thus this proposal was blocked.

42. In December 1984 Noboru Takeshita—one of the new leaders—organized a "study group" (*Sōseikai*) within the Tanaka faction with Kanemaru's assistance. The faction was essentially divided into two parts. At the end of February, when Tanaka hid from the political scene because of a brain infarction, this group gradually increased its power and the Tanaka faction became the "Takeshita" faction.

43. One of the postal tribe's prominent leaders was a chairman of the PARC postal committee, Akira Fukita.

44. The final decision reached by the three party leaders that followed the major line of the compromise plan between the ministries was as follows: (1) the MPT would be able to use ¥2 trillion (= $13.83 billion; $1 = ¥144.64 in 1987) of postal savings funds for investment in the 1987 fiscal year and this fund would amount to a total of ¥15 trillion until the 1991 fiscal year; (2) the maximum amount of individuals' deposits would be raised from ¥3 million to ¥5 million (= $20.74 to $34.57 thousand); (3) the deposit interest would be connected with changes in the market interest; (4) post offices would be allowed to sell government bonds up to ¥1 trillion (= $6.91 billion).

45. The number of vice chairmen had increased rapidly from four or five to fifteen as the tax issue was increasing in importance under the budget deficit.

46. The positions of core members of the LDP TSRC were assigned to each faction according to the faction's numerical power inside the LDP: five for Tanaka (including those who were closer to Takeshita); four each for Nakasone, Abe (previously Fukuda), and Miyazawa (previously Suzuki); one for Kōmoto; and one for independents.

47. This complaint was especially heard inside the Miyazawa faction (*NK*, October 10, 1986).

48. The members of the "Dietmen's Study Group on Fiscal Reconstruction" criticized the large-scale indirect tax in general, but did not single out the Japanese-style VAT which the LDP TSRC was deliberating as an object of criticism.

49. For example, the largest opposition party, the socialists, lost twenty-seven seats and won only eighty-five in the HR in the simultaneous elections. Therefore, very little could be done against a bill to privatize the Japan National Railways (JNR) in the previous session, even though the labor union of the JNR had provided important organized support for it.

50. For example, the JSP TSRC (an organization of the Japan Socialist Party that corresponds to the LDP TSRC) proposed the tax reform package in late November as a private plan by chairman Masao Hori, which included the value-added tax with invoices for the purpose of tax equity (*NK*, November 23, 1986). No socialist members mentioned this plan after public opposition to the VAT was apparent.

51. The MOF confirmed the introduction of this measure in late November (*NK*, November 20, 1986).

52. The assumed measures were compression of the number of income tax brackets from fifteen (ranging from rates of 10.5 percent to 70 percent) to five (ranging from rates of 10 percent to 50 percent); the introduction of a Japanese-style VAT with a 5 percent rate; the abolition of the Maruyū system—a 20 percent tax on interest income below ¥400 thousand and a 40 percent tax at the source on interest income above ¥400 thousand (= $2.37 thousand; $1 = ¥168.52 in 1986); and a ¥120 thousand (= $712) tax deduction for a housewife in the household of a salaried worker.

53. Curiously enough, the election results at the level of cities, towns, and villages (on April 26), immediately after the government's formal decision to drop the sales tax bill, were fairly good for the LDP.

54. Both tax councils presumed the use of invoices because the other candidate of a multistage tax, which would use the accounting method, was the same as the general consumption tax proposed under the Ōhira administration, the introduction of which the Diet resolution in 1979 had directly denied.

55. A bureaucrat who was involved in the reform process admitted that the MOF did not expect this problem (Ozaki 1987a, 46–49).

56. Ishi (1989) assesses that "this exemption level was . . . approximately 12–20 times [larger] in comparison to the counterparts in the EC countries and Korea" (306).

57. This unified organization was formed the previous June.

58. Consumer groups also began to organize grassroots opposition. The National Federation of the Consumers' Cooperative Society (*Seikatsu Kyōdō Kumiai*) made simple calculation methods in March, and recommended through their nationwide chain stores and members' activities that households should estimate their own taxes after the reform and find the increases for themselves (*Asahi*, March 8, 1987).

59. On February 5, Gotō, the head of Nisshō, stated that Nisshō largely accepted the introduction of the sales tax, but tried to postpone its introduction and modify

the system (*NK*, February 6, 1987). A day later, however, pressure from small and medium-sized businesses among its members forced him to change this statement and say that the sales tax should not be introduced.

60. The estimate by the Economic Planning Agency (EPA), however, showed that the tax reform would push up 0.1 percent of the GNP and increase consumption only by 0.3 percent in real terms annually from 1987 to 1990 (*NK*, February 18, 1987).

61. These two vice chairmen previously had opposed the new indirect tax, but accepted it at the time of the party resolution.

62. Even the Japan Socialist Party did not insist on opposition to the ceiling problem, though the reduction of defense expenditures was one of the most important aims of its party policies.

63. The opposition parties did not have effective financial measures for income tax reduction or for the abolition of the Maruyū system. In late March, they publicized their alternative plan for tax reform but it was not realistic, especially in terms of financial measures for the tax reduction.

64. The CGP did not significantly increase its number of seats, and the DSP even decreased the total votes in the unified local elections.

65. The hardliners on the party side were the chairman of the LDP PARC, Itō, who had been a close and long-time friend of the late Ōhira, and some leaders of the LDP TSRC, especially Yamanaka.

66. These six LDP leaders were Takeshita, Abe, Itō, Chairman of the Diet Affairs Committee Takao Fujinami, Chairman of the LDP Members' Organization of the House of Councillors Yoshihiko Tsuchiya, and acting LDP Secretary General Sōsuke Uno.

67. The LDP vice president, Kanemaru, began to imply this on April 16.

68. In the fall, during the GTSRC's deliberations, the MOF estimated that the new tax would raise about ¥4 trillion (= $ 27.65 billion; $1 = ¥144.64 in 1987) of revenue under a 5 percent tax rate, with a ¥20 million (= ¥138.27 thousand) tax-exemption point, or that a 1 percent tax rate would lead to approximately ¥0.8 to ¥1 trillion of revenue (= $5.53 to $6.91 billion). In late November, while the LDP TSRC began to lean toward the adoption of the Japanese-style VAT, the MOF publicized the estimate that the new tax would yield ¥2.9 trillion (= $20.05 billion) under a 4–5 percent tax rate and with a ¥50 million (= $345.69 thousand) tax-exemption point (*NK*, November 27, 1986). The MOF did not explain the discrepancy between the two numbers until the LDP issued its "Major Line"; *Asahi Shimbun* pointed out that the MOF had not explained this difference (*Asahi*, December 18, 1986), and *Nihon Keizai Shimbun* guessed that the MOF had included the revenue loss of the sales tax resulting from the high tax-exemption point and the tax-exempted transactions in this difference (*NK*, December 4, 1986). After the LDP's "Major Line," the MOF provided a detailed explanation which said that the sales tax would raise an annual revenue of ¥5.8 trillion (= $40.1 billion) with a 5 percent tax rate, a ¥100 million (= $691.36 thousand) tax-exemption point, and forty-three

tax-exempted items, that is, about ¥1.16 trillion per 1 percent of tax. The MOF explained that the ¥2.9 trillion of revenue that had been estimated previously was the result of subtracting the revenue from the existing excise tax (about ¥2.9 trillion) from ¥5.8 trillion (*NK*, December 24, 1986). Masaaki Homma, one of the main figures of the Forum, however, estimated that the revenue from the sales tax would amount to ¥7 trillion instead of ¥5.8 trillion (*Asahi*, July 24, 1987).

69. For example, some junior members of the LDP expressed apparent distrust of the MOF after the sales tax bill was dropped in the Diet (*Asahi*, July 24, 1987).

70. Hayao (1993, chap. 4) argues that Nakasone's leadership had an important impact on the tax reform in the late 1980s. I agree with Hayao in the sense that Nakasone had his own view on the tax policy and succeeded in reflecting it in the 1987 reform. However, I do not think that Nakasone's leadership contributed to introducing the broad-based consumption tax. Though Nakasone changed his mind and came to support the sales tax enthusiastically, his effort in the later stage of the reform was not enough to restore the damage caused by his election pledge against a broad-based consumption tax, such as the sales tax.

CHAPTER SIX

THE THIRD ATTEMPT: INTRODUCTION OF THE CONSUMPTION TAX
AND THE SECURITIES TRADING SCANDAL

1. Usui was an assistant director in the tax bureau at the time of the general consumption tax proposal. He was also a director in charge of the sales tax proposal, and was to be involved in the consumption tax proposal as a director supervising the whole tax reform.

2. The MOF's support for the new tax in terms of the rectification of tax inequity was expressed frequently and widely reported. For example, see the series article "Zeisei Kaikaku Sono Kōzu Ge" (*Asahi*, December 16, 1987).

3. For example, in March 1986, the MHW argued for the need of a special account for social security expenditures, expecting a large amount of stable revenue from the new tax. But this proposal produced no cooperation between the MOF and the MHW.

4. The new chairman of the LDP PARC, Michio Watanabe, was the exception.

5. This latent contradiction between the demand for smaller government and the claim of tax increases became apparent in the GTSRC interim report in April 1988. The report contended that the reform *should not aim* to increase the level of the tax burden, but at the same time it acknowledged a certain increase in the tax burden and in social security contributions.

6. Takayama (1992, 86–93) presents supporting evidence for this, three years after the introduction of the sales tax. He argues that a majority of elderly people enjoy a comparable or even higher living standard than younger generations, while a small number still suffer from a lower standard of living.

7. Some economists indicate that financing social security with a broad-based

consumption tax would elevate the level of "social welfare" as measured by rates of capital accumulation and savings compared to financing with an income tax (Noguchi 1987b; Homma, Atoda, and Otake 1988). Their economic analyses are too complicated for nonspecialists to understand that financing pension programs by a broad-based consumption tax would actually lead to a substantial decrease in the level of pension benefits (Hatta and Oguchi 1990, 126–27).

8. The MOF immediately responded that raising the proposed revenue by these measures was "unrealistic." For example, the opposition's proposal for capital gains taxation on securities would require an individual identification system that was likely to cause public opposition. In the early 1980s, the opposition parties had opposed the introduction of an identification-card system, the so-called green-card system, as an invasion of privacy, and the public had supported their opposition. Moreover, the opposition's proposal did not necessarily respond to the public's expectation for rectification of tax inequity. They excluded certain special tax treatments from their proposal, which were frequently referred to as tax policies that represented "tax inequity": special treatment in taxation for religious corporations, medical doctors, and self-employed businesses, known as "quasi-corporation systems." These groups constituted crucial parts of organized support for the opposition, as well as for the LDP.

9. The JCP requested a tax reduction that would be financed by cutting defense expenditures in half.

10. This leadership change attracted the media's attention because the head of the Seibu Saison group, Seiji Tsutsumi, as a member of the GTSRC, had once expressed his support for a large-scale indirect tax. In addition, Takaoka had been promoted from vice president to president of Seibu immediately before Shimizu's term ended, and thus was qualified to become president of the association (*Asahi*, January 28, 1988).

11. The executives of Nisshō reported that "a majority of answers supported the reform including the introduction of a new indirect tax" without specifying the type of new indirect tax. These reported results did not include percentages or numbers of each answer (*NK*, March 18, 1988).

12. This method allows corporations to regard a certain percentage of the amount of sales as added value. This simple taxation method was an attractive choice to alleviate opposition from small and medium-sized distributors who had been most worried about the tax authority's investigations of their businesses through the taxation. *Asahi Shimbun* reported that under Nakasone's cabinet, Vice President Kanemaru had once asked the leader of the distribution industries to accept a 1 percent turnover tax as a compromise, and had obtained a positive response from the industries (*Asahi*, "Sugata Miseta Shingata Kansetsuzei," March 26, 1988).

13. Securing financial resources for the aging of society was given as a second reason for reform in the interim report because some GTSRC members wanted to stress the need for administrative reform to coincide with the tax reform and were afraid of increasing spending pressure.

14. A bureaucrat who was deeply involved in the consumption tax proposal highly praised Katō's role. That bureaucrat met Katō for the first time at a conference on the tax system in the summer of 1988. After the meeting Katō came to understand the MOF's proposal of the new tax (according to my interview with MOF bureaucrats during the summer of 1989). Katō also frankly admitted that he had changed his position. He explained that he had opposed the sales tax because he thought it went against administrative reform, but he had come to believe that the new indirect tax would be compatible with administrative reform ("Zeisei Kaikaku no Teiryū," *Asahi*, May 1, 1988).

15. The word *darakugata* became popular to symbolize the government's concession to special interests, as well as the disagreement between the MOF and the GTSRC. Ogura later stated that he strongly suggested the council's preference for the EC-type VAT, but the tax bureau continued to resist his suggestion ("Zeisei Kaikaku no Teiryū," *Asahi*, April 30, 1988).

16. A group of junior members who had opposed the sales tax, the "Study Group on the New Tax" (*Shinzei Kenkyūkai*), began to study the tax system in general, and invited high-ranking MOF bureaucrats to their meetings once a week in March ("Danmen 88 Zeisei Kaikaku," *Asahi*, May 18, 1988). This showed that they were more flexible in accepting the new tax, and were trying to find the best way to compromise.

17. While the MOF estimated a tax reduction for average households with incomes of more than ¥2.74 million (= $21.38 thousand; $1 = ¥128.15 in 1988), the private research groups of the Policy Planning Forum (*Seisaku Kōsō Hōramu*), Shizuoka University, and the JSP, the CGP, and the DSP showed tax reductions for households with more than ¥2.77 to ¥3.29 million (= $21.62 thousand to $25.67 thousand) of annual income. The JCP results predicted tax reductions for households with more than ¥5.5 million (= $42.92 thousand). The MOF regarded the tax increase for a single person as part of a lifelong burden, and said that the increased burden for some working couples was exceptional.

18. The income tax cut amounted to about ¥3.1 trillion (= $24.19 billion; $1 = ¥128.15 in 1988) in the final government proposal. The tax increase from the new tax, if subtracted from a tax cut by the abolition of excise taxes on commodities, was estimated to be about ¥2.0 trillion (= $15.61 billion).

19. I was able to confirm this in interviews I had with several bureaucrats in the summer of 1989. The MITI, as well as some LDP members, served as intermediators between the special-interest groups and the MOF. In interviews during the same period, the MITI bureaucrats who had been involved in tax reform stated that the transformation to an EC-type VAT was unrealistic because of the special-interest groups' opposition.

20. Because of the natural increment of revenue that was expected later, the government's promise was achieved with a 3 percent tax rate on the initial budget of the 1990 fiscal year.

21. I confirmed this point in my interview with an MOF bureaucrat during the

summer of 1989. He worked in the tax bureau when the decision on the tax rate was made.

22. At the beginning of January the MOF had already formulated a rough plan for the new broad-based consumption tax: as a basis for discussion in the GTSRC, a VAT that would be levied on all commodities and services with tax rates of 3 percent, that would exclude distributors with annual sales under ¥20 million (= $156.07 thousand; $1 = ¥128.15 in 1988), and that would allow businesses with annual sales of less than ¥2 billion (= $15.61 million; $1 = ¥128.15 in 1988) to regard 0.6 percent of their sales as the tax (*NK*, January 12, 1988).

23. Of course, the unclear situation of taxation with the accounting method could work against the interests of distributors because it might force weak competitors to pay the tax themselves without shifting it to the price. Ironically, faced with the installation of the new tax after the passage of tax bills, the government had to suffer criticism from both consumers and distributors.

24. The number of distributors and manufacturers below the tax-exemption point was expected to be 68.2 percent of the total number.

25. The result also depends on whether a majority of these corporations would employ the simple method.

26. Because of public criticism, a revision of the special tax treatment for medical doctors was added to the reform at the final stage, but the special treatment for "quasi-corporations" was left untouched.

27. A tax based on "quasi-capital gains" from the sale of securities, which most taxpayers were expected to use, was especially compromising because it would consider a certain ratio of sales as profit and make this "quasi-capital gain" the basis for a flat rate of taxation without regulating the tax return. This measure was not a tax on capital gains in an accurate sense, but was similar to the existing tax on securities transactions. In the final reform plan, a separate tax based on a tax return would be 26 percent of the profits from a sale (20 percent capital-gain tax at the national level and 6 percent at the local level), and a separate tax at the source would consider 5 percent of the sale price as a quasi-capital gain; 20 percent of this ratio, that is, 1 percent of the sale price would be the tax amount.

28. For example, the opinion polls by *Asahi Shimbun* in June 1988 reported that 28 percent of respondents supported the new indirect tax and 54 percent opposed it. In addition, 77 percent did not think that the tax inequity would be improved as a result of the reform (*Asahi*, June 26, 1988). Almost at the same time, *Nihon Keizai Shimbun* conducted opinion polls and reported about 30 percent support for and 50 percent opposition to the new tax—results that were similar to those reported by *Asahi Shimbun*. These results also showed that only 4.9 percent of respondents valued the measures for the rectification of tax inequity, and 22.3 percent expressed a negative reaction (*NK*, July 3, 1988).

29. The polls by *Nihon Keizai Shimbun* asked respondents why they supported or opposed the consumption tax. Results showed public confusion about the tax reform's effect on welfare. About 60 percent of supporters regarded it as a stable

financial source necessary for the approaching aging society, and about 60 percent of respondents who were opposed to the tax questioned the heavier burden on low-income people (*NK*, July 3, 1988).

30. In terms of the tax reform's impact on local governments, the MOF and the MHA agreed that local governments would share responsibility with the national government for financing ¥790 billion (= $6.16 billion; $1 = ¥128.15 in 1988) from the total tax reduction. Because the existing excise tax that provided revenue to local governments was to be integrated into the consumption tax, they also agreed that a fifth of the revenue from the consumption tax would finance local governments as a local allocation tax and 24 percent of the remaining four-fifths of the revenue would be given to them as a local transfer tax in an average year.

31. In addition to their different attitudes toward the tax bills, more implicit disagreements existed between the JSP, which welcomed the resolution of the House of Representatives and a general election, and the middle-of-the-road parties, which feared an election in the near future. The CGP wanted to avoid a general election because of the party's involvement in another securities trading scandal. The DSP did so because the chairman of the party, Saburō Tsukamoto, had been included in the list of people who bought Recruit Cosmos stock before it was offered to the public.

32. According to the opinion polls by *Nihon Keizai Shimbun*, the number of those outrightly opposed to the consumption tax and the number of those inclined to oppose the tax increased, respectively, from 24.8 percent and 25.0 percent in June 1988 to 26.3 percent and 29.3 percent in September. Among the 52.6 percent of total respondents who opposed the consumption tax in September, 52.7 percent had opposed it in June but 32.3 percent had changed their attitude from reservation to opposition because of the Recruit problem; 5 percent now opposed the tax reform because of this problem, although they had supported it before (*NK*, September 26, 1988).

33. Hiromasa Ezoe resigned immediately after the disclosure of the problem in July 1988.

34. When the party was threatened by public criticism, Tsukamoto lost the support for his leadership inside the party, as well as from labor unions as a major support organization.

35. According to the opinion poll by *Asahi Shimbun*, in November 1987, immediately after the formation of the Takeshita cabinet, the approval rate was 44 percent and the nonapproval rate was 24 percent. After about a year, in October 1988, immediately before the LDP's forced voting in the HR special committee and the Recruit special committee's examination of the former president of Recruit as a witness, the rates remained roughly the same—41 percent and 31 percent, respectively. But in December, the approval rate dropped to 29 percent and the nonapproval rate rose to 47 percent. This trend continued. On the day following his declaration of resignation, the approval rate was as low as 7 percent and the nonapproval rate climbed as high as 84 percent. Other opinion polls showed similar trends.

36. Various opinion polls showed that the consumption tax and the Recruit problem became the two biggest issues in the election. For example, when asked to choose three election issues from thirteen options, 65.8 percent of respondents chose "the tax system" and 43.1 percent chose "the political ethics" related to the Recruit problem (according to opinion polls by Jiji Tsūshinsha in March 1989). These rates far exceeded the 36.3 percent of respondents who chose "the price" as an election issue (*Jiji Yoron Chōsa Tokuhō*, April 11, 1989). Kabashima's (1992) close analysis confirmed that the election in 1989 was exceptionally issue-oriented and that the consumption tax was a far more important issue than political ethics. The liberalization of agriculture, which was rapidly politicized immediately before the election, also had likely influenced the defeat of the LDP because farmers are well organized and important supporters of the party.

37. According to opinion poll by *Nihon Keizai Shimbun* in March 1990 after the general election, 47.6 percent of respondents supported the "freezing" or "abolition" of the system, and this rate almost equaled the 49.4 percent of respondents who supported the existing system, the LDP's revision plan of the consumption tax system, or further modification of such a plan. Compared to corresponding polls conducted earlier by the same newspaper, these results showed that support for the abolition of the plan had begun to decrease (*NK*, March 26, 1990).

38. In January 1990 the results of Jiji Tsūshinsha opinion poll showed that 32.7 percent of respondents praised the bills for the abolition of the consumption tax and alternative financial measures by the opposition parties, while 58.2 percent of respondents supported the LDP's revision plan (*Jiji Yoron Chōsa Tokuhō*, February 11, 1990).

CHAPTER SEVEN
CONCLUSION: BUREAUCRACY, PARTY, AND THE POWER OF RATIONALITY

1. Takako Doi considers that the party's failure to appeal to the public on tax issues was the main reason for the election's defeat and regrets that her party did not present a viable alternative to the government tax reform in order to maintain popular support ("Watashi no Rirekisho," *NK*, September 29, 1992).

2. All these countries except Canada introduced the VAT before Japan. See Table 1.1.

3. For example, see OECD 1987, 118.

4. Anne Swardson, "Canada's Value-Added Tax: Cautionary Tale for Clinton," *Washington Post*, April 16, A6, column 4.

5. From an interview with a bureaucrat of the Treasury of New Zealand in October 1992.

6. Hatta (1988, 12–16) summarizes this position and clarifies its relation to the government's presented aims for "rectification of tax inequity." He then argues that this position is justified only when the reform to improve the income taxation directly is proved to be impossible.

7. From an interview with a bureaucrat of the Treasury of New Zealand in October 1992.

8. This was because of the inherent difficulty in determining the appropriate value on which the tax was charged at the wholesale stage.

9. Article 42 of the Commodity Tax Law (*Buppinzei Hō*) enacted in 1962 stipulated that the tax should be listed separately from the price. But the tax had usually been included in the price, and this divergence between law and practice was rarely developed into a political problem.

10. It is impossible to include the interests of self-employed people and small and medium-sized businesses in the conservative coalition that supported the introduction of the new tax. The introduction of the new tax itself clearly went against their interests, although the government made many compromises with them in the tax-filing measures of the new system. The new tax required them not only to do more paperwork in filing their taxes, but also to present more information on their business incomes; tax-exempted businesses also feared that taxed firms would exclude them from transactions. They were clearly better off without the new tax. This was why self-employed people joined the consumer opposition that appeared upon the introduction of the new tax.

11. If one includes self-employed people in "the public," the opposition to the new tax had more contradictory claims. The consumers felt that the incomplete tax-filing measures gave the taxes they paid to the distributors as a benefit, while the distributors argued that they had to pay taxes at the expense of their profits without shifting the tax burden to consumers because of price competition. The consumers and distributors criticized the new tax for contradictory and opposing reasons, but temporarily agreed on the abolition of the system immediately after the introduction of the new tax.

12. This system also met the MOF's interest in controlling a fund of postal savings that was under the Ministry of Posts and Telecommunications. According to the MOF, the savings whose interest was exempted from income taxation amounted to about 60 percent of total personal savings in the mid-1980s. The most notable tax-exemption measures were the "Maruyū" system, under which the interest earned from deposits at banks, securities companies, and other private financial institutions (under ¥3 million) was exempt, and tax exemption of the interest earned from postal savings. More than 90 percent of tax-free personal savings were included in both measures. Three other tax-free investment incomes included national and local bonds under ¥3 million, savings for the formation of employee's assets under ¥5 million, and postal installment savings for housing under ¥0.5 million in the mid-1980s.

13. The most implicit reason, which had no verifiable evidence but was popularly believed, was that this system might destroy the underground economy whose stock and flow of funds evaded the tax. The politicians, especially of the LDP, were believed to depend on contributions from those who benefited from this kind of underground economic activity.

14. In April 1983, when the funds in banking deposits began to flow to investments in gold and zero-coupon bonds that could be exempted from taxation, the opposition assumed this was a market response to the enhancement of taxation on savings and criticized the introduction of the green-card system, believing it would distort economic activities.

15. On this point, both the pluralists and rational choice theorists may provide another explanation. Emphasizing the autonomy of the LDP from bureaucratic influence, they may relate the introduction of the VAT to the LDP's long-term interest—to secure a financial source for its constituencies' service. They may also attempt to connect the VAT with an interest of one of the LDP's important allies— for example, major business associations (Ramseyer and Rosenbluth 1993, 53–55). But there are counterevidences to them. First, the VAT was introduced when the Japanese government had a clear prospect for eliminating reliance of deficit bonds to supplement revenue (the VAT—called the consumption tax—was introduced in April 1989; from the 1990 fiscal year, the Japanese government stopped issuing deficit bonds for the first time since the mid-1970s). Moreover, the issuance of bonds itself had had persistent support from LDP politicians before the MOF indicated the risk of relying on it. Second, the new tax was not in the interest of major business associations in the first place. As already shown, they supported the VAT in order to avoid the concentration of a tax burden on large-scale corporations.

16. This number included two members who could not attend any meetings of this Diet session because of illness, thus the number of members who were intentionally absent from the voting was sixteen.

17. Among seven next-generation leaders under Takeshita and Kanemaru in the former Takeshita faction, Keiwa Okuda and Kōzō Watanabe quit the faction with Hata. Ozawa and Ryūtarō Hashimoto remained with Kajiyama and Obuchi.

18. The election system was added to the agenda because the HR's multimember district system with single nontransferable votes was considered to require more money for candidates to win elections.

19. Rational choice theorists point out the same backbenchers' dilemma, but they tend to explain that the LDP organizations are designed to solve this dilemma.

20. For example, both former Prime Minister Toshiki Kaifu and the late Takeo Miki, who served as prime minister in the mid-1970s, came from this faction.

21. It is interesting to note the LDP's response to this coalition government's proposal. Some leaders criticized a tax increase under the name of a "people's welfare tax." But other leaders saw the proposal as combining an income tax reduction and a consumption tax increase in order to prevent the government's budget from going into a deficit. These two different views inside the LDP did not develop into an intraparty conflict simply because the government withdrew the proposal, and the proponents of each view together began to criticize the government as irresponsible for reversing its policy.

22. Here, the reader may be reminded of the U.S. tax reform in the mid-1980s. This reform was implemented based on a report by a group of tax experts. It suc-

285

ceeded in applying theoretical principles to a reform that had been considered politically unfeasible. However, some scholars pointed out that institutional and structural factors cannot explain the political success of this reform. Rather, they attribute its success to the power of the ideas and workings of experts and policy entrepreneurs who are not usually important participants in the policy-making process
(Conlan et al. 1990).

# Bibliography

NEWSPAPERS AND PERIODICALS

*Newspapers*

*Asahi Shimbun* (Tokyo)
*Globe and Mail* (Toronto)
*Mainichi Shimbun* (Tokyo)
*New York Times*
*Nihon Keizai Shimbun* (Tokyo)
*Sankei Shimbun* (Tokyo)
*Wall Street Journal* (New York)
*Washington Post*
*Yomiuri Shimbun* (Tokyo)

*Periodicals*

*International Financial Statistics* (Paris)
*Jiji Yoron Tokuhō* (Tokyo)
*Zaisei Kinyū Tōkei Geppō* (Tokyo)
*Zenkoku Yoron Chōsa no Gaikyō* (Tokyo)

BOOKS

Aaron, H. J., ed. 1981. *The Value Added Tax: Lessons from Europe.* Washington, D.C.: The Brookings Institution.
———, ed. 1982. *VAT: Experiences of Some European Countries.* Deventer, Netherlands: Kluwer Law and Taxation Publishers.
Aaron, H. J. 1987. "The Impossible Dream Comes True: The New Tax Reform Act." *The Brookings Review* (Winter): 3–10.
Aberbach, J. D., R. D. Putnam, and B. A. Rockman. 1981. *Bureaucrats and Politicians in Western Democracy.* Cambridge, Mass.: Harvard University Press.
Aberbach, J. D., E. S. Krauss, M. Muramatsu, and B. A. Rockman. 1990. "Comparing Japanese and American Administrative Elites." *British Journal of Political Science* 20, no. 4: 461–88.
Alt, James E., and Kenneth A. Shepsle. 1990. *Perspectives on Positive Political Economy.* New York: Cambridge University Press.
Altfeld, M. F., and G. J. Miller. 1984. "Sources of Bureaucratic Influence: Expertise and Agenda Control." *Journal of Conflict Resolution* 28, no. 4 (December): 701–30.
Andō, H. 1987a. *Sekinin to Genkai (Jō).* Tokyo: Kinyū Zaisei Jijō Kenkyūkai.

Andō, H. 1987b. *Sekinin to Genkai (Ge)*. Tokyo: Kinyū Zaisei Jijō Kenkyūkai.

Aranson, P. H., and P. C. Ordeshook. 1981. "Regulation, Redistribution, and Public Choice." *Public Choice* 37, no. 1: 69–100.

Arnold, R. D. 1979. *Congress and the Bureaucracy*. New Haven, Conn.: Yale University Press.

Arrow, K. J. 1963. *Social Choice and Individual Values*. New York: Wiley.

———. 1987. "Rationality of Self and Others in an Economic System." In R. M. Hogarth and M. W. Reder, eds., *Rational Choice: The Contrast between Economics and Psychology*, 201–15. Chicago: The University of Chicago Press.

Becker, G. S. 1962. "Irrational Behavior and Economic Theory." *Journal of Political Economy* 70, no. 1: 1–13.

———. 1983. "A Theory of Competition among Pressure Groups for Political Influence." *Quarterly Journal of Economics* 98, no. 3: 371–400.

Bendor, J., and T. M. Moe. 1985. "An Adaptive Model of Bureaucratic Politics." *American Political Science Review* 79, no. 3: 755–74.

Bendor, J., S. Taylor, and R. Van Gaalen. 1985. "Bureaucratic Expertise versus Legislative Authority: A Model of Deception and Monitoring in Budgeting." *American Political Science Review* 79, no. 4: 1041–60.

Berger, S. D. 1981. *Organizing Interests in Western Europe: Pluralism, Corporatism, and the Transformation of Politics*. New York: Cambridge University Press.

Blais, A., and S. Dion, eds. 1991. *The Budget-Maximizing Bureaucrat*. Pittsburgh: University of Pittsburgh Press.

Bradford, D. F. 1980. "The Case for a Personal Consumption Tax." In J. A. Pechman, ed., *What Should be Taxed: Income or Expenditure?*, 75–126. Washington, D.C.: The Brookings Institution.

———. 1986. *Untangling the Income Tax*. Cambridge, Mass.: Harvard University Press.

Braybrooke, D., and C. E. Lindblom. 1963. *A Strategy of Decision*. New York: The Free Press.

Brennan, G., and J. M. Buchanan. 1980. *The Power to Tax*. New York: Cambridge University Press.

Buchanan, J. M. 1960a. "'La scienza delle finanze': The Italian Tradition in Fiscal Theory." In *Fiscal Theory and Political Economy: Selected Essays*, 24–74. Chapel Hill: University of North Carolina Press.

———. 1960b. "Positive Economics, Welfare Economics, and Political Economy." In *Fiscal Theory and Political Economy: Selected Essays*, 75–89. Chapel Hill: University of North Carolina Press.

———. 1972a. "Toward Analysis of Closed Behavior Systems." In J. M. Buchannan and R. D. Tollison, eds., *Theory of Public Choice*, 11–23. Ann Arbor: University of Michigan Press.

———. 1972b. "Fiscal Policy and Fiscal Preference." In J. M. Buchanan and R. D. Tollison, eds., *Theory of Public Choice*, 76–84. Ann Arbor: University of Michigan Press.

————. 1975. *The Limits of Liberty: Between Anarchy and Leviathan.* Chicago: University of Chicago Press.

Buchanan, J. M., and G. Tullock. 1962. *The Calculus of Consent.* Ann Arbor: University of Michigan Press.

Buchanan, J. M., and R. E. Wagner. 1977. *Democracy in Deficit: The Political Legacy of Lord Keynes.* New York: Academic Press.

Cain, B., J. Ferejohn, and M. Fiorina. 1987. *The Personal Vote: Constituency Service and Electoral Independence.* Cambridge, Mass.: Harvard University Press.

Calder, K. 1989. "Elites in an Equalizing Role: Ex-Bureaucrats as Coordinators and Intermediaries in the Japanese Government-Business Relationship." *Comparative Politics* 21, no. 4: 379–404.

————. 1988. *Crisis and Compensation: Public Policy and Political Stability in Japan, 1949–1986.* Princeton, N.J.: Princeton University Press.

Calvert, R., M. D. McCubbins, and B. R. Weingast. 1989. "A Theory of Political Control and Agency Discretion." *American Journal of Political Science* 33, no. 3: 588–611.

————. M. J. Moran, and B. R. Weingast. 1987. "Congressional Influence over Policy Making: The Case of FTC." In M. D. McCubbins, and T. Sullivan, eds., *Congress: Structure and Policy*: 493–532. Cambridge: Cambridge University Press.

Campbell, C., and G. J. Szablowski. 1979. *The Superbureaucrats: Structure and Behaviour in Central Agencies.* Toronto: Macmillan of Canada.

Campbell, J. C. 1977. *Contemporary Japanese Budget Politics.* Berkeley: University of California Press.

————. 1985a. "Governmental Responses to Budget Scarcity: An Introduction." *Policy Studies Journal* 13, no. 3: 471–75.

————. 1985b. "Governmental Response to Budget Scarcity: Japan." *Policy Studies Journal* 13, no.3: 506–11.

————. 1992. *Policy Change: The Japanese Government and the Elderly.* Princeton, N.J.: Princeton University Press.

Cohen, M. D., J. C. March, and J. P. Olsen. 1972. "A Garbage Can Model of Organizational Choice." *Administrative Science Quarterly* 17, no. 1: 1–25.

Conlan, T. J., M. T. Wrightson, and D. R. Beam. 1990. *Taxing Choices: The Politics of Tax Reform.* Washington, D.C.: Congressional Quarterly.

Cowhey, P., and M. D. McCubbins, eds. Forthcoming. *Structure and Policy in Japan and the United States.* Cambridge: Cambridge University Press.

Cox, G., and M. D. McCubbins. 1993. *Legislative Leviathan.* Berkeley: University of California Press.

Crozier, M. 1964. *The Bureaucratic Phenomenon.* Chicago: University of Chicago Press.

Curtis, G. L. 1988. *The Japanese Way of Politics.* New York: Columbia University Press.

Dahl, R. A. 1961. *Who Governs?* New Haven, Conn.: Yale University Press.

Dahl, R. A. 1971. *Polyarchy: Participation and Opposition.* New Haven, Conn.: Yale University Press.

———. 1982. *Dilemmas of Pluralist Democracy: Autonomy and Control.* New Haven, Conn.: Yale University Press.

De Menil, G., and R. Portes. 1987. *Economic Policy: The Conservative Revolution.* Cambridge: Cambridge University Press.

deHaven-Smith, L. 1988. *Philosophical Critiques of Policy Analysis: Lindblom, Habermas, and the Great Society.* Gainesville: University of Florida Press.

Dogan, M., ed. 1975. *The Mandarins of Western Europe: The Political Role of Top Civil Servants.* New York: Wiley.

Downs, A. 1957. *An Economic Theory of Democracy.* New York: Harper & Row.

———. 1967. *Inside Bureaucracy.* Boston: Little, Brown.

Dungan, P., J. M. Mintz, and T. A. Wilson. 1990. "Alternatives to the Goods and Services Tax." *Canadian Tax Journal* 38, no. 3: 644–65.

Eavey, C. L., and G. J. Miller. 1984. "Bureaucratic Agenda Control: Imposition or Bargaining?" *American Political Science Review* 78, no. 3: 719–33.

Elster, J. 1989. *Solomonic Judgements: Studies in the Limitations of Rationality.* New York: Cambridge University Press.

Evans, P. R., D. Rueschemeyer, and T. Skocpol, eds. 1985. *Bringing the State Back In.* New York: Cambridge University Press.

Feldman, A. M. 1980. *Welfare Economics and Social Choice Theory.* Boston: Martinus Nijhoff.

Feldman, M. S. 1989. *Order Without Design: Information Production and Policy Making.* Stanford, Calif.: Stanford University Press.

Fenno, R. F. 1977. *Home Style: House Members and Their Districts.* Boston: Little, Brown.

Fiorina, M. P. 1977. *Congress: Keystone of the Washington Establishment.* New Haven, Conn.: Yale University Press.

———. 1982. "Legislative Choice of Regulatory Forms: Legal Process or Administrative Process?" *Public Choice* 39, no. 1: 33–66.

Fischer, F. 1980. *Politics, Values, and Public Policy: The Problem of Methodology.* Boulder, Colo.: Westview.

———. 1987. "Policy Expertise and the 'New Class': A Critique of the Neoconservative Thesis." In F. Fischer and J. Forester, eds., *Confronting Values in Policy Analysis: The Politics of Criteria,* 94–126. Newbury Park, Calif.: Sage.

———. 1990. *Technocracy and the Politics of Expertise.* Newbury Park, Calif.: Sage.

Friedman, D. 1988. *The Misunderstood Miracle: Industrial Development and Political Change in Japan.* Ithaca, N.Y.: Cornell University Press.

Fujita, S. 1987. *Zeisei Kaikaku: Sono Kiseki to Tenbō.* Tokyo: Zeimu Keiri Kyō-kai.

Fukuda, Y. 1987. *Zeisei Kaikakuheno Ayumi: Fukuda Yukihiro Taidanshū.* Tokyo: Zeimu Keiri Kyōkai.

Gerth, H. H., and W. Mills. 1958. "Introduction: The Man and His Work." In M. Weber, *From Max Weber: Essays in Sociology*, 3–31. New York: Oxford University Press.

Goode, R. 1980. "The Superiority of the Income Tax." In J. A. Pechman, ed., *What Should Be Taxed: Income or Expenditure?*, 49–74. Washington, D.C.: The Brookings Institution.

Gourevitch, P. 1986. *Politics in Hard Times*. Ithaca, N.Y.: Cornell University Press.

Groenewegen, P. D. 1988. "Tax Reform in Australia and New Zealand." *Government and Policy* 6: 93–114.

Hadley, E. M. 1989. "The Diffusion of Keynesianism in Japan." In P. A. Hall, ed., *The Political Power of Economic Ideas*, 291–310. Princeton, N.J.: Princeton University Press.

Hall, P. A. 1986. *Governing the Economy*. New York: Oxford University Press.

———. 1989. *The Political Power of Economic Ideas*. Princeton, N.J.: Princeton University Press.

Hammond, S. W. 1983. "The Members of the U.S. Congress." In F. R. Valeo and C. E. Morrison, eds., *The Japanese Diet and the U.S. Congress*, 155–70. Boulder, Colo.: Westview.

———. 1989. "Congressional Caucuses in the Policy Process." In L. C. Dodd and B. I. Oppenheimer, eds., *Congress Reconsidered*, 4th ed. Washington, D.C.: A Division of the Congressional Quarterly.

Hart, O. 1990. "An Economist's Perspective on the Theory of the Firm." In O. E. Williamson, ed., *Organization Theory: From Chester Barnard to the Present and Beyond*, 154–71. New York: Oxford University Press.

Hart, O., and B. Holmstrom. 1987. "The Theory of Contracts." In T. Bewly, ed., *Advances in Economic Theory*. Fifth World Congress, Cambridge: Cambridge University Press.

Hashiguchi, O. 1977. *Shin Zaisei Jijō*. Tokyo: Saimaru Shuppankai.

Hatta, T. 1988. *Chokusetsuzei Kaikaku*. Tokyo: Nihon Keizai Shimbunsha.

Hatta, T., and T. Oguchi. 1990. "Nenkin Kaikaku." In Gendai Keizai Kenkyū Gurūpu, ed., *Nihon no Seiji Keizai Shisutemu*, 103–40. Tokyo: Nihon Keizai Shimbunsha.

Hayao, K. 1993. *The Japanese Prime Minister and Public Policy*. Pittsburgh, Pa.: University of Pittsburgh Press.

Heclo, H. 1977. *A Government of Strangers: Executive Politics in Washington*. Washington, D.C.: The Brookings Institution.

———. 1984. "In Search of a Role: America's Higher Civil Service." In E. Z. Suleiman, ed., *Bureaucrats and Policymaking*, 8–34. New York: Holmes and Meier.

Heidenheimer, A., H. Heclo, and C. T. Adams. 1990. *Comparative Public Policy: The Politics of Social Choice in Europe and America*. New York: St. Martin's.

Hirshleifer, J. 1976. "'Comments' on Peltzman." *Journal of Law and Economics* 19, no. 2: 241–44.

291

Homma, M., N. Atoda, and F. Otake. 1988. "Kōreika Shakai to Koteki Nenkin no Zaisei Hōshiki." *Financial Review* (March): 50–64.

Igarashi, H. 1989. "Nakasone Motoshushō niokeru Rīdashippu no Kenkyū." *Leviathan* (Fall): 167–82.

Inoguchi, T. 1983. *Gendai Nihon Seiji Keizai no Kōzu*. Tokyo: Tōyō Keizai Shinpōsha.

———. 1990. "The Political Economy of Conservative Resurgence under Recession: Public Policies and Political Support in Japan, 1977–1983." In T. J. Pempel, ed., *Uncommon Democracies: The One-Party Dominant Regimes*, 189–225. Ithaca, N.Y.: Cornell University Press.

Inoguchi, T., and T. Iwai. 1987. *"Zoku Giin" no Kenkyū*. Tokyo: Nihon Keizai Shimbunsha.

Institute for Fiscal Studies. 1978. *The Structure and Reform of Direct Taxation: Report of a Committee Chaired by Professor J. E. Meade*. London: Allen and Unwin.

Ishi, H. 1987. "The Impact of the Shoup Mission." In H. M. van de Kar and B. L. Wolfe, eds., *The Relevance of Public Finance for Policy-Making*, 237–320. Detroit: Wayne State University Press.

———. 1989. *The Japanese Tax System*. Oxford: Oxford University Press.

———. 1993. *The Japanese Tax System*. 2d ed. New York: Oxford University Press.

Ishida, H. 1963. "Hoshutō no Bijyon." *Chūō Koron* (January).

Ishikawa, M., and M. Hirose 1989. *Jiminto: Chōki Shihai no Kōzō*. Tokyo: Iwanami Shoten.

Itō, D. 1980. *Gendai Nihon Kanryōsei no Bunseki*. Tokyo: University of Tokyo Press.

Ito, T., and A. O. Krueger, eds. 1992. *The Political Economy of Tax Reform*. Chicago: University of Chicago Press.

Izumi, S. 1983. "Diet Members." In F. R. Valeo and C. E. Morrison, eds., *The Japanese Diet and the U.S. Congress*, 61–78. Boulder, Colo.: Westview.

Iwai, T. 1990. *Seiji Shikin no Kenkyū*. Tokyo: Nihon Keizai Shimbunsha.

Jin, I. 1986. *Ōkura Kanryō*. Tokyo: Kōdansha.

Johnson, C. 1975. "Japan: Who Governs? An Essay on Official Bureaucracy." *Journal of Japanese Studies* 2, no. 1: 1–28.

———. 1982. *MITI and the Japanese Miracle: The Growth of Industrial Policy, 1925–1975*. Stanford, Calif.: Stanford University Press.

Kabashima, I. 1992. "89 nen San'insen—Jimintō Taihai to Shakai Taishō no Kōzu," *Leviathan* 10: 7–31.

Kaizuka, K. 1987. "Zeisei Kaikakuron." *Keizaigaku Ronshū (The University of Tokyo)* 53, no. 2: 16–24.

———. 1988. *Zaiseigaku*. Tokyo: Tokyo University Press.

———. 1989. "Zeisei Kaikaku no Nichibei Hikaku." In K. Iwata and I. Tsuneo, eds., *Nihon Keizai Kenkyū*, 137–50. Tokyo: University of Tokyo Press.

Kakizawa, K. 1979. *Nagatachō 1 Chōmeno Kokkaigiin wa Jingasa o Kabutta Ta-nukito Iwareru "Mainichiga Senkyosen" ni Kurushimu Awarena Senryōtachi.* Tokyo: Gakuyō Shobō.

———. 1983. "The Diet and the Bureaucracy: The Budget as a Case Study." In F. R. Valeo and C. E. Morrison, eds., *The Japanese Diet and the U.S. Congress*, 79–98. Boulder, Colo.: Westview.

Kalt, J. P., and M. A. Zupan. 1984. "Capture and Ideology in the Economic Theory of Politics." *American Economic Review* 74, no. 3: 279–300.

———. 1990. "The Apparent Ideological Behavior of Legislators: Testing for Principal-Agent Slack in Political Institutions." *Journal of Law and Economics* 33, no. 1: 103–31.

Kaplan, E. J. 1972. *Japan: The Government-Business Relationship.* Washington, D.C.: U.S. Department of Commerce.

Kato, J. 1991a. "Public Pension Reforms in the United States and Japan: A Study of Comparative Public Policy." *Comparative Political Studies* 24, no. 1: 100–26.

———. 1991b. "Seisaku Ketteikatei Kenkyō no Riron to Jisshō—Kōteki Nenkin Seido Kaikaku to Iryōhoken Seido Kaikaku no Keisu o Megutte." *Leviathan* 8: 165–84.

Katō, Y. 1982. *Nihon no Yosan Kaikaku.* Toyko: University of Tokyo Press.

Katzenstein, P. 1985. *Small States in World Markets.* Ithaca, N.Y.: Cornell University Press.

Kawaguchi, Y. 1987. *Kanryō Shihai no Kōzō.* Tokyo: Kōdansha.

Kawakita, T. 1989. *Ōkurasho.* Tokyo: Kōdansha.

Kay, J. A. 1987. "Tax Reform in Retrospect: The Role of Inquiry." In H. M. van de Kar and B. L. Wolfe, eds., *The Relevance of Public Finance for Policy-Making*, 67–82. Detroit: Wayne State University Press.

Kiewiet, D. R., and M. D. McCubbins. 1991. *The Logic of Delegation: Congressional Parties and the Appropriations Process.* Chicago: University of Chicago Press.

Kingdon, J. W. 1984. *Agendas, Alternatives, and Public Policies.* Boston: Little, Brown.

Kishiro, Y. 1985. *Jimintō Zeisei Chōsakai.* Tokyo: Tōyō Keizai Shimpōsha.

Kitchen, H. M. 1987. "Canada." In J. A. Pechman, ed., *Comparative Tax Systems: Europe, Canada, and Japan*, 341–402. Arlington, Va.: Tax Analysts.

Koh, B. C. 1989. *Japan's Administrative Elite.* Berkeley: University of California Press.

Komiya, R. 1990. "Economic Policy Makers in the Japanese Government." In R. Komiya, ed., *The Japanese Economy*, 361–90. Tokyo: University of Tokyo Press.

Kōsai, Y. 1981. *Kōdo Seichō no Jidai.* Tokyo: Nihon Hyōronsha.

Krauss, E. S. 1984. "Conflict in the Diet: Toward Conflict Management in Parliamentary Politics." In E. S. Krauss., T. P. Rohlen, and P. G. Steinhoff, eds., *Conflict in Japan*, 243–93. Honolulu: University of Hawaii Press.

Kubouchi, Y. 1984. "Tax Burden on Corporate Income: An International Comparison." *Keidanren Review* 87.

Kuribayashi, Y. 1987. Ōkurasho Shuzeikyoku. Tokyo: Kōdansha.

———. 1986. Ōkurasho Shukeikyoku. Tokyo: Kōdansha.

Kwack, Tae-Won, and Lee Kye-Sik 1992. "Tax Reform in Korea." In T. Ito and A. O. Krueger, eds., *The Political Economy of Tax Reform*, 117–36. Chicago: University of Chicago Press.

Levitt, Barbara, and James G. March. 1990. "Chester I. Barnard and the Intelligence of Learning." In O. E. Williamson, ed., *Organization Theory: From Chester Barnard to the Present and Beyond*, 11–37. New York: Oxford University Press.

Lin, C. 1992. "An Appraisal of Business Tax Reform in Taiwan: The Case of Value-Added Taxation." In T. Ito and A. O. Krueger, eds., *The Political Economy of Tax Reform*, 137–53. Chicago: University of Chicago Press.

Lupia, A., and M. D. McCubbins. Forthcoming. "Designing Bureaucratic Accountability." *Law and Contemporary Problems*.

Mann, T. E. 1986. "United States Congressmen in Comparative Perspective." In E. Suleiman, ed., *Parliaments and Parliamentarians in Democratic Politics*, 223–48. New York: Holmes and Meier.

March, J. G., and J. P. Olsen. 1984. "The New Institutionalism: Organized Factors in Political Life." *American Political Science Review* 78, no. 3: 734–49.

———. 1989. *Rediscovering Institutions: The Organizational Basis of Politics*. New York: The Free Press.

Masujima, T. 1985. "Advisory Councils with Consultancy Function in Japan— Analytical Study of the Provisional Commission for Administrative Reform." Mimeo.

Mayhew, D. R. 1974. *Congress: The Electoral Connection*. New Haven, Conn.: Yale University Press.

McCormack, G., and Y. Sugimoto. 1986. *Democracy in Contemporary Japan*. Armonk, N.Y.: M. E. Sharpe.

McCubbins, M. D. 1985. "The Legislative Design of Regulatory Structure." *American Journal of Political Science* 29, no. 4: 721–48.

McCubbins, M. D., and G. W. Noble. Forthcoming a. "The Appearance of Power: Legislators, Bureraucrats, and the Budget Process in the U.S. and Japan." In P. Cowhey and M. D. McCubbins, eds., *Structure and Policy in Japan and the United States*. Cambridge: Cambridge University Press.

———. Forthcoming b. "Perceptions and Realities of Japanese Budgeting." In P. Cowhey and M. D. McCubbins, eds., *Structure and Policy in Japan and the United States*. Cambridge: Cambridge University Press.

McCubbins, M. D., and F. M. Rosenbluth. Forthcoming. "Party Provision for Personal Politics: Dividing the Vote in Japan." In P. Cowhey and M. D. McCubbins, eds., *Structure and Policy in Japan and the United States*. Cambridge: Cambridge University Press.

294

McCubbins, M. D., and T. Schwartz. 1984. "Congressional Oversight Overlooked: Policy Patrols versus Fire Alarms." *American Journal of Political Science* 2, no. 1 (February): 164–79. Reprinted 1987 in M. D. McCubbins, and T. Sullivan, eds., *Congress: Structure and Policy*, 426–40. Cambridge: Cambridge University Press.

McCubbins, M. D., and T. Sullivan, eds. 1987. *Congress: Structure and Policy.* Cambridge: Cambridge University Press.

McLure, Charles E., Jr., and George R. Zodrow. 1987. "Treasury 1 and the Tax Reform Act of 1986: The Economics and Politics of Tax Reform." *Journal of Economic Perspectives* 1, no. 1: 37–58.

Milgrom, P., and J. Roberts 1988. "Economic Theories of the Firm: Past, Present, and Future." *Canadian Journal of Economics* 21, no. 3 (August): 444–58.

Miller, G. J. 1977. "Bureaucratic Compliance as a Game on the Unit Square." *Public Choice* 19, no. 1: 37–51.

Miller, G. J., and T. M. Moe. 1983. "Bureaucrats, Legislators, and the Size of Government." *American Political Science Review* 77, no. 2: 297–322.

Mills, C. W. 1959. *The Power Elite.* New York: Oxford University Press.

Miyajima, H. 1989a. *Zaisei Saiken no Kenkyū: Saishutsu Sakugen Seisaku o Megutte.* Tokyo: Yūhikaku.

———. 1989b. "Koremade no Zaisei Saiken o Ginmisuru." *ESP* (July): 19–23.

Miyake, I. 1977. "Yūkensha Kōzō no Hendo to Senkyo." *Annual Report of the Japanese Political Science Association,* 259–302.

Mizuno, M. 1988. *Zaisei Saiken to Zeisei Kaikaku.* Nagoya: University of Nagoya Press.

Mochizuki, M. M. 1982. "Managing and Influencing the Japanese Legislative Process: The Role of Parties and the National Diet." Ph.D. diss., Harvard University.

———. 1985. "The State and Democracy in Contemporary Japan: A Review of American Political Science Literature." *Journal of Modern Japanese Studies* 7: 335–56.

———. Forthcoming. *Conservative Hegemony.* Berkeley: University of California Press.

Moe, T. M. 1984. "The New Economics of Organization." *American Journal of Political Science* 28, no. 4: 739–77.

———. 1987. "An Assessment of the Positive Theory of Congressional Dominance." *Legislative Studies Quarterly* 12, no. 4 (November): 475–520.

———. 1990. "The Politics of Structural Choice: Toward a Theory of Public Bureaucracy." In O. E. Williamson, ed., *Organization Theory: From Chester Barnard to the Present and Beyond,* 116–53. New York: Oxford University Press.

Monroe, K. R. 1991. *The Economic Approach to Politics: A Critical Reassessment of the Theory of Rational Action.* New York: Collins Harper.

Moser, P. K., ed. 1990. *Rationality in Action: Contemporary Approaches.* New York: Cambridge University Press.

Mueller, D. C. 1989. *Public Choice*. Cambridge: Cambridge University Press.

Murakami, K. 1967. "Zaisei Kōchokuka no Yōin to Dakaisaku." *Kinyu Zaisei Jijyō*.

Murakami, Y. 1982. "The Age of New Middle Mass Politics: The Case of Japan." *Journal of Japanese Studies* 8, no. 1: 29–72.

———. 1987. "The Japanese Model of the Political Economy." In K. Yamamura and Y. Yasuba, eds., *The Political Economy of Japan*, Vol. 1: *The Domestic Transformation*, 33–90. Stanford, Calif.: Stanford University Press.

Murakawa, I. 1986. "Jimintō Zeisei Chōsakai to Seifu Zeisei Chōsakai." In K. Uchida, ed., *Keizai Seisaku Kettei Katei no Kenkyū*, 87–118. Tokyo: Nihon Keizai Kenkyū Sentā.

Muramatsu, M. 1981. *Gendai Nihon no Kanryōsei*. Tokyo: Tōyōkeizai Shinpōsha.

———. 1987. "In Search of National Identity: The Politics and Policy of the Nakasone Administration." *Journal of Japanese Studies* 13, no. 2: 307–42.

Muramatsu, M., and E. S. Krauss. 1984. "Bureaucrats and Politicians in Policymaking: The Case of Japan." *American Political Science Review* 78, no. 1: 124–46.

———. 1987. "The Conservative Party Line and the Development of Patterned Pluralism." In K. Yamamura and Y. Yasuba, eds., *The Political Economy of Japan*, Vol. 1: *the Domestic Transformation*, 516–54. Stanford: Stanford University Press.

———. 1990. "The Dominant Party and Social Coalitions in Japan." In T. J. Pempel, ed., *Uncommon Democracies: One-Party Dominant Regimes*, 282–305. Ithaca, N.Y.: Cornell University Press.

Nakajima, Y. 1990. "Tokurei Kōsai Izon karano Dakkyaku: Heisei 2 nendo Yosan nitsuite." *Fainansu* (Finance) (March): 4–12.

Nakamura, T. 1980. *Nihon Keizai: Sono Seichō to Kōzō*. 2d ed. Tokyo: University of Tokyo Press.

New Zealand Government. 1984. *Goods and Services Tax: A Booklet Explaining Measures Announced in the 1984 Budget*. Wellington, New Zealand: V. R. Ward Government Printer.

———. 1985. *Statement on Taxation and Benefit Reform 1985*. Wellington, New Zealand: V. R. Ward Government Printer.

Nihon Keizai Shimbunsha Henshubu. 1983. *Jimintō Seichōkai*. Tokyo: Nihon Keizai Shimbunsha.

Nihon Keizai Shimbunsha. 1992. Ōkurashō no Yūutsu. Tokyo: Nihon Keizai Shimbunsha.

Niskanen, W. A., Jr. 1971. *Bureaucracy and Representative Government*. Chicago: Aldine.

———. 1991. "A Reflection on 'Bureaucracy and Representative Government,'" In A. Blais and S. Dion, eds., *The Budget Maximizing Bureaucrats: Appraisal and Evidence*, 13–32. Pittsburgh: University of Pittsburgh Press.

Noguchi, Y. 1980. *Zaisei Kiki no Kōzō*. Tokyo: Tōyō Keizai Shinpōsha.

———. 1984. *Nihonzaisei no Chōki Senryaku*. Tokyo: Nihon Keizai Shimbunsha.

———. 1985. "Nihon no Kigyō no Zeifutan." *Kikan Gendai Keizai* (Spring): 48–64.

———. 1987a. "Public Finance." In K. Yamamura and Y. Yasuba, eds., *The Political Economy of Japan*, Vol. 1: *The Domestic Transformation*, 186–222. Stanford, Calif.: Stanford University Press.

———. 1987b. "Kōteki Nenkin no Shōrai to Nihon Keizai no Taigai Pahōmansu." *Financial Review* (June): 8–19.

Nordlinger, E. A. 1981. *On the Autonomy of the Democratic State*. Cambridge, Mass.: Harvard University Press.

Nordlinger, E. A., T. J. Lowi, and S. Fabbrini. 1988. "The Return to the State: Critiques." *American Political Science Review* 82, no. 3: 875–901.

Okimoto, D. I. 1988. "Political Inclusivity: The Domestic Structure of Trade." In T. Inoguchi and D. I. Okimoto, eds., *The Political Economy of Japan*, Vol. 2: *The Changing International Context*, 305–44. Stanford, Calif.: Stanford University Press.

———. 1989. *Between MITI and the Market: Japanese Industrial Policy for High Technology*. Stanford, Calif.: Stanford University Press.

Organization for Economic Co-operation and Development. 1981. *Long-term Trends in Tax Revenues of OECD Member Countries, 1955–1980*. Paris: OECD.

———. 1987. *Taxation in Developed Countries*. Paris: OECD.

———. 1988. *Taxing Consumption*. Paris: OECD.

Olsen, J. P. 1972. "Public Policy-Making and Theories of Organizational Choice." *Scandinavian Political Studies* 7: 45–62.

Ornstein, N. J., T. E. Mann, and M. J. Malbin. 1990. *Vital Statistics on Congress*. Washington, D.C.: Congressional Quarterly.

Ōtake, H. 1979. *Gendai Nihon no Seiji Kenryoku Keizai Kenryoku*. Tokyo: San'ichi Shobō.

———. 1984. *Nihon Seiji no Soten*. Tokyo: San'ichi Shobo.

Ozaki, M. 1987a. "Uriagezei Hitorigatai: Jō." *Fainansu* (Finance) 23, no. 6: 43–52.

———. 1987b. "Uriagezei Hitorigatai: Chū." *Fainansu* (Finance) 23, no. 7: 55–65.

———. 1987c. "Uriagezei Hitorigatai: Ge." *Fainansu* (Finance) 23, no. 8: 66–74.

Page, E. C. 1985. *Political Authority and Bureaucratic Power*. Brighton: Wheatsheaf Books.

Pechman, J. A. 1980. *What Should Be Taxed: Income or Expenditure?* Washington, D.C.: The Brookings Institution.

———. 1987. *Comparative Tax Systems: Europe, Canada, and Japan*. Arlington, Va.: Tax Analysts.

———. 1988. *World Tax Reform: A Progress Report*. Washington,, D.C.: The Brookings Institution.

Peltzman, S. 1976. "Toward a More General Theory of Regulation." *Journal of Law and Economics* 19, no. 2: 211–40.

Pempel, T. J. 1978. "Japanese Foreign Economic Policy: The Domestic Bases for

International Behavior." In P. J. Katzenstein, ed., *Between Power and Plenty*. Madison: University of Wisconsin Press.

Pempel, T. J. 1975. "The Dilemma of Parliamentary Opposition in Japan." *Polity* 8, no. 1: 63–79.

———. 1982. *Policy and Politics in Japan: Creative Conservatism*. Philadelphia: Temple University Press.

———. 1987. "The Unbundling of 'Japan, Inc.': The Changing Dynamics of Japanese Policy Formation." *Journal of Japanese Studies* 13, no. 2: 271–306.

———. 1990. "Introduction. Uncommon Democracies: The One-Party Dominant Regime." In T. J. Pempel, ed., *Uncommon Democracies: The One-Party Dominant Regime*, 1–32. Ithaca, N.Y.: Cornell University Press.

———. 1991. "Japan and Sweden: Polarities of 'Responsible Capitalism,'" in D. A. Rustow and K. P. Erickson, eds., *Comparative Political Dynamics: Global Research Perspectives*. New York: Harper Collins.

Pempel, T. J., ed. 1990. *Uncommon Democracies: The One-Party Dominant Regime*. Ithaca, N.Y.: Cornell University Press.

Pempel, T. J., and K. Tsunekawa. 1979. "Corporatism without Labor." In P. C. Schmitter and G. Lehmbruch, eds., *Trends toward Corporatist Intermediation*, 231–70. Beverly Hills: Sage.

Peters, B. G. 1991. "The European Bureaucrat: The Applicability of Bureaucracy and Representative Government to Non-American Settings." In A. Blais and S. Dion, eds., *The Budget Maximizing Bureaucrats: Appraisals and Evidence*, 303–54. Pittsburgh: University of Pittsburgh Press.

Piore, M., and C. Sabel. 1984. *The Second Industrial Divide*. New York: Basic Books.

Polsby, N. W. 1975. "Legislatures." In F. I. Greenstein and N. W. Polsby, eds., *Handbook of Political Science*, Vol. 5: *Governmental Insitutions and Processes*, 257–319. Reading, Mass.: Addison-Wesley.

———. 1986. *Congress and the Presidency*. 4th ed. Englewood Cliffs, N.J.: Prentice-Hall.

Putnam, R. D. 1973. "The Political Attitudes of Senior Civil Servants in Western Europe: A Preliminary Report." *British Journal of Political Science* 3: 257–90.

———. 1977. "Elite Transformation in Advanced Industrial Societies: An Empirical Assessment of the Theory of Technocracy." *Comparative Political Studies* 10, no.3: 383–412.

Ramseyer, J. M., and F. M. Rosenbluth. 1993. *Japan's Political Market Place*. Cambridge, Mass.: Harvard University Press.

Ridley, F. F. 1966. "French Technocracy and Comparative Government." *Political Studies* 14, no. 1: 34–52.

Riker, W. H. 1984. "The Heresthetics of Constitution-Making: The Presidency in 1787, with Comments on Determinism and Rational Choice." *American Political Science Review* 78, no. 1: 1–16.

Ripley, R. B. 1983. *Congress: Process and Policy*. 3d ed. New York: Norton.

Rogers, J. M. 1988. *The Impact of Policy Analysis.* Pittsburgh: University of Pittsburgh Press.

Rohde, D. A. 1991. *Parties and Leaders in the Postreform House.* Chicago: University of Chicago Press.

Rohde, D. A., and D. A. Shepsle. 1973. "Democratic Committee Assignments in the House of Representatives: Strategic Aspects of a Social Choice Process," *American Political Science Review* 67, no. 3 (September): 889–905. Reprinted 1987 in M. D. McCubbins and T. Sullivan, eds., *Congress: Structure and Policy.* Cambridge: Cambridge University Press.

Romer, T., and H. Rosenthal. 1978. "Political Resource Allocation, Controlled Agendas, and the Status Quo." *Public Choice* 33, no. 4: 27–43.

Rose-Ackerman, S. 1978. *Corruption: A Study in Political Economy.* New York: Academic Press.

Rosenbluth, F. 1989. *Financial Politics in Contemporary Japan.* Ithaca, N.Y.: Cornell University Press.

Samuels, R. J. 1987. *The Business of the Japanese State.* Ithaca, N.Y.: Cornell University Press.

Sartori, G. 1976. *Parties and Party Systems: A Framework for Analysis.* Cambridge: Cambridge University Press.

Satō, S., and T. Matsuzaki. 1986. *Jimintō Seiken.* Tokyo: Chūo Kōronsha.

Satō, S., K. Kōyama, and S. Kumon. 1990. *Postwar Politician: The Life of Former Prime Minister Masayoshi Ōhira.* Tokyo: Kodansha International.

Schmitter, P. C., and G. Lehmbruch, eds. 1979. *Trends toward Corporatist Intermediation.* Beverly Hills: Sage.

Schoppa, L. J. 1991. "*Zoku* Power and LDP Power: A Case Study of the *Zoku* Role in Education Policy." *Journal of Japanese Studies* 17, no. 1: 79–106.

Shepsle, K. A. 1979. "Institutional Arrangements and Equilibrium in Multidimensional Voting Models." *American Journal of Political Science* 23, no. 1: 27–59.

———. 1986. "Institutional Equilibrium and Equilibrium Institutions." In H. F. Weisberg, ed., *Political Science: The Science of Politics.* New York: Agathon.

Shepsle, K. A., and B. Weingast. 1981. "Structure-Induced Equilibrium and Legislative Choice." *Public Choice* 37, no. 3: 503–19.

Shindō, M. 1989. *Zaisei Hatan to Zeisei Kaikaku.* Tokyo: Iwanami Shoten.

Silberman, B. S. 1993. *Cages of Reason.* Chicago: University of Chicago Press.

Simon, H. A. 1953. "Notes on Observation and Measurement of Political Power." *Journal of Politics* 15, no. 4: 500–16. Reprinted in Simon 1987a, *Models of Man.*

———. 1955. "A Behavioral Model of Rational Choice," *Quarterly Journal of Economics* 69. Reprinted in Simon 1982, *Models of Bounded Rationality,* and Simon 1987, *Models of Man.*

———. 1956a. "Rational Choice and the Structure of Environment." *Psychological Review* 63, no. 2: 129–38. Reprinted in Simon 1982, *Models of Bounded Rationality,* and Simon 1987, *Models of Man.*

Simon, H. A. 1956b. "A Comparison of Game Theory and Learning Theory." *Psychometrika* 21: 267–72. Reprinted in Simon 1982, *Models of Bounded Rationality*, and Simon 1987, *Models of Man*.

———. 1964. "Rationality." In J. Gouldand and W. L. Kolb, eds., *A Dictionary of the Social Sciences*, 573–74. New York: The Free Press.

———. 1976. *Administrative Behavior*. 2d ed. New York: Macmillan.

———. 1982. *Models of Bounded Rationality: Behavioral Economics and Business Organization*. Cambridge: M.I.T. Press.

———. 1983. *Reason in Human Affairs*. Stanford, Calif.: Stanford University Press.

———. 1985. "Human Nature in Politics." *American Political Science Review* 79, no. 2: 293–304.

———. 1987a. *Models of Man: Social and Rational*. New York: Garland.

———. 1987b. "Rationality in Psychology and Economics." In R. M. Hogarth and M. W. Reder, eds., *Rational Choice: The Contrast between Economics and Psychology*. Chicago: University of Chicago Press.

Simon, H. A., D. W. Smithburg, and V. A. Thompson. 1962. *Public Administration*. New York: Knopf.

Simons, H. C. 1938. *Personal Income Taxation*. Chicago: Chicago University Press.

Seidelman, R., and E. J. Harpham. 1985. *Disenchanted Realists: Political Science and the American Crisis, 1894–1984*. Albany: State University of New York.

Skocpol, T. 1979. *States and Social Revolutions: A Comparative Analysis of France, Russia, and China*. Cambridge: Cambridge University Press.

———. 1985. "Bringing the State Back In: Strategies of Analysis in Current Research." In P. B. Evans, D. Rueschemeyer, and T. Skocpol, eds., *Bringing the State Back In*, 3–37. Cambridge: Cambridge University Press.

Skowronek, S. 1982. *Building a New American State: The Expansion of National Administrative Capitalism*. New York: Cambridge University Press.

Smith, R. M. 1988. "Political Jurisprudence: The 'New Institutionalism,' and the Future of Public Law." *American Political Science Review* 82, no. 1: 89–108.

Steinmo, S. 1989. "Political Institutions and Tax Policy in the United States, Sweden, and Britain." *World Politics* 41, no. 4: 500–35.

Stepan, A. 1978. *State and Society: Peru in Comparative Perspective*. Princeton, N.J.: Princeton University Press.

Steven, R. 1983. *Classes in Contemporary Japan*. London: Cambridge University Press.

———. 1990. *Japan's New Imperialism*. Armonk, N.Y.: M. E. Sharpe.

Stinchcombe, A. L. 1990. *Information and Organizations*. Berkeley: University of California Press.

Stigler, G. J. 1971. "Theory of Economic Regulation," *Bell Journal of Economics* 2, no. 1: 3–21.

Stockfisch, J. A. 1987. "The Value-Added Tax as a 'Money Machine.'" In

C. E. Walker and M. A. Bloomfield, eds., *The Consumption Tax: A Better Alternative?*, 225–37. Cambridge: Ballinger.

Stone, D. A. 1987. *Policy Paradox and Political Reason*. Glenview, Ill.: Scott, Foresman.

Suleiman, E. N. 1974. *Politics, Power, and Bureaucracy in France: The Administrative Elite*. Princeton, N.J.: Princeton University Press.

———. 1978. *Elites in French Society: The Politics of Survival*. Princeton, N.J.: Princeton University Press.

———, ed. 1984. *Bureaucrats and Policymaking: A Comparative Overview*. New York: Holmes and Meier.

———. 1986a. "Introduction." In Suleiman, ed., *Parliaments and Parliamentarians in Democratic Politics*, 3–7. New York: Holmes and Meier.

———. 1986b. "Toward the Disciplining of Parties and Legislators: The French Parliamentarians in the Fifth Republic." In Suleiman, ed., *Parliaments and Parliamentarians in Democratic Politics*, 78–105. New York: Holmes and Meier.

———, ed. 1986. *Parliaments and Parliamentarians in Democratic Politics*. New York: Holmes and Meier.

Suleiman, E. N., and J. Waterbury, eds. 1990. *Political Economy of Public Sector Reform and Privatization*. Boulder, Colo.: Westview.

Sugisaki, S. 1989. "Zeisei Kaikaku no Gaiyō." *Fainansu* (Finance) 24, no. 11 (February): 17–59.

Takayama, N. 1992. *Nenkin Kaikaku no Kōsō*. Tokyo: Nihon Keizai Shimbunsha.

Tanimura, H. 1987. "Yosan Hensei to Naikaku Kinō Kyōka Mondai." *Fainansu* (Finance), 23, no. 6: 53–63.

Tsebelis, G. 1990. *Nested Games: Rational Choice in Comparative Politics*. Berkeley: University of California Press.

Tsuji, K. 1969. *Nihon Kanryōsei no Kenkyū*. Tokyo: University of Tokyo Press.

Tullock, G. 1965. *The Politics of Bureaucracy*. Washington, D.C.: Public Affairs Press.

Tversky, A., and D. Kahneman. 1987. "Rational Choice and the Framing of Decisions." In R. M. Hogarth and M. W. Reder, eds., *Rational Choice*, 41–66. Chicago: University of Chicago Press.

U.S. Treasury Department. 1977. *Blueprints for Basic Tax Reform*. Washington, D.C.: U.S. Government Printing Office.

Usui, N. 1987. *Kansetsuzei no Genjō*. Tokyo: Ōkura Zaimu Kyōkai.

Valeo, F. R., and C. E. Morrison. 1983. *The Japanese Diet and the U.S. Congress*. Boulder, Colo.: Westview.

Webber, C., and A. Wildavsky. 1986. *A History of Taxation and Expenditure in the Western World*. New York: Simon and Schuster.

Weber, M. 1958. *Essays in Sociology*. New York: Oxford University Press.

———. 1978. *Economy and Society*. Berkeley: University of California Press.

Weingast, B. R. 1984. "The Congressional-Bureaucratic System: A Principle-

301

Agent Perspective (With Application to the SEC)." *Public Choice* 44, no. 1: 147–91.

Weingast, B. R., and W. J. Marshall. 1988. "The Industrial Organization of Congress; or, Why Legislatures, Like Firms, Are Not Organized as Markets." *Journal of Political Economy* 96, no. 1: 132–63.

Weingast, B. R., and M. J. Moran. 1983. "Bureaucratic Discretion or Congressional Control? Regulatory Policymaking by the Federal Trade Commission." *Journal of Political Economy* 91, no. 5: 765–800.

Whalley, J., and D. Fretz. 1990. *The Economics of the Goods and Services Tax.* Canadian Tax Paper No. 88. Toronto: Canadian Tax Foundation.

Wicksell, K. 1958. "Finanztheoretische untersuchungen." Partially translated in R. A. Musgrave and A. T. Peacock, eds., *Classics in the Theory of Public Finance.* London: Macmillan.

Wildavsky, A. 1988. *The New Politics of the Budgetary Process.* Boston: Scott, Foresman.

Williamson, O. E. 1975. *Markets and Hierarchies: Analysis and Antitrust Implication.* New York: The Free Press.

———. 1985. *The Economic Institutions of Capitalism.* New York: The Free Press.

———. 1988. "The Logic of Economic Organization," *Journal of Law, Economics, and Organization* 4, no. 1: 65–93.

———. ed. 1990. *Organization Theory: From Chester Barnard to the Present and Beyond.* New York: Oxford University Press.

Wilson, J. Q. 1989. *Bureaucracy: What Government Agencies Do and Why They Do It.* New York: Basic Books.

Winter, S. 1986. "How Policy-Making Affects Implementation: The Decentralization of the Danish Disablement Pension Administration." *Scandinavian Political Studies* 9, no. 4: 361–85.

Winter, S. L., and W. Hettich. 1988. "Political Checks and Balances and the Structure of Taxation in the United States and Canada." In A. Breton, G. Galeotti, and P. Salmon, eds., *The Competitive State,* 39–56. Dordrecht, The Netherlands: Kluwer Academic Publishers.

Wright, J. R. 1985. "PACs, Contributions, and Roll Calls: An Organizational Perspective." *American Political Science Review* 79, no. 2: 400–14.

Yakushiji, T. 1987. *Seijika tai Kanryō.* Tokyo: Tōyō Keizai Shimpōsha.

Yamaguchi, J. 1987. Ōkura Kanryō Shihai no Shūen. Tokyo: Iwanami Shoten.

———. 1989. *Ittō Shihai Taisei no Hōkai.* Tokyo: Iwanami Shoten.

Yanaga, C. 1968. *Big Business in Japanese Politics.* New Haven, Conn.: Yale University Press.

Yanagisawa, H. 1977. "Chūki Zeisei no Yukue," *Zaisei Kinyū Tōkei Geppō* (August): 1–8.

———. 1985. *Akaji Zaisei no 10 nen to 4 nin no Sōritachi.* Tokyo: Nihon Seisansei Honbu.

Yanow D. 1990. "Tackling the Implementation Problem: Epistemological Issues in Implementation Research." In D. J. Palumbo and D. J. Calista, eds., *Implementation and the Policy Process: Opening Up the Black Box.* New York: Greenwood.

Zysman, J. 1983. *Governments, Markets, and Growth: Financial Systems and the Politics of Industrial Change.* Ithaca, N.Y.: Cornell University Press.

# Chronology of the Tax Reform Process
## from 1975 to 1991

THE TAX REFORM MOVEMENT UNDER THE ŌHIRA ADMINISTRATION

**1975**

7 November     The Diet passes a supplementary budget providing for the special issuance of ¥2.29 trillion (deficit) bonds due to a ¥3.879 trillion revenue shortfall.

**1977**

4 October     The Government Tax System Research Council (GTSRC), in its interim report, proposes the introduction of a general consumption tax.

**1978**

7 December     The Ōhira cabinet is formed.

26 December     The LDP Tax System Research Council (TSRC), in its proposal for an annual revision of the tax system for fiscal year 1979, asks for the introduction of a general consumption tax.

27 December     The GTSRC issues its "Major Line of the General Consumption Tax."

**1979**

19 January     The cabinet endorses the "Major Line of the Tax System Revision" for fiscal year 1979, including the introduction of the general consumption tax in 1980.

26 September     Prime Minister Ōhira, on a stumping tour, withdraws the proposal to introduce a general consumption tax from the 1980 fiscal year.

7 October     General election is held. (The LDP gains only 248 seats of 511 in the House of Representatives; the party manages to maintain a bare majority by the entrance of successful conservative independents to the party.)

21 December     The Diet issues a resolution on "fiscal reconstruction," stipulating that elimination of deficit bonds should not depend on revenue increases from a general consumption tax.

## ADMINISTRATIVE REFORM

**1980**

17 July          The Suzuki cabinet is formed.

28 November   The Diet passes special legislation to establish the Second Provisional Council for Administrative Reform.

**1981**

16 March        The Council for Administrative Reform begins deliberations.

5 June           The cabinet endorses the imposition of a zero-ceiling on the general account of the ministries' budget.

**1982**

9 July            The cabinet endorses the imposition of a minus-ceiling on the general account of the ministries' budget.

30 July          The Council for Administrative Reform decides on the Basic Report on Administrative Reform.

## THE TAX REFORM MOVEMENT UNDER NAKASONE'S ADMINISTRATION

**1982**

27 November   Nakasone's cabinet is formed.

**1983**

15 March        The Council for Administrative Reform ends its two-year term.

**1984**

19 December   Both the GTSRC and the LDP TSRC, in their proposals for the 1985 fiscal year tax system revision, propose the need for a structural tax reform.

**1985**

20 September  The GTSRC receives an inquiry from Prime Minister Nakasone about a structural tax reform.

**1986**

25 April         The GTSRC issues its interim report, including individual and corporate income tax reforms (resulting in a tax reduction).

6 May            The LDP TSRC decides on individual and corporate income tax reforms (resulting in a tax reduction).

14 June          Prime Minister Nakasone, on a stumping tour, makes a public promise "not to introduce a large-scale indirect tax."

| | |
|---|---|
| 6 July | Simultaneous elections of the House of Representatives and the House of Councillors are held. (The LDP obtains a record-breaking three hundred seats in the House of Representatives.) |
| 29 July | Three alternative plans for the new indirect taxes, including an EC-type value-added tax, are proposed by a subcommittee of the GTSRC. |
| 28 October | The GTSRC issues its final report on structural tax reform, including an income tax reduction and the introduction of a new consumption tax. |
| 5 December | The LDP TSRC decides on the basic direction of the tax reform, choosing a value-added tax system as the new consumption tax and naming it the "sales tax." |
| 23 December | The introduction of the sales tax is proposed in a GTSRC report and in the LDP TSRC's "Major Line of the Tax Reform." |

**1987**

| | |
|---|---|
| 3 February | Tax reform bills for the 1987 fiscal year, including the sales tax, are endorsed by the cabinet. |
| 10 February | The tax bills are submitted to the Diet. |
| 27 May | The 108th session of the Diet ends. The tax bills are dropped. |
| 31 July | Revised bills on individual and corporate income tax reforms are submitted to the Diet. |
| 19 September | The Diet passes bills to legislate the income tax reduction and the elimination of tax-exemption of savings. |

THE INTRODUCTION OF THE SALES TAX UNDER THE TAKESHITA CABINET

| | |
|---|---|
| 16 October | The LDP and the government decide on the introduction of a structural tax reform in the near future. |
| 6 November | The Takeshita cabinet is formed. |
| 12 November | The GTSRC receives an inquiry from Prime Minister Takeshita about a structural tax reform. |

**1988**

| | |
|---|---|
| 8 February–3 March | Public hearings on a structural tax reform are organized by the GTSRC in twenty places throughout the country. |
| 25 March | The GTSRC makes a preliminary plan for the tax reform. |

| 5–15 April | The LDP TSRC organizes hearings with industrial groups. |
| 11–14 April | Public hearings are organized by the GTSRC in five places. |
| 28 April | The GTSRC issues its interim report. |
| 14 June | The LDP TSRC proposes to introduce a new value-added tax, the "consumption tax," in its "Major Line of the Tax Reform." |
| 15 June | The GTSRC issues its final report. |
| 28 June | The "Major Line of the Tax Reform" is approved by the cabinet. |
| 29 July | The tax bills are submitted to the 113th provisional Diet session. |
| 16 November | The tax bills are passed by the House of Representatives. |
| 24 December | The tax bills are passed by the House of Councillors. |

AFTER THE IMPLEMENTATION OF THE NEW CONSUMPTION TAX SYSTEM

1989

| 1 April | A new system of consumption tax begins. |
| 23 July | The election of the House of Councillors is held. (The LDP obtains only 36 seats out of 126.) |

1990

| 18 February | The general election of the House of Representatives is held. (The LDP obtains 275 seats out of 512. The Japan Socialist Party (JSP) increases its seats from 83 to 133 but the middle-of-the-road parties decrease their number of seats.) |
| 26 June | The 118th special session of the Diet ends and both the bill to revise the consumption tax system (submitted by the government) and the bill to abolish the system (submitted by the opposition parties) are dropped. |
| 14 December | The LDP and the opposition parties fail to agree on a revision of the consumption tax system because they cannot agree on the tax exemption of foods. |

1991

| 22 April | After a large loss of seats in the unified local elections, the JSP accepts a revision of the consumption tax system. |
| 8 May | The 120th ordinary session of the Diet ends and the bill to revise the consumption tax system passes with the support of all parties. |

# Index